# CALIFORNIA EDITION
## of
# HILL OF THE HAWK

PALA MISSION



Scott O'Dell

LIMITED AND SIGNED

*First Edition*

# HILL OF THE HAWK

SCOTT O'DELL



THE BOBBS-MERRILL COMPANY
*Publishers*
INDIANAPOLIS NEW YORK

*To*

Anne of El Nido

# HILL OF THE HAWK

# 1

THIRTY-NINE days out of Santa Fe and riding hard, a pack train dropped downward through the Cajon.

It wound like a great gray snake between topes of pine and alder, down from ledges of blue-shadowed snow where the air bit and sparkled and the rising wind smelled of rain, past bronze benchlands of chaparral, down through cottonwood bottoms green with the leaves of early summer, across a swift, cold-running stream, over a rise and another, into a valley that rolled away to far mountain ramparts lost in a stormy haze.

They rode hard—four men in dirty buckskin, mouths rimmed white with alkali, red-eyed and thin-tempered, with forty jaded horses; two of the men against the approaching storm, one for reasons of his own, the other because the pack train was worth sixteen thousand in Spanish gold delivered at Los Angeles, and worth nothing unless it was.

Grady Dunavant sat watchful in the saddle. A thousand miles lay behind him. The Apache, the poisoned arrows of Pima and Cocopa, the waters of the Gila and Colorado that could swallow a pack train in a few swift minutes, the endless desert and its dry marches where flesh fell away from bones and tongues swelled black between the teeth. Behind him, thank God, all of it. By late afternoon, with luck, he would be in the pueblo, his goods safe in Kate Howland's corral. Only ten hours more. But those ten hours lay through Spanish country. A dozen leagues in which danger awaited him. Ambush, confiscation, arrest—any one of them or all, depending on unknowable factors.

His eyes swept the valley. Willows and sycamores that marked the serpentine of the Santa Ana, plunging in spate toward the mountain ramparts and the sea. Red cattle grazing on lush grass. Smoke from a sheepherder's hut. A stallion and a herd of mares running before the wind in mating play. A flight of snow-white geese circling for water, high up against the sun, like flakes of tinsel. The King's Highway deserted, except for a single cart moving eastward. A cone of yellow dust, rising out of nothing, careening along parallel to the train and then fading out again.

He saw nothing else. No armed band of *vaqueros.* No blue-coated soldiers from the frontier garrison. It was a good beginning. Shoving his hat back from his forehead, a young man, lean-hipped and straight-backed, with gray eyes deeply set, he filled his lungs with the sultry west wind.

He looked at the river looping away toward the Temescals, the hills blue with chaparral, the June grass like a sea stretching beyond the reach of the eye. He looked at the great valley that lay below him, the drifting cattle, the rolling leagues where not a house rose to meet the gaze, where no plow marked the earth. He had seen all this before. He had seen it twice before, coming out of the desert and down from the Cajon, but now as then what he saw was new as if he were looking at it for the first time. And now, as before, his blood ran strong in his veins. Someday, he thought, he would no longer come skulking out of the mountains to ride, furtive and watchful, through the land. Someday, when the Spaniard no longer ruled California, he would ride like a man, over acres that belonged to him.

He looked long at the valley as he dropped downward to meet the river; through cracked lips he made the vow and repeated it aloud above the creak of saddle leather and the thud of hoofs.

Thunderheads towered above the Temescals, nudging ponderous shoulders toward the sun. The sky was covered now with a milky haze and scattered windy rags of clouds. Riding west from the river, upward from the quiet bottomlands, Dunavant faced the storm that drove down from the mountains. He lowered his head slightly as the wind struck, not moving his body, and looked ahead to where ranch buildings showed in the unnatural light.

Above the wind he could hear the clatter of the pack train behind him, the soft curses of Boyd and Lampson anticipating the storm, anticipating also his decision not to halt and seek shelter. As usual, there was nothing from Mr. Fraser, but in his mind he saw the sandy, close-cropped mustache above the firm lips, the spare face which the sun could redden but not tan, the blue, secretive eyes, and knew that the Englishman—whatever his reason—agreed with the decision to press on.

Dunavant closed his mind on the resentment behind him, as palpable as the wind, which did not need curses or sullen coughs to give it expression, and on the mystery of Mr. Fraser. Taking his eyes from the ranch, he looked ahead along the King's Highway, now partly obscured by a racing scud.

At a distance of a mile or more, between rifts in the scud, he saw what he took to be a line of cattle moving at right angles to the trail. He was not cautious by nature, rather the reverse—a hard-fisted young man with an Irish disdain for consequences—but on this morning, with a valuable cargo behind him, Camilla Howland waiting in the pueblo, and Mr. Fraser offering a handsome bonus for every day under forty-five between Santa Fe and Los Angeles, he felt compelled to remove the glasses from the saddle horn.

The column, which to his eyes showed the familiar movement of drifting cattle, under magnification became a line of horsemen heading south, with objects interspersed among them that would be either carts or travois. Dunavant's lips tightened. If the objects were travois, the horsemen would be Indians; Spaniards if they were not. He wiped the lenses on his shirt, and, waiting an instant of clear vision, brought them into sharper focus. The objects now seemed to be carts, drawn by oxen, moving presumably away from the ranch.

Lowering the military glasses, holding them in one gloved hand against the saddle horn, he waited for another chance to bring them to bear on the column, but the scud had lowered and thickened, driven by an increasing wind. He could no longer see beyond a quarter of a mile. He put the glasses away and slung over the horn the battered leather case, stained with sweat, with the letters spelling out across the hollowed lid, through a rime of white alkali dust, LIEUT. GRADY C. DUNAVANT.

He was again conscious of the sounds behind him, momentarily changed in tone and subject. Boyd and Lampson had seen the horsemen and had decided on the fact that they were Spaniards, on their destination, on everything apparently except their names. At any moment he expected to hear them attempt to solve this final riddle. He was tempted to inform them that it was not yet certain that the column was composed of Spaniards, that his eyesight was equal to theirs, the glasses superior.

Instead, he withdrew the rifle from its sheath beside his right leg and held it across the saddle, ready for use.

Behind him the conversation continued, reaching his ears against the storm and his will. Grady's face darkened under its heavy tan. On the last leg of a thousand-mile journey, during which he had been unable to convince them of the simplest needs of caution, it was now too late to hope for success in this latest instance. He didn't propose to jeopardize the party, however. Their lives were their own; theoretically, if they wished to lose them in the final few miles to Los Angeles, it was their responsibility. But his own interests aside, now that he had brought them safely through dry marches, river crossing difficult any time, doubly so in this season of flood, through Indian country where death could lurk behind every rise, he'd be damned if he would permit them to take the column for granted.

"Boyd—" it was the Kentuckian, as always, who seemed to be the more positive of the two—"if your rifle isn't ready, I advise you to see that it is. The horsemen may be Spaniards. It's possible they aren't. It's also possible that the Spaniards are unfriendly. I've known them to be."

Dunavant shouted his words down the wind, not turning in the saddle, barely turning his head. If anything was said in reply, he didn't hear it, but he did hear Boyd swear as the rifle stuck in its sheath, the dry, mocking laughter of the other.

"That goes for you also, Lampson."

Mr. Fraser, the Englishman, was capable of taking care of himself.

The horizon had shut down and the wind was slackening, oppressive now with the feel of rain. The heat increased.

Grady Dunavant looked down at his own rifle. It held a good charge, carefully prepared. Ordinarily, he liked to load on the moment, preferring this against traveling with powder and ball which could be exploded by some slight accidental jar. In fact, throughout the journey he had traveled with an empty rifle. Only two hours before, coming through the Cajon into Spanish country, he had prepared the charge and asked the men to do likewise. He hadn't bothered to explain something which wouldn't be understood by either Boyd or Lampson, that Indians of whatever tribe were predictable, that the California Spaniards, Spaniards anywhere, were not. He might have told them that before he knew differently, four years ago in '42, when he was certain he knew what the Spaniards were about, this certainty had led to his arrest, shipment in chains to the port of San Blas and imprisonment for a year in the fortress of Tepic. He was glad now he had kept his counsel, for nothing would have been accomplished, except that Lampson would have made the rest of the journey unbearable with questions.

Beside the trail the young leaves of the cottonwoods, quick to move in the slightest wind, hung limp on their pale stems. As the wind died away, there was the smell of willows fringing the river, and the smell of the river itself, of cattle and grass. Rain hung above the King's Highway.

In the sudden quiet, mingled with the noises of the pack train, he heard the thud of hoofs, the rumble of carts, and shortly afterward he saw off to his right, moving toward the trail, a line of horsemen and carts, and in the carts, women. His lips relaxed. Spaniards didn't go out on forays with carts full of women, nor in the circumstances would they be seeking trouble. He relaxed in the saddle, but held his rifle ready across his knees.

With a feeling of annoyance, he realized that the line of Spaniards was converging upon the trail. In another quarter of a mile the two caravans would meet. From what he could see of the Spaniards' caravan, it extended for a half mile at least—probably twice that distance, judging by the sounds. Should he pull up and wait for them to pass in front of him or continue on? He felt the gaze of Lampson and Boyd, pressing against his shoulder blades, asking the same question. Mr. Fraser, the Englishman, also watched with his pale-blue eyes.

Dunavant made his decision quickly, out of bitter memories of Tepic and Texas, with no thought given to caution. It was to go on and let the Spaniards wait for him, wait the fifteen minutes beside the trail, while the pack train wound slowly past, wait in the rain and if not the rain, then in clouds of yellow dust. He felt the silent approval of Mr. Fraser, though the Englishman for some curious reason didn't share his opinion of the Spaniards.

Setting his spurs, he stepped up the gait of his horse and the gait of the train, and saw as he did so two horsemen disengage themselves from the caravan. One rode a palomino with a flowing golden mane and four white feet; the other a blue gelding. They came in a swinging curve toward him, riding shoulder to shoulder at a gallop, with the horsemanship which belonged only to the California Spaniards.

Dunavant, beneath the down-turned brim of his hat, seemingly incurious, watched them closely.

The two horsemen crossed the trail in front of him, spun together in a short arc, circled back at full speed and came to a stiff-legged halt, barring his way. They stood there obscured for a moment in rising dust.

Dunavant sat stiff in the saddle, the muscles gathering along his legs, his hands tightening on his rifle. He made no effort to rein down his horse. The two Spaniards were now only fifty paces away. Through the clearing dust he could see that they were both dressed in black leather jackets and trousers, and black, low-crowned hats. They both carried coiled *reatas* on their peaked Spanish saddles and ancient muskets beside their stirrups. As he watched them, riding forward, one of the horsemen leaned down and withdrew a musket from its antelope sheath.

Grady Dunavant's thumb went slowly to the hammer. His hand spread and, with his thumb still pressing down, a finger curved softly over the trigger. He wondered if Lampson and Boyd had loaded. He thought about Mr. Fraser and crossed him off as an unknown quantity. That left three—three Americans against an unknown number of Spaniards. He felt no qualms. He hadn't wanted trouble, but pack train or no pack train, no Spaniard who ever lived was going to block his path with an ancient musket. The anger in his gray eyes was as cold as the steel under his fingers.

He spurred his pony into a trot, listening to the gathering momentum of the train behind him. The horseman, who had withdrawn the musket and now held it raised across the neck of the palomino, stood a pace in advance of the other. Dunavant placed his forearm along the stock of his rifle for leverage; as he made the motion, his thumb suddenly relaxed, his finger slid from the trigger.

He was still a dozen paces away and the air hadn't cleared, but his eyes were not mistaken. The Spaniard, who at a distance, in the dust and haze, had looked like a young man, was in reality a girl, dressed the same as the youth beyond her, with black hair falling from beneath her wide hat around her shoulders.

Dunavant reined down his horse and came to a halt. He slipped his rifle into the scabbard, sat erect and with an instinctive gesture, which in no way lessened his anger or softened his cold, direct glance, touched the brim of his hat. His lips did not move.

The girl returned his glance. At first, as he drew up a few paces from her and raised his hand, her expression was one of surprise, a fleeting emotion which passed across her mouth rather than her gaze. To Dunavant it was as if she had, like him, expected someone else to appear there on the trail. It was a look which disregarded the dirty buckskin, the rimed mouth and reddened eyes and the thin, unshaved cheeks, for the man beneath. It wasn't pity or exactly interest or a woman looking at a man. It was all of these things and none of them.

The next instant, swift as the shadow which now fell across the trail, the emotion left her face. Her look became guarded and hostile. You are a trespasser, her eyes told him plainly. An American trespasser.

You are a stranger who rides arrogantly through a country which does not belong to you. You are the enemy and I look at you only to show my hatred—for no other reason except this.

She held the ancient musket in her hand, resting on the high-peaked Spanish saddle. She did not speak.

Dunavant fought down an impulse to spur his horse around her. He swallowed hard on his anger and said, "This is not to my liking." He waited for her to answer.

The girl sat with her wide shoulders set squarely against him. She looked at him with eyes that were tawny-colored and flecked with brown, a shade darker than those of the youth standing beyond her. She looked at him and made no reply, but her eyes said, "I am here to prevent your passing."

"I am not greatly impressed with the musket," Dunavant said. "I doubt that it will shoot or that you could use it if it did."

The girl remained silent.

Anger again rose in his throat. "The next time you decide to halt a pack train, my advice is to wear a dress. You might be mistaken for a man."

Color showed along the girl's high cheekbones. She raised one hand, brushed back her hair in a quick gesture, and then again lowered her hand to the barrel of the musket. She looked at him steadily and said nothing.

"Except for the fact that you're a girl—and judging from your garb and your actions this is only a presumption—I wouldn't be sitting here."

The colored heightened in her cheeks, and her full lips were suddenly compressed, but she didn't answer him. Dunavant was on the point of speaking when the youth said over her shoulder that the caravan had reached and passed the trail. The girl glanced around to confirm his words. Then she looked at Dunavant. For an instant her eyes held the same unguarded look he had seen when she had first ridden up. Her expression changed as it had done before, and in a soft, slurring accent he had never heard outside of Santa Fe, with sudden mockery and contempt, she said the single word, "Gringo."

Wheeling her horse into a gallop, she left him standing there in the middle of the trail, with a retort on his tongue and heavy clouds of dust already beginning to drift down upon him from the caravan.

# 2

THROUGH thickets of manzanita the line of horsemen and carts wound up the trail. The valley lay behind them, shadowed by a haze of breathless heat. Above them the upper reaches of the slope and the crests of the hills that rose beyond were banked with clouds. They traveled slowly for the way was steep, to the creak of saddle leather, the clatter of bit and rowel, to the screech of solid wooden wheels turning against wooden axles.

In the lead rode Don Saturnino de Zubaran on a bay stallion. The size of the man made the horse seem small.

He sat well back in the saddle, his legs thrust forward, the wheels of his Spanish spurs brushing the June grass. He was a man in his early fifties, with the shoulders and neck of a mountain bull. His head was long, broader at the base than the top; the brows, nose and jaw bony beneath tight-stretched, leathery skin. His long hair was braided and bound at the ends with rawhide. Holding the reins loose against one thigh, he watched the storm gathering in the south.

Throughout the morning, before they had left the ranch, small clouds had blown in from the sea until cloud had piled upon cloud against the Temescals in rearing thunderheads. Now as if by sheer weight, they had broken across the mountain barrier and were moving ponderously upon the valley below. A flickering, uneasy light showed along the horizon.

Saturnino turned to the priest who rode a step or two behind him on a flop-eared donkey, his cowl thrown back and the skirt of his robe pulled up on thin, hairy legs.

"There is no wind yet, but when it comes we will have the storm," he said. "The service should be brief."

"Don Cristóbal was a man of many deeds," the priest replied. "A brief service, therefore, is not appropriate."

"The more deeds the less reason for words."

The priest scratched his bald crown. "The words will not be directed to God, but to those who are here to pray and profit by Don Cristóbal's example."

"My father's virtues are known to all," Saturnino grumbled. "They require no elaboration. Remember that a storm approaches."

"God will stay the storm," Father Expeleta said.

Saturnino was silent. The priest was a stubborn man, hardheaded and evasive, impossible to argue with. Besides, he had ridden many miles from the pueblo on his flop-eared donkey in order to exercise his oratory. Saturnino decided to say nothing more, though he was worried about the storm and doubted very much that God was.

"This is an unfortunate time for Don Cristóbal to be taken off," the priest said. "During a season beneficent beyond memory. With bad news from the North and more to be expected at any moment."

The priest was determined to be as stubborn about this matter as he was about the storm. "The news is exaggerated," Saturnino said emphatically. "It is hatched by politicians who have nothing better to do."

"The news comes from General Castro," Roque de Zubaran, who rode beside the priest, broke in. He was a young man not yet twenty, with the long, narrow head of his father, but of slighter build, his shoulders narrow and sloping, and his bones delicately joined. "Castro says that Captain Frémont has returned from Oregon, is now on the Sacramento."

"Castro is a politician dressed in the uniform of a general," Saturnino replied. "After the battle at Cerro del Gavilán, you will remember, he sent out the story that he had driven the gringos from the hill, inflicting heavy losses. Later we learned from Sandoval, who participated in the battle, that Captain Frémont had simply left the hill unmolested and ridden north."

Saturnino shifted his weight in the saddle and glanced sidewise at his son, encouraging him to answer, but the youth, looking down at his hands, kept his counsel.

It was the priest who spoke. "I recall only General Castro's story."

Saturnino disregarded Father Expeleta's words, waiting patiently for something from his son, though he knew it wouldn't come. For ten years and more he had made every effort to develop a spirit of independence in the youth, to encourage him to express his opinions, but unsuccessfully. One remark in opposition, and Roque retired into a brooding silence. This trait galled Saturnino almost as much as his timidity. He had sent Roque out with his sister to halt the gringo pack train, but it was the girl who had finally accomplished it.

"Why did you stand behind your sister this morning," Saturnino said, his patience at an end, "and permit her to do the talking?"

"Nothing was said," Roque replied.

"It was done, however, and you had no part in it."

The youth was silent.

Looking up at the shifting light along the horizon, Saturnino swore under his breath.

Young Jorge, with an oxgoad over his shoulders and a bang of black hair hanging in his eyes, shuffled along behind the three men. He was giving scant attention to their talk or the beasts that bore Doña Carlota, his grandmother. The conversation in front of him was of no interest; the oxen were obedient—if they faltered, Doña Carlota and her parasol could be counted on. His mind, therefore, was fixed on something else.

At the moment it was on his father's stallion, a flashy beast that lifted its hoofs as if it were treading on hot rocks. In some ways he liked his own gelding, which was smaller and better against Indians. But you weren't chasing Indians every day. A curvetting beast to ride betweentimes would be fine, particularly if Señor Frémont came poking his nose into the valley—it would be just the horse to impress the gringos on their broken-down nags.

His thoughts turned from the stallion to his grandfather, who lay in the cart rumbling along behind him, with his hands folded and weights upon his eyes. At a time like this, Jorge shouldn't be concerned with anything else. Dutifully and with a sharp twinge of conscience, he decided to think about Don Cristóbal de Zubaran.

Someone was always dying on the Hill of the Hawk—one of the servants, the child of a servant, a *vaquero* or one of the family—but this was the first time he had lost a grandfather. There would be a greater profusion of sugar cakes and skulls of panocha, and more candles in the chapel, on this occasion, which would be agreeable. But there were things which wouldn't be so agreeable now that Don Cristóbal was gone. Henceforth when he wanted to take his fighting cocks to El Monte, he wouldn't be able to tell his grandfather, who always believed everything he said, that he was going to the river to snare quail. He would have to ask permission of his father, who would not grant it; nor would he believe the quail story.

Yes, life would surely be different without Don Cristóbal. And to think that he hadn't appreciated him when he was alive! The very day that his grandfather had fallen sick, he had wiggled out of going to the hills to gather herbs for medicine, because of something else that he had wanted to do. The corners of his mouth drew down at this memory, and in an excess of remorse, he decided to expiate this sin by being nicer to his grandmother. It would be difficult, considering the nature of Doña Carlota, but he would do it, or at least try.

He crossed himself and, to seal his new resolve, gave the off oxen a jab with the goad, and began once more to think about Don Saturnino's stallion. In the midst of his reverie, he heard the shrill voice of his grandmother.

"We travel fast now without the goad," she cried. "It is I who will be ready for burial, if the pace is not lessened."

Jorge made no reply, for whatever he said would lead to an answer—he had already made a vow against this. Properly, he should not be walking along with a goad in his hand, leading a cart; he should be riding his gelding up in front with the men of the family. It was a long time before he could gather his thoughts and fix them again upon the buckskin stallion.

Doña Carlota drew hard on her cornhusk cigarette. She decided that as soon as they arrived back at the ranch she would lay out a strict course of discipline for her grandson, Jorge—he had been flying around like a catamount long enough. She would teach him the manners she had been unable to teach him when her husband was alive. She would also do the same for some other people she knew.

The old lady looked at her granddaughter. From beneath the red parasol, which she carried because everyone had expected her to carry the black one, she fixed her sharp eyes on the girl riding beside the cart. She was still annoyed over the way her granddaughter had rushed out, at the bidding of Don Saturnino, and halted the Americans. Luz had wisely stayed away from her, thinking that the episode would be forgotten, until this moment.

"What did the American say when he saw you standing there on the trail, with a musket in your hand, like some stupid *vaquero?*"

The girl's long legs hung loose outside the stirrups. She looked straight ahead and answered calmly, "I don't remember what the gringo said."

"The word 'gringo' is something to be used by a sheepherder," Carlota said. "By someone who knows no better."

"I don't remember," Luz replied, evading the subject, "what he said because I didn't take the trouble to listen."

Carlota sniffed through her thin nose. "I knew you would not remember so I asked your brother."

Luz brushed her rowels against the grass, started to hum a tune, and then stopped in embarrassment. She continued to look straight ahead.

"I have no wonder," Carlota said, "that he thought you were a man."

"He learned soon enough that I wasn't."

"The knowledge was not sufficient to cause him to become speechless."

"You don't know what it was sufficient to do."

"If it had been me, it would have brought you a slap," Carlota said. "He probably desired to give you more than one."

The girl looked at Carlota; her eyes flashed. "I would have shot him if he had." She nudged her palomino forward out of hearing.

She looked at her father riding ahead up the slope. Her eyes still flashed. "Gringo!" she said again. But as she said it the thin sun-dark face of the gringo rose between her and her father. She saw the wide mouth, and the gray, deep-set eyes looking at her from the shadow of his hat. Beneath the dirty buckskin she saw the lift of his shoulders, the hands long and sinewy on the rifle. Luz brushed a wisp of hair from her face. Shifting uneasily in the saddle, she shoved her feet into the stirrups. "Gringo!" she said. She was surprised at the lack of conviction in her voice.

Doña Carlota ground out her cigarette on the bottom of the cart and vowed that, when she was through with Jorge, she would begin on her granddaughter. After that, now that she was mistress of the Hawk, on her son, who, for the silly reason that a worthless wife had run away with an American, had brought up his daughter with a hatred of all Americans. It was a task to exhaust the patience and skill of Saint Gregory, but she would manage it or leave many broken heads in her path.

She turned and glanced down the slope at the caravan plodding along behind her. Every aunt, every uncle, it seemed to her, was there on the slope. And every cousin, five times removed, on both sides of the family, their servants, the relatives of the servants, brats and dogs, from Santa Barbara in the north to San Diego in the south, and hangers-on she had never in her life laid eyes on.

She groaned. By what special device of the devil, she asked herself, did she have to be burdened with this crowd? By what dispensation and at whose invitation had the whole countryside become involved in the burial of Don Cristóbal? After all, he had been her husband—a fine man as men went—and it was wholly her own affair. She should have gone out early in the morning with a *vaquero* and buried him herself, as she had buried her first son.

But this was now beyond her power to change; the problems of Jorge and Don Saturnino and Luz belonged to the future. It was her bodily discomfort which concerned her at the moment. The fact that she had been routed out of bed at dawn, that a storm was gathering, that because her son was in a hurry—there was a pretty new girl at the ranch he was probably worrying about—he had set a pace that was fast jolting the life out of her.

She looked critically at the caravan struggling up the hill. The Peralta family, riding in a cart with a black, tasseled canopy. The city De Zubarans. She raised her voice above the creaking wheels and commanded Jorge to bring the oxen to a halt. She would show her son, and the Peraltas and the Malaspinas. She would show them, one and all, that the mistress of the Hawk was Doña Carlota de Zubaran.

Roused out of his dreaming, Jorge halted the oxen.

He leaned on the goad and watched his grandmother crawl out of the cart—nimbly for her years—and walk slowly, looking neither to one side nor the other, across the trail, and along the hillside to the nearest clump of bushes.

He looked down the slope and saw that all the carts had come to a stop. People were standing up, craning their necks to see what had happened. He hoped that no one would think badly of his grandmother; he was sure they would not, knowing her as they did. But at least she might have chosen a larger bush.

Don Saturnino was riding along with his eyes on the gathering storm, half listening to Father Expeleta, when he was aware that the clatter had ceased behind him. Jerking his stallion to a halt, he rose in the stirrups. He shaded his eyes and glared down the slope at the silent wheels and the motionless horsemen. He discerned nothing to account for the halt. Then, closer at hand, under his very nose, he saw a figure, carrying a red parasol, saunter across the hillside. It was his mother.

Saturnino dropped in the saddle and dug his rowels into the stallion's flanks. "Angels of Christ!" he shouted to the morning. "*Jesús María* and all the Saints!"

The glade was filled with smoky haze. Above the giant oak, thunderheads had overrun the sun. Beneath the oak, the crosses scattered among the grass were rayed with deflected light.

Saturnino stood with his legs thrust apart, hands knotted behind him, muffled to the eyes in his black poncho. He looked around him at the sky, the unmoving leaves, the half circle of mourners, and finally at the crosses. Winter rain had washed away the lime, and sun had whitened and checked the wood. They looked stark there with the live, spring grass growing around them. They reminded him suddenly of his own mortality. For an instant his eyes clouded. Then he flexed the muscles of his legs and glanced up. His yellow eyes confidently swept the glade.

Beneath the oak Father Expeleta had opened his breviary and was reading, the words issuing from his cowl like words out of a cavern, mixed with the distant rumble of thunder and the sound of weeping.

Saturnino looked at the priest and then at the half circle of mourners—everyone was crying except his mother. The noise sent a chill into the marrow of his bones. He shifted his feet restlessly. The sobs seemed to grow louder, louder than the priest's words and the sound of the thunder.

Saturnino lifted his hand and snatched the poncho from his mouth. "Enough! Enough of the weeping," he bellowed so all would hear. "I will tell you when to weep."

The sobbing ceased. The priest's words rolled through the glade. Thunder boomed on the horizon.

Saturnino looked at the sky again, the light receding into the sky's upper reaches, the trees moving now in a faint wind, and once more at the crosses in front of him. He looked from one to another, remembering each one, and by his memory giving each a moment of precarious life: Guero, who had lived a year and died in a fit of coughing; Delfina with the curly hair and laughing mouth—it was twelve years now since she had been thrown to her death, and those years had not changed his belief that a girl should be taught to ride as soon as she was old enough to walk; there was Arturo, his brother, and Aunt Petra, Lucienda and Nieves, dead of smallpox; Doña Petra's husband, Felipe, killed by Indians at the Cajon because he was a man of great courage; Doña Beatriz, his first wife, and a frigid, excessively religious woman she was too.

There were others that he could not recall, and many graves of Indian servants and their children—in a full lifetime a man should not be asked to remember everyone. But there was one that should be here and was not; his face twisted with anger at the thought of her, and wherever she was he wished her dead.

His gaze moved across the markers, resting at last upon one which was chiseled with the date 1837. His eyes were motionless for a brief moment. Then they raised and sought out the girl who stood a few steps beyond, under the oak. She was looking at him and as their eyes met he remembered with sudden warmth her part in the scene on the trail that morning; it made up in a measure for his son's timidity.

A sudden wind swept through the glade, bending the tall grass and fluttering the robes of the priest, who was talking now in Latin. The wind ceased and after a while blew again, this time so gently that the grass failed to stir. The haze grew heavier and there was a breath of dampness in the air.

Saturnino's gaze moved on from his daughter to the woman beside her. She stood with her hands hidden beneath a shawl, erect and unmoving as a pillar of stone. But her black eyes darted here and there, resting upon the tethered horses and yoked oxen, the circle of friends and relatives, on the priest and on him, missing nothing.

Looking at his mother, her eyes undimmed by age, her unyielding carriage, at the thin, obdurate mouth and the flinty nose, like the beak of a parrot, he measured her as one measures an antagonist. She had always ruled Don Cristóbal and she had ruled him. Don Cristóbal was now in his grave, but he, Don Saturnino de Zubaran, was very much alive. She had delivered the first thrust coming up the trail, but the conflict had just begun. He was prepared and ready.

Beyond Doña Carlota stood his two sons, the younger one engaged at the moment in surreptitiously pinching his brother. Saturnino withdrew the poncho from his mouth and was on the point of correcting his son, when he saw Carlota turn slowly and hiss through her teeth. The boy straightened as if he had been kicked. Saturnino frowned and gave his attention to Father Expeleta. The priest, no longer speaking in Latin, had begun his discourse on Don Cristóbal's life.

There were mutterings of thunder over the mountain and the priest raised his voice. ". . . Honorably he bore arms against the tyrant Napoleon, and served the viceroy of New Spain with distinction."

Father Expeleta paused as the thunder rolled closer, drowning out his words, and waited for the rumbling to diminish.

"It is well to remember Don Cristóbal now," the priest went on, "for these are days when great distress may fall upon the land."

Saturnino grunted in the folds of his poncho. It was clear that the priest still clung to his belief that a conflict between the Americans and Spaniards was inevitable. Saturnino grunted again, louder this time. The politicians had no intention of making war. They invented rumors, issued manifestoes, uttered bloody threats against the invader. But in the end they did nothing. Their cowardice filled him with rage and distrust.

He glanced around for his cousin's son, and, not seeing him, listened once more to Father Expeleta. He was saying, ". . . for these days when men are tempted to vengeance."

Saturnino shifted his weight impatiently. He was being counseled by the priest, through the example of his father, to alter his convictions, to assume an attitude of moderation toward the foreigners who had come into the country. To condone their illegal and arrogant actions!

He looked at a tall, heavy-set man standing on the fringe of the throng. His name was Wolfe and he was a friend of Don Cristóbal. He had come at no one's invitation, least of all, Saturnino's. He stood there apart from the rest, overdressed in his Spanish clothes, and uneasy, as if aware that he was an interloper.

Saturnino looked back at the priest, listening carefully as he continued with his counsel.

Suddenly Saturnino's yellow eyes took fire. "Death," he said in an even voice. "Death to the gringos!"

The priest went on calmly. Wolfe did not move.

The last of the earth had been thrown into the grave, and two Indians were arranging a double layer of rocks against marauding beasts, when Saturnino heard above the priest's final words the sound of hoofs moving at a brisk Spanish walk. The sound came from the north, ceased for a time as the sand of the small arroyo was crossed, and then began on the uptrail. With no more to judge from than the sound of the hoofs, the pace and rhythm of the riding, Saturnino knew that the horse was his gray stallion, the rider his cousin's son.

Saturnino watched him dismount and join the mourners under the oak. Julio's round face was serious and there was a restlessness in his gaze which had nothing to do with the occasion. More rumors, Saturnino thought. Even a proclamation from Governor Pico. There had been many lately . . . it was time for another.

Saturnino looked at the priest, who had closed the pages of his breviary. On the horizon the thunder had ceased, and quiet crept over the glade. The mourners lifted their eyes. He freed his chin from the poncho and said in a voice loud enough for everyone to hear, "The time has come to weep."

Saturnino strode through the glade, swung into the saddle, and turned his horse toward the trail. He had not gone a dozen paces when Julio de Zubaran stepped in front of him.

"There is no need to open this now," Julio said, handing him a letter, sealed with wax and fastened with the red, official ribbon of the governor. "I will tell you what it contains."

Saturnino stuffed the letter in his pocket. He could not read—reading and writing were feminine accomplishments, which he looked upon with contempt—but he was nevertheless pleased that he had been saved the pretense.

"I'll talk briefly because I have yet to see Palomares and I must return to the pueblo before night." Julio glanced at the heavy clouds churning over his head. "The letter contains a summons from Governor Pico. You are commanded to muster weapons and horses, and await a call to gather in Los Angeles within the next two weeks."

Saturnino frowned. "What is it that transpires this time?"

"The Americans are massing troops on the Sacramento. It's the governor's intention to ride north with a large force and join General Castro."

"More likely he goes to fight Castro."

"This time it's to fight the Americans."

Saturnino gave Julio a searching look. Was it possible that Governor Pico was finally going to act? That this was not just another proclamation, another gesture to placate those who like himself had become infuriated at the governor's laxness toward the gringos, a foray against General Castro rather than against the invaders?

"If this is another ruse," Saturnino said threateningly, "someone will pay for it."

"I bring you the news of the American activities on the Sacramento as it came two days ago from Monterey. As it came again yesterday by courier from San Francisco. And I can assure you that Governor Pico intends to act."

Saturnino gathered himself in the saddle. His heavy jaw thrust forward. "Then death to the gringos," he said in a hoarse whisper. "And no rest for any Spaniard until they are driven into the sea."

Don Saturnino rode out of the glade and down the trail alone. Below him lay the ranch, the meadowlands and shallow arroyos, the winding streams bordered with willows, the broad channel of the Santa Ana curving down the mountains. There below him was the mesa, an upthrust of land flat as a table, oval in shape and a quarter of a league in extent. On it stood the house, the great hollow rectangle of limewashed walls, solid as a fort and actually a fort with its own ironbanded gate, the revetments at each corner from which the enemy could be enfiladed, the walls pierced by few windows and those small, mere loopholes strategically placed, the thick three-foot walls impervious alike to arrow or bullet.

He hunched his powerful shoulders. His gaze took in the house and corrals, the streams and river, the roaming, wide-horned cattle, with one sweeping glance. All that his eyes encompassed lay under his protection. He would protect it with his life. When he arrived home he would have his daughter write a letter to Governor Pico, accepting the summons, and send it to the pueblo by Roque. Afterward he would gather horses, see to the conditioning of muskets and lances. Then he would have the pit deepened for the making of powder. In the morning he would give orders for the saving of all urine in the house, the collection of weeds, ashes, chicken dung, bones and refuse from the slaughter. He would be ready when the call came.

Thunder rolled and the first drops of rain began to hiss around him. He looked off into the west where the dust of the pack train still hung in the quiet air. His mouth twisted in a smile, remembering how the pack train had been halted on the trail, and deliberately, as expression of his contempt and the contempt of all Spaniards, by a girl.

"Death to the gringo!" he said to himself. "And may the day soon come when they no longer raise dust on the King's Highway!"

# 3

Trees writhed and grass bent to the wallowing wind. A bluish-gray tongue curled down from the south hills, changed shape and fanned out over the lowlands. Lightning forked through it, thunder crashed, and gray wedges of rain, one wedge following another until they were finally joined, advanced across the trail.

Grady Dunavant rode steadily into the west.

The packs were secure against the rain—they had weathered a dozen violent storms since Santa Fe. They would be impervious to this last one. The same held true for Lampson muttering behind him, and Boyd, who had left his place in the train and was now riding up. Mr. Fraser, as was to be expected, made no comment.

"There's a ranch off east," Boyd said, pointing.

Dunavant showed no surprise that after more than a month of correction he still didn't know one direction from another. "East?" he repeated.

"Over there." Water was dripping from Boyd's hat and his stubborn Kentucky chin. "By the oaks."

"I've seen it."

"We can get out of the rain."

"We'll keep moving," Dunavant said.

The storm wouldn't last longer than an hour at this time of year, but with the end of the trip in sight an hour was not to be wasted. By riding on, the cargo would be delivered in Los Angeles before nightfall, as well as Mr. Fraser and his damned collapsible English oven which delayed every meal or tossed it into the fire. Lampson and Boyd, God bless them. He wondered if they would be glad to see the last of him, and if their pleasure would match his. Undoubtedly it would. The thought was somehow pleasing; it was proof to him that he had done a good job against odds and with little help.

Boyd, still grumbling beside him, finally gave up and rode to the rear. There had been no point in explaining to the Kentuckian, if he didn't know after the encounter on the trail, that you didn't ride up to a Spaniard's home seeking shelter and expect to be welcomed in; that one time, years ago, you could or thought you could, but not in these latter times, certainly not now after this morning.

Dunavant, leaving the men to curse behind him and cough in throats which were no longer dry, bent his shoulders against the driving rain. It had been three hours since they were stopped on the trail, but the anger lumped in his stomach hadn't grown any smaller. He still could see the girl sitting there in the middle of the King's Highway, looking at him with an eye as cold as the muzzle of the ancient musket pointed across the saddle horn. He could hear her voice now above the drumming of the rain, and the derisive word gringo spoken in a slurring accent. He could taste the bitter dust as she had ridden away, the dust of the caravan. He imagined again the Spaniard on the buckskin stallion wondering if his gesture of contempt in sending a girl out to halt the pack train had been understood.

Yes, every part of it—you on the buckskin stallion; you with the musket, in leather trousers—and it still rankled. The worst of it was he never would have another chance to confront either one of them. Nothing would give him more satisfaction than to meet them again on the trail, particularly the girl with her haughty mouth and female assurance. Sometime when he wasn't in a hurry and there was no cargo to worry about. He hadn't missed the look in her eyes when she had ridden up. He had seen the look before in Taos and Santa Fe and New Orleans and St. Louis. He knew what it meant. For all her Spanish pride, her hatred of the gringo, the musket and the leather trousers, there was soft flesh underneath. A woman who could be reached with time and a little patience.

But he would never have this pleasure, unfortunately. He would have to chew on his anger and digest it.

The sky had lightened to a thin gray. The gray had paled to gold and now as they rode down the sandy banks of the San Gabriel it was a clear, pulsing blue.

Dunavant considered riding on, but it was the ten minutes out of every hour when they walked and led the saddle horses—a cavalry practice which he had instituted at the beginning of the journey, which he had not deviated from in a thousand miles, and which as much as any one thing had brought them through safely. This time they would halt, but not for the horses, since they were within easy distance of the pueblo.

"We'll be here for a few minutes," Grady told Lampson and Boyd. "I am going to change clothes. You can do the same."

Boyd looked at him from the saddle and said, "I thought we were an hour out of Los Angeles."

"An hour and a half." Dunavant took fresh clothes from his kit. "Possibly longer, Boyd, if we spend time debating." He slipped off his trousers and shirt. "Buckskin has a habit of shrinking as it dries."

It was a poor excuse and Dunavant knew it, but it wasn't necessary or possible to explain why, after having ridden in wet buckskin on several previous occasions, he was now changing into his best clothes.

"If we'd taken shelter at the ranch back there . . ."

"Then," Dunavant said, walking down the bank, "we wouldn't be here."

The river was icy cold with melted snow from the mountains, and while he was trying to wash himself and breathe at the same time, Mr. Fraser waded out beside him. It was the first time he had seen the Englishman without his clothes. Somehow, at other times, Mr. Fraser gave the impression of fragility, but standing there braced against the current, in spite of his white skin, the color heightened by his red face and red hands, in spite of a certain womanly reticence, he revealed that his body was long-muscled and hard. Dunavant had often wondered how old the Englishman was, settling after deliberation on the age of forty. But looking at him now, he changed his mind and decided that Fraser was nearer his own age, thirty. The matter could be concluded by a simple question, but remembering an occasion at the start of the trip when he had asked Fraser how long he had been in the United States, he refrained from asking it.

"This is the first time in the water since we left Santa Fe," Fraser said, showing, surprisingly, no reaction to the icy river.

Mr. Fraser took a bath every day in a leather horse bucket, but he apparently didn't count this. There had been one time, however, that he had forgotten. "Not counting," Dunavant reminded him, "the dive in the Gila."

"Yes, that." Mr. Fraser grinned and sluiced a handful of water over his face. "You know you damned well saved my life. Another moment or two and I'd have been a dead one."

Nothing had been said on the Gila, and nothing since; Dunavant was glad to know that Mr. Fraser had really appreciated the rescue all the time. It was possible, he thought, walking toward his clothes, that if the trip had been twice as long, by the end he might be able to learn the Englishman's age, and a few other things that puzzled him.

Mr. Fraser didn't have to shave now—he shaved every morning in cold water and clipped his mustache with a pair of diminutive scissors; so he was dressed and ready before Dunavant had finished with his beard. He sat his horse a few yards away, a neat man and, Dunavant was forced to admit, glancing at him from time to time over the top of the mirror propped on the saddle, a strikingly handsome man, with his high color, blond hair and spare, emotionless face. Handsome and intelligent both. Mr. Fraser, sitting there on his horse looking in well-bred indifference at the mountains, knew why Grady was dressing and shaving, as surely as if he had been told.

In the saddle Grady reconnoitered the crossing. The river ran swift and discolored, but it wasn't the current that bothered him as much as the quicksand. He chose a place a hundred yards below the crossing he had made two years ago when he had lost three horses and their loads in the shifting sand, and headed his pony on a slight angle upstream. From the far bank he signaled Boyd to proceed, watching tensely as the pack train moved into the water, sagged a little as the current struck, but came on.

As the train wound up the beach, he allowed himself a moment of congratulation that the last physical hazard had been passed. The moment was dimmed only by the sudden knowledge that he had water in his new boots, that he shouldn't have changed clothes before the crossing. But this error, he concluded, was permissible in the circumstances—it had been two years almost to a day since he had seen Camilla Howland.

The willows, shining in the hot sun, fell behind. The trail stretched away in a sweeping crescent through hills yellow with mustard. Shoving his hat back from his forehead again, he flicked his pony into a fast walk.

Through the windless dusk, Grady Dunavant rode into Los Angeles. He sat straight in the saddle, his legs long in the stirrups, with one hand loose at his side. He rode up the twisting path from the river with the air of a man leading a column of cavalry rather than a pack train.

Beneath the down-turned brim of his hat he appeared to see nothing, but his eyes took in everything around him. A new planting of grapes had been made on the flat land northeast of the pueblo; the old ones, leafing out, showed in a tender mist of green on both sides of the trail. Irrigation ditches ran full, branching out among small farms where beans and corn were already high. The new planting of grapes, the old ones heavy with growing clusters, the full ditches, the early produce, should mean a contented populace. In the milpas men carried rattles instead of muskets to ward off thieving crows. This indicated that the pueblo was low on powder and ball, less disposed, therefore, to use them frivolously on a passing American. Along the approaches to the town he saw no sign of a soldier. Smoke hung blue and peaceful above the flat roofs.

Dunavant smiled in the shadow of his hat and flicked his spotted pony into a trot. Behind him the lead horses picked up momentum, the pace passed quickly along the line, and with the jingling of hawk bells and harness and a clatter of hoofs and shouts from Boyd and Lampson, the pack train bore down upon the plaza, past the great mud-colored Church of Our Lady of the Angels.

Horsemen and people afoot stood aside for the train to pass but no one spoke a greeting. On the face of every Spaniard and peon, Dunavant saw a look of unconcealed hostility. His smile did not change. He glanced at the buzzards circling in the last of the day's light. He glanced with indifference at the faces smoldering with hatred. Someone, as he turned down the lane toward Kate Howland's, called him a Yankee pig without a mother. His smile broadened. To hell with all the Spaniards! The cargo was safe!

The corral was empty except for two Mexican hostlers, who came forward on bare, shuffling feet to take his horse. He knew them both from the last trip; they spoke, but with a coolness that a liberal tip did not change. To hell with them also! He leaped to the ground and, standing beside the gate, counted each horse, going over in his mind the contents of every pack. Silverware. Silk from China by way of Mexico. Ladies' dresses. Shoes. Trinkets and beads and carved images and rosaries. Chocolate. Coffee. Woolen goods from the Navajos.

The last horse trotted into the corral. Dunavant stepped forward, with the relief of a man who snaps the lock on a chest of treasure, and closed the gate. He thrust his hands into his pockets and stood there in the dusk watching Lampson and Boyd and the two hostlers struggling with the packs. Thirty-six thousand dollars were deposited to his account in St. Louis, the results of two trips to California, three to St. Louis and two into Mexico. The present cargo had cost him a trifle under seven thousand; even allowing for the fact that Kate Howland was a sharp trader, it would bring him sixteen thousand, minus five hundred to both Lampson and Boyd—a net of eight thousand dollars.

He rolled a cigarette, lighted it and drew deep on the bitter smoke. Counting the deposit in St. Louis, the sum came to forty-four thousand dollars. It was enough to buy the largest ranch in California, to buy cattle and horses, to build a house and fill it with fine furniture. More than enough, actually, but the plan was impractical. He had been arrested before. He could be arrested again and his holdings, if he had any, confiscated. Someday, however, he would own a ranch. He saw it in his mind's eye, a rambling house, with a stream flowing through lush acres and cattle on a hundred hills. Again, standing there in the corral, he repeated the vow he had made at the Cajon.

In the midst of this tableau, Mr. Fraser cleared his throat and spoke, coming toward him out of the dusk. "Doesn't this call for a drink, Mr. Dunavant? The last leg of the journey. The parting of good company. And all that sort of thing."

"The best the house affords, Mr. Fraser."

Dunavant excused himself—the Englishman was a great stickler for formalities—and walked over to where Lampson and Boyd were unloading the packs. There was no point in advising them about their conduct in the pueblo, but he did it anyway, adding a word about the game of *chusa,* which they would find in the tavern and elsewhere.

"A knee shoved against the leg of the table can make the ivory ball fall where it's wanted. People have lost a year's earnings at the game."

It wasn't necessary to say that he had. Boyd replied that he could beat any game he'd ever seen, and Lampson, as Dunavant left them, mumbled something of a similar nature.

The tavern, which formed one side of the corral and a wing of the rambling *fonda,* was filled with lamp smoke and the sour smell of wine spillings, a long narrow room with walls washed white with gypsum, hung with pictures of sailing ships. The floor was hard and glossy black, made of earth mixed with ox blood. At the far end of the room was a small bar and suspended over it, above the squat figure of an Indian, was the head of a wolf, yellow fangs bared in a grimace of ferocity. At rough-hewn tables were Mexican soldiers, Spanish ranchers and, sitting by themselves in a corner, three American sailors listening to a blind Indian picking at a guitar.

Dunavant, at the bar, found it necessary to raise his voice, for the din was considerable. "*Aguardiente* or wine, Mr. Fraser?"

The Englishman chose the former, they touched glasses and downed the fiery native brandy, Dunavant gingerly and Mr. Fraser at one long gulp, with no more evidence of distress than he had shown standing in the snow water of the San Gabriel.

They had another drink, and while Dunavant was recovering his breath, Mr. Fraser said, "I presume you'll be here for a few days." Dunavant nodded. "We can arrange our accounts then at your leisure." The Englishman's pale-blue eyes traveled slowly over Dunavant. "No doubt other things occupy your thoughts at the moment." He smiled faintly, a surprising thing for him to do—Dunavant recalled nothing of the kind during the entire trip. "I understand your anxiety to be about other matters."

Dunavant held out his hand, glad of the chance to be on his way and the Englishman took it in a warm grip, saying, "I offer my blessing to you both."

Dunavant had mentioned the matter only once, and then briefly, the first day out of Santa Fe. The Englishman had a good memory.

"Thank you, Mr. Fraser," he said.

Grady Dunavant walked down the passageway which led from the tavern into the store. Mrs. Howland was not behind the counter or sitting on the high stool working on her ledger. He went out into the passageway again, along it to the north wing of the inn, and knocked on a door in the rear of the establishment. At the sound of his fist on the oak panel, a voice shouted, "Wipe your boots and come in." His boots were clean, but knowing Kate Howland he wiped them anyway, making a suitable commotion as he did so.

She was sitting in a rocking chair, looking into space, her long jaw cupped in her hand. At first she didn't move, but when she recognized him she jumped to her feet, strode across the room and clasped his hand with the hard grip of a bullwhacker.

"Stab me, if it isn't Grady Dunavant!" She steered him toward the sofa and seated him with a bony poke of a finger. "I was just sitting here rocking and pining for someone to talk to." She straightened the pillows and sat down opposite him. "When did you come?" Before he could answer, she said, "Getting deaf as a post or I'd heard you in the corral."

"Or coming up from the river. A pack train can be heard at that distance."

He was thinking of Camilla, not of her mother's deafness, of the girl with the red-gold hair whom he had half expected to find waiting for him when he had ridden down the lane and into the corral. Every day of the trip he had thought of her, picturing her there beside the gate, with the light shining on her hair, sometimes in a white dress, sometimes in a yellow one, but always standing at the gate. She hadn't been there, however, and she wasn't here. Actually, he was not surprised. She had talked about going East to visit her aunt. It was possible, as he had cautioned himself daily, that she had gone and not yet returned, that none of the three letters he had written had reached her.

"Overslept this morning," Kate Howland was saying, "and haven't caught up yet. Celebrated my wedding anniversary last night. Thirty-five years a bride and widow. Drank a bottle of Rose of Peru all by myself."

Dunavant sat forward on the sofa. Without further ceremony, he said, "Where is Camilla?"

"Time flies, doesn't it? One minute you're young and the next you're old and have a headache." She stood up and fussed with the curtain at the window, saying over his shoulder, "It's been a pretty day, with the rain and all. I like the rain better than the sun. The glare's enough to put your eyes out. Sometimes I wish I had never left Boston." She blew her nose loudly into a large colored handkerchief.

Dunavant raised his voice and repeated the question.

"Camilla? Oh, she's getting ready for the fandango tonight. She'll be along presently." Mrs. Howland straightened a rug with the toe of her boot. "What did you bring me this time, young man? More Navajo rugs, I hope. Sold the last ones inside a week. All except this one. I saved it out because it was the prettiest."

Dunavant leaned back against the cushions. "A full line," he said brightly, thinking of Camilla. After two years, he was here in Los Angeles and Camilla was in her room dressing. "Everything I brought before, Mrs. Howland."

A hen set up a sudden clamor somewhere out behind, and Kate Howland bounced to her feet. "That's Sarah. If you'll excuse me I'll fetch her in. Thievery's been going on lately and I've taken to bringing her in of nights." She took something from a vase on the table. An egg. She held it up for him to see. "Sarah lays them every day, speckled nice as a picture."

With swinging skirts she disappeared, and after a little he heard her through the partitions crooning and talking nonsense to the hen.

Dunavant let his eyes wander over the room. He was surprised that nothing had been changed in his absence, how every detail associated with the thought of Camilla was the same. Against the far wall was the table with a black marble top and carved brass feet; over it the mirror and in the center of the mirror the painted scene of green bluffs, a river winding among trees, and handsome cavaliers and their ladies strolling beside a phaeton. On each side of the mirror were portraits in oil. The one on the right was of Mr. Howland, captain of the *Allure*. There was a small picture of the ship in the background and in front of it sat the master, erect, disciplined, with commanding eyes that by some nasty trick of the painter's art followed you wherever you turned in the room. The other portrait was of his wife, plucking at the strings of a golden harp. It was difficult to imagine Kate Howland with a harp, the woman who had taken over the inn after the captain's death and had run it successfully with the help of a few Indians and Mexicans.

He glanced toward the door and the hallway which led to Camilla's room; finally he got up, crossed the room and listened, pressing his ear against the door. There was a faint sound of someone singing. Camilla! He lighted a cigarette and was strolling around, thinking that this was a good time to tell Kate Howland he was going to marry her daughter—he really should have told her before he left two years ago—when she burst into the room, her skirts slapping against her legs. She was carrying a wicker cage in which a Dominique hen teetered and squawked.

"Sit down, young man. We'll have supper in a jiffy. Camilla came back from New York with a lot of newfangled ideas. Takes her as long to put on her shoes now as it takes me to dress from the skin out."

Mrs. Howland set the hen in the corner and covered her with a shawl.

"You wouldn't know Camilla, she's so changed. Girls grow up, Grady Dunavant. Faster, I guess, in New York. But they grow up anywhere. And a good thing too. For the race, that is. If they didn't, if they stayed freckle-faced, pig-tailed and slab-sided, with no more in front than a couple of small apricots, the world would be in a pretty pickle."

He had never thought of Camilla growing up; she remained to him as he had seen her last, quite different from what her mother had just described. But however she had changed she was still the girl he was going to marry.

"Mrs. Howland," he said, deciding to waste no more time about the matter. "When I was here before Camilla and I talked about——"

"You'd scarcely know her. She walked in the room here when she came back from the East and I had to look twice." Mrs. Howland sat down in the chair and began to rock. "I'll swear it nearly knocked me off my perch. But what did knock me off was something else. You'd never guess, Grady Dunavant." She looked at him with her sharp blue eyes, wagging her head from side to side, and clucking in her throat. "You'd never guess."

He grinned and shrugged his shoulders and waited for her to finish.

"You know what! She got herself engaged."

"Engaged?"

"In New York. Without saying anything. Not a word in any of her letters. Just up and got engaged to a young man she met at a dance. Met him, danced with him, and got engaged, all in one night. He's an Englishman. Name's Fraser. Peter Pomeroy Fraser. Did you ever hear of him?"

Dunavant gulped. In the whole world there wouldn't be more than a couple of Peter Pomeroy Frasers.

"He's on his way to California now," she said.

Dunavant gulped for the second time. In the United States and on his way to California, there was not more than one Englishman by that name. And he was not on his way. He was here, under Kate Howland's roof, was Peter Pomeroy Fraser.

"Isn't it the silliest thing you ever heard of in your life?" Mrs. Howland asked.

Dunavant found his voice. "It is," he replied.

Kate Howland suddenly quit rocking, leaned forward, gripping the arms of the chair, and gave him an outraged glance. "I'll have a talk with this Mr. Fraser when he comes, you can bet. And if he's not a lot better than he sounds, a lot better than any Englishman I've ever seen, there'll be no wedding."

Dunavant looked down at Mrs. Howland sitting there with her eyes snapping. He saw Mr. Fraser floundering around in the swirling waters of the Gila, nearer dead than alive, and himself risking his life to drag him to safety. He remembered the determination with which he had kept the pack train moving from dawn until night, not only in his own interest, but also under the spur of the Englishman's great hurry to reach Los Angeles, the bonus for every day saved from the regular schedule. He saw Mr. Fraser bathing in the icy waters of the San Gabriel and dressing himself meticulously for his entry into the pueblo.

He recalled Peter Pomeroy Fraser at the bar, his handshake and blessing. Dunavant thought of all these things and began to laugh.

"It's not funny, Grady Dunavant. You'd laugh on the other side of your face if you had a daughter who treated you to a piece of silliness like this. Meeting a man once and . . ."

"There's nothing to worry about," Dunavant said. "Whether you like Mr. Fraser or not." He picked up his hat from the table. "I am going out to the corral to see about my goods—if they're stealing chickens nothing is safe. I may not be back for supper but I'll be at the fandango tonight, wherever it is." He walked to the door and opened it. "And don't worry about Camilla or Peter Pomeroy Fraser," he said.

# 4

It was eleven o'clock by Grady Dunavant's watch as he made his way through the warm night toward the fandango at Jacob Kroll's. His tan, tight-fitting coat, with its brown velvet lapels, was carefully brushed. A hard, brown hat sat on his head at a jaunty angle. His boots, polished to a mirrorlike brightness, tossed sharp, clear echoes against the mud walls.

He walked rapidly down the deserted lane, for at the last minute while he was sitting in his room polishing his boots, a Mexican official had knocked on the door and insisted upon checking over his invoices. A bottle of wine had loosened the Mexican's tongue but had not kept him from forcing Dunavant to return to the corral to go through the cargo item by item, until everything had been checked off. As a consequence, he was now two hours late for the fandango.

Lights showed in the houses of the rich that ringed the plaza; a dull glow came through the doors of the Church of Our Lady, and beyond in a narrow lane he saw the glare of pine torches at Jacob Kroll's. His irritation with the Mexican official evaporated before the more pressing problem of Camilla Howland. It had been foolish of him, two years ago when he had last talked to her, not to see to it that there was a definite understanding between them, also with her mother. It would have prevented the ludicrous scene earlier in the evening with Kate Howland and the situation confronting him, which for some reason didn't seem so funny now as it had when it had burst upon him in Mrs. Howland's parlor. But that was in the past, like a good many other things, an oversight which no longer amused him but could be remedied.

Oxcarts, tethered horses and a few carriages cluttered the lane in front of Jacob Kroll's. From the patio, shut off from the lane by a high wall, he heard the squeal of violins, the dragging notes of guitars, the sound of women's laughter. Candles in thin paper covers threw colored reflections against the smoky night sky. With the confident air of an aroused and determined man, he knocked on the door and was let into a hall, which led through a series of halls into a large room furnished in dark woods, blue velvet curtains and blue rugs. In the center of the room hung a great crystal chandelier, sparkling with pendants.

Dunavant paused before a door that led out into a patio crowded with dancers, long enough to catch a glimpse of Camilla's red-gold hair, and the slender figure of Mr. Fraser. He smiled to himself, noting the proprietary look on the Englishman's red face—little did Mr. Fraser know that his marriage to Camilla would never take place, not if she had to be shanghaied aboard ship—and then he crossed the room to where Kate Howland and Jacob Kroll were sitting beside a punch bowl.

Mrs. Howland wore dangling blue earrings and a blue dress which was a shade lighter than the rugs. He had not gone back to supper and had not talked to her since, but, walking across the room, as he met her gaze he was aware before she spoke that she was delighted out of her wits with the Englishman.

"Why didn't you tell me that Mr. Fraser came in with you today?" Kate Howland said accusingly. "He's the most charming young man imaginable."

"Very cultivated," Dunavant said with a touch of irony, which was lost on Mrs. Howland. He pictured her chagrin—it would equal Mr. Fraser's—when her daughter informed her of the change in plans, or if not then, when Camilla was spirited away from under her nose. "And very charming," he added.

Jacob Kroll stood up and forced a cup of punch into his hand. He was a short, potbellied little man with thin legs and grizzled hair cut close over a round skull. Dunavant had met Kroll only once before, but he was well acquainted with the man's history. He was a retired sea captain, a widower who had been in California for ten years, variously occupied as a rancher, a dealer in hides and an importer of goods. During this period he had been arrested several times for failure to pay adequate excise taxes. He was known among his friends as a sharp trader, and among the Spaniards as a smuggler, a restless, dangerous character.

"Glad you could come," Kroll said, in a quarter-deck voice which belied his appearance. "We've just been talking about you. Something has turned up that we think you'll be interested in."

"I've worked my last for a while," Dunavant said. "Eight years on the trail entitles a man to a rest."

Kroll pushed a chair toward him. "This is not work. Far from it. If

I were younger and more favorably known among our friends, the Spaniards, I'd undertake it myself."

Dunavant, though he was not interested in what Jacob Kroll had to say, sat down. He looked at Kroll but his mind was on the dancers. The music stopped; he could hear the sound of voices and laughter drifting in from the patio.

Kroll offered him a thinly veined cigar out of a silver case and lighted one himself. "I understand you've been in the army," he said. "An officer in the cavalry during the fight in Texas."

Dunavant didn't bother to correct the date, but his eyes narrowed; he wondered how Kroll knew about Texas and the cavalry.

"You were in the fight, weren't you?" Kroll persisted.

"I don't see how this has a bearing on anything," Grady said bluntly, "but I *was*, in '36."

Kroll squinted over his cigar at Dunavant, puzzled at his tone. "Yes, I remember now. The year I came here." He motioned for an Indian to fill the cups. "This is what I have in mind."

The music had begun again, soft and faraway, a waltz. Dunavant forgot Kroll.

"You've noticed a difference in the Spaniards since you were here two years ago?" Kroll was saying.

Grady nodded.

"You've noticed it, but do you know the reason?"

"They've always been unpredictable. I wouldn't attempt to gauge their temper now or explain it. It varies from season to season. With the weather, possibly, or the crops."

Kroll shook his head. "It's neither one. Both are the best in memory. The reason is deeper and immediate." He paused and fixed his eyes dramatically on Dunavant. "Captain Frémont is in California. On the Sacramento with a small army!"

"Think of it. Captain Frémont!" Mrs. Howland cried. "I've read about him in the New York papers Camilla brought home." She lapsed into a momentary dream, her eyes lifted to the ceiling. Then she said with a loud sigh, "He must be a dashing figure. The pale, serious face. The flashing gaze."

Dunavant squirmed in his seat. He didn't share her enthusiasm about the Pathfinder, or Kroll's interest in his presence on the Sacramento with a small army. Frémont's exploits had been overrated; what he had done had been done before, by better men, without fanfare, and without the help of Senator Benton, the captain's father-in-law. He looked toward the door which led into the patio. He wasn't in the least concerned with what Frémont was doing. He was even less concerned with what Jacob Kroll had to say.

"Captain Frémont has already met the Spaniards in a skirmish at Gavilán Peak, near Monterey," Kroll said. "That was early in March. The engagement was indecisive. Afterward Captain Frémont retired to the Sacramento. Later to Oregon. Yesterday we received word that he's back on the river at Sutter's Fort."

"But with no authority to attack the Spaniards," Mrs. Howland broke in. "Or even the authority to provoke them into attacking him."

Grady Dunavant finished his punch and set the cup on the table. In Santa Fe he had heard rumors of a possible war with Mexico. It was discussed freely there among the Americans, editorially in the newspapers that were brought in from the East, and reportedly among the members of Congress, particularly by Senator Benton. Polk himself had campaigned in '44 on a platform which advocated the annexation of Texas and Oregon. He had beaten Henry Clay, who held the opposite view. It was now said that President Polk was in favor of taking not only Texas and Oregon, but, after weighing the temper and wishes of the American public, New Mexico and California as well.

"Authority to attack the Spaniards," Jacob Kroll said, "has not been given officially. But it's my belief that it exists unofficially. Apparently it lies behind Frémont's coming to California and his skirmish at Gavilán. His activities now on the Sacramento would bear me out."

Grady, beginning to follow the thread of the conversation, straightened his brocaded waistcoat and glanced at his watch.

Kroll said, raising a hand to detain him, "What we want of you is this. Frémont will make an attack at Sonoma or Monterey as quickly as he's ready, using irregulars recruited along the Sacramento. I am certain of it. But this action won't affect the situation here where much of the Spanish strength and the government is located. We need to attack in Los Angeles at the approximate time Frémont moves in the north."

"And hold the town until Captain Frémont can arrive to relieve us," Kate Howland said.

"We need someone to organize resistance here among the American settlers," Kroll continued. "Someone who's qualified by experience to raise and handle a force of fifty men, which is all that will be required. We already have a good supply of powder and ball. But we lack a leader."

Kate Howland leaned forward. "You're the man for the job, Grady

Dunavant. You'll look dashing at the head of an American army. As dashing as Captain Frémont."

Dunavant glanced at Mrs. Howland sitting on the edge of her chair, prim in her blue taffeta dress. There was a veiled, conspiratorial gleam in her eyes, a hard, practical look that had little to do with her romantic words. He took out his watch again.

"We have lived for many years," Kroll said, "persecuted by the Spaniards. Heavily and illegally taxed. In constant fear of arrest and seizure of our means of livelihood. You yourself were arrested and imprisoned at Tepic. The American flag has been insulted on numerous occasions. The time has come to end this tyranny. You can help to do it, Lieutenant Dunavant."

Dunavant got to his feet, his hands clenched at his sides. He stood for a moment, looking down at Jacob Kroll. The room spun around him.

"That name—the rank—I no longer use or wish anyone else to use. What you know, Mr. Kroll, you will please forget."

He turned and left Jacob Kroll standing there on his short legs staring at Kate Howland, who, without words for once, sat with her earrings swinging and her bony bosom heaving violently. He left the hall and made his way into the garden, his mouth set in a straight line.

Ash trees flanked the central courtyard. Finding an inconspicuous place with a clear view of the dance floor, he waited. After a moment he singled her out from the maze of dancers. She was in the arms of a Spaniard, one of the few present as far as he could see—a young man in a blue, gilt-trimmed uniform, with black sideburns slanting down his round cheeks. Fraser, fortunately, was not in sight.

He caught brief, tantalizing glimpses of her as she appeared and disappeared among the dancers on the crowded court. The curve of her small waist. A white expanse of shoulders. Her small feet in gold slippers. The lanterns suspended between the trees on rawhide strings and moving gently in the breeze which had sprung up, glowed on her red-gold hair. They made her dress seem as unsubstantial as the smoke beginning to drift across the sky.

He stood there for a time watching her, lost in the memory of the long months without her, months in which a chance smile or a tune remembered and heard again or a flowering shrub or a mountain wind had evoked her image and her presence. The touch of her fingers. The lilt of her voice. Her lips touching his. He watched, never taking his eyes from her. Once when she danced close by, he heard the rustle of her silk dress. It's not the rustle of the trees on the Cimarron, he thought, nor the wind in the long prairie grass of the Platte—it's the sound of her skirts, here in this garden!

His gaze followed her wherever she went on the tiled court, and then suddenly he saw Fraser, talking to a group of women at the opposite side of the garden.

The memories faded, and with a shock that was as physical as a blow, he realized that he was wasting precious time. He glanced toward the musicians who sat on a draped platform at one end of the court. Intent and sweating, they showed no signs of ceasing. He straightened his cravat, left the trees and walked into the court. It was not the accepted, the polite thing to do, but he was not in a polite mood. He threaded his way through the whirling dancers, like a starved man stalking a deer in the forest.

Camilla saw him as he strode up, and disengaged herself from the grasp of the Spaniard. She was smaller than he remembered her, with a languid grace as she moved toward him which he had never seen before, and in that moment, as she held out her hand to him, he was sharply aware of the change her mother had spoken about. The pressure of her fingers was as languid as her movements, different from the boyish handclasp of old. Her hair was curled in dozens of ringlets and piled high, so that her head seemed to droop a little, as if too heavy for the slender neck. Her freckles were no longer visible under a light dusting of rice powder.

She introduced the young Spaniard in the gilt-trimmed uniform. "Julio de Zubaran is an aide to Governor Pico," she said. "He's one of the few Spaniards in Los Angeles who thinks well of us Americans."

De Zubaran smiled and said in Spanish, looking from Dunavant to Camilla, "I think very well of them. Some more than others, señor." He smiled again and, to Dunavant's relief, disappeared.

"You've neglected me," Camilla said, as they danced away under the shifting lights. "Shamefully!"

"I've been talking to your mother and Jacob Kroll."

"Yes, and I know what about. I've heard nothing else since I came back from New York, until I am sick of it. But don't tell Mother. She takes it very seriously." Camilla lifted her eyes reproachfully. "But that isn't what I mean. You've been here since dark and never even bothered to come to see me."

"I did. You were dressing when I was there."

Camilla drew her breath in. "Mother didn't tell me a word about it. She's getting awfully forgetful, poor dear."

"Your mother," he said pointedly, "had other things on her mind."

She looked at him in wide-eyed innocence, as though she hadn't the slightest idea what he was talking about, and asked him if he'd had a nice trip. Her tone was so light she might have been asking about an hour's ride he had taken to gather wild flowers. It was so maddeningly inconsequential that he was overcome with a sudden doubt. Was this the girl he had fallen in love with? The girl who had never been entirely out of his thoughts during any day of the two years since he had seen her? The girl who had become in that brief time a sophisticated woman, full of wiles and graces?

Then he quickly realized that he was foolish to hold onto an image formed two years ago, and his doubt vanished. There were natural changes to be expected, even desired, in a girl then seventeen. The changes which had seemed strange at first—the elaborate coiffure, the absence of freckles, the sweetly rounded figure, the sophistication—had really increased her charm. Looking at her as she moved lightly in his arms, breathing the scent of her hair, he found her suddenly the most beautiful woman in the world.

She asked him again about the journey from Santa Fe.

"You've probably heard the details already," he said.

She smiled quickly and squeezed his hand. "Not from you." She gave him a lingering glance and waited for him to answer.

Dunavant was silent. He would tell her about the journey, about this and about other things as well, as soon as they were alone. He knew exactly what he would say, and in the event that she was really serious about the Englishman, he also knew what he was going to do—everything was clear in his mind. But as the waltz ended, and he was getting ready to lead her away into the garden, Mr. Fraser appeared at his elbow.

A few minutes later he found himself standing among the trees drinking punch and listening, of all things, to a long-winded anecdote related by the Englishman who after many weeks of silence had suddenly become loquacious. He stood there beside Camilla with the grim patience of an impatient man, wondering why he had not had the good sense to leave Fraser back on the trail, floundering around in the flood waters of the Gila. From the first moment he had laid eyes on him, when the Englishman had come to the inn that evening before the pack train set out from Santa Fe, when Mr. Fraser had walked into the room and offered a fancy figure to be taken to Los Angeles as quickly as possible, without offering any explanation for his haste, he should have been suspicious. Suspicious or not, he should have left him in the Gila.

He drank two cups of Jacob Kroll's punch and watched the smile playing at the corners of Fraser's mouth, a smile which said, I know what's in your mind, but go ahead, old boy, and see what it gets you. He returned the smile, drank another cup of punch and was beginning on the fourth when Julio de Zubaran strolled up and introduced a young Spanish woman with a pale, oval face, framed by black hair braided in a crown.

It was a chance he had not expected but he seized it without delay, as if it were planned and Yris Llorente were his confederate and not an attractive woman seeking a dance with one or the other of two young men. In the midst of the flowery Spanish introduction, as the violins started up in a lively tune, he told her that Mr. Fraser was a newcomer to the pueblo and was very desirous of learning the intricacies of the jota. It was done quickly. Before the Englishman had time to say anything or to give him more than a well-bred glance of surprise, he had Camilla's arm and was walking toward the lower end of the garden.

Deaf to the entreaties that she already had the dance engaged with someone or other, he did not stop until they reached the low wall at the bottom of the garden, masked by bushes and trees from the court. The night was now clear of smoke and the far mountains showed dark against a sky flooded with stars. Beyond the wall, the dull orange of candle flames burned in the huts scattered among the vineyards. Someone was picking on a guitar. The music floated up to them on the wind, louder than the music from the court.

The lanterns in the garden cast only dim reflections where they stood, but he could see her face against the night, turned slightly away from him, her chin raised and her blue eyes watching him in the simulation of innocence he had seen earlier, as if she were determined to show him that she still didn't have the faintest notion what he had been talking about while they were dancing or why at the moment she was here with him alone. Languidly lifting her hand to her hair, she asked him again about the journey from Santa Fe.

There was a self-possession about her gesture and the way she spoke that made him forget his carefully planned words. "The only part you're interested in you already know," he said. "What you don't know is that you're not going to marry Fraser."

She turned her head slowly until she was facing him but in her eyes there was not the smallest trace of dismay—as far as any visible effects of his statement were concerned, he might have been commenting on the weather. She opened her fan and moved it lightly before her face.

"You've chosen someone else for me?" she said, smiling. "I hope he's handsome and rich and not too old. Jacob Kroll, for instance. Or is it Julio de Zubaran?"

"It's not Peter Pomeroy Fraser!"

He spoke quietly, but with a finality that amused her. She laughed softly and folded her fan, holding it against her cheek.

"Have you told Mr. Fraser?" she asked.

"You can when you go back," he said.

"And if I don't choose to?"

She stood with her back to the low wall, her wide skirts billowing around her and the glow of the lanterns on her red-gold hair. She looked at him as if he were some stammering, indecisive youth whom she could parry, instead of a man eleven years her senior in age and twice that in experience, who had come a thousand miles to marry her and had little time for phrases or idle flirtation, who refused to take any arrangements she had made with Fraser seriously.

"Then I'll tell him," he said. "But it won't be as graceful as if it came from you."

She opened her fan again. "You've been away for two years," she said idly.

"Less two days," he corrected her. "It seems longer, Camilla."

She lowered her lashes at the warmth in his voice, and though he had the sudden feeling that the gesture was an automatic response to his words, without emotion or meaning, the qualm quickly passed. She was in a difficult position. It was a position of her own making, but it was up to him to get her out of it as gracefully as he could.

"I looked for you last year," she said.

"I intended to come but I found that I could make more money by going to St. Louis. It was a very successful trip. The one I have just finished was successful, too. We can have the finest ranch in California."

"I don't like California," she said. "I hate it. And I don't like ranches or smelly cows." She fanned herself for a moment. "Naturally, when you didn't come back I thought you had changed your mind . . . about everything."

He tried to keep the impatience out of his voice. "I said I'd come back. You certainly knew that I would, after all our plans."

"I was terribly disappointed," she said, "and humiliated."

A little catch came into her throat. It was something about her which had not changed; it was always there when she was hurt. And now, as always before whenever he heard it, tenderness choked him.

"I'm sorry. I thought you would understand," he said.

As he was about to go on with his apology, he stopped and looked at her. She must have known what was in his mind, for she evaded his eyes, glancing toward the courtyard.

"I have this dance," she said. "We can talk afterward."

She picked up her skirts and started past him, but he reached out and took her hand. She dropped her skirts and, pulling away from him, squared her shoulders.

"What will everyone think? Me being here with you alone the whole evening," she said. "It's very embarrassing."

She looked embarrassed, but he was certain that it was not for this reason. "When I was here before you told me you were going to New York on a visit. That was partly why I went to St. Louis." He hesitated, thinking perhaps it would be better not to drive her into the corner, but something in him made him continue. "You were there last summer, weren't you, Camilla?"

She looked at him defiantly and said nothing.

"You were in New York and not here," he said, anger creeping into his words. "So you couldn't have been humiliated by me not coming."

Her blue eyes did not waver.

"You're perfectly horrid. You take everything I say and twist it around. . . ."

The little catch had come into her voice again, and in spite of himself, in spite of everything—the lie he had caught her in—the old tenderness swept over him.

She took a step back from him, clicking her fan open and stood there fanning herself, her profile dimly outlined against the night. The movement of the fan roused small gusts of perfume. She was only a few short steps from him. In one stride he covered the distance, lifted her from her feet, up and against him, and kissed her hair. Her body was light in his arms, her hair soft against his mouth. It was the moment he had waited for during long months on the trail.

The stars wheeled over his head unnoticed. He did not hear the music or the sound of the guitar from the vineyard. He was not aware of anything while he held her. It was not until he set her lightly on her feet that he realized he had been holding a person without life or emotion. She straightened her hair where he had mussed it. She looked at him with eyes that were sea-cold. Her face was white with anger.

She said slowly, "I suppose this is an apology for your horrid insinuation. It's to make me forget that you have called me a liar. It's to make up for all the humiliation you've caused me. For not coming back when you promised you would, whether I was here or not." She paused and then said with icy calm, "I am in love with Mr. Fraser and I am going to marry him."

The next moment she had picked up her skirts and was running through the trees.

Dunavant watched her go. The gleam of her golden shoes on the garden path. The whisper of her skirts among the bushes as she ran. A scent of her perfume remained behind her in the garden. She was gone.

He stood looking after her, surprised not only at what she had done and said, but also at the fact he was still standing here, swearing bitterly, but doing nothing. He could follow her into the garden and take her away from whomever she was dancing with. He could punch Fraser in the nose if he interfered. He could wait until the dance was over—there were many things he could do, that he had planned to do if this happened. But suddenly they were all inadequate beside the inescapable fact that he had been jilted for someone else. Persistence, boldness, ingenuity, might win Camilla, but when he had won her, then what? Irrelevantly, he remembered that she didn't like California.

He made and lighted a cigarette. And then without smoking, he crushed it out against the wall and walked rapidly through the garden. He saw a white blur on the path ahead of him and knew before he reached it that the handkerchief belonged to Camilla. He didn't stop to pick it up.

# 5

DUNAVANT paused on the shallow steps and looked down into the lane. Servants were lighting fresh torches on either side of the door for the guests who were beginning to leave the fandango, but the sound of violins and voices and laughter still came from the garden behind the wall. He stood for a moment listening to the revelry, his thin face pale beneath its deep tan. Then he walked down the steps and started toward the inn.

He had reached the middle of the lane when a carriage rolled up noiselessly behind him, continued on for a way and came to an abrupt halt. Then the door of the carriage opened as he passed. He saw gloved fingers on the handle of the door, holding it open. The light of the pine torches did not reach into the carriage, and he could make out only the vague glimmer of white shoulders leaning toward him out of the darkness, a blurred impression of lips against the dark interior.

"The lane is dusty," a voice said. "I'll be glad to take you where you're going."

For an instant, until the girl spoke, thinking that it was Camilla, he did not slacken his pace. But the voice was low-pitched and Spanish; he had heard it before. The carriage had not moved. He retraced his steps, and as he drew closer recognized the girl to whom De Zubaran had introduced him earlier in the evening, Señora Yris Llorente.

He removed his hat. "I've been riding for a thousand miles," he said. "I enjoy walking for a change."

"It's not safe for an American to walk at this time of night," she replied and leaned back against the cushions, leaving the door open. "But I shouldn't have said that for you'll think it is a challenge. You shouldn't. You've already proved your courage by being in Los Angeles at all."

Dunavant hesitated. Actually, he preferred to walk. He had no desire to talk to anyone, to improve his acquaintanceship with Señora Llorente or to be obligated to her. But on a sudden impulse, seeing the white gleam of her shoulders, thinking with sudden bitterness of Camilla, he stepped into the carriage and swung the door shut. The Indian driver spoke to the horses. The carriage rolled slowly down the lane, the wheels turning quietly in the dust. The seat was narrow, and though he couldn't see her face he could feel her arm against his, moving gently with the sway of the carriage.

Doña Yris rested her head against the satin cushions. "I saw you when you rode into the plaza at dusk," she said suddenly. "You sat very straight in the saddle and very serious, looking to neither side, giving no heed to the insults shouted at you. There is an American, I thought, who comes here after a dangerous journey, as a thirsty man to an oasis. But there is no oasis. He will find here in this unhappy land nothing to quench his thirst or comfort him."

She spoke slowly, as if she were not sure that he understood Spanish well enough to follow her, in a dreamy voice which was more insinuating than her words, which gave him the impression, in spite of her youthful appearance, of a woman practiced in the arts of seduction.

"I saw you riding through the plaza and my heart went out to you," she said.

"You must have been watching from behind barred windows," he replied with a touch of gallantry, "or I would have seen you."

"You saw me at the fandango and left me for Señorita Howland," she said accusingly.

"My apologies. I am a man of poor discernment."

"Who speaks more gracefully than he acts."

They were approaching the inn; instead of answering her, he thought, I can go inside and play *chusa,* lose as I always do, or get drunk on bad *aguardiente.* I can go to my room, which smells of gypsum and its previous occupant, and lie on one of the hard boards, which Kate Howland calls a bed, lie throughout the night and toss, and not sleep, and watch the dawn come up.

He could do any or all of these things, or he could ride through the night with Doña Yris. The lantern, hanging above the door of the inn, shone into the carriage. He turned and looked at the girl beside him. There was a faint glow from the brilliants that threaded her hair; a reflection from them lay across her forehead. Her wide mouth was pale in the light of the lantern and her eyes were large and dark—black or deep brown, he couldn't tell which.

"I'm staying at Kate Howland's," he heard himself say. "But it's not a night to sleep."

"We can ride and watch the stars," she said, but a moment or two later, as the driver turned the horses into a lane that curved back toward the plaza, she gave a direction in Indian dialect, and the carriage drew up in front of a massive, iron-studded gate. "Perhaps you would like to come in and talk. Or if you'd rather we can ride."

The door was opened to them by a fat Indian woman holding a candle cupped against the wind. He found himself in an enclosed courtyard, banked with shadowy masses of millefleur roses. The air was sweet with the heavy fragrance of some night-blooming shrub. A concealed fountain tinkled among the shrubbery. The house was larger than it had seemed from the lane, stretching away in a series of dark, rambling rooms, the windows barred with iron.

Doña Yris led the way through the courtyard and down a passage where a doll-like Virgin, dressed in red silk, looked down from a niche, into a small hall. The room was overcrowded with furniture of the Boston trade and heavier, ornately carved pieces from Mexico City. The rugs scattered over the blue-tiled floor were ones he had brought on his last trip from Santa Fe. Two perfumed candles burned in a six-branched candlestick. The Indian woman lighted the remaining four and padded out of the room. The candlestick, he recognized after a moment, was the one he had given Camilla.

Doña Yris opened a gold case set with yellow diamonds, offered him a *cigarro,* took one herself, and lighted it at the table.

As she bent forward, with the glow of the candles shining on her black hair, a knife suddenly turned in him. The anger which he thought he had left in Kroll's garden flared through him. For an instant, looking at the candlestick and the light falling not on Camilla, but on a girl he didn't know and very likely would never see again, he was seized with an impulse to rush out of the house and find Camilla wherever she was. To haul her, protesting and screaming, in front of the nearest priest and marry her at the point of a pistol, if necessary. And then go back and give Mr. Fraser, Peter Pomeroy Fraser, a punch in his well-bred face.

Through the window came the sound of violins at Jacob Kroll's. He was aware that the girl was beside him on the sofa. "How long will you stay in the pueblo?" she asked.

"Not long," he said, forgetting his earlier gallantry. "No longer than necessary."

"You speak with feeling. Perhaps it's some disappointment over business. Perhaps it's something else."

He knew without looking at her that she was smiling.

"You were worried at the fandango," she said. "Your mood has not improved."

She was silent as a servant came in, bearing a tray and two tall goblets of wine. The man was short and the color of mahogany, with one arm, and the small, steady eyes of a lizard. He set the tray on a low table in front of the sofa and went slowly out of the room, making no sound with his bare feet. Dunavant had the impression that he went no farther than the passageway and was standing there by the ivory Virgin, listening.

"This will lighten your mood," Doña Yris said, handing him a goblet of the amber liquid. "You'll forget your worries, whatever they are, and perhaps your wish to leave. Although I don't blame you for wishing to. It's not pleasant here for an American, or safe."

"It's hard to remember when it was."

"But it is worse now that Captain Frémont is in California." She sipped her wine, and he noticed that her lips were not pale as he had thought in the carriage, but heavily carmined. They were the lips of an experienced woman, seductive and wise, like her voice, yet with a certain quality of freshness. "You have heard about Captain Frémont?"

"I know nothing about his movements—they're hard to keep up with."

"And neither do I, really. Except that everyone is greatly excited—the peons, the military, the rancheros, Governor Pico." She withdrew her shawl from her shoulders and tossed it over the back of the sofa. Her dress, given an ivory sheen by the candles, was cut square and low at the neck, with lacy frills. "It seems very silly, all this excitement over one man."

He agreed, but with a tinge of annoyance at the turn of the conversation. He hadn't come here to talk about Captain Frémont or Governor Pico. With champagne in crystal goblets, the scent of *dama de la noche* floating into the room, with a beautiful girl whose voice and every movement promised mysterious delights, he could think of more exciting things than the Pathfinder and the swarthy Pío Pico. He frowned, rubbing his chin, and told her that some of the rugs on the floor he had brought from Santa Fe two years ago.

She displayed little interest in the rugs and finally rose and crossed to the open window, pulling the velvet curtains. She walked quickly and lightly, with the vibrant grace of a dancer, her high, wooden heels, painted a glossy scarlet, clicking on the tiles. Somewhere in the past, he thought, watching her as she came back to the sofa, in Havana or Lima or Mexico City, she had been a dancer. He could imagine her in the intricate figures of an Arroganese jota. He could see her arms rigid at her sides, the turning of her lithe hips, her head leaned back and her eyes half closed. He could hear the stamping of her heels to the throb of the guitars, the muted whisper of the castanets.

Placing his empty goblet on the table, he said, "I'd like to see you dance."

Doña Yris looked at him curiously. "And how did you know that I dance?"

"I'm a connoisseur in these matters."

She smiled for an instant and then went back to the subject of Captain Frémont, pausing to snap her fingers for the servant, who appeared too quickly to have been anywhere except in the passageway. She gave orders to refill the goblets and was silent until he returned and had left the room again. He gave Dunavant a flicking glance from his black eyes as he disappeared.

Doña Yris crushed out her *cigarro* and said, "I wouldn't speak this way to everyone, but, frankly, it would be a good thing if Captain Frémont put an end to the Mexican regime." Picking up her goblet, she looked at him for several moments. "You don't think me disloyal for saying this?"

He shook his head, and began to wonder, drinking his wine, what had prompted her confession.

"Perhaps indiscreet is a better word," she said.

"Considering that you don't know me, it is."

She answered him instantly. "I have no fear of the authorities. None. They are all pigs and stupid." She made a hissing sound to express her contempt. "I would not blame the Americans if they seized the Governor's Mansion and threw Don Pío into the street."

He lighted his *cigarro* and said nothing, hoping by his silence to end the discussion, but she went on as before. He found himself not listening to her. He tried, instead, to fathom the reason for her concern and her reason for singling him out for her confidences. It was natural that the corrupt Mexican Government had enemies among the Spaniards, though few if any were as outspoken as the girl beside him.

He drank his wine and wondered if her enmity were only professed? Was it an attempt to lead him into some incriminating admission? He thought about the lizard-eyed servant, still lounging, he was certain, in the passage. He wondered about Señor Llorente, whom she had mentioned. Was the señor dead or alive, in the town or elsewhere? He remembered that he had met her through De Zubaran who was an aide to Governor Pico. She could easily be acting under his instructions—in this connection he recalled the coincidence of their meeting in the lane, her ready acceptance of his suggestion that they ride and, later, the invitation which had brought him here to the house.

"If Don Pío is removed," she said, "it will not be the work of Spaniards. If it is done, it will be done by the Americans—by men like you."

"Perhaps by men *like* me," he said, "but not by me, I'm afraid. I'll be on a ship when this happens. On my way to the Isthmus of Panama." Or somewhere! he thought.

Then she said something that gave him a start. "If you're not arrested before the ship sails."

"There's a chance," he said calmly. "I was arrested once before."

"It was four years ago."

He didn't betray his surprise that she knew this, but it added another suspicion to the ones he already held. "It won't be so easy this time," he said.

"No. There are people to help you now. Jacob Kroll. Señora Howland. I myself."

He was about to say that he required no one's help, but decided against it. Instead he rose, picked up his hat and said that he still had work to do before he went to bed. She made no effort to detain him, but when they reached the courtyard she stopped before the gate and laid her hand lightly on his arm.

"Even if you wish to leave, there will be no ship for ten days or so, possibly longer. I am lonely here. If you will come back, it will make me happy."

He promised that he would, without the slightest intention of doing so, but her hand on his arm did not relax.

"How I wish I were leaving this accursed country also!" she said sighing. "The fleas and dust. The vile scraping and sawing which passes for music. The men without courage or spirit. The frumpy women, old in their twenties, with hordes of children clawing at their skirts. This forsaken pueblo without a theater or a *paseo* or bullfights or a place to gamble except with reeking peons breathing down one's neck." She made a gesture of disgust, increasing the pressure on his arm. "How I wish for the day! But it will come soon and then I will live again."

She was silent beside him, a shadowy figure against the massed foliage of the courtyard. Her hand was hot where she clasped his arm. Mingled with the scent of the night flower was the heavy fragrance from her bodice. He saw her profile dimly against the light in the sky, her delicately flaring nostrils, the blur of her lips, and above the lacy frill of the dress, the swell of her breasts like half-moons rising out of a foamy sea. She turned her head slowly, with the brilliants threaded through the black braided hair, and then, twisting her body as if in the beginning movement of some voluptuous dance, she was in his arms.

Through the clamor of his blood, he felt her mouth beneath his. It was like a flower of fire, and her body was like fire, running the length of him, stronger than the wine in his veins. For a long moment she strained against him, breathing in little sighs, her head thrown back and her eyes closed, breathing and saying words he did not understand. And then she went limp in his arms and he thought she had fainted. But unexpectedly she slipped away from him. She stood looking at him. Her face was indistinct in the darkness. She said nothing, breathing calmly again. He had the feeling that she was an actress playing a well-rehearsed role.

"Come back," she said finally. "And exercise care while you remain in the pueblo." She slid back the bolt in the gate. "Come back soon. Tomorrow."

He opened the iron-studded gate and let himself out into the lane. Blowing from the north, from the direction of Jacob Kroll's, the wind no longer carried the sound of music. The light of the pine torches had faded from the sky. Pausing before the gate, he glanced along the dark defile which wound on into the plaza. The lane was deserted save for a single figure which was gone in the moment he stood there. He heard the bolt slide shut behind him, the voice of Doña Yris whispering a last word of parting and caution.

As the great gray church loomed out of the night, the empty plaza ringed with silent, shuttered houses, he smiled to himself at her warning. The scene at the gate had only served to deepen the suspicions which had grown steadily since he had entered the house. He was certain now that the danger lay not in the streets he was walking through, but behind him in the garden with its tinkling fountain concealed among masses of half-wild shrubbery and its cloying scent of night flowers; in the candlelighted passageway, its doll-like Virgin and the lounging, bare-footed servant; in the person of Yris Llorente herself, with her dancer's body which was young and yet as old as the knowledge of sin.

He walked deliberately across the plaza. It was a rash impulse that had sent him there in the first place, but the time spent with Yris Llorente had served its purpose—the sharp edge of his anger was dulled, thanks to the girl and her excellent wine. If his visit had increased the urgency of his leaving the pueblo, that was something to worry about tomorrow. He had no regrets. The pressure of his Colt was hard and reassuring against his thigh.

He left the plaza and turned into the lane which led to the inn. He became aware that someone was behind him, walking at a gait faster than his own. He did not increase his steps. He did not turn until the man was a few paces from him. A young man of medium height, dressed in a blue uniform with gold markings and a sword suspended from a silver chain. It was Julio de Zubaran.

"I am walking in your direction," he said. "If you'll permit me, señor, I'll walk with you."

The distance to Kate Howland's was short and they walked it in silence except for the clanking of De Zubaran's sword. Under the lantern that shed a small pool of light in the narrow doorway, Dunavant stopped and looked at the Spaniard, waiting for him to speak. He wondered if De Zubaran were the man he had seen when he was leaving the house of Yris Llorente.

"If you are remaining in the pueblo," De Zubaran said, "there are things which it may be to your advantage to know. I hesitate to speak because I am sure you're *simpatico.*" His Spanish was quick, slurred, difficult for Grady to understand. "But I rely on your forbearance."

"My stay here depends on a ship to take me away."

"We shall be sorry to see you go," De Zubaran said, smiling.

"I shall be sorry to leave," Dunavant replied, matching the other's tone.

The Spaniard fiddled with his sword. "There are various Americans here in Los Angeles—not many, I am happy to say—who have been encouraged by Captain Frémont's presence on the Sacramento to conspire against Governor Pico. It is a dangerous activity. Your being at Jacob Kroll's this evening led me to think that you might be concerned with these schemes."

"I was there for another reason entirely," Dunavant said, growing impatient. "You were there also."

"Likewise for another reason." The Spaniard held his sword and bowed. "Forgive me, señor, for intruding upon your time and accept my sincere wishes for a pleasant stay in the pueblo."

He stood up, still holding his sword—a stout young man with a quick smile—and looked at Dunavant. His eyes were a deep, burning yellow. Meeting them for the first time, Dunavant instantly thought of the girl on the golden palomino, with the ancient musket and the haughty insolent mouth, who had halted him on the trail that morning. De Zubaran was related to her, he was certain, for the eyes were the same. He looked at the Spaniard with sudden anger.

"Good night," he said.

The Spaniard bowed again and said nothing.

# 6

Dunavant opened the door of the tavern and stood for a moment surveying the room. The crowd had thinned out since he had left for the fandango; those who remained at the tables—several Spaniards in wide hats and silver spurs, a peon or two, a soldier, with his head buried in his arms, snoring—were in various stages of advanced drunkenness. A motley group, still on their feet, were drinking and laughing at the far end of the tavern. They grew silent as he approached, but made room for him at the bar. They stood aside with grudging glances, turned their backs on him and began to talk in lower tones.

He ordered a brandy and drank it, looking up at the grinning head of the wolf. The stuffed animal, with its malevolent eyes and bared yellow fangs, though it was a prized belonging of Kate Howland, a sort of mascot, became as he looked at it a symbol of the pueblo's hatred and the hostility around him. He drank another brandy, wondering how he was going to spend the time before the ship sailed without getting into a fight, or a dozen of them, without being thrown into the *juzgado*. He could stay in his room or, better yet, go to San Diego, which, being more than a hundred miles away from the seat of the government, might be in less of a ferment.

Finishing his drink on this decision, he was putting his cup down when a girl, who had been talking to a soldier at one end of the bar, slid up to him and slipped one arm around his waist.

"Your face is serious, señor. You have worries."

Dunavant laughed. This was the second time within an hour that he had been accused of having a long face.

"My name," she said, showing white, pointed teeth, "is Narcisa. I possess many surprises."

Looking at Narcisa he did not doubt her boast. She was young and her red dress lay tight and thin against the deep brown of her skin. The face tilted toward him was broad, pretty, supported on a neck as round and sturdy as the bole of a tree.

"Come with me, señor. You will forget your seriousness."

Forget, Dunavant thought, the dream fashioned during long days and nights on the trail, on the South Platte, the Cimarron and the Gila, out of a vision of red-gold hair and blue eyes? Go with you to some weed-strewn hillside or frowsy hut and there in your arms pretend that it is someone else? Forget? Sardonically he smiled to himself and took an onza from his pocket. He pressed it into the hand resting on his hip and left the bar.

The gaming room, as he passed it on his way down the short passage which connected the tavern and the hotel, was crowded, and through the open door came the subdued murmur of voices and the clink of coins. He walked on deliberately toward his quarters, and, reaching them, let himself in. He lighted a candle and stood for a moment glancing around at the small, evil-smelling room, and then on a sudden impulse snuffed out the candle, closed the door and retraced his steps along the passage. In his present mood he would rather lose all he owned than face the night in that barren cell, with its narrow bed and one chair.

The *chusa* game was unattended; the dozen or more players were clustered around a long table in the middle of the room. By the light of two lamps, sending up a reek of sperm at either end of the table, he saw that about half the number were rancheros—wealthy landowners from the amount of silver on their high-peaked hats and velvet jackets—the rest, officers of the garrison. Among the officers was Julio de Zubaran. Their eyes were fixed on the cards; no one looked up as Grady Dunavant came into the room.

The dealer, standing on the far side of the table, was masked by the players. The monte game at Kate Howland's was always banked by one of the customers, usually one of the rancheros, but as the dealer called a *sota* and *rey* of swords, there was something about the even drawl of the voice that was neither local nor entirely Spanish. The words sent a sudden chill through Dunavant. It isn't Colonel Curel, he thought. In New Orleans at the Café dez Zouaves or playing écarté at Madame Gigon's, dancing calinda under blazing flambeaux, or riding at the head of Mexican cavalry on the San Saba, but not here, thousands of miles away, in Kate Howland's, dealing Spanish monte.

He drew closer to the table and through a gap in the wall of players caught a glimpse of the man bending over the cards. A thin, chalky white face, in which French and Spanish blood were aristocratically blended. A thin mouth and a black, short, square-cut beard. It is not

Colonel Curel, Dunavant still insisted to himself. The light is not good and it is someone who looks like Curel.

But at that moment the other glanced up slowly from the table, paused with his eyes level to Dunavant's shoulder and then, as if forced by some inner compulsion rather than what he saw, raised them. In the dim room their gazes met.

"You have traveled far," Curel said in his precise English.

"No farther, señor, than you."

Two of the players made a small space between them and Dunavant shouldered his way into it. He looked across the table at Cesaire Curel standing with the cards in one slender hand, the other resting on his hip, balanced lightly on his feet with the sureness of an expert swordsman. He looked steadily into the dark morose eyes. One thing was certain, he thought: there was no longer any doubt that war was imminent. The hostility which he had met on the trail that morning, and later in the pueblo; Kroll's conspiracy and the open remarks of Yris Llorente, Captain Frémont on the Sacramento—were only straws in the wind. The presence of Curel in Los Angeles put the final seal upon it, for his thin, slightly hooked nose could smell out war half a continent away, particularly if it could be turned to advantage. His being here was no coincidence; Cesaire Curel could be nowhere else in the world.

"It is a surprise," he said.

"A surprise," Dunavant replied.

Curel's eyes drifted away to the players, pausing briefly at each one, while he shuffled the forty-card deck with a slow flourish. His eyes drifted back. "Do you join us, Lieutenant Dunavant?" He indicated eight piles of gold onzas, ten coins to a pile, stacked beside him. "We are wagering part or all, at your pleasure."

Dunavant's mouth tightened at the name, but he said nothing. He looked at the small, white effeminate hands shuffling the cards. His thoughts raced backward into the past, to Texas and the Sabine, the morning on the Saba when he had ridden out with Chapman who was going home after the war was over to his new wife and the baby he had never seen; and John Rogers talking always in the heat about the cool waters of the Chesapeake; and Sessions who was going back to Tennessee to buy mules for the ranch Sam Houston had promised everyone; and tough young McCutcheon who was worrying whether there would ever again be any fighting in the world, after the fighting in Texas was over—afraid there wouldn't be. These and ninety others riding out under a blazing sky to meet the Mexicans and the man who now stood beyond the table. He thought of the moon rising on the line straggling back in retreat, and Chapman gone, and Rogers and Sessions and McCutcheon, all dead in the arroyo, with thirty-five of their comrades lying dead and unburied.

"You are cautious, señor." Curel laid the cards down for a cut. "Your business has not been prosperous or perhaps for some other reason?"

"For some other reason," Dunavant said evenly. He cut the cards twice and glanced openly at the edges before handing them back. "For many other reasons," he added.

Curel's morose flickering gaze rested on him for an instant. Then with the deck held in his left hand, he drew off two hole cards and placed them in the center of the table. The bottom layout showed a seven of swords and a *caballero* of cups. The two cards, which he removed from the top of the deck for the other layout, were the four and five of clubs.

"Your bets, gentlemen," Curel said in Spanish.

Dunavant drew out five coins and placed them beside the layout of the sword and cup, resisting the temptation to double his bet. There was a reasonable chance that the deck was not marked, but his respect for Curel's luck remained. Everyone of the eight men who were playing the hand was wagering more, though none of them apparently had been winning. Three or four hands should give him the clue.

Curel took in the table with a sweeping glance, and with a movement of his thin wrist, exaggerated in its slowness, turned the deck face up. The top card was a deuce of coins. No other cards of the same suit showed in either of the layouts. He tossed the deuce away, gathered in all the money and, turning the deck over, began to make a new set.

Without taking his eyes from the yellow and vermilion cards, he said, "I am not surprised to find you here, Señor Dunavant, present circumstances and future probabilities being what they are. California offers many opportunities for one of your talents."

Curel spoke quietly, not interrupting the placing of the new layouts, but whether from the quality of his voice or the fact that he was speaking in English, Dunavant was suddenly aware of the hostility of the other players. Nothing was said and no one looked at him, but the air had become heavy with restraint.

"The opportunities, whatever they are, don't tempt me," he said, placing another small bet. And then in Spanish he added, "I'm leaving for San Diego tomorrow afternoon. From there to Panama."

The small white hands dropped a card on the table. "*Sota* of swords," Curel said in his Castilian lisp, losing to everyone.

"I'll leave the opportunities to you," Dunavant said.

A faint smile showing above his black beard, Curel paid off the wagers, discarded the *sota* and began on a new layout. Then he said, again in English, "I am sorry to decline your offer. You see a man traveling for his health, to escape the New Orleans summer, under strict orders to refrain from all forms of excitement. I regret that this is so. Also your immediate departure. For nothing would please me more than that we should find ourselves once more ranged against each other on the battlefield." He finished the layout and, waiting for the wagers to be placed, looked at Dunavant. "On one side, Lieutenant Dunavant. On the other, Colonel Cesaire Curel. *Virgen santisima!* It would be like old times."

If there had been any doubt about Curel's reason for being in the pueblo, it was gone now, not because of his words or the casual manner of his speaking, but from the unexpressed challenge which lay beneath them. He was here for one purpose. It was written clearly on his face.

The hand was played without Dunavant's participation. He stood watching the smoke curling up from the lamps, the tall shadow of Curel thrown against the white wall, the silent, hostile Spaniards around him. He saw De Zubaran glance toward the door and, following his gaze, a squat, one-armed figure entered the room and stood beside the doorway. It was Yris Llorente's servant.

"Like old times," Curel said, stacking his winnings. "Perhaps by now you have learned the art of establishing a forward vidette. As I remember it was the ignorance of this art which led to your—shall we say?—difficulties."

Dunavant made no reply, but his hands tightened in his pockets. It would be foolish to throttle Cesaire Curel here in Mrs. Howland's gaming room, surrounded by Spaniards, any one of whom would deem it a pleasure to thrust a knife between a gringo's ribs. It would be simpler to do it outside, tonight in the inn, or in some dark lane. Or better, in the full light of day, so that as his fingers sank in the Creole's neck he could watch the face constrict and purple under pressure.

"An interesting encounter," Curel said. "With certain advantages on your side. The Spaniards have powder of an inferior quality and their weapons are muskets and lances. They rely, I am told, mostly on the latter, on the lance, and their horsemanship. *Por Dios!* It would be like leading an army of medieval Spain. You would have an edge, Lieutenant Dunavant, which, considering the outcome of our last meeting, I would be glad to accord you."

Dunavant knew now as he stood there with the table between them, not raising his voice to silence Curel, that he would never throttle him. There had been other chances and other provocations in the past, in New Orleans. He had not seized them. He realized that he never would. It would gain nothing for him to kill Cesaire Curel. It would not wipe out the memory of Rogers or Chapman or McCutcheon or the others. Or of Major Gilson.

With a sudden, involuntary movement he turned, half expecting, now that Cesaire Curel was here out of the distant past, to see the egg-shaped figure of Gilson. Gilson of the Fourth Raiders, chewing on the stub of a cigar, his campaign hat squarely on his head, the dusty gray hair curling low over the collar of his tunic. The little martinet, with the bitter, sun-squinted eyes and the face of a bigot, who fought pedantically by the book and who would rather lose a battle than violate a principle. Major Gilson, with a Bible in his hip pocket, handing out punishment, which he called justice, with the omnipotence and fury of an Old Testament prophet.

Instead of on Gilson, his eyes rested on the squat figure of Yris Llorente's servant. The Indian had not moved; he still stood beside the door, leaning one shoulder against the wall. His gaze was narrowed and sleepy in the yellow light of the lamps. Apparently, he was not interested in the game or the players or Dunavant; apparently, in nothing. But why was he here? Had he come on his own initiative or at the orders of his mistress? And if he had been sent here, why?

Grady's speculations were interrupted by the appearance of two Americans. They came down the passageway from the tavern, their voices, raised in a raucous ditty, preceding them into the room, and took up positions at one end of the table. They were sailors or hide droghers—lean, hard-mouthed young men, and drunk. Clutching a handful of octagonals in each fist, they glanced at Curel, the half circle of Spaniards, finally at Dunavant, and wanted to know if the game was on the level.

"When I find out," Dunavant said, placing a small bet on the five and six of cups, "I'll let you know."

A shadow passed across Curel's face or it might have been the flicker of the lamp, for he said nothing, his gaze lowered, while the two sailors placed their wagers on the suit Dunavant had chosen. With the same slow, expert movement of his wrist, holding the deck and selecting the gate card all with one hand, he drew.

Dunavant, waiting for the card, noticed that all the Spaniards had wagered on the same layout and what was significant, on the opposite layout. They were betting against him rather than Curel. He was not surprised at the outcome, at the *rey* of swords which fell upon the table.

"It is always better," Curel said, addressing the sailors, "to use your own judgment. The lieutenant here is often unlucky. In cards as in other things."

Cold anger gathered in Dunavant's throat. He buttoned his tan coat deliberately. Watching Curel pick up his own and the sailors' money, pay off the other bets and begin another shuffle, he saw for the first time the slight bulge at the Creole's hip. Very likely it was the ivory-handled pistol with the short ugly, over-and-under barrels—a clumsy weapon but one which Curel used with consummate skill. He glanced at the servant beside the door, at Julio de Zubaran and the rest of the Spaniards. He coolly weighed his chances in a fight.

"I regret that you lack a taste for the encounter," Curel said. "It would be very interesting. Even with lances and muskets." He held out the deck for a cut. "It is unfortunate, *mal suerte,* that you leave and that I travel for my health."

Dunavant, gazing steadily across the table, ignored the cards.

Curel shrugged. "Perhaps a game of écarté would suit you better, lieutenant."

The small, effeminate hand still held the cards toward him. It would be easy to grasp the thin wrist, twist the arm in the doeskin jacket, reach at the same time for the double-barreled pistol.

"Or a game of three-card monte," Curel said.

He could do all this in a brief moment before the other was aware of his intention, but the chance that the Spaniards would stand and watch Curel choked before their eyes was a remote one. They would fall upon him like hornets, out of an already strained and overripe hatred. A broken head and a month or two in the *calabozo* was the best he could expect.

For an instant before he turned away from the table he debated about warning the sailors openly against a deck from which the dealer could choose a suit to meet any necessity. (There were no signs of daubing or shaving, or any odor of slick-ace, but he was certain that the deck was cold.) Instead, his warning was indirect. "If I play again," he told Curel, "I'll bring my own cards."

It was a provocation, spoken against his better judgment, in blind, sudden anger. The moist lips glistened in the light. The dark eyes grew somber. The hand, holding the deck, dropped to the table and rested there; the slender fingers worked slowly, ruffling the edges of the cards. The faint clicking was the only sound in the room.

"Señor Dunavant," Curel said, making a visible effort to control his voice, "you see a man who is not easily provoked. It is not because of magniminity. Or any softness of the heart. I refrain because I still entertain hopes for the encounter. I spare you, being a man who gambles on long odds, for another time."

"Until then, colonel, wherever it is!" Dunavant replied, not knowing that he was making a decision, or that, having been made, it was a decision which one of them would come to regret. *"Hasta luego,"* he said.

*"Hasta luego,"* Curel answered. "Until then, señor."

Dunavant stepped back from the ring of players; he was almost to the door when he heard Curel, speaking in English, ask for bets. There was a moment's silence, followed by an oath from one of the Americans, a hot answer in Spanish, not from Curel, and then a rending crash as the table struck the wall, the clink of coins rolling across the floor, a sudden splash of light that illuminated all corners of the room as the lamps fell and flared. Then partial darkness and another moment or two of complete silence.

He stopped in the doorway and glanced back over his shoulder, past the squat figure of the servant who now stood alert, his arm at his side. The room was lighted by a pool of oil sputtering on the earth-and-blood floor. In the brief silence the shadows thrown on the wall were as fixed as if they had been painted there.

It was only a step through the door and into the passageway; fifty feet down the passageway to his room. His calculations of the success of any fight put up by three Americans and more than a dozen Spaniards, half of them armed with swords, all of them with knives, against the finest pistol shot he had ever known, had not changed since he had made them five minutes before. The chance of success remained nil.

But in that instant of indecision something happened which put an end to his caution. A shadowy figure, a sword rattling at his heels, emerged from the melee at the far end of the room—the welter of curses, the sound of a chair striking someone's skull—and advancing quickly across the floor, collided with him. He was thrown off balance, and as he tried to recover, the swinging sword tripped his legs. Lying flat, he kicked the man in the middle of the back and propelled him through the door. Two more figures ran past him as he lay there; the last one he caught with his foot and spilled into the passageway.

On his feet again, he gave up all thought of escape. He rubbed his chin where it had struck the wall; it was numb, but the numbness was pleasant. The anger that had been fermenting for hours broke through in a hot flood. He stood with his shoulders hunched, blocking the doorway. Fighting mad, he peered into the room. Cesaire Curel was there somewhere, a few paces away.

The pool of sperm burning against the far wall had been trampled underfoot and the room now was a smoky heaving darkness, filled with curses in two languages, grunts, the scuffling of feet, repeated gasps of someone being choked. But no one came toward the door. He looked around for the servant who had been standing beside him when he was tripped by the sword and, not seeing him, made his way, one fist extended, a groping step at a time, toward the sounds. He might not find Curel, but he'd find someone.

It came from behind, without the slightest warning, a breath on his neck, and before he could turn, a long arm circled his throat, dragged him backward off his feet. He went down hard, with a wrenching twist that took his wind. But lying there on the floor, free for an instant, he reached out, found a leg and lifted, putting all his weight behind it. The man fell, not away from him as he had intended, but on him, a squat, heavy body which he recognized even in the darkness, before he felt the coarse clothes, as that of Yris Llorente's servant. His suspicions about her had been accurate.

The man was powerful and silent. A heavy blow with his elbow against the servant's belly brought forth not the slightest sound. A short cutting blow to the chin produced the same results; the man was made of iron. Dunavant rose to a knee, preparing to use his feet, and was almost upright when the long arm had him by the throat. The fingers, as stiff as oak fagots, shut off his breath. With the first pressure, he was on his feet and staggering for a hold, but the grip did not relax. Together they fell, Dunavant raining blows against the flesh as solid as the wall.

Then the Indian spoke for the first time, a few mumbled words of dialect, a word or two in Spanish. Dunavant could not reply. The air trapped in his lungs was on fire. Points of fire glittered in the darkness, and he heard, as if from a great distance, the fighting at the other end of the room.

The sudden light in the doorway was his head exploding, a reflection of the consuming fire in his chest. The woman standing there with a long-barreled rifle, the folds of her blue dress glinting, was death itself. But as she spoke, her voice through the darkness engulfing him was vaguely familiar.

"Goda'mighty," Kate Howland shouted. "Get out, before I shoot ever' last one of you."

Dunavant, calling on the Virgin, struck a final blow before the figure in the doorway faded and night closed upon him.

He was lying on a bed and a candle was burning on the bureau. His head was the size of a pumpkin and his lungs ached with every breath, but he *was* breathing—he was alive, sore in every bone, but alive!

He raised himself to one elbow and, recognizing the clothes thrown over the chest, his rucksack against the wall, he saw that he was in his own room. There was no sound. A light wind fluttered the curtains at the window. He was in his own room, but how had he got here? The last thing he remembered was lying on the floor with fingers around his neck, choking. The light. The figure in the doorway with a blue dress. The fight. By God, he was here, somehow, and the fight was still going on.

Throwing his feet over the side of the bed, he sat up. The room dipped and turned, slid away and then steadied. In a moment he would be ready to go back and finish things.

He was aware that someone else was in the room. His head was clear now and he was sure that he was not alone. Whoever it was sat there behind him in the rawhide chair, watching him. Somehow he knew who it was before he turned around.

The servant was smoking a reed cigarette, holding it in his one hand and looking straight ahead, his lizard eyes sleepy and inscrutable. There was a small discolored puff over one ear, but nothing else to show that he had been in a fight.

Dunavant got to his feet, doubling his fists, took two unsteady steps toward the Indian, and stopped.

"Fight over," the servant said.

"The hell it is," Dunavant said. "The hell it is."

"Fight over," the Indian repeated, puffing on the cigarette as if he had never smoked one before. "Señora Howland say finish."

"Señora Howland hasn't anything to say about what I'm going to do."

"Fight over," the servant said again.

Dunavant took another step toward him, steady on his feet now.

The Indian did not move. "Señora Llorente say come. Come. Stay. Watch. Guard señor."

Dunavant's mouth dropped open. *"Nombre de Dios!"* he shouted. "You were sent here?"

"Señora send."

"You come here as a guard and end up by damned near choking me to death?"

"Six men hurt. Three stabs. One head bust. Two arms," the Indian said. "Señor only choke."

"Why didn't you say something before?"

"No chance talk. Anyway, señor no believe. Choke better."

"I've got a good mind to give you a punch in the nose."

"Many punches," the Indian said. "No feel."

Dunavant looked around for a chair to use instead of his fists; the Indian was sitting in the only one in the room; he could hardly ask him to relinquish it for the purpose he had in mind.

"Better you sleep," the Indian said between puffs.

"Better you shut up," Dunavant replied.

He sat down on the bed, rubbing his skinned knuckles, his anger divided impartially between the one-armed, iron-sided Indian and the woman who had almost cost his life and, worse, had prevented him from cracking a few Spanish heads. Then slowly simmering down, his anger took a different and more intense turn. He recalled the bitter experiences of Texas, the galling defeat on the San Saba with victory in his grasp, the court-martial and Major Gilson mouthing pious platitudes, his arrest in Los Angeles and the year in the prison of Tepic. He recalled the encounter that morning on the trail—the arrogance of the Spanish girl with the musket and the tawny-yellow eyes, the contemptuous glances as he had ridden through the Calle Principal. His anger, increasing with each memory, finally fixed itself upon Cesaire Curel.

It brought him to his feet. It guided his steps as he paced the small room. There was a debt he owed his men—Rogers and Chapman and the others. A debt of a different kind to Major Gilson wherever he was. A debt, incidentally, he owed himself to wipe out the memory of Gilson and the court-martial and the defeat on the river. Finally, there was a score to settle with the man with the black square-cut beard and the white hands. He had already made a pact with Curel at the card table. The time had come to keep it.

Dunavant opened the door and strode down the passageway. He could hear the Indian padding along after him, but he didn't turn around. Before a room at the end of the passage, he pulled up and knocked. The door swung open after a moment and Kate Howland stood peering out at him, a candle in one hand and the long-barreled rifle in the other. Her eyes were shooting fire. She was in a flannel nightdress, with her hair done up in curlers, and she looked mad enough to chase bears with a switch.

"You've come to apologize," she snorted. "It better be good, young man. Breaking up my furniture and everything. Acting like a Comanche."

"I've come about the proposition Kroll made tonight." He saw that her jaw was relaxing a little. "I've decided to accept—if it's still open."

Her eyes got as mellow as they ever were and she lowered the rifle. "It's open," she said, "and I'll take the acceptance as an apology. Glad now that I didn't shoot you, like I had a mind to."

He backed away, seeing a look that made him know that she was going to start talking about Camilla at any minute, and said good night.

The servant was standing in the passage a few steps away. Dunavant passed him without a word, wondering if from now on, wherever he went, the Indian planned to follow him. At least, he would get rid of him for the night. Opening the door of his room, he slipped quickly inside, but before he could close it, he felt pressure on the other side and a copper-colored foot was thrust through the small opening.

Dunavant yanked the door open. "What the hell do you want now?"

"Sleep," said the Indian.

"Sleep outside."

"Sleep inside better," the man replied, walking through the door.

Dunavant swore and slid the bolt. He lacked the strength to throw the Indian out, if he had ever had it, the strength even to argue.

"Do you want to sleep in the bed?" he asked politely.

"Sleep floor," the Indian said, lying down in front of the door. "Sleep here. Señor no get out."

Dunavant sat down on the bed and swore again. "What's your name, *hombre?* Since we're going to be *compañeros*."

"Tepeyollotl."

"Let's just call you Joe," Dunavant said. "And go to sleep."

He took a brown leather book, dog-eared and no larger than his hand, from the rucksack beside the bed, dropped some candle grease on the headboard, set the candle in it and stretched out. The book was the *Military Maxims of Napoleon Bonaparte.* He opened it to page one and began to read.

# 7

Julio de Zubaran, having left Kate Howland's at the moment the fight started, and stopped for a drink at *La Golondrina,* was now making his way toward his home in the Calle Principal.

He walked jauntily, whistling to himself, bouncing up slightly on his heels at each step, but the jauntiness of his manner was not a true reflection of his mood. It was, in fact, merely an attempt to repair the indignity of his hasty departure from the gambling room, the wound to his pride caused by the kick administered by the gringo Dunavant, the rent in his trousers resulting from the fall in the passage. Actually, he was very depressed.

The clean night wind blowing in from the sea, the clank of his Toledo sword, the two gold onzas he had won at monte resting in his pocket, did nothing to lighten his mood. Or the knowledge that his departure, as undignified as it was for one who was an aide to Governor Pico, had probably saved him from the consequences of a common brawl.

His feeling of depression was heightened by the fact that he had always had a certain admiration for the gringos. Under three successive governors, he had formed this admiration, maintaining it in spite of censure from his friends and superiors, often at the loss of prestige, and even danger to his position and future.

It was true that this admiration was in some measure due to other things than any particular merit he had found in the American adventurers who had come to the pueblo. A trip to Washington and New York six years before had something to do with it, for, seeing the size of these cities, the energy and power that had built them, he had become convinced that in event of war between the two nations, his country could never emerge the victor. And, once convinced, he had made it a point to protect himself and his interests against this eventuality.

In the last three months, since war had become inevitable, he had redoubled his efforts to increase his number of friends among the Americans and to make new ones, at the same time scrupulously performing the duties of his office.

The efforts had not been easy. Governor Pico had warned him on several occasions about his actions, and likely would have asked for his sword if it had not been that the governor, feuding with General Castro in the north, in disfavor among the populace, and beset by the encroaching gringo, was in no position to risk the displeasure of the powerful De Zubaran family. His attendance at Jacob Kroll's fandango had been made against Pico's wishes. It would be necessary to make excuses to the governor tomorrow; to invent a piece of information which would justify his reason for going.

He would have to invent it because he had learned nothing. The conspiracy which Jacob Kroll was hatching was already known to Governor Pico, who was waiting until the proper time to spring the trap, until all the names of the Americans who were going to join the movement were learned—a matter which shouldn't take more than a day or two. The information he had hoped to gain from Señora Llorente had come to nothing, since she had slipped away under his eyes, before he had had a chance to talk to her. He had followed her through the streets, seen her and the gringo, Dunavant, enter the house, the gringo come out after an hour, but there was little or nothing in this to attract the governor's attention.

The talk with Señor Dunavant had turned up nothing, either, beyond the fact that the gringo, in the face of all efforts to be friendly, to warn him against participating in Kroll's scheme—even going so far as to hint that the authorities were aware of it—had taken no pains to conceal his enmity. The feud between the gringo and Curel over the card table was apparently one of long standing. The gringo's remark that he was leaving for San Diego the next day was routine information which would be reported by Lieutenant Morales, who also had heard it there in the gambling room.

No, there was nothing to tell Governor Pico when he saw him tomorrow. The knowledge that he would be forced to tax his ingenuity between now and then, combined with the wind at the moment whistling through the rent in his trousers, deepened his depression.

Major de Zubaran circled the church and, as his eyes fell on the open door and lighted altar beyond, he was tempted to enter and spend a few minutes on his knees. At this point he noticed a light falling in the lane at the opposite side of the plaza. It came from Señora Llorente's. The hour was late, but the light showed that she had not yet retired. He might be able to learn something from this woman which he could pass on to the governor.

He turned away from the church, crossed the plaza and knocked on the iron-barred gate. His mood grew lighter at the prospect which lay before him—something really important might yet turn up.

A great deal of mystery surrounded Señora Llorente. She had been in the pueblo not more than a month and yet no one knew much about her. Some said she was from Mexico City; others had different views, among the latter Captain Piedra of the sloop *Chubasco,* who had brought her to San Pedro from Acapulco. It was Piedra's opinion that she came originally from Callao, where she had been mixed up in the bloody revolution of the previous year; he knew a man who had seen her there, a person of reliability and himself an exile, who said that she had been responsible for the death of General Ortega and his entire staff.

The knock was not answered and De Zubaran used the hilt of his sword a second time.

But one thing about Señora Llorente was certain: whether she was from Mexico City or Callao in Peru, she was a woman of intelligence, familiar with both sides of the conflict taking shape in California. And besides her intelligence, she was a woman of flashing beauty, superior in charm to anyone he had ever seen. He regretted as he stood there, listening to footsteps approaching through the courtyard, that he was already engaged, though this in itself was not an immediate handicap.

Señora Llorente's voice inquired his name; he gave it, and the door swung open on heavy hinges.

As he entered, he was momentarily startled by a man who was standing just inside the deep embrasure of the gate, hat in hand, presumably about to take his departure. The man was in the shadows, his face hidden, and the major thought for an instant that it was one of his fellow officers. But a moment later the figure stepped into the light and he recognized the slender build, the fashionable, well-fitting clothes, the square-cut beard of Cesaire Curel.

Curel bowed. "I see that you are no worse for the brawl, Major de Zubaran."

"And you likewise," Julio said, wondering how the other had managed to arrive so quickly.

"For the reason that I didn't remain," Curel said. "There is nothing more dangerous than a fight in the dark, where things happen beyond your control, where it is easy to do injury to a friend. *Caspita!* I have no taste for these affairs." He walked through the gates and turned. "I trust that no one was hurt. None of your friends. Or Señor Dunavant. Particularly Señor Dunavant, whom I wish to see again. Did you stay for the finish?"

Julio struggled with the truth. "I left shortly after you did," he said finally, "contenting myself with a couple of blows of the sword."

"Not against Señor Dunavant, I hope."

"I am not sure," Julio said, wondering at Curel's continued solicitude for the gringo, which at first he had taken as a joke. "Only that it was a gringo who received the blows."

"If it had been Señor Dunavant, you would have known for sure," Curel said cryptically. He bowed and said good night to Yris Llorente.

"I haven't intruded?" Julio apologized.

"Not at all. I was merely walking home and stopped for a word with an old friend. I will see you in the morning at the Governor's Mansion, Major de Zubaran."

Señora Llorente had said nothing during the conversation at the gate, so Julio was puzzled when upon reaching the *sala* she turned and faced him, her eyes shadowed beneath the heavy lashes.

"What is this affair at Howland's in which you risk your life with such abandon?" she asked.

Julio was puzzled as much by the tone of her voice as by the intense look she gave him, but, as he was a vain man where women were concerned, his puzzlement was brief. He decided that both things were the result of her interest in his safety. While he had seen her only twice since she had arrived in the pueblo, and only for a few minutes at each meeting, he didn't find it hard to believe that she had become enamored of him, even though she was a woman of great charm and beauty, who was sought after by all the officers of the garrison and by the governor himself.

Stroking the silky ends of his mustache, he described the fight at the card table in some detail, adding a few embellishments of his own to enliven the scene and the role he had played. "It was nothing," he said, pausing to light a cigarette. "Since the gringos have been pouring into the pueblo, these affairs are commonplace."

She leaned back against the table, her hands supporting her weight, and studied him for a moment. She was dressed in a peignoir—he presumed that she had been preparing for bed when Curel had arrived—of heavy yellow silk. Open at the throat and revealing the startling pallor of her skin, it lay like a sheath across her stomach and the sinuous curves of her hips.

Julio's depression disappeared; his blood began to race madly through his veins; he debated whether to press his advantage or to wait. Settling upon the latter course, since he was not quite certain that her feeling for him had ripened to the proper point, he stood there drawing on his cigarette, and through the rising smoke devouring her with his eyes.

"Three Americans," she said, "and more than a dozen Spaniards. The odds then were not against you."

Her words were spoken lightly and without any trace of mockery, but he couldn't escape the feeling that his account of the story had failed in some respect. "It was nothing," he said, smiling. "A brawl, distasteful to me in every way, which I was happy to leave at the first opportunity."

"After two blows of your sword."

"Two or three," he said.

"Directed at Señor Dunavant?"

"It was dark and I wouldn't be sure."

She straightened and in the movement, almost violent in its nature, as her peignoir swirled back from her thigh, he saw in a silken sheath fastened to her garter a thin blade with a silver filigreed handle. She stood looking at him for a long moment, her eyes blazing.

"If I thought you had struck him," she said then in a voice cold with passion, "I would kill you."

Somehow Julio managed to smile. "It could have been one of the other two Americans, as Curel said."

"It could have been!"

Before he had a chance to say more, Yris Llorente snatched the candlestick from the table. Faced with ordinary dangers, Julio was not a coward, but there was something about an enraged woman, with or without a blade in her garter or a heavy candlestick in her hand, that struck terror to his soul.

It was beneath his honor as an officer and a hidalgo to take the sensible course and bolt for the door. He therefore compromised by taking several steps backward. But as she advanced toward him, the candlestick held in her hand, he suddenly gave up all pretense.

He was at the door in time to step through it and into the courtyard as the candlestick, followed by a shower of maledictions, crashed at his heels.

Once outside the gate, he hurried up the lane, cursing himself for ever having mentioned the fight, and crossed the plaza without looking back. But as he reached the door of his home, he heard behind him, clear in the quiet night, the sound of running feet. He glanced over his shoulder. From the lane he had just left, a figure emerged, wrapped in a long, dark riding cloak, and, skirting the plaza, disappeared toward Kate Howland's. There was no mistaking who it was or where she was going.

His spirits suddenly brightened. The evening, after all, had not been wasted. He would have a very interesting piece of information to pass on to Don Pío Pico in the morning.

At noon the next day, Julio sat at his desk in the Governor's Mansion. The red velvet curtains were pulled back on their brass rings. Waves of heat, reflected from the tarred roofs of the houses that enclosed the plaza, came through the open window. In the last hour he had talked to fifteen people who had come to air grievances or ask favors of the governor. Only one person remained to be seen, his cousin, Roque de Zubaran.

Leaning back in his chair, Julio lighted a cigarette, and let his eyes drift over the ceiling, the red carpet, the plush chairs, the heavy, gold-framed mirrors on the walls. He was familiar with Roque de Zubaran's business, and since the young man had become quite impossible of late—the result, he presumed, of Don Saturnino's efforts to make a hidalgo out of a quiet, studious, musically inclined youth—it would do him good to cool his heels.

Julio glanced at the buzzards wheeling through the hot sky, and smoked his cigarette slowly to a stub. Then he nodded to the soldier standing inside the door and occupied himself with the papers on his desk while his cousin entered the room. At the proper moment, he glanced up and gave him a businesslike greeting in which he was careful to include no hint of familiarity.

Roque fished a letter from his jacket. "This is from Don Saturnino. It's about a summons."

"The summons?"

"The one you brought to the ranch yesterday."

Julio opened the letter and spread it out on his desk. It was written in firm strokes, the words boldly formed in straight-running lines, an extra flourish beginning each sentence. He could see Don Saturnino pacing up and down the saddlery on his stout legs while he dictated it, and Luz sitting with a fresh quill, putting down what she was told, except for the flowery phrases. He could hear her reading the letter when it was finished, her voice husky but full of sudden changes, as Saturnino stood with his feet thrust apart, grinning as if he had written it himself.

Thinking of the girl, he forgot the letter and her brother in front of the desk. Momentarily he forgot also Señora Llorente and the wound she had inflicted upon his pride, the wound which had caused him a sleepless night of twisting and turning. Luz de Zubaran, his betrothed, a woman potentially superior in every way to the mysterious, hot-tempered señora!

Of course, there were certain things about Luz that needed his attention. For one thing, she cared nothing about elegant clothes or the social life of the city. She preferred instead a pair of leather trousers and hours in the saddle, roaming the hills or roping *mesteños* with the *vaqueros,* on a horse that anyone in his right mind would never ride. But these are small things, to be overlooked in a girl with a father who had brought her up to do everything he did. They would probably tax his patience, but the result would more than justify the effort—he would make her over into the most charming and beautiful woman in the pueblo, including Yris Llorente.

Julio pushed the letter aside without reading it and looked at his cousin. For a moment he considered having Roque come back later to deliver the letter personally to Governor Pico—Don Pío was engaged for the time being; but observing that the young man was dressed in the garb of a *vaquero* and looked like he had just come in from twisting a cow's tail, he gave up the idea.

"I'll see that the governor gets the message."

"What shall I tell Don Saturnino?" Roque asked.

"Tell him that I have the letter and will see that it's delivered to Governor Pico," said Julio impatiently.

"Nothing else?"

"Nothing."

Roque, fingering his hat, turned to leave.

Julio stopped him, suddenly struck by an idea. "Before you go, what happens with *los Alacranes?* You and Malaspina and the rest?"

Roque hunched his narrow shoulders and his thin face took on the look of a conspirator. "The activities of the *bando* are secret," he said.

"Even from the governor?"

"Even from him."

Frowning at his cousin's bravado, Julio rose and walked to the window and looked out into the square. "There's a man, a tall blond gringo by the name of Dunavant, who travels south to San Diego tomorrow along the King's Highway. He will pass the Hill of the Hawk. It may be that he travels on the following day or possibly not at all. But if he does, I suggest that *los Alacranes* investigate his reasons for traveling and his destination. Whatever you see fit to do has the sanction of the governor."

"Your suggestion is a command," Roque said.

Julio glanced at his cousin, surprised by the grace of his remark. "And when you return to the ranch, convey my greetings to the family, to your sister particularly.

He turned and, as the door closed behind Roque de Zubaran, he again looked through the window. Two horsemen were trotting lazily out of town on the North Trail, the sun flashing on their bridles and silver headstalls. A woman with a basket on her head and a child in her arms shuffled toward the church. A peon, squatting against the wall, rose up out of the shade and found a patch of sun. On his gray, long-eared donkey, returning from the Hill of the Hawk, Father Expeleta jogged across the plaza.

The glare from the plaza caused a faint throbbing behind his eyes—he had drunk far too much punch last night—and he was about to leave the window when he saw a man hurrying up the lane from Jacob Kroll's. The hot dancing light prevented good vision, but he was obviously a gringo, for only a gringo would be hurrying in the noon sun.

As the man came closer, he saw that it was Señor Dunavant. He moved with long, swinging strides, his wide shoulders set forward as if he were prepared to shove someone out of the way. An Indian, with one arm, followed in his dust.

Julio, being in the other's line of vision, took a step back from the window, experiencing as he did so a resurge of the feeling that had prompted him to tell Roque about the gringo, a feeling made up of the slighting way he had been treated when he had offered his friendship outside the tavern, the indignity of the kick which had ruined his best uniform, the blow to his pride suffered at the hands of Señora Llorente.

As he watched the gringo cross the square, the feeling, which had been formless at first, began to take definite shape. As the man approached and glanced up at the Mexican flag flying over the mansion, giving it a sidelong look in which Julio read unmistakable contempt, the feeling hardened. His admiration for Americans, which he had prided himself on for many years, in that moment became an active dislike.

He was suddenly clear in his mind about Señor Dunavant. The fact that Yris Llorente had rushed to the inn to see him, when he had stupidly implied that the gringo had beeen injured, did not mean anything necessarily, for her connection with Jacob Kroll's conspiracy had not been established. Indeed, Governor Pico had given Lieutenant Morales a dressing down when the latter had voiced his suspicions of her. But this, with the fact that he had just seen Señor Dunavant coming from Kroll's house, his whole manner as he had crossed the plaza, his contemptuous glance at the Mexican flag, added up to one thing.

Julio pulled the curtains shut and began to sort the papers on his desk. He had little faith in the Scorpions and their horrendous name, or in Roque, their leader, a timid young man for all his show of bravado, who would not have had the position he held except for Don Saturnino's power in the valley. They would probably stop the gringo and talk to him, give him a bad moment or two and in the end permit him to go, no worse for the encounter. It would be better to report what he had seen to Lieutenant Morales. The arrest of Señor Dunavant before he left the pueblo would place him in the custody of an officer noted for his hatred of the gringos and his resourcefulness in expressing it.

He left the desk and walked to the small, barred window which opened on the patio. The angle of the window prevented him from seeing Governor Pico, but he could hear his voice, the voice of Colonel Curel offering an occasional word in reply.

Julio was puzzled by Cesaire Curel. The colonel had arrived from Mexico City on the same ship with Yris Llorente, but he had come in no official capacity and with only vague allusions, in his letter of introduction from President Paredes, to numerous services performed in the interests of the Mexican Government. There was no doubt, however, about his loyalty to the cause or his desire to see every gringo driven from the soil of California.

The puzzling thing was what Colonel Curel hoped to gain by joining in the conflict. He was not an officer in the Mexican Army, though he had been during the war in Texas. He was not even a citizen of the Republic. Could it be that, like so many of the other adventurers who had come to the country, he was interested only in gaining a grant of land? It didn't seem sensible to Julio, for who would deliberately risk his neck in a cause that already seemed lost simply to acquire cattle and a ranch of rolling hills?

About the third man sitting at the table in the patio, there was no question.

The Englishman, Señor Fraser, who had arrived in the pueblo yesterday in the pack train from Santa Fe, was here for a definite reason. As an agent of Great Britain, he had come to confer with Governor Pico about placing California under British protection. It was a plan which Pico had entertained for many months, which he had publicly announced several weeks before in Monterey, and which he had been quietly working for ever since, against those who favored an American, a Russian or French Protectorate.

The hour for these maneuvers seemed late, as they had since Frémont had appeared in California and Commodore Sloat with the American Navy at Mazatlán, a thousand miles to the south. He had expressed this opinion to Governor Pico in the past. Thinking of his experience last night, the gringo swaggering out of Jacob Kroll's and across the plaza, he now regretted that he had. In the future he would use his influence—and it was considerable, backed as it was by the influence of the De Zubarans—against the Americans.

Abruptly he left the room and walked down the passage toward the patio.

The day was hot and Don Pío Pico sat in his shirt sleeves, under a ramada of peeled willow poles, at one end of a table set with fresh linen and well-polished silver. His hat was pulled down to shield his eyes from the stray sun which filtered through the willow lattice. Colonel Curel, in a fawn-colored jacket, sat across from him, and on the opposite side of the table, the Englishman, Fraser, dressed in somber black. In front of them were platters of barbecued beef, dishes of peppers, lentils and frijoles, a large bowl of tomato sauce.

Julio seated himself at the table.

"The *salsa* is good," Don Pío said, giving him a curt nod.

On his return from the frontier, Julio had brought back a basket of little pocket tomatoes from one of the Indian milpas. They were no particular delight to the eye, but they were out of season for the pueblo, and within their crisp, greenish-brown husks was firm, rich meat.

"*Chile verde* is a treat for this time of year," he said, determined that his gift should have full appreciation.

Governor Pico was silent while he speared meat onto his plate and poured himself a cup of claret. Then, sipping and munching, he turned his small, black eyes on Julio. "Besides the tomatoes, Major de Zubaran, what did you bring from the frontier? What response to my summons?"

"The response was mixed. Two expressed willingness to join the expedition into the north. . . ."

"Two?" Governor Pico thundered. "What of the others?"

"Four expressed reluctance. One refused."

An Indian girl brought a tray of food from the outdoor oven and Julio paused to fill his plate. "These men on the frontier," he explained, "are out of touch with events in the pueblo and elsewhere. News reaches them slowly or not at all. When it does it finds them busy rounding up cattle, slaughtering, or chasing Indians. What happens in the north doesn't concern them because it is hundreds of miles away."

Governor Pico spread his broad hairy hands in a gesture of resignation. He glanced from Curel to Fraser, as if to ask them to witness the trials the government was forced to endure.

"Why is it," he blustered, "that I should have to go begging for arms and men? Am I the governor of California or a mendicant peon? Am I the one who is responsible for the safety of the country? Am I the one who is in a position to appraise the danger, or are they?"

Mr. Fraser, sitting stiffly in his somber black coat and black cravat, raised pale-blue eyes from his plate. "Your experience isn't unique, Governor Pico. It is shared by all leaders who attempt to arouse the citizenry in time of danger."

Pío Pico's dark, Negroid face flushed. "They will be aroused soon enough. I will dispatch soldiers to the frontier to impress them with the fact that a summons from me calls for neither reluctance nor refusal."

These threats Julio did not take seriously; he doubted that the Englishman, with his skeptical eyes, did either. Threats had been made in the past by Governor Alvarado and Governor Micheltorena, by Don Pío himself. The truth was that the ranchers on the frontier were too strong to be intimidated. Don Pío knew this; his threat was the outburst of a man speaking for effect, and in anger. It was a good time, he realized, to give the De Zubarans a boost.

"As you know, Governor Pico, the frontier follows the lead of Don Saturnino de Zubaran. He has pledged his support to the cause. It will be unnecessary to send soldiers. Don Saturnino will see that they fall in line."

The governor's temper was improved by these remarks, and finishing his claret, he said, "We find ourselves, Señor Fraser, suddenly threatened by hordes of Yankees. The wagons of that perfidious people have already crossed the continent, scaled the almost inaccessible summits of the Sierra Nevada and penetrated the fruitful valley of the Sacramento."

Julio ate his food and waited for Don Pío to come to the point. What he was saying, almost the exact words, he had listened to before at the meeting of the Junta in Monterey. Judging from the bored expression on the Englishman's face, he also had heard much of it during the hour they had been talking in the patio.

"Already," the governor said, "are these adventurous land voyagers seeking to spread themselves over a country which seems suited to their tastes. They have begun to cultivate farms, erect mills, saw up lumber, build workshops and a thousand other things which seem appropriate to them, but which the Californians despise."

Don Pío paused, sopped up the last of his sauce with a folded *tortilla* and popped it into his mouth. After a moment he said, "By ourselves we cannot save the country from this swarm of rapacious insects. We can slow their progress, which I propose to do. But we cannot exterminate them alone, without help. Several weeks ago in Monterey, as I have told you, I pronounced for annexation to England. My proposal was received with some disfavor. But I propose it again here and to you."

The Englishman's expression of boredom did not change. "I have already explained the position of my country: our controversy with the United States over the Oregon territory and our determination to do everything within our power to prevent them from taking over California. Before I left Santa Fe I received word from our agents in Mexico City that Admiral Seymour and the British squadron, led by the *Collingwood,* were on their way to San Blas. We are therefore prepared for action. I suggest that your attitude be conveyed to Admiral Seymour without further delay."

"The Pacific Squadron of the United States is at Mazatlán, a hundred miles from San Blas," Colonel Curel broke in, "commanded by Commodore Sloat. It is a powerful fleet."

"Inferior in every way to the British—in size and firing power," Fraser said, suddenly coming to life. "The American flagship *Savannah,* for instance, carries fifty-four guns to the *Collingwood's* seventy-four."

An Indian girl brought dishes of custard, sprinkled with burned sugar, and four glasses of angelica. Governor Pico finished the dessert and drank his wine. He touched his lips with the corner of his napkin, raised a hand—each finger of which was adorned with a silver ring—to his mouth and politely belched. Then he glanced at the Englishman.

"The Mexican ship, *Chubasco,* is now loading at San Diego," he said. "It will sail within the week for Mazatlán. I will see that a cabin is prepared for you. From Mazatlán you can reach San Blas and Admiral Seymour in three days by horseback." He turned to Colonel Curel. "You can proceed as far as San Diego with Señor Fraser and there use your talents to reorganize the garrison, which, from all reports, is in a bad condition, and also to repair the fortifications."

Colonel Curel fingered his square-cut beard. "I am at your service," he said in his soft drawl.

Julio rose from the table as the three men began to discuss the details of the coming conflict; he had business of his own with Lieutenant Morales who would be eating now at La Golondrina. Before he had reached the door, Governor Pico's voice stopped him.

"Major de Zubaran, you will accompany Colonel Curel and Señor Fraser to San Diego, where you will introduce the colonel to the officers of the garrison. Afterwards you will accompany Señor Fraser to San Blas. Make your preparations accordingly."

"Yes, sir," Julio said calmly, but as he left the patio and walked toward the tavern, he grew pale and his stomach began to churn at the thought of the long sea voyage. He had made the trip the previous summer and swore that he would never make it again. But he was in a corner. The governor was in no mood for trifling. There was one advantage, however, in going to San Blas: he would be away from California while much of the fighting was taking place.

# 8

Father Expeleta, rising from his nap, left his quarters in the rear of the church and climbed the six wooden steps to the little room from which the ponderous bell was rung.

He was still weary from his long journey to the Hill of the Hawk, and unrefreshed by his afternoon sleep, but the ringing of the bell was a duty he did not care to delegate. Without a certain skill and patience, which he had not been able to teach any of his helpers, the instrument gave out jangling ungodly sounds, as if it were being rung by the Devil himself.

Grasping the rawhide rope in his knotty hands, the old priest bent his weight. His joints creaked and snapped as the rope tightened but, biting down on his tongue and gathering all his strength, he tripped the bell and swung it to the highest point of its arc. This was the ticklish part of the business—getting off to the proper start—so he held his breath and said a short, silent prayer. To his delight but not to his surprise, for the prayer was said to the patron saint of all bell ringers, the first note broke forth clear and true on the evening air, followed by notes of equal clarity and resonance.

Of course, his trained ear detected in the sounds spilling out of the iron-throated bell a flaw, a mere whisper of discordance. It was always there no matter how hard he tried to deny it or how much skill he exercised in the ringing. When he had first heard it, several years before, he had attributed this small discord to a flaw in the casting, but later on he had arrived at the belief that it came from a different source. The bell had been given to the church by a young couple, who had flouted family and ecclesiastical law, in expiation of their sin. Gradually he had come to the conclusion that the gift had not absolved the sin, and that the discord remained as a warning to all those who did not heed the laws of God and man. The conclusion and, unfortunately, the warning were both weakened by the fact that no one could hear the discord except himself.

As the last notes of *Ave Maria* died out and the final echo came back from the hills, Father Expeleta walked to the small window and, leaning his thin wrists on the sill, looked down upon the pueblo.

The streets and lanes were almost deserted. The town was quiet; even from the Calle de los Negros, that haunt of thieves, gamblers and loose women, he heard no sound, not a guitar, a voice, a scream or a pistol shot. Crows that had been quarreling with bands of half-wild dogs over refuse, rose, while he watched, and winged toward the sycamores by the river. Evening smoke laid a blue veil over the roofs. Now that the bell was still, pigeons flocked back to nest in the belfry. Cattle were drinking along the irrigation ditches. Vineyards and fields gave off the sweet breath of growing things, and beyond them the far mountains lifted their crests into a serene cloudless sky. Below the mountains the great valley, bathed in a dusky haze, stretched away past the reach of his vision.

It was a peaceful scene but, looking out upon it and thinking of the ominous shadows beginning to fall across the pueblo and the whole of California—as, indeed, he had not ceased to think since the summons to war had come in the midst of the services yesterday morning—Father Expeleta crossed himself.

Many things had happened since he had arrived in California from Spain thirty-eight years ago. He had seen the missions prosper under Spanish viceroys and the early Mexican governors, and then, through the connivance of powers beyond his control, fall into decay. He had watched the long and bitter struggle between the Spanish ranchers and the Mexican overlords. During the past few years he had witnessed the steady encroachment of the Americans. And now, in his seventy-first year, came the shadows of war, the first, fearful blowing of trumpets.

The death and burial of Don Cristóbal de Zubaran seemed, as he stood there looking down upon the town and the distant mountains, a fitting end to an old and good way of life, the portent of a future which no man could foresee. The storm was gathering. The first warnings flickered along the horizon. Soon the lightning would strike. There was no point in wishing that he were a younger and more vigorous man. He had withstood other storms; with God's help he would withstand this. "Thou art Peter," he said to himself, "and upon this rock I will build my church."

Father Expeleta left the window, retraced his steps and entered the refectory.

The air in the small, candle-lighted cell was filled with spicy odors;

in front of his plate were bowls of steaming food. He had not eaten since dawn, and in spite of himself his thin nostrils quivered, his eyes twinkled and his mouth began to water at the sight of the laden table. He sat down quickly, but to make up for his greediness he took a sparing amount from each bowl, and as a further penance, mixed up everything on his plate—the sweet with the sour, the meat with the garbanzos, the garbanzos with the corn, stirring everything thoroughly with his wooden spoon until nothing was recognizable.

"To mortify the flesh," he explained to the new sacristan, who had entered the room and stood watching him beside the door. "*Aequam servare mentem.* To preserve an unruffled mind."

"There's a woman in the confessional," the sacristan said. "I explained that you have just returned from a long journey."

"Did you say that communion is not until Sunday week?"

"I said this also, but she is insistent and in a state of agitation."

Father Expeleta went on with his eating. The request was irregular; he was tired and extremely hungry, and furthermore he knew the identity of the woman—no one except the one he had in mind would make such a request at this hour and time. Besides, he did not approve of the supplicant, her background or imperious ways. Like a stone tossed into a quiet pond, her arrival in the pueblo had set up a series of ripples which had reached into many homes. But, his food suddenly losing its savor, he placed his spoon on the table and went into the church.

After he had closeted himself, and seated his tired bones on the hard bench of the confessional, he waited, thinking of his food growing cold. As the first words came through the grating, rich, throaty and invested with the vanity of a proud and beautiful woman, he realized that his surmise had been correct.

"To God Almighty and the Blessed Virgin, I, Doña Yris, confess to having coveted a string of pearls and a pair of earrings and the beauty of the woman who possessed them."

"When did this sin of covetousness take place?"

"Last night at a *baile.*"

"You have many pearls. Abundance makes poor."

"Yes, Father."

"And then?"

"I confess to using a lash on an impertinent servant."

"Words suffice and cut deeper."

"Yes."

"And thereafter?" the priest asked, with a touch of impatience, doubting that the woman had come here for these ingenuous reasons.

"I confess to anger, which tempted me sorely and which led me to drive a friend from the house."

"*Furor arma ministrat.* Rage supplies arms." The priest, who had again begun to think of his neglected supper, pricked up his ears. "Continue," he said. No sound coming from beyond the grating save a faint rustling, he repeated his command.

"I accuse myself of contemplating an action which is against the interest of our country."

"Who is the man that causes this temptation?" the priest asked, making a shrewd appraisal of the situation.

"An American."

Father Expeleta pressed closer to the grating. "Of what does the temptation consist?"

There was a short period of silence beyond the wall and again the rustle of silk. He was suddenly conscious of a thin but pervading odor of perfume sifting down upon him from the grating. Against his will the scent erased time and he was a youth once more, standing beneath a balcony in the city of Córdova. Quickly he made two thrusts of a finger, driving Beelzebub away, and said under his breath, "*Vaya, vaya,*" for good measure. "Go!"

Señora Llorente was speaking ". . . and during the afternoon I learned that this—this American is to be arrested by Lieutenant Morales."

"Is he one of the plotters?"

"I don't think he is, Father."

"But whether he is or not, you are tempted to warn him of the arrest?"

"Yes."

The priest pulled on his lower lip. He had not thought when he was looking down on the pueblo a moment or two before, pondering his part in the coming conflict, that he would be called on so soon to take a stand. What counsel was he to give? Perhaps the man *was* an enemy. Should he be allowed to escape and thereby be free to continue his activities? If he was not a conspirator, his arrest would be an injustice, another provocation to all those who wished to see Governor Pico deposed.

"The role of an informer is never a happy one," he said evasively.

"I have no fear for myself."

"Love is often a seducer of right."

"*Jesús María!* Who speaks of love?"

"The epithet is not becoming," the priest said, certain from the quickness of the reply and her tone that she was trying to throw him off the trail. "If not love, then friendship, and in either case I counsel restraint. If the man is guilty of conspiracy, he is also prepared to accept the consequences of his act. If he is not guilty and is still arrested, he may not have long to languish in jail. Since he is an American and here in the pueblo, he is a man of resource. In the middle course you will go most safely. *Medio tutissimus ibis.* Counsel neither the pursued nor the pursuer."

Rising from the bench, Father Expeleta absolved the girl and, though thinking of his food grown cold, the irregularity of the occasion, the haughty nature of the supplicant, gave her only a mild penance, suggested that she be prompt for communion, and slowly made his way toward the refectory, beginning already to doubt the wisdom of his advice. His doubts were somewhat lightened by the knowledge that in all likelihood Señora Llorente would not heed the advice he had given.

Doña Yris, once more in her house off the Calle Principal, sat combing her hair, tilting her head as she brushed one side and then the other, and glancing at herself in the large gilt-framed mirror. It was a wonderful mirror. The frame with its fat-bellied cupids, leafy scrolls and festoons of fruit and flowers was very gay. Her image, even in the shifting light of the candles, came back from the glass without distortion, not as in most mirrors where one looked like someone else.

She was glad she had insisted upon bringing it from Mexico City as she had all the other furnishings in the small boudoir. Two months had gone by but she could still see the astonishment on the face of Cesaire Curel when she had told him that she would not set foot outside the city unless he arranged for her to take all her most intimate furnishings, things she had bought in Paris when she had gone there six years ago as the bride of Don Francisco Llorente. They were riding through the *paseo* and Colonel Curel had turned and said, "*Por Dios,* no!" After that she didn't speak to him for three days and in the end—it was he who gave in and not she—everything that she wished to bring was crated up and packed on donkeyback to the port of Acapulco and carried by ship to San Pedro, thence by oxcart through the hills to Los Angeles.

How glad she was that they were here—the escritoire with its lid which folded shut, the red-lacquer table, the bits of crystal and jade, the diminutive bed, once owned by the Marquesa of Monte Alba. For whenever she could no longer stand the heavy dreariness of the rest of the house and its countless rooms filled with tasteless furniture, she could come here to the pink and gold boudoir and imagine herself back in Mexico City or even that she had never left it. And whenever, as now, there was a reason for looking one's best, it was nice to be sitting in front of a mirror that was flawless and yet subtly flattering.

Not that she absolutely needed the impersonal assurance of a mirror; despite her years—she was already twenty-eight, an age when most Spanish women were beginning to show the ravages of time—and the dry brilliant sunlight of California which was so hard on the skin, she looked no different than she had six years ago when she had danced at the Teatro Imperial and officers had fought duels over her and when, under the very noses of the city's most beautiful women, she had married the owner of the fabulous and ill-starred El Tigre, the greatest silver mine in all the provinces.

No, she thought, studying her reflection in the gilt-framed mirror, there was little if any change. Her hair was still blue-black and lustrous—the one gray strand she had plucked out night before last did not count. The pearly pallor of her skin was undiminished. Her dark eyes, made darker by the contrast of her coloring, still held the look of both fire and innocence which men found enchanting. It was only her mouth that she was not sure about. There was a little strain around the corners, the faintest shadow of sadness.

*"Un pocito triste,"* she said, changing the expression of her mouth for the moment by smiling. And no wonder, with all the misfortune of the past three years. In the name of the Virgin, no wonder. The silver treasure of El Tigre suddenly cut off by an underground flood. The long months of waiting for machinery from New York, only to have it lost in a storm within sight of Tampico. Again months of waiting and debts piling up. And then in the midst of everything, the death of Don Francisco—vigorous for a man of his years when he went to bed, and dead when the bells of Santa Brigida rang for Mass next morning. Yes, there was reason for the look of sadness. It was surprising that her mouth was not hard, *dura, muy dura.*

Dividing her hair, she pulled the two plaits forward over her bare shoulders and began to braid them. Catalina, the maid she had brought north with her from Mexico, usually did this, but she had sent the girl with a letter for Señor Dunavant. It was long past the time when Catalina should have returned. Being of a flirtatious nature, she had likely stopped somewhere to talk to one of the pueblo louts. A box on the ears was what she would receive when she got back.

Her hair braided and wound in a tight crown on top of her head, Doña Yris pierced it with pins set with small diamonds and began to rouge her lips. The diamond pins, the diamond-studded little box for cigarettes, a necklace of pearls and a few hundred gold onzas were all that she had managed to save out of Don Francisco's holdings. After the debts had been paid and the vultures had flown away, these and the house on the Avenida which she would never sell.

It was then that the affair with Cesaire Curel had commenced, though really it had commenced before, on the night at the opera when he had sat next to her and Don Francisco in an adjoining box and had never taken his eyes from her. Don Francisco, incensed at the familiarity, had accosted Curel when they were leaving, a quarrel had followed, and for a time it looked as if the duel, which her husband insisted on, would take place. But certain of Don Francisco's friends, who were powerful in the government, knowing Curel's skill with weapons, forced Curel to leave the city. He did not go far, no farther than Cuernavaca, and he was back the week after her husband's death.

She wished now, as she finished with the rouge and studied her mouth in the mirror, that he had never come back, that the duel had been fought and by some miracle of fortune he had been killed. It was not that she hated Cesaire; everything would be simpler if she did. The truth was, she was bored with him, with his square-cut beard and the admiration for it which led him to fasten it in a silken bandage when he went to bed. Bored with his swagger and conceit, the perfume he used, the clothes he ordered from a tailor in New Orleans, the pride in his small feet and his taste for shoes that made them look smaller.

But beyond the plain fact of her boredom was anger—anger with herself at having been attracted to him in the first place, at having returned his glances at the opera, at her simple belief, when he had come to see her after Don Francisco's death, in the tales of the vast properties he owned in Cuba. She had believed them like any innocent schoolgirl, and other tales as well—the trip to Paris and Madrid, the theater he was going to build for her in Havana, the wife he was divorcing as soon as a dispensation could be arranged. *Por Dios!* She, Yris Llorente y Machado!

And above everything—her boredom and anger and the gnawing

regret that she hadn't returned to the stage—was the madness which had brought her to the flea-bitten pueblo of Los Angeles.

Her mouth looked gayer now that it was brushed with rouge, and she rose from the little gold chair in her red high-heeled shoes and her long, black, dancer's stockings and stood regarding herself in the mirror. The reflection of her body was, like her face, reassuring. The high full breasts showed not the slightest evidence of the child of Don Francisco which she had suckled until its final breath. Her waist was as small and sinuous, the line from hip to ankle as clean as the first night she danced in Havana and the stage was a litter of flowers and men's hats.

What unkind star had guided her steps across those of Cesaire Curel? What fever had blurred her grasp of realities? And what madness had left her at the mercy of a passion which was to end here thousands of miles away from her home? Which was to end in boredom, but not until she had given up what well might be her last opportunity to dance again—given up the hot wine of fortune and fame for a tepid adventure in the interests of a man she was bored with, of other men she didn't know, and a government which was corrupt.

She drew the shift over her shoulders and sat down again at the mirror, wondering as the sound of steps came from the garden what word Catalina was bringing back from the inn. The note she had written was brief. She had withheld all of the information she had managed to gain from Lieutenant Morales when he had called on her three hours ago. She had simply asked the American to come immediately. But would he, being as suspicious of her as he seemed to be? Would he not, instead, take the letter for a warning, and leave the pueblo without seeing her? Perhaps he had left already.

She had begun to deepen the shadows around her eyes when this last thought struck her. She paused, her fingers tightening on the small brush, and stared into the mirror. At this very moment, while she was dressing to receive him, he might be riding away, away under the cover of night, out of the pueblo.

The footsteps in the garden drew closer; she heard the door into the *sala* open and shut. Soon she would know. The sound of steps faded out toward the far wing of the house. Perhaps Catalina was going to the kitchen to get something to eat—the fool was always eating. For an instant she was seized with an impulse to follow her and box her ears, but she realized that the girl was innocent. She had been told to deliver a note; probably she had delivered it and had returned and was now hungry.

Shrugging, she made a pretense of forgetting Catalina and any message she may have brought, but when several minutes passed without the maid's appearance, her thoughts turned again to the American. She had been heedless to write the letter at all. She should have taken Father Expeleta's advice and let what was to happen, happen. It was none of her business whether he was arrested or not. It was, actually, a silly impulse which had led her to disregard the priest's advice, for while Cesaire Curel had left for Santa Barbara, the town was alive with officers, any one of whom might see the American enter the house.

"Stupid!" she said under her breath, and as she said it again for good measure, making a face at herself, she heard the door open behind her and saw, with a sudden shock of surprise, the clear reflection of Cesaire Curel advancing across the room, his shoes sparkling in the candlelight, his sullen lips compressed in anger.

He came noiselessly toward her and kissed the nape of her neck. "Your servants seem to be asleep or dead. I'd still be standing outside except that I remembered the gate in the garden and found it open."

At the touch of his lips, even in her state of excitement, an involuntary shudder ran through her body, which she did her best to conceal by a shrug. "I didn't expect you, since you told me last night that you were leaving for the North. Both of the servants are out on errands. One of them must have left the gate unbarred." She spoke casually, though her heart was pounding. "It was probably Catalina," she said.

"A dangerous and careless oversight, with the town full of cutthroats."

He seated himself behind her so that he could observe her image in the mirror. Leaning forward, she deepened the shadows over her eyes, her face intent, her mind apparently absorbed with what she was doing. She didn't dare to meet his gaze. If she did he would certainly know what she was thinking, see the consternation and panic written there.

"What happened to change your plans?" she asked.

"*Nombre de Dios!* What happens I don't know, except that the man listens to the advice of officers who are excited as he is, and as ignorant of strategy."

She touched the corners of her eyes lightly with the brush. She must think clearly, very clearly. When she had sent the letter to Grady Dunavant telling him to use the small gate hidden among the vines at the bottom of the garden, because it opened unobtrusively into a vineyard, when she had unlocked the gate herself, she had reckoned on many things, but not on Curel.

"One minute it's Santa Barbara. The next, something else. Tomorrow, if Pico does not have another idea, I leave for San Diego."

She must act more cleverly than she had on any stage in any role she had ever played. Somehow, without arousing his suspicions—and he was suspicious of every breath she took—she must get him away, out of the house. But how? If only Catalina would come! If she only knew whether . . .

He was on his feet now, pacing up and down behind her, moving with his quick, graceful strides.

"For a gold onza," he said, "I'd let Pico have his war and be damned."

"There are two gold onzas in the desk," she answered.

"I am not joking."

"Neither am I. I am sick of the pueblo and everything and everybody in it. Pico and Major de Zubaran and Captain Ramirez, even your friend, Lieutenant Morales." Suddenly, looking in the glass, she saw him stop and glance at her. For the first time she met his gaze, held it an instant and then shifted her eyes slowly. It had been a try in the dark, almost accidental, but she knew it had been successful. "Particularly, your *friend*, Morales," she added.

He resumed his pacing, cursing the change in plans and Governor Pico, saying nothing about Morales, but she wasn't fooled. If she were patient, her words would take root; he would ponder what she had said and after a time come back to it.

She rose and went into the alcove just off the boudoir and slipped into her dress. When she returned, Curel, leaving the door open behind him, had left the room; she heard him walking down the passage, the click of his boots sharp on the tiles. He had thought over what she had said about Morales and was on his way to the *sala* to look around for evidence that the lieutenant had been there during the afternoon. Fortunately he would find it.

For an instant she stood holding her breath and then instead of following him, she hurried out of the room, let herself quietly through the door into the courtyard and ran toward the lower end of the garden. Curel had probably barred the gate when he entered, but if he hadn't, if it were open, and the American had come—all during the time Curel had been pacing up and down she had sat in dread of this happening.

She pressed through the shrubbery, found the wall and fumbled in the darkness among the tangled vines until her hand rested on the gate. It was locked. She tried it twice to make doubly certain, and then retraced her steps along the winding dirt path till she reached the courtyard and the light that came through the window of her room. In the light, waiting for her, was Curel.

"I told you that I locked the gate," he said, when she was still several steps from him.

"You didn't, and I just this minute closed it."

He grasped her arm as she passed him and dragged her around, facing him. Very quietly he said, "Perhaps you went to open it for your friend, Morales."

"Perhaps," she answered him, and she was about to ask him why he didn't walk back and see, but before she could say the words, he turned and went striding off through the garden.

She waited, smiled to herself while she listened to him stumbling among the shrubbery; his steps pause at the wall, a moment of silence, then the steps once more, coming toward her in the darkness.

"Did you find everything to your satisfaction?" she said as he stopped in front of her.

He ignored her question. "Why didn't you tell me that Morales was here this afternoon?"

"You can be quite tiresome at times," she said, using a tone that always enraged him. "Very."

He seized her arm again. "Answer me. Why didn't you say something about Morales?"

"Should I? Is it necessary for me to report every breath I take?"

"You don't deny that the fool was here?"

"You bore me very much," she said, finding the words strangely easy to say. "And you're hurting my arm."

"Deny it, if you can."

"I deny it and I repeat that you are very tiresome."

He released her arm and thrust a hand in front of her face, palm up. In it were the ends of three cigarettes. "What do you say to this?" He stood towering over her, his eyes black in the light from the window.

"They look like the ends of cigarettes," she said.

"Yes, and the kind that only Morales smokes. In the whole pueblo no one else uses a Peruvian cigarette, and for a reason, except this *cabrón*."

"I find their aroma pleasing."

There was a moment of silence, in which he threw the cigarettes angrily on the ground, and she heard a knock at the gate. At first she thought the sound came from the bottom of the garden, and though she was certain that the American wouldn't make a noise when he came, her breath caught in her throat. The knock was repeated; it was at the gate which gave on the lane. She turned deliberately from Curel and crossed the court, slid the heavy bolt and, hearing Curel's steps behind her as Catalina slipped in, she whispered to the girl, "Go inside."

Leaving the gate open, she stood looking out into the lane.

Still behind her, Curel said, "Are you waiting for your friend?"

She made no reply.

"Perhaps, since you are obviously surprised that I am not in Santa Barbara, and since you are dressed so ravishingly, I should say, your lover."

She whirled on her heel and, with all her strength, struck him across the mouth. It was not the first time she had struck him, but it was the hardest. A moment elapsed while he gathered his composure, and then he bowed and said softly, "You will regret this, Doña Yris."

He went dramatically past her and into the lane. She watched him until he was out of sight before she closed the gate. He would come back. He would return after an hour, drunk, as he always had in the past.

Holding her skirts, she ran toward the house, her heart suddenly pounding. "What word has he sent?" she kept saying as she ran. "Will he come? Where is the maid? Catalina!"

# 9

In the hot smoky light of a dripping lamp, Grady Dunavant finished packing his rucksack. He examined the barrel and firing mechanism of his Colt and slipped the pistol into the holster beneath his coat. Everything that he wasn't taking on the trip had already been placed in Kate Howland's care; she held also the payment for the goods he had brought in yesterday. After turning out the lamp, he went outside to the corral, where his spotted pony, newly shod, grained and fresh after a day's rest, was tied to the hitch rack.

At the corral gate, seated in the saddle, with his rucksack fastened behind him, he stood looking down the trail that led east out of town. Fog was beginning to roll in from the sea, curling over the low hills to the west and spreading out toward the river bottoms. Before long, he saw, it would lie heavy on the valley beyond.

Both Kroll and Kate Howland had suggested that he wait until morning, not thinking of the fog, simply of the difficulty of traveling at night. He had decided against them, out of restlessness and a sheer desire to get on with the mission he had undertaken. Besides this and the wisdom of masking his destination under the cover of darkness was the feeling that his movements were being watched, a feeling which had grown throughout the day. When he had gone to Kroll's two hours ago, for the last time, he had felt it, and also when he returned to the inn. At the moment the Indian servant was standing in the corral, watching him.

He was still not clear in his mind about the Indian, who had slept at the door last night and had tagged along after him all day, or about his mistress, Doña Yris. Though Jacob Kroll had been very definite in insisting that she, as well as Colonel Curel, was working with Governor Pico, and though he thought so himself, there was much about the situation that was puzzling.

The most puzzling was the letter which had arrived while he was packing. Why should she ask him to come to the house immediately to learn something that might be to his advantage, why for that matter had she delegated the servant to serve as his bodyguard—peculiar as the Indian's idea of the role was—when it was pretty plain that she was serving the Mexican Government? It could be a ruse to get him to the house and into some sort of a trap, but this didn't make sense. He had been around the pueblo all day; if they had wanted to arrest him they could have done so a dozen times. She might still hope that he could be drawn into making some incriminating remark, but after her lack of success last night it wasn't probable.

Chill and thick, the fog swirled out of the west. There were two river crossings to make before dawn, a series of small arroyos where it was easy for a horse to stumble or to lose the way. Inside an hour the whole countryside would be blanketed. For several minutes he sat there debating what to do, and then, out of stubbornness, he picked up the reins and rode through the gate.

The inn was barely visible as he circled it, but as he reached the far wing he saw through the mist a dull gleam of light in Camilla Howland's window. He glanced at the light once, then looked away. At noon when he was settling his accounts with her mother, Camilla had come into the store. She came in because she knew he was there, and had stood around pretending to be looking at the things he had brought from Santa Fe, giving him quick looks from under her lashes. He had tried to get away without having to speak to her, but she was directly in his path as he went out, and there was nothing to do but stop.

She had looked very charming in a yellow dress with big puff sleeves and a bonnet of the latest mode—very pretty and she knew it. The conversation had been short and mostly about the weather, but somehow, from the way she acted more than from anything she said, he got the impression that things between her and Mr. Fraser were not so satisfactory as they had been the night before. Something had happened to cool her ardor. She was full of talk and smiles and he had a hard time getting away.

Now, as he rode up the lane, leaving the light in the inn behind him, he felt the same relief he had in the store when he had said good-by to her; he was in no mood for either a flirtation or a warmed-over passion. It would be a long time, he thought, before he was.

He rode at a quick trot, wrapped in the swirling mist, the pony's hoofs soundless in the dust, but he had the feeling, which had been with him on and off all day, that he was being followed. At the first turning in the lane, he pulled up and listened, and then, hearing nothing, went on.

There was no doubt that the servant was trailing along after him, but the Indian would get tired of that fairly soon, long before he had covered the hundred miles and more to the pueblo of San Diego.

Wan lights showed briefly through the drifting fog. In the white darkness of the deserted lane, the silent clustered houses seemed to press in on him, and he began to imagine, before he left them for the open plaza, that behind every barred window someone was watching. Again he reined in and waited, listening. . . . There was no sound, not even the barefooted, familiar shuffle of the Indian.

He sat there staring into the fog. The shortest way to San Diego led through the plaza at this point and down the lane in which Doña Yris lived. When the letter from her had come he had dismissed it without an instant of serious thought; a few moments before, riding out of the corral, his intention was to take a longer trail which would avoid the necessity of passing her house. But now, on a hunch, he took neither way. Circling the plaza and the church, he reached the adobe rubble that marked the rear of the Campo Santo, and there, a good quarter of a mile from the nearest lane, tethered his pony to a tree.

On foot, after skirting the back of the church, groping over the uneven slope, he reached the vineyard, the high wall that enclosed Doña Yris' garden, and finally the gate. There, with his hand grasping the latch, he hesitated, wondering what excuse he would give her for coming. His actions were not those of a person who was only in the pueblo until he could find passage on a ship to take him away. Wasn't her letter an assumption that he was one of Kroll's henchmen? And his presence here an admission of the fact?

He tried the gate. . . . It was open, but he did not move from where he stood. For some reason, seeking an excuse, seeking an answer to the enigma of the letter, the Indian who had become his bodyguard, to the mystery of the girl herself, he remembered the scene in the garden last night, her flaming hatred of the pueblo, the impassioned ardor with which she had clung to him, her kisses, the parting words of caution. And suddenly, feeling the blood racing through his veins, realizing that he had not come here for information, on a hunch, as he had thought, but for another reason entirely, he wondered if he hadn't found the clue to everything—the servant, the letter and the girl.

She met him at the door, and when he saw the red dress, which revealed every curve of her lithe body, the red flower in her braided hair, when she spoke to him in a low stirring voice, and when on reaching the *sala*, she turned and faced him, her eyes dark and intense, he was certain of her purpose in sending the letter.

"Where did you leave your horse?" she asked him.

Her tone was dramatic, and he smiled to himself, saying, "Behind the Campo Santo, where no one will see it."

"Did you notice anyone when you came in?"

"No one, except the Indian. But I've been seeing him all day and last night. Your concern for my safety almost cost me my life."

She stood with her back to the table as she had the night before, and as then the candles shimmered along the edges of her hair, along her bare shoulders and the graceful serpentine lines of her hips. Looking at him, her eyes more intense now, she did not return his smile.

"You are still in danger," she said.

She was, he thought, a fine actress, but the role she was playing was transparent. "I am sure of that for you are a very beautiful woman. However, danger often inspires courage."

She was looking beyond him at the door, silent, pretending that she hadn't heard him.

"You saw no one on your way here?"

He shook his head, he wondered how long she was going to keep up the pretense.

Suddenly she said, lowering her voice as though she were a conspirator, instead of a woman dressed with every thought and care given to her beauty, as though they both were conspirators and not a man and a woman, "They have made plans to arrest you tonight at Kate Howland's."

"They—whoever they are—will be disappointed."

"It's Lieutenant Morales."

"Perhaps, since you've been so kind as to furnish me with a bodyguard, you will also give me shelter."

It was only a step to her side, and before she could answer, he took her in his arms. The words that were on her lips faded out against his, and for a moment she gave up the role she was playing, holding him with all her strength, and whispering endearments. Then she pushed him away from her.

"You must go," she said. "Now!"

"I've just come," he replied, but for the first time there was a curious, compelling quality in her voice, which cut through his excitement like a knife.

At the same moment he heard steps in the passageway behind him;

he supposed that, tired of the fog and his lonely outpost, it was the Indian again. But before he could turn, looking at the girl, he saw her eyes suddenly fix on some object beyond him.

Curel said. "You forgot, señor, to lock the gate when you came in."

He stood in the doorway, his mouth curling at the corners in a slow, insinuating smile. He looked at neither of them.

"Was I supposed to lock it?" Grady asked in a level voice.

Curel left the doorway and took two steps into the room. Ignoring the question, he bowed to the girl. "You forgot also, señora, though it's apparent that you remembered to open it."

"I lock it or leave it unlocked as I wish," Doña Yris said.

Watching her, the surprise, the shock of Curel's entrance still with him, Grady saw a face that was cold and self-possessed.

"You left once," the girl said. "And you were not invited to come back."

Curel, with a casual gesture, took a burning taper from the niche in the wall beside him and lighted a cigarette. He smoked for several moments in silence, and then remarked, almost absent-mindedly, "I make my own invitations as the occasion demands."

His tone and self-possession matched the girl's, but beneath his words and the casual way he stood against the wall, one leg crossed over the other, watching the smoke curling from his cigarette, Grady Dunavant read anger, a calculating anger, contained yet deadly. He had thought at first, the moment Curel had appeared in the doorway, that his entrance had been premeditated, that Curel was here at Doña Yris' bidding, and the coldness between them was assumed. It had seemed then as if they were both playing a part for his benefit. But he saw now, studying Curel, that he had been wrong.

Doña Yris made some excuse and walked into the passage. When she had left the room Curel stood away from the wall; for the first time he raised his eyes. In his glance was deliberate surprise, as if he had forgotten that Dunavant was there, or as if he had not seen him before this moment.

"We meet again, Lieutenant Dunavant——"

He was dressed, Dunavant noticed, in the uniform of a Mexican artillery officer, a short white coat, a white linen mameluke, and black half boots, open in front. A heavy sword was suspended at his side.

"And this time," Dunavant said, "I observe that you're not traveling for your health."

"And I observe that you are not on your way to San Diego or to

Panama." Curel brushed the ends of his beard with the back of a pale hand. "I was never taken in by that story. A man of your intelligence should be able to think of a better one."

"Such as yours."

"My story was not meant to be believed. That, señor, is the difference between us."

Curel's gaze was cold and opaque; the mocking smile again showed around the corners of his mouth. Returning his glance, standing squarely before him, Dunavant thought, Here is the man who was responsible for the death of Chapman and Sessions and McCutcheon and Rogers. For them and the deaths of thirty-five others. This is the officer who offered amnesty to thirty-nine American soldiers on the San Saba and, when they surrendered, less than a half hour after their rifles were stacked, butchered them and left their bodies unburied.

"Since you are not leaving for Panama," Curel said, "you will have to think of another excuse for your continued presence. But perhaps you already have one. A better one, I trust, than before."

"No excuse is needed," Dunavant said, lowering his voice, letting his words express his anger. "But if one should be, I'll not make it here or to you."

The smile disappeared from the corners of Curel's mouth. The muscles of his shoulders moved visibly under his tight tunic, and one hand went slowly to the gold hilt of his cavalry sword. The gesture, Dunavant knew, was deliberately deceiving, for in no circumstance would he use a weapon which was effective on horseback but not in a crowded room where a chair could parry any blow and ultimately do more damage. Curel was aware of the Colt; if Curel used anything, it would be the double-barreled pistol, and he would have to unfasten the lower button of his tunic to reach it—a matter of a second; but Curel was also aware that this second would be one he could not rely on.

"I am a man who is not easily insulted, as you know, Señor Dunavant. We will permit your change of plans to pass and your reasons for remaining in the pueblo, both of which are obvious and therefore do not lend themselves to excuses. But you will explain something else?"

Curel paused as the girl came to the doorway and stood there a few steps behind him. Without glancing at her, he said, "You will explain your presence in this house."

An uncontrollable anger seized Dunavant, but before he could speak, Doña Yris said from the doorway, "He came here at my invitation, on a matter which doesn't concern you. He was leaving as you arrived."

Over Curel's shoulder, Dunavant saw her make a movement with her hand, swift yet unmistakable in its urgency—go, the gesture said, go at once!

Against every instinct of caution he hesitated. Then, seeing her gesture swiftly repeated, he looked from her to Curel and saw in his opaque eyes a hatred which was greater than the old hatred between them. Realizing the reason for it, he swallowed his pride, walked to the table and picked up his hat.

He looked at Curel again; he was still looking at him when through the window that opened on the courtyard a loud knocking sounded at the gate. There was a moment's silence in the room during which the knocking was resumed. Dunavant glanced toward the girl, but she had quietly left the doorway; he could hear her steps on the tiles, the door open, then steps in the courtyard. A shadow passed the window.

As he walked by Curel, the other bowed, and said, "*Hasta luego,* señor, I leave you to the ingenuity of Lieutenant Morales, a man who lacks my patience, and whose success with the *baqueta* is well known. Give my regards to the lieutenant when you meet him." He was silent until Dunavant was in the passage and then he called after him, "Do not forget to go out by the lower gate."

The knocking had ceased as Dunavant reached the front door but, closing it behind him, while he was pondering Curel's words, he heard a clamor in the lane—a confused sound of shouts, and voices giving directions. The directions were precise and military. He heard the clank of swords and the running of feet. And then, fully aware of the meaning of Curel's words and the clamor outside the walls, he saw the girl standing at the gate.

There were streamers of fog between them; an instant afterward the fog drifted and he could no longer see her. The house, he realized, was surrounded; the gate Curel had mentioned would certainly be guarded. Hurrying across the courtyard, he found Doña Yris standing where he had last seen her, talking, apparently for the first time, to a man on the other side of the gate. In a calm voice she was asking who it was. The answer came back, "Lieutenant Morales."

The suspicion came to him that the whole thing—the letter, Curel, the act now going on in front of him—was after all a trap. But as the thought flashed across his mind, the girl spoke again, repeating her question. As she did so, her hand grasped his arm and propelled him into the heavy vines beside the gate. The answer this time was touched with impatience.

Pressed against the wall and half hidden by the vines, holding the Colt cocked in the hand resting along his thigh, he heard the bar slip, the hinges groan and give. The clamor in the lane died out and in the silence Morales walked through the gate. He stood three paces away, his back turned to Dunavant, and offered his apologies. When he was finished, he explained why he had come and apologized again for the intrusion.

"He is no longer here," the girl said.

Morales stammered. "We followed him to the other gate half an hour ago. Both gates have been guarded since."

"Your guards have been asleep." The words were full of annoyance.

There was a moment of silence. Morales cleared his throat. Without much effort Dunavant could have put his hands around the officer's neck, but three or four soldiers stood outside the gate shuffling their feet and whispering.

"You will pardon the necessity," Morales said, "that impels me to search the garden. Not that I doubt your honesty, you understand, but it is possible that the gringo, having discovered that the lane was guarded, in the fog succeeded in scaling the wall."

"You are welcome," the girl said. "Take care, though, not to trample the flowers."

"*Adelante!*" Morales said, and at the command three soldiers rushed through the gate, carrying muskets.

"The garden follows the wall," Doña Yris said, "and remember about the flowers."

"The most beautiful flower is in front of me," Morales said, bowing, and started off with his three men.

Dunavant did not move; his hand was wet where it grasped the butt of the pistol. The door of the house opened and he caught a brief glimpse of Curel standing on the first step, peering into the garden. Morales and the soldiers had disappeared in the fog. The girl still held the gate open. Outside, a dozen paces away, someone was whistling.

He moved cautiously out of the vines to avoid tripping, past Doña Yris, who said nothing and did not look at him, and through the gate. He heard the gate close at the same instant he saw the soldier standing in the middle of the lane, his hands on the muzzle of his rifle. The man, still whistling, watched him approach, and it was not until Dunavant was two short steps away that he stiffened. The blow with the pistol caught the soldier above the temple and he went down without a sound. Somehow in falling his finger touched the musket's trigger. The explosion crashed through the narrow defile.

At the juncture of the lane and the plaza, Dunavant stopped running. The fog was thinner here where there was some wind to stir it, and he could see the glow from the interior of the church. Keeping close against the houses, he hurried away from the noise that had grown into an uproar behind him, a babel of random shots and curses, and shouts of "*muera, muera . . . el cabrón . . . muera!*"

Where the street narrowed into a half circle around the church, though the sounds were becoming fainter he broke again into a run. He did not stop until he saw through the fog the dim white crosses of the Campo Santo.

# 10

RIDING his pinto horse and leading another he had picked up during the night, Grady Dunavant headed east along a trail that paralleled the King's Highway. The sun was above the hills but the fog had not yet burned out and the Sierra Madres were a misty line against the sky. The breeze that drifted down from the mountains was chill with dawn.

He carried his field glasses slung to the pommel, his Colt at his hip, and enough food on the cantle to last a week. Dressed in a long gray coat and gray trousers, with a heavy gold chain looped across his flowered waistcoat, he might have been taken for a dealer in hides or a supercargo from a Boston ship.

"One or the other, as the occasion demands," Jacob Kroll had said at their last meeting. "The Spaniards still have to sell hides and buy goods. They'll not molest someone they want to do business with."

The remark had been made before the whole garrison had turned out to chase him through every lane and street in the pueblo. But as far as he knew it was still valid. He had made a wide circle around the town and ridden a half mile through the river to confuse his tracks. There was no evidence when he headed east shortly after midnight that he was being followed. Now, six hours later there was still no evidence. It was likely that they thought he was hiding in some dog hole in the town. And it was unlikely, even if they thought he wasn't, that they would attempt to follow him—not enough men could be spared from the garrison, particularly at the moment, to undertake a chase. However, he had stayed off the King's Highway, and though the trail he was on was brushy, he would stay off it for another day.

Through a copse of willows he rode down to the stream he had crossed two days ago, the snow-fed San Gabriel. The water had cleared since the storm, but it still ran swift, over a changing, sandy bottom. A mile upstream from his old tracks, he made a quick crossing. On the far bank, in a bend where the river widened and ran more slowly, he dismounted and watered his horses. He took a strip of jerked beef from his rucksack to chew while he rode, mounted and started back for the trail.

In a creek which fed into the river, a herd of cattle stood knee-deep, drinking—small, red, wide-horned beasts that lifted their heads and looked at him with angry, bloodshot eyes, backing away a grudging step at a time, water dripping from their muzzles. Even a Spanish steer, he thought as he passed them, could smell out a gringo.

And like the steers, every Spaniard between the San Gabriel and San Diego would look at him in the same way, in spite of his gray coat and flowered waistcoat.

During the week he had allotted for his trip to San Diego and back, he would encounter little else in a country uneasy with fear and hostility. He was prepared for it; he even took pleasure in the thought, for it served to whet his determination. Senator Benton in Washington could orate about Manifest Destiny. Thousands of people in thousands of white cottages in Vermont and Maine and Connecticut could long to see the eagle's wings spread to the Pacific. Kroll and Kate Howland, thinking of ledgers and loans and interest, could do the same. His own feeling was simpler.

He wanted to see the Spaniards beaten into the earth, along with their Mexican overlords and all the others who espoused their cause of intimidation, cruelty and hatred. But this feeling, as with all simple passions, needed to be fed. Like a burning fire, it needed replenishing. It was one thing to lead a revolt which would cause the shedding of blood, against those who were friends or at least indifferent. It was another to go out against an avowed enemy, who constantly reminded you of his enmity, of old scores long unsettled.

And this was fortunate, for the job would require determination. The Spaniards had begun to organize their forces; the time, therefore, was short. The Americans in Los Angeles who could be relied on were few, not more than twenty men, far fewer than Kroll had claimed. It was necessary, consequently, to gather an additional force in San Diego and recruit as many as possible on the way. Another factor was present—he had learned from Kroll that Governor Pico was strongly in favor of handing the country over to the British and that the British fleet was now at San Blas. Yes, determination as well as luck, and, at the moment, the assurance that he wasn't being followed.

The sun was hot over the green hills, pouring down toward him in a stream of light. It shone on his gold watch chain and the well-tailored broadcloth of his suit and his gray, hard-finished hat and his polished boots, which this time he had managed to keep out of the water at the crossing. In the quiet morning the gold coins in his rucksack jingled softly. Except for the Colt, the look in his eyes and the set of his thin jaws, there was nothing about him to suggest his purpose in traveling the King's Highway.

The trail, churned by the hoofs of cattle, led up a steep bank through a tunnel of willows. When he came out of the willows there were five horsemen ranged across the trail in front of him, ten paces away. They wore green flat-rimmed hats, with tall conical crowns, the narrow bands worked in silver. On the middle fingers of their right hands were wide green rings, woven of grass or some glossy material. They were the same young men he had seen yesterday morning in the plaza, when he was walking back from Jacob Kroll's.

He said, "*Hola,*" and pulled up his horse.

His greeting was not answered. One of the horsemen slowly circled around behind him and stood near the opening in the willows which went down to the river. Among the four who were left in front of him was a youth with narrow shoulders and a dark, high-cheeked face. He sat stiffly in the saddle, a pace or two in advance of the others. As Dunavant pulled up his pony, he saw that the young man was the one who had accosted him on the trail.

"My name is Roque de Zubaran," the youth said. "Around me are my friends who also are from this valley."

Before De Zubaran spoke, Dunavant, meeting the brilliant yellow eyes fixed on him, knew that the youth was related to Major de Zubaran; the knowledge he kept to himself. As he had thought, the major was related to the girl with the musket. Now that Dunavant was entering the country where he had met her before, now that her brother or her cousin or someone who was related to her was standing in the middle of the trail staring at him, she would probably ride out of the trees. He wanted to see her again, even in the circumstances.

"Where do you go?" De Zubaran asked.

"To Jim Wolfe's."

"What is your business?"

Dunavant was silent. He had doubted when he first saw the band of youths blocking the trail that they had any connection with the pueblo and the search, but he still didn't like De Zubaran's tone, his look, or the look of the others, or the fact that one of them stood behind him.

He said, trying to keep his voice cool, "I'm a dealer in hides."

"It's early for hides."

"I've bought hides at this season before."

"Not at the Hill of the Hawk."

"Well, you'll have hides later on. I'll be glad to contract for them—" Dunavant was surprised at the readiness of his words—"at the usual rates."

De Zubaran hesitated as if he had not expected the offer. Leather creaked and he shifted in the saddle. He glanced around at his companions and then back at Dunavant.

"We have nothing to sell," he said. "Either now or later."

Holy Hell! Dunavant said to himself.

He looked at the four youths in front of him, from one to the other in a careful, unhurried appraisal. They all had *reatas* looped and tied to their high pommels; two carried smoothbore muskets; one had a nine-pound Hawkins rifle; De Zubaran an old-fashioned, bellmouthed buffalo gun with a tasseled stopper in the muzzle.

There was something comical about their appearance, the nondescript weapons, the self-conscious way they sat their saddles, the green identical hats and woven rings—like boys playing at highwaymen—that made him want to grin in their faces. If it hadn't been for the search which was going on for him at the moment, he would have laughed.

"I've explained my business," he said, picking up the reins.

De Zubaran took a firmer seat in the saddle. "Our business remains. It is to investigate all foreigners who travel this valley. We investigate until we are satisfied."

"Satisfied with what?"

"Just satisfied."

De Zubaran's horse was nervous, and he turned it in a short circle and brought it back again, facing Dunavant.

"I am a dealer in hides. I have many ranches to visit," Dunavant persisted.

Dunavant saw a look of indecision come over De Zubaran's face, and he was about to ride on, when another member of the band spoke up. He had bulging eyes and long black sideburns slanting down his cheeks.

"You weren't a dealer in hides two years ago. Then you were a Santa Fe trader. Before that you were arrested for instigating trouble and went off to the prison at Tepic."

"Not a prison," Dunavant said. "A vermin-infested stink hole."

"You did not like it, *hombre?* Why, man, do you return?"

Dunavant said nothing to the youth with the sideburns; his reply, as he again picked up his reins, was a direct glance at De Zubaran. At this open acceptance of the leadership which had been taken from him for the moment, De Zubaran's face showed sudden pride. He looked at his three companions, muttered something that Dunavant didn't understand, and made a motion with his head toward the one standing among the willows.

"You may go," he said to Dunavant. "But we are not satisfied, remember, and neither have we forgotten."

With no further word all the youths wheeled their mounts as one and disappeared upriver into a clump of oaks.

Dunavant rode on at a trot, but before he had gone a half mile he heard hoofs behind him. The sound faded for a time, and then he heard it again, muffled in the heavy grass. He did not look around; he rode steadily, not increasing his gait. They would follow him to Jim Wolfe's and when he left. As he rode out of the valley, other youths would stop him, youths probably like these, with down on their cheeks and ancient weapons. Anger burned deep in him. Some of it showed in his gray eyes fixed on the trail and the golden morning settling over the hills.

The trail led into rolling hills dotted with oaks and cattle grazing in deep grass; by late morning the cattle increased in number and at the open end of a steep-sided box canyon he came to branding fires beside a makeshift corral filled with wild horses. Around the fires were a dozen or more *vaqueros,* sweating in the air that was rank with the stench of burning hair and flesh. From Kroll's description he had a fairly accurate idea about the location of Jim Wolfe's ranch, but he halted at the first fire and asked directions of two men kneeling in the grass. One of them did not look up; the other did but failed to speak.

Dunavant suppressed an oath and rode on. At the corral several men leaning against the bars, and two on horseback, all of whom had undoubtedly heard the question, watched him approach. They looked at him and also said nothing. One of the men on horseback, a powerfully built Spaniard, with a long bony face, he recognized as the man he had encountered the morning he had ridden out of the Cajon.

He was passing the corral, his indifference studied and complete, when someone among the group asked him why he did not stay in the pueblo where he knew the directions. It was a full moment until he realized that the words had been spoken by a girl, and that he had heard the voice before.

Without turning his head, he caught a brief glimpse of her out of the corners of his eyes before the corral shut off his view. She was one of the figures on horseback, standing beyond the powerfully built Spaniard. It was the girl with the musket. She was not looking at him—she was looking straight ahead at nothing—but he touched the brim of his hard gray hat in mock appreciation of her advice.

In silence, sitting ponderously in his high-peaked saddle, Don Saturnino watched the horseman until he dropped out of sight. Then he turned and looked at the girl who sat beside him.

"Well spoken, *hombre*," he said, his small eyes hot with pride. "The gringo rides away with a flea in his ear." He glanced at the men standing around the corral and broke into a laugh. "That's good—'Why don't you stay in the pueblo where you know the directions?'" He looked at each man in turn, his heavy shoulders heaving with laughter. "You never heard better, eh, Vejar?"

Vejar laughed and nodded his head; everyone was laughing, Saturnino noticed, except Mayorga. The old man never laughed at anything, but this was not the present reason for his long face. He was the one rancher in the valley who still professed a liking for the gringos, even to the point of refusing to heed the summons of Governor Pico.

"You don't think this funny, old man?"

"It is not a good time to bait the Americans," Mayorga said, not taking the cigarette from his mouth.

"Then why didn't you speak up and answer his question?"

Mayorga puffed on his cigarette.

Saturnino glanced around at the other men. "He thinks that the gringos will take over California and make him alcalde. Eh, Mayorga? Mayor of Los Angeles."

"I am a raiser of cattle and I wish to remain one—that is all."

"You are an old man, and a fool, but if you should live twice your age, you will never live to see the gringos rule this valley."

"From the claw you may infer the lion," Mayorga replied and said nothing more.

Saturnino laughed, though the edge had been taken off his pleasure, and repeated what his daughter had said. After all the fun had been wrung from the situation, he thrust his feet in the stirrups and wheeled his stallion.

"Well, *hombre*, let's be off. We work while Mayorga dreams of being an alcalde."

Following after him at a gallop, Luz glanced toward the horseman trotting up the far rise. She saw him reach the crest and stand there looking around. He was trying to locate the ranch of Jim Wolfe, but he would not see it from where he was. It was a league off to his right, hidden behind a spur of hills; she hoped he would never find it.

She tucked a strand of hair under the broad brim of her hat, untied the *reata* and looked ahead at the herd of wild horses grazing in the canyon. Already that morning they had cut out twelve of the best *mesteños,* roped and led them to the branding fires. There were at least this many good ones left, out of the original herd of seventy wild horses driven down from the Temescals. There would have been more if the *vaqueros* who were guarding the mouth of the box canyon had not gone to sleep and allowed part of them to escape. The best one, however, the one she wanted for herself, was still there—a young stallion with a white blaze and wild hazel eyes. It was grazing far up in the canyon, with one of the tame mares they had driven in for lures.

She shook out the *reata* and, when her father swerved and plunged to a halt as he came to the line of *vaqueros* guarding the entrance to the canyon, rode on around him. He was stopping to tell the men about the gringo and what she had said to him. He called to her, but she kept on, pretending she hadn't heard.

She shook out the loop and held it loosely, riding at a slow trot around the main herd and toward the young stallion. She was glad that she hadn't stopped to hear the story again, for somehow it was no longer amusing. Mayorga was a stupid old fool and she would pay him back one of these days for what he had said, for not laughing; but, remembering how the gringo had touched his hat, she wished now that she hadn't said anything. It would have been better if she had remained quiet and by her silence shown her contempt.

She looked over her shoulder. He was still standing up there on the crest, gawking around, in one direction and then another, with something held up to his eyes. She supposed it was the glasses she had seen fastened to his pommel when she had first met him, in the leather case with a name printed on it. She hadn't been close enough then to read the name—just the letter D. It probably stood for *Diablo,* Devil, or something as ridiculous—*Diantre,* perhaps.

Well, Señor D, she thought, snatching her eyes away from him, gawk all you want—you'll see nothing, even with your fine glasses.

The stallion was facing up the canyon and though he heard her he did not deign, in his pride, to turn. But as she came within roping distance and he saw that the mare was not going to take alarm, he left her with airy grace and moved on. Luz followed him at a jog, the *reata* hidden, allowing him to gain a little, yet keeping him between her and the steep canyon wall, away from the main herd, which she did not wish to stampede.

The crest and the man standing on it were in front of her now. As she jogged along, keeping one eye on the stallion, she saw him put the glasses away and move off. He was going straight to the east. The sun glinted briefly on his polished boots and he was gone. In the wrong direction, she thought, smiling, hoping that it would take him the rest of the day to find the ranch.

But a moment later, where the canyon opened into the valley, and the stallion, sensing freedom, broke into a lope, she did something which surprised her, and which she thought about the rest of the day. She had planned to run the stallion to her left into country that was clear of brush; instead she turned him in the opposite direction, toward the crest where the gringo had been standing.

The *mesteño* was gaining on her, though he still had not made a run for it. She set herself firmly and confidently in the saddle. She enjoyed this moment before the chase started, secure in the knowledge that her horse had the endurance to run down any mustang she had ever seen. She let the stallion gain, enjoying the moment to the full, and then she set the heavy, six-pointed rowels. Her horse leaped and the chase at last was on.

She was close enough to throw a loop before she reached the crest. She held back for the swale on the other side, not because the gringo was there, she told herself, but because there was less brush. A branch of buckthorn slashed across her cheek and ended her speculations. She let the gelding have its head, galloped over the crest and down the other side, past the gringo and his two horses, into the level, brush-free swale.

Fifty yards, a hundred, and then, though she usually gave a beast a better chance for freedom, she swung the noose. It spun, opened, hung for a moment in the bright air, settled with a slow beautiful motion. At the first sign that the loop had caught, she made a swift hitch around the pommel and, once her fingers were clear, as the gelding automatically drew up, she braced herself for the shock.

The stallion, reaching the end of the rope in headlong flight, paused in mid-air, his head went down, and in a wrenching somersault, he landed on his back. He was on his feet in an instant, breathing hard, his nostrils distended and blood-red, while he pulled at the rope which she had shortened. He snorted, arched and strained his neck against the tightened noose, and then dashed for her. She veered aside and brought him up short again, four feet pawing the air. He stood up trembling, getting his wind, and bolted once more, this time to the side.

The gringo and his two horses were in the stallion's path now, a short distance away; he stopped and sheered off in the opposite direction. Again she threw him heavily, and in the few moments that he lay there breathless, even before she could jump from her horse, the gringo had run up and slipped a half hitch over the stallion's nose.

Her cheeks flamed at this interference; anyone could throw a mustang, but few could make the hitch too. "I did not ask for your help," she said. "I would take the hitch off if it weren't for hurting the horse."

"And yourself," the gringo said.

"Next time you can mind your business. You're a long way from where you're going. Your energy might be more gainfully spent. . . ."

"He's a beauty. Black to match your hair, if not your temper."

The stallion was up, and without another glance at the man standing there in the swale, Luz started back toward the corral. The beast whinnied and tugged at the rope and stopped for a moment, stiff-legged. She looked back at him and could see by his eyes that this was a last protest and that he would follow. The gringo, now in his saddle, was still watching her.

"Jim Wolfe's is a league away," she said. And then as she rode on through the swale, she called over her shoulder on a sudden impulse, "To your right, beyond the next wooded spur."

Grady's eyes followed her through the swale and up the short rise. A good match, he thought, sitting there—the *mesteño* and the señorita, the wild black stallion and the black-haired girl—a very good match indeed.

He waited until she turned around, as he knew she would. With exaggerated deference, he touched the brim of his hat again, spoke to his pony and started off toward Jim Wolfe's at a fast trot. He grinned to himself as he rode; he was still grinning when, topping the wooded spur, he saw the ranch house below him, dazzling white in the hot noon sun.

# 11

Dunavant sat talking to Jim Wolfe and his wife Rica. Wolfe had his chair tilted against the wall, the wheels of his Spanish spurs hooked over a mahogany rung. His wife sat on a stool at his feet. Dunavant judged that she was about half her husband's age, slender, with small hands and feet, and dreamy eyes set in a small heart-shaped face. He marveled at the difference between her and Meadow-in-the-sun, Wolfe's first wife—a broad-beamed, bandy-legged Snake squaw, ugly as sin. Wolfe, he concluded, probably marveled too.

Life had changed for the old mountain man. Dunavant had known him on and off for ten years, had employed him as a hunter on two trips to St. Louis. He looked at Wolfe's silver spurs, the velvet trousers slashed up the leg to show yellow drawers, the ruffled shirt with pearl studs, the brocaded, silver-buttoned waistcoat, and thought about the last time they had met. It was in Santa Fe and Wolfe was coming back from the Wind River Mountains, loaded with beaver. His leather trousers were shrunken halfway up his legs then and his jacket was black with grease. In those days his spurs were made of iron.

Yes, things had changed for Jim Wolfe. But more than the fancy clothes, the great rambling house stuffed with furniture, the new wife sitting demurely at his feet, was the change in the man himself. The gaunt hard-bitten frame was now enveloped in fat. The lean jaw and hollow cheeks were gone, and in their place was smooth flesh, pink and shining with good living. Only his eyes were the same—they were still the small hard eyes of a trapper.

Dunavant looked at Wolfe and his Spanish wife; he felt uneasy. At noon when they were eating dinner he had told Wolfe about the proposed attack on the Spaniards at Los Angeles, but before he had gone very far, she had come in and Wolfe had given him a wink, as much as to tell him to say nothing more while she was present. He remembered now that neither Kate Howland nor Jacob Kroll had shown much enthusiasm when Wolfe's name was mentioned. He was beginning to wonder if their lack of enthusiasm was not justified.

An Indian brought in three silver mugs of wine and passed them around on a silver tray.

Wolfe drank his wine off at a gulp. "I'll never forget the rendezvous at Salt Lake. That was before your time. And us trappers and two thousand Snake Indians beat the Blackfeet in a two-day free-for-all. And General Ashley hove in from St. Louis with fifty mule, mostly packed with drinking liquor. That was sure a mighty fine ruckus." Wolfe studied the silver cup in his hand. "Never thought then I'd be drinking wine off my own place. I just squash the grapes and let them set for a spell. Makes a pretty brew."

Dunavant agreed, watching Mrs. Wolfe—usually at this time of day Spaniards went off for a siesta. Jim Wolfe launched into another story and by the time he had finished, his wife was beginning to look sleepy. Presently she rose, excused herself and left, giving her husband a coy look as she walked across the room.

Wolfe waited until the door had closed behind her. Then he turned to Dunavant. "You never know what she understands and what she don't. It's best to say nothing." He rested his arms on his broad thighs and cupped a hand over his knee. "Now here's the way I look at things. The country's ripe for revolution. All we have to do is to set back and watch. The Californians are mostly in favor of kicking the Mexican Government out. If we just keep our shirts on and let them alone, they'll do it soon—in a month or two."

"By then there'll be a British flag flying over California," Dunavant replied. "Possibly sooner if nothing is done."

"It's only Pico that has a hankering for the Britishers."

"Yes, but Pico is governor. He's in power and he is conspiring now with England. The English fleet has been in Callao and there's word that it's on the way north to San Blas, if not already there."

*"No es nada."*

"It's nothing," Dunavant said impatiently, "until the country is overrun and you're paying taxes to an English King."

Wolfe shook his head.

"You're sure then about the British?"

"Not about them. Just the Americans." Wolfe thumped his thigh. "We'll kill every Britisher that sets foot in California."

"You'll fight against the British, but not with the Americans. Is that it?"

"Not exactly. It's like this. Everybody around here is a relation of everybody else. An aunt or an uncle or something—maybe it's only a godfather or a *compadre,* but it's always something. I'm hitched to a girl that's connected with the Gamboas—they're big medicine around Los Angeles. If I get mixed up in a ruckus and anything goes wrong, I'll be a cooked goose."

Dunavant took a drink of wine. "Nothing is going wrong. The plans are laid in the North. In two weeks they will be completed here—down to the last detail."

Wolfe shook his head. "Even if it's all planned and nothing goes wrong, it still don't look right for a man to go out shooting at someone that might be a relation. I'd have a lot of explaining to do to my wife if I accidentally put a hole in one of her uncles or cousins. She's not like my first wife—and by the way, don't say anything about me being married before. When Meadow-in-the-sun got on a tear and shouted fit to deafen a man, I'd just lop me off a good length of cottonwood and larrup her a couple. But you can't gentle Doña Rica that way. Fact is, she just don't gentle at all—it's best not to rile her in the first place."

Jim Wolfe rubbed a hairy hand across his forehead. "No, my advice is to set in the shade of a tree and let the Californians do the fighting. They're beginning to warm up already. Pico is spouting fire. The older Spaniards are cleaning out their muskets and the young bucks are riding around loose, taking pot shots at everything that moves. They're sore at the Americans now, but pretty soon they'll get sore at each other."

"I met some of them on the trail this morning," Dunavant said. "One—De Zubaran—lives around here."

"Over on the Hawk. They're a touchy bunch, the De Zubarans. I ran into them first in '43. I'd been trapping north of Sutter's Fort and when I started back for Santa Fe I come down this way and fell in with some trappers that had been working the headwaters of the Sacramento. They had half a dozen Piutes from the Colorado trailing along. We camped over near the Santa Ana and from there you could see the De Zubaran place perched up on the mesa and the corrals stringing out behind it, filled with fat horses.

"The Piutes got to talking about the horses, and I had a feeling that they'd been up there before nosing around. But they had a lot of respect for the De Zubarans—I gathered that from the way they talked—and they wouldn't have gone up there if it hadn't been for the trappers, who had ran into a bad spring, besides losing most of their pelts gambling Spanish faro.

"It was coming on sundown when the trappers first started talking, beginning where the Piutes left off, and when I was getting ready to bed for the night they up and asked me what I thought of it. I said I thought it was plumb crazy. I didn't say nothing about me having a good trip and my saddlebag being full of money or that I had no hankering to get stuck with a lance or that I was planning to come back next year. I just said I thought it was plumb crazy.

"Well, I bedded down and about midnight I was jarred out of sleep by horses running. It sounded like all the horses in the world. There was a moon and I could see them pouring off the hill. I knew without thinking much just what was going on, and I knew the only thing for me was to get the hell out of there. They rode fast, the Piutes and the trappers, driving the horses, and I didn't catch up until they hit the foothills.

"It was daylight then and you could see dust rising down in the valley along the trail we had just come over, and I knew we was being followed. They was moving faster than us, but we had a three or four-hour start, and they didn't catch us until about noon of the second day. We had gone up a pass out of the desert and was coming into a big valley when we see them off to our left. They had took a short cut and had us cut off. There was about a dozen of them—*vaqueros* and the De Zubarans—strung out one behind the other.

"Well, I still didn't have no taste for the business, and I kept figuring as we forted up how best to get out of it with a whole skin. Just happened that luck was with me. About dusk, after skirmishing all day, they made a sortie, the De Zubarans riding out ahead. We drove the others back, but old Don Cristóbal got trapped in a box canyon. The Piutes took him off his horse and was going to scalp him right there, but I knocked a couple of them over the head with my carbine and sent him back to his own camp. When night came we slipped away and rode till sunup before we stopped."

Jim Wolfe shook his head and grinned. "That was back in '43. The next year when I came here and got hitched, me and old De Zubaran got to be friends—he sorta felt that I saved his life and I guess I did. But his son, Saturnino, never would speak—figured I was nothing but a horse thief and a gringo to boot. Yep, they're a touchy lot. . . ."

The door opened softly, Doña Rica looked at her husband and after a moment disappeared. Jim Wolfe colored around the ears and got to his feet.

"Let them fight among themselves, is my advice. Before the end of summer Pico and the Mexican Government will be thrown out."

"By the Americans," Dunavant said. "And before the end of summer."

Dunavant was waiting in the parlor while Jim Wolfe took his siesta. The curtain had been drawn against the sun; the room was cool and in semidarkness. There was no sound inside the house or outside in the courtyard, where even the trees were silent in the windless afternoon.

He made a cigarette, feeling the sudden premonition of sleep, got up out of the large chair he was in and sat on a rawhide stool. The fact that he had not slept last night and had eaten a larger meal than he was used to, with wine, did not give him the excuse of taking a siesta like a damned Spaniard.

He smoked with great concentration, weighing the results of his talk with Wolfe. After the siesta was over, the two of them were riding to the next ranch to see Juan Mayorga, who Wolfe thought might be interested in helping the cause. The trip had some of the aspects of a wild-goose chase, but he decided that whether the Spaniard could be persuaded to help or not, it was smart to meet him. In guerrilla warfare, which the conflict would be, every ranch house where food and horses could be found on short notice, should be known. From Wolfe himself, though he liked a fight, nothing much could be expected as long as his Spanish bride was around.

Getting to his feet, Dunavant took the heavy watch from his waistcoat. It was three o'clock—another hour before he could expect Wolfe. He went to the door and looked out into the courtyard. A breeze had come up from the sea, rustling the cottonwoods. He wound his watch with a gold key, closed the door and sat down again on the stool.

The breeze grew into a steady wind, as he sat there smoking and rolling one cigarette after the other. And then suddenly above the whipping of the curtains at the window, he heard the thud of hoofs. He stood up, buttoning his coat over the Colt. A moment or two later a knock sounded on the door. He said nothing and did not move.

The knock sounded again. Then the door opened slowly and two figures stood on the threshold outlined against the sun slanting into the courtyard. They were slender and tall, of equal height; they looked like twin brothers. They stood peering into the dim room.

*"Hola,"* he said.

*"Hola,"* the two answered immediately, speaking together, so that their greeting seemed to be one, an echo of his own.

One of the two figures closed the door, and both of them came forward, walking slowly as if not sure of themselves. There was little light in the room, but Dunavant could see that they were dressed alike in leather jackets and leather, tight-fitting trousers and carried broad-brimmed hats in their hands. They wore rowels that clinked on the tiles as they walked. He was certain now that they were Spaniards and brothers.

"We have come out of the sunlight," one of them said. "We cannot see well, but it is well enough to see that you are not Señor Wolfe."

The voice was young, with a slurring accent that stirred his memory. The one who had spoken came closer and Dunavant saw that it was a boy of fifteen or so. He had a long, narrow face and yellow eyes; they were like the eyes of Julio de Zubaran.

"Wolfe is sleeping," Dunavant said.

The boy stood awkwardly for an instant, blinking. Then he looked over his shoulder and said something which Dunavant didn't understand.

"We will wait for Señor Wolfe," the one behind the boy said.

It was the voice of a girl. Dunavant opened the curtains. When he turned around she had come forward into the light. She was older than the boy, by four or five years, and had heavy hair that fell to her shoulders. Her hair was black, streaked red in places by the sun. Her shoulders were wide and in the leather trousers her legs were long and slender. She had large eyes, set wide, the same color as those of the boy, though darker, more the color of amber, and flecked with brown. She was the girl he had watched going over the hill, leading the stallion, the girl who had stopped the pack train.

"This is my brother Jorge," she said. "My name is Luz de Zubaran."

The words were spoken deliberately. They said, The name De Zubaran is known and respected in this valley, and beyond this valley. It is a name to be feared by everyone whoever he is. She stood in the middle of the room and looked at him steadily, as if she had never seen him before.

"You're Señor Dunavant," she said. "I know from my brother, Don Roque, who has already talked to you."

"On the trail. An interesting talk." Dunavant made a slight bow. "I am glad of a chance to thank you for the directions."

"They do not require thanks," the girl said. "Directions are given to everyone, *even* gringos."

"They weren't given by the *vaqueros.*"

"*Vaqueros* are usually without manners. When they possess manners, their feelings are the stronger of the two."

"Yours were not," he said.

"No. But not for the reason you think."

"I haven't thought about the reasons. The directions were sufficient. If you sit down, I'll call Wolfe."

The girl, holding her wide-brimmed hat tight in her hand, made no movement toward the chair he offered. She looked at him with the same expression of guarded hostility he had seen when they had first met. He wanted to return the look, but he didn't; he looked at her and smiled.

"A Spaniard," she said, "is never disturbed during siesta."

"Since when has Wolfe become a Spaniard?"

"Since he married a Spanish girl."

"I see," Dunavant said.

"You act as if there were some blame attached to being a Spaniard." She spoke in a low voice, but the words, flung at him like a challenge, carried fire. "They are good people and lead a good life."

He let her win the argument by default. "In any event," he said, "night is the proper time to sleep."

"As for that," she replied, her eyes going over his features, "a long siesta now would do you no harm."

She smiled for the first time, a quick, amused smile that made his ears color. He glanced at the boy who had been standing beside her through all this. The boy was looking at him without appearing to.

He said, "My brother says you were arrested and sent off in a ship to Mexico."

"To Tepic," Dunavant said lightly, as if he had gone there on a vacation. The boy looked at him for a moment in frank curiosity, his hatred for gringos struggling with a reluctant admiration for someone so infamous as to be thrown into prison. Then the girl told him to go outside and amuse himself with the horses. She waited until the door closed behind him, not taking her eyes from Dunavant.

"My brother also said that you are a friend of Señor Kroll."

Grady kept his temper and a determined silence. He wondered why she had come. She had known that he was here at Wolfe's, she certainly hadn't come to say the same things he had heard from her brother a few hours ago, to lecture him as if he were a schoolboy.

She took a step toward him. "If my brother had said nothing, I'd still know that you are a friend of Kroll. I knew it the first time I saw you and later this morning. And now as you stand there. It is in your face. Like Kroll, you hate all Spaniards."

"Not *all* Spaniards," he said pointedly.

The words, to his surprise, did not soften her. She looked away from him a moment, watching the light on the hills. The wind stirred a strand of hair across her face and she thrust it back impatiently. Then she looked at him again, her tawny eyes suddenly bright.

"Why is it that you——" She started to say gringos and stopped. "Why is it that you come here to California? Beyond the mountains is a country which belongs to you. I have never seen it and never hope to. But I've heard about it from those who have. The Spaniards don't go there to cause trouble. Why is it then that the Americans come here?"

Dunavant looked at his watch and made a show of winding it. He put the watch back in his pocket and straightened the gold chain across his waistcoat. He wished that Jim Wolfe would appear. He also wished for Senator Thomas Hart Benton and James Buchanan and President Polk himself, to explain their theory of Manifest Destiny. He had got himself, damned if he hadn't, into a full-fledged debating society.

"The Spaniards don't go to your country to steal horses," the girl went on, "nor to incite Indians. Nor do they cross the mountains to make trouble. To spill blood. To molest women . . ."

Before he could check himself, he said, "I've yet to see the woman in California whom I'd be tempted to molest."

He expected anger from her but she laughed instead.

"There are none," she answered him, "whom you could have without molestation."

She looked at him openly now, standing with her hat held in both hands behind her back, the wind moving her hair and the slanting sun filling it with shadows. Her teeth, he noticed through his anger, were white—even and white as bleached bone. Her skin, burned by the sun, was the color of honey, except where her jacket was open at the throat. She looked at him and smiled. In her smile was amusement again and pride and assurance, the open knowledge, that, in spite of what he had said, he found her attractive.

He returned her look, but without smiling. He was overcome with the desire to break her pride, with the same desire which had seized him the first time on the trail. He wanted to deny that he found anything about her worthy of his notice, whether it was the shadows in her hair which changed with the movement of the wind, or the color of her skin, or her eyes, or the way she stood there with smiling contempt for what he had said, like a duelist who permits his rival to strike first and at will, confident of his own skill and the superiority of his weapon. He forgot completely the role he had started to play.

"One reason for this is that in California it is difficult to tell the women from the men," he said, glancing at her trousers. "When you came in I thought from your age and the way you are dressed that you and the boy were twin brothers."

She was still smiling. "You know better now. And my age is not the same as my brother, as you can observe. And the clothes are worn because I am on horseback. For other occasions—those of importance—I dress differently."

"Where I came from women always dress like women," he said. It was the best he could manage. He started to walk past her. "If you will pardon me, I'll tell Wolfe that you're here."

"What I have to say I can say to you."

Dunavant stopped as she took a pair of spurs from her pocket. They were made of silver, etched with a running design, and had five-pointed rowels.

"These belonged to Don Cristóbal, my grandfather," she said. "Before he died he asked me to give them to his friend, Señor Wolfe. There is nothing further to say about the spurs because my grandfather said nothing else. And there's nothing I wish to add."

Dunavant took the spurs from her. "In other words, you don't approve of the gift."

"No."

"Or of Wolfe?"

"No."

"Then why did you come?"

"Because I was asked to."

"You could have sent a *vaquero*."

"Don Cristóbal asked *me* to come. I am here."

"You could have come another time."

She began to put on her hat, tucking her hair slowly into the high crown. She looked at him as she did so. "You think I came because you are here. You think that having met you twice on the trail—riding along in your fine clothes, with your eyes contemptuous, seeing nothing but everything—that having met you twice I wished to meet you again."

Grady said nothing.

She dropped her hands to her sides. "Yes, that is what you believe. Spanish men have great conceit. And so does the stallion. And the male peafowl. But the conceit of the male gringo exceeds them all."

"It didn't prevent you from coming here," Dunavant said. "It isn't too great for that."

He crossed the room and opened the door and stood looking out into the sunlit courtyard. She went by him silently, except for the small sound of her rowels touching the tiles, but when she reached the *portale,* she suddenly turned. She was no longer smiling.

"Of course I came because you were here. But not because I admire you or your conceit. Neither one nor the other impresses me." She settled a thin braided strap under her chin. "I came because I knew that you are not what you pretend to be."

"I am still a dealer in hides."

The sun shone in her eyes but she looked at him steadily. "I came to warn you that you are in danger."

"The warning is unnecessary," he said. "Any American who travels California, whatever his business, is in danger. From a lance or a musket shot. And what is worse, from talk and threats from those who have nothing better to do."

She spoke as if she had not heard him. "Leave the country or permit us to live in peace. If you don't, you will regret it."

Dunavant closed the door and stepped out on the *portale.* "I'll neither leave now nor regret it," he said calmly. "And if my business were not hides, I'd consider your warning an invitation to stay here long enough to see the end of Mexican rule."

He was standing a short distance from her and saw her eyes go dark, her full lips tighten and then relax into a forced smile. She raised her head and looked at him for a long moment. Her smile slowly froze. Deliberately she took a braided quirt from her silver-studded belt, and, though he knew what she was going to do, he didn't move until she lifted her hand. Then he grasped the quirt, caught the arm which she raised to ward him off, and forced her hands behind her back.

As she strained against him, her face was close to his. He could see her mouth, the gleam of her teeth, in a grimace that was more rage than pain. Her hair smelled of horses and sunlight. She held her breath and drew her head as far away from him as she could. And then she raised her head and stopped struggling and stood rigid in his grasp. For an instant she looked at him, breathing quickly through parted lips. She looked at him, her eyes narrowed and afire, as if he were a mortal antagonist whom somehow she must vanquish. In that moment, on a sudden impulse but deliberately, he relaxed his hold and at the same time kissed her on the mouth.

He stepped back from her, waiting for the fury to break. To his surprise she did not move. She stood with her feet apart and looked at him and said quietly in a voice edged with scorn, "I thought there was no woman in California you would be tempted to molest."

"I've changed my mind," he replied. "Just now."

She made a brief ceremony of straightening her wide-brimmed hat and then looked at him again. "I've not changed mine. I said there wasn't a Spanish woman whom you could have without molestation. It is still true."

He saw her glance at the quirt he held in his hand. "I'll keep it until you feel differently."

"That will be a long time," she said. "Longer than you will live." She drew the back of her hand across her lips and spat. "As for this, I'll stop at the nearest stream and wash."

"There's one about a mile to the north."

"That far, unfortunately," she said, and whirled on her heel.

She moved quickly down the *portale*, with the rocking gait of one long accustomed to the saddle. Her toes, in the yellow, stitched boots, turned in as she walked. Her spurs caught the sun and flung it against the white walls. Without looking back, she opened the door which led outside, slammed it after her, and a moment later he heard the sound of hoofs galloping away.

# 12

Late that night Grady lay in bed, holding the travel-stained book of Napoleon's maxims propped up on his knees. His watch on the chest beside him said three o'clock. He had slept for five hours and was now waiting for dawn.

Dogs were barking in the courtyard. Off at a distance, at intervals when they paused for breath, he could hear the barking of a coyote—three sharp yips, the third yip sliding into a long ascending note. Then at a greater distance and fainter, another coyote answering. Chickens roosting in the trees outside the window muttered uneasily.

He turned a page of the book and read, "Bold men should not be sought for among those who have anything to lose." That, he decided, covered Jim Wolfe. Shortly after Luz de Zubaran had ridden away, Wolfe had appeared sleepy-eyed and stretching to announce that it was too late to see Mayorga—they'd make the trip the first thing in the morning when they had more time. "You can't rush a Spaniard," Wolfe had said, yawning. Dunavant read the passage again, concluding that Napoleon had had someone like Jim Wolfe in mind when he wrote it.

He read on, turning a half-dozen pages, but he didn't find anything that covered the situation with Luz de Zubaran, unless it was the part which went, "Rashness succeeds often, still more often fails." What he had done was rash all right, with any girl, but especially with a Spaniard at a time when all the country was on edge and everyone was looking for an excuse to shoot a gringo, when he wasn't sure whether or not he was being followed. Whether he had failed remained to be seen.

The print began to blur. He closed the book, snuffed out the candle and lay with his hands folded behind his head, watching the moon going down, breathing the smell of the cottonwoods and the river. He thought about the other times in the past when the same sort of rashness had pitched him headlong into trouble—the time he had lost three wagons filled with goods at the crossing of the Platte because he didn't like the man who advised against it; the fight in Taos over a girl he had never seen before and never saw again; the duel at Natchez over a card which by the laws of chance could not show up but did; the battle on the San Saba under Major Gilson.

He thought of other times when, according to his mother, the Irish blood he had inherited from his father had led him into trouble. But it was the night on the Ohio that his thoughts finally dwelt on, a night like this one, hot, with a wind smelling of trees and the river sedges. The house was quiet, except for a few stray noises. There was no sound from the next room where his two older brothers were sleeping. They had come in late when everyone else was in bed, sneaking up the stairs with their shoes in their hands, trailing the strong sweet odor of Monongahela. But down the hall he could hear his grandfather breathing, thin and whiny like a faraway trumpet. Outside, in the dog run, one of the hounds was scratching fleas, thump-thumping his foot on the puncheons. Another hound was barking down by the creek, pausing and barking again in a halfhearted way.

Then he heard another sound. It was not in the house nor the fields nor the forests beyond. The last of the geese had gone over a week before, so it wasn't the geese and their honking far in the sky, lonely and yet not lonely to the ears. It was something else, something he had heard before, last night and every night for a month. He listened, knowing that he would hear it again.

Finally it came. Far off at first. A sound which grew louder and from the river. A sound as lonely as geese calling, and like them, not lonely. It was a horn, a boat horn, a boat on the river, drifting past the farm, down the hushed Ohio. The horn quit blowing, but he could hear the squeal of fiddles, a man's voice and laughter, loud, then faint, then no more.

Now that spring was settled it seemed as if everyone was on the move, everyone except the Dunavants.

Another boat horn wound nearer and he pictured himself on the boat, drifting with the current, the helm clasped in his hand, his eyes on the moon-swept river, alert for snags, drifting into the west toward the big river and St. Louis. After a time he wasn't so alert and the next thing he knew sun was flooding his room and his mother was standing at the bottom of the stairs calling, "Grady."

He took his time dressing, dawdling with his shoes, for the hired man had gone into Shelbyville to get married and would be away for a week, which meant that he would have extra chores to do. He made as much noise as he thought he could get away with, but his brothers didn't stir. His mother came to the stairs again and wanted to know in a soft firm voice if he was going to take all morning.

Downstairs in the kitchen, he stretched and yawned in the sun that came blasting through the open door, glancing at the new hired girl, and then at his mother.

"What has got into you, Grady?" his mother inquired. "You've been moping around for the last month."

"I'm growing," he said, putting as much into his voice as he could.

"Grady Dunavant, don't let me hear any more of that kind of talk. You're so big now that you couldn't grow another inch."

He felt bigger suddenly, and as his mother said, he was big enough already. He yawned again and waited for a moment. Then he went over to the stove, giving the hired girl a look out of the corners of his eyes, and took a pinch of salt from the crock.

"I'm glad to see that you don't have to be told about that every morning," his mother said.

He went outside, broke a twig from an apple tree, salted the end and scrubbed his teeth, taking his time. Then he took a pail down from the peg, milked the cow and came back to eat.

"Where's Father?" he asked when he had finished breakfast.

"He's gone to Teal's and won't be back until noon."

"I can go hunting, then."

"You can when the potatoes are hoed," his mother said.

"Mr. Owens will hoe them when he comes back from Shelbyville. They'll take a whole day."

"Yes, the way you move around."

"They don't need hoeing yet. They haven't been in the ground long enough."

"Those are your father's instructions," his mother said. "The sooner you start, the sooner you'll be done."

He moved slowly across the room, dragging his heels. He stopped at the doorway and without thinking or meaning to, said, "Well, I'll hoe the potatoes, but I'll not be here to eat them."

He had taken three steps when he heard his mother call his name. He took two more steps before he turned around. His mother was standing in the doorway, her face red and her hands on her hips.

"What did you say?" she asked as sweetly as if she wanted to know the time of day.

"Nothing," he muttered.

The sun had sucked the moisture from the grass, but the flanks of the long-furred cows, grazing in the shade of the beech, were still wet. The potato plants showed glossy in the sun, ankle-high and twice as numerous as yesterday, it seemed—four long, wiggling rows that didn't end until they reached the riverbank.

Safely out of sight and hearing of the house, his ears red, he paused and said, addressing the morning, "Goda'mighty." Then he grasped the hoe, so that his knuckles showed white, and began on the potatoes. The blade glinted in the sun; it went *chunk-chunk* as it cleft the earth; it could be heard everywhere on the Dunavant acres, as was his intention.

When he came within view of the house, he doubled back on the next row. The sun was hot, drawing mist from the river. The mist rose like steam and seeped through the sycamores and beeches and the tangled branches of the water maple, and lay in a pearly stratum over the field. Sweat poured down inside his shirt, his lungs were dry, but he didn't stop until he reached the end of the row.

He wouldn't have stopped then if it hadn't been that through a gap in the trees he saw a flatboat far out on the river. He watched it drift past him and disappear behind the trees as quietly as it had come. He wiped his forehead on his sleeve and turned back to the potatoes.

Suddenly, above the *chunk* of the hoe, he heard a voice. It was unfamiliar. It came from behind him, from the river. Turning around, he saw a boat, halfway between a flatboat and a pirogue, close inshore and moving slowly. On the afterdeck, one bare foot cocked up on the gunwale, was a girl. She was looking at him and he judged it was she who had called. He said nothing, waiting for her to speak again. She had yellow hair, which looked snarled from where he stood, and a ragged calico dress that showed her bony knees.

"Hello, farmer boy," she said.

"Hello," he said, though the "farmer boy" made him mad, and for a moment he had decided to say nothing.

"How's the potato crop?" she asked, simpering and showing teeth that had never been washed.

"Fair," he said.

The boat was so close now that he could almost jump from the bank onto the deck. The girl had blue eyes, faded out and big. She looked at him from the ground up, smiling. There was a bandy-legged man, standing behind her at the helm, smiling too, and ornery-looking enough to be her father.

The girl spoke again, still looking him over. She said, "You'll never get rich, hoein' potatoes." Then she said something under her breath to the man behind her and looked at Dunavant. "Hoein' is bilious work," she said. "Bad for the bowels, so I hear."

The flatboat drew even with him. He noticed that the girl's knees were caked with dirt.

She said, "We could use a likely-looking boy, such as you." She smiled her prettiest, never taking her eyes off him, as if he were a sure-enough prize. "You'd find us real obligin' oncet you got to know us."

"I have hoeing to do," he said firmly.

"Let your daddy do the hoein' and come along," she said. "We'll treat you right."

He kept silent. He wanted to go to St. Louis and the Western lands, and someday he might, if his grandfather, who had fought every war the United States had been in and who had influence at Washington, didn't send him off to West Point in the meantime. He wanted to go down-river, but not with this outfit.

The bandy-legged man thrust his head over the girl's shoulder and said, "Mebbe he don't like our looks." His eyes blinked and looked red, as if he had been drinking.

"It ain't that," the girl said, giving her shoulder an annoyed twist in his face. "He's jes bashful, ain't you, farmer boy?" She was rubbing it in.

The name made his neck burn. "It isn't that," he said. "Your old man is right—I don't like your looks."

The smile on the girl's face went away quick. And the man thrust his bald head out again over her shoulder. "Why, you clod-bustin' sonofabitch," he said. "I got a mind to jump out of this here boat and slit your ears."

He was leaning on his hoe when the bandy-legged man said this. He dropped the hoe and started down the bank. The boat had drifted past him, but not far. He jumped from the bank and reached it in three strokes. He grasped the stern and pulled himself up on the deck. He was waterlogged and slow on his feet, but he reached the man as he was bending down to pick up an oar, lifted and threw him against a crate of chickens. The girl was running around the deck, swearing, and the chickens were cackling, and with all the commotion he didn't hear the snag-toothed boy come out of the cabin.

The next thing he knew, the morning exploded into a thousand pieces. When he woke up it was night, two days later, and he was drifting down toward the Mississippi. But he wasn't at the helm. He was lying on his back out on the deck, with the biggest headache he ever had, before or since. . . .

Dunavant looked out the window. The moon had dropped behind the hills. The dogs had gone off somewhere and the coyotes were quiet. He could no longer smell the cottonwoods or the river. He was lying here in a strange country, trying to sleep, because of that morning on the Ohio. That was long ago, in his first youth, but he still hadn't learned anything, apparently.

He turned over on his side in the big four-poster bed and closed his eyes. The bed had been purchased in Boston, according to Wolfe, and had been sent around the Horn by ship. After almost two months of lying on the ground and a night on the hard pallet furnished by Kate Howland, it was a welcome change. But it was so soft he couldn't sleep.

He got up, went to the window, stooped down and looked out. The moon had set. The air was growing chill. Day was not far off. There was no point in waiting for Jim Wolfe to make up his mind about taking him to see Mayorga; it might be today or tomorrow or the day after. At first he had thought that Wolfe was simply a mountain man who had grown soft with good living, but this wasn't true. As Luz de Zubaran had said, he had become a California rancher, a Spaniard.

While he was shaving, he could see the first graying of the sky, the mountains building up in the north. By the time he had dressed and gone out to pack one horse and saddle the other, an Indian was making a fire in the outdoor oven. Dunavant left a message with him for Jim Wolfe. Then he mounted his pinto and, leading his pack horse, rode through the gate.

He headed south along the rolling hills. The gray was lightening in the east. The mountains were as blue as a gun barrel. A fine day was coming—was standing there now beyond San Gorgonio. With luck and hard riding, he'd make fifty of the one hundred and twenty miles before nightfall.

A cock quail called from deep in the chaparral. Dunavant called back and grinned as he was answered. He listened to the jingle of pack and bit and spur. He smelled the sweet, stinging odor of mesquite. He thought without envy of Jim Wolfe sleeping beside his pretty Spanish wife. And of Camilla Howland. It was curious, but he felt pretty calm about Miss Howland. It was as if a part of him, an extra sense, had known all along what would happen. Even some of his anger had simmered off; his one regret was that he hadn't taken a poke at Peter Pomeroy Fraser. He thought about Joe, the servant, whom he had managed to leave in the pueblo, and of Yris and her dancer's body and puzzling loyalties. (He didn't have to think about Cesaire Curel—the black, square-cut beard and morose eyes were never wholly out of his mind.) Lastly, of the De Zubaran clan who might be waiting for him over the next rise.

Let them wait, he said to himself.

His rifle was sheathed beside the stirrup; the Colt lay against his thigh—anyone knew that one well-armed American was equal to ten Spaniards. He looked ahead along the trail, cocked his hat back on his head and took a deep breath of the cool dawn air.

The sun was up when he approached the Santa Ana, shining on the sycamores and the low-growing willows which fringed the river. Ahead of him the King's Highway was deserted, except for straggling steers and a cart rumbling slowly into the bottoms. To his left were the ranch buildings he had seen in the rain. The walls glimmered white through thin ground mist. Smoke rose from the inner court and curled away over the gray roofs. At the gate stood a row of saddled horses. He was certain, from Jim Wolfe's description, that it belonged to the De Zubarans.

Reining in his pinto, he sat there on the slope looking down at the thick-walled house. He took his field glasses from the case and studied the house in detail. From what he had learned in Los Angeles and from Jim Wolfe, Spanish resistance in the valley would be led by De Zubaran. It would be centered here at the Hill of the Hawk, on this mesa, behind the fortresslike walls he was now looking at.

The house was built in the shape of a hollow square, about two hundred feet to a side, the walls low and broken by two small windows on the side he was facing. A large gate, the same height as the walls. Flankers at each of the corners. At the corner nearest him, the flanker was extended upward into a watchtower. An object on the tower caught the sun. He sharpened his glasses. It was a brass swivel gun mounted on a wooden platform, placed to command all approaches to the mesa.

He put away the glasses, took a pad of paper and a crayon from his rucksack and, resting the pad on the pommel, made a quick sketch of the house. The roof sloped toward the central courtyard. From the texture and color he presumed that it was made of tule bundles set down in pitch. A fire-tipped arrow would set the roof ablaze, but it would be difficult to get close enough to shoot an arrow.

The flankers were rifle-slotted and cleverly arranged to cover all directions; anyone who succeeded in reaching the walls would be enfiladed. The gate was constructed, by an extension of the roof, so that it was impossible to scale under fire. There were no trees on the mesa. Not a stump or rock. It was as flat as a table. A force of a hundred might storm the walls, but he wouldn't have that many men—he'd be lucky to raise half the number. A six-inch cannon set up where he was standing could overpower the swivel gun on the tower, but a six-incher would not be available—no cannon of any caliber, in fact.

Dunavant slipped the pad and crayon inside his coat and began to whistle off key. He studied the house on the mesa—it was really a fortress—and thought about Edward the Third and his seven-foot sword; how he won his first victory over the French; and how the Dauphin, realizing that he was no match for the invading army, had wisely retired his forces to fortified towns—to castles in effect much like the one before him—and permitted the English to roam a deserted countryside.

Something of the kind could take place here. It could but it wouldn't, for there was a solution to the problem. Before he returned from San Diego he would have it.

He picked up the reins, and then on second thought dropped them. A fifteen-minute ride would bring him to the gate. It was now pretty certain that he was not being pursued by soldiers from the pueblo garrison. He had not been accosted on the trail by the De Zubaran clan as he half expected to be, but it was still a long ride out of the valley. He had told Luz de Zubaran and her brother that he was buying hides, and though the offer had been refused in one case and ignored in the other, it might be wise to make it again, to old De Zubaran himself.

The time lost would be regained by not being forced to take precautions against ambush at every clump of trees, ravine and bend in the trail, for a man who openly came to your house could not under the Spanish code be followed and ambushed when he left. Unpredictable in most things, the Spaniard was a firm believer in this.

There were objections to the idea, but as he sat there enumerating them, he remembered the quirt he had put away in the rucksack, and thinking of the quirt, he thought of the girl. The next instant he was riding down the hill, toward the house on the mesa.

# 13

Don Saturnino left his room and crossed the *portale*. He walked to the well in the center of the courtyard and stood under the blue ash tree, surveying the morning.

The sky was clear. It was not long after dawn, but the sun was already lusty. It beat against the hard earth of the courtyard and bounced off the leaves of the ash tree. The sun glistened on the snow fields of San Antonio, far off above the roofs, and its dark belts of oak and pine.

His eyes surveyed the courtyard. The smoke rising from the ovens. The glow of the forge. The squat figure of Mitla at the bellows. Guadalupe, the new Indian girl, sweeping the *portale*. The eagle preening its plumage beside the well. His eyes drifted slowly around the four sides of the courtyard. When he was satisfied that everything was in order, he shouted for Tiburcio. Then, though he saw his servant running toward him, buttoning his breeches as he ran, Saturnino raised his voice and shouted again. The last shout was not for Tiburcio alone; it was also for all those who had not yet risen on the Hill of the Hawk.

The Indian arrived out of breath.

"How would you like to be sent to the mountains to chop wood?" Saturnino asked. Tiburcio replied that he would not like it. "Then see that you rise hereafter with the sun."

Tiburcio nodded and let the jug into the well. He pulled it up, dripping, and held it while Saturnino sloshed himself, rinsed out his mouth and took a long gulp of the cold water. Tiburcio gave his master a length of coarse cloth, and while he was drying himself, spread a blanket on the ground and pulled up the rawhide stool. Saturnino sat down, and the Indian loosened the long hair, arranged it over Saturnino's back and spread the ends out on the blanket, where it lay glistening like the tail of a horse.

Tiburcio knelt on the ground, his black eyes narrowed, and began to comb the heavy hair. He grunted and hissed between his teeth as he worked, but the sounds did not disturb Saturnino, whose eyes and attention were focused on the girl who was sweeping the *portale*. She moved with a steady graceful rhythm, her hips stirring gently. He had bought her from the Santa Rosas, a tribe of Indians for whom he had no great admiration, but she was prettier than common, with a wild hot look in her eyes that stirred his blood.

The girl passed out of his vision. "What do you accomplish?" he asked Tiburcio. The day was advancing and he was anxious to be on his way to Los Angeles. No further word had arrived from Governor Pico. There was a rumor that the plans for a foray into the North had been delayed. He wished to learn if the rumor were true and, if it was, to lend the weight of the De Zubaran influence against it. There had been too much delay already to suit him. "Are you yet alive? Do you live and breathe?" he asked the Indian.

"Knots," Tiburcio announced.

"Before long, if you do not hurry, there will be other knots. The knots will be on *your* head."

Tiburcio grunted, his tongue fast between his teeth, and went on with his combing.

"And see that you exercise more care than last time," Saturnino said, "when the braids came untied as I was riding through the plaza in front of many people."

The Indian grunted again, wiped the sweat from his broad nose, twisted the hair into a braid and secured the ends with rawhide. He stood up and wound the braid in a tight bun on top of his master's head, leaving a short queue behind, which he tied with a black ribbon. Into the bun he thrust three pins of polished horn. Then he walked around Saturnino and studied his handiwork from all sides.

"How does it appear in your eyes?" Saturnino asked.

"Good," Tiburcio said. "But it can be made again."

"I lack time for further practice."

Tiburcio placed a black silk handkerchief over Saturnino's hair, pulled it tight and drew the four corners back and tied them behind, close to the right ear, in a decorative knot. Then he stepped back, fixed his small eyes on the sky, and waited for the pinch of tobacco. The pinch was larger than customary.

"Much thanks," he said. "May you go with God. And may your hair fall not in the street."

"Angels protect you if that transpires," Saturnino said. "Now, my breakfast."

The sun filtered down through the leaves of the blue ash, across Saturnino's broad shoulders and around his feet, in bright, shifting patterns. He could hear the whisper of the broom moving nearer on the opposite side of the courtyard, nearer, nearer, but it was beneath his dignity to look around. He sat watching the sun patterns at his feet, waiting for her to appear again.

Tiburcio brought four bowls and placed them on a stool. Saturnino removed the lids one after another, sucking in his cheeks at the sight of the steaming contents. Pink beans cooked with chili and slivers of fresh beef, garnished with strong goat cheese. *Tortillas* as thin as the knife blade in his garter. Thick syrupy chocolate, beaten to a bubbly froth. *Trepes de leche* from a yearling cow, cooked over an open fire. The King of Spain ate no better than Don Saturnino de Zubaran!

Smacking his lips, a fine dew of anticipation on his forehead, he spread his powerful legs, drew the stool and its contents toward him and set about the business of eating. He folded a *tortilla* and scooped up a mouthful of beans. The chili, prepared precisely to his taste, made sweat pop out on his upper lip; it created the right conditions for a deep draught of the golden frothy chocolate. His strong jaws worked rhythmically; pausing now and then to mop his face, he finished the beans and sent Tiburcio off for another bowl.

On the *portale,* the girl had drawn even with him; she was now not more than a dozen paces away, swinging the broom in wide languid arcs. He fixed his yellow eyes on her in an appraising glance. The sun shone on her bare arms and feet. Her skin was lighter than the skin of any Indian he had ever seen. She was also taller, with a fine column of a neck. Her skirts were kilted up to her knees, revealing sturdy calves. His practiced eye told him that her thighs were likewise sturdy, that between them she could easily crack the hard husk of a mountain nut.

Tiburcio set the fresh bowl of beans in front of him, but Saturnino kept his gaze on the girl. The work she was doing was the most menial task the ranch afforded. She had been here only a week, however, and it was yet too soon to see that she was given something more suitable. Until she had served a proper apprenticeship, the other Indian women would resent his interference. Not only the Indians, but Doña Carlota, as well. The resentment of both the Indians and Carlota was more than one man could support.

He sent Tiburcio off to get his tinderbox, which was in his jacket, and when he was gone, called the girl to his side. She stood in front of him, firmly on her sturdy legs, her head raised, looking at him with her wild dark eyes, her broad face proud and expressionless.

"Come closer," he said. "What I wish to say I do not wish to shout." The girl did not move. Spirit, he thought pleasantly. "Do you like it here on the Hill of the Hawk? Do things please you? Do you have a good place to sleep? Is the work too difficult?"

"I like to go home to the mountains," the girl said in dialect.

"You have a sweetheart there?"

The girl shook her head. "I like it in the mountains."

"You will like it here," he said. "Soon you will wish to stay."

"No," the girl said. "Sometime I will run away."

Saturnino laughed. "It is a long distance to the Santa Rosas. You will be overtaken before you go far. I will send *vaqueros* out to bring you back."

"When I go I will never come back," the girl said proudly.

He liked her pride, her way of frank speaking, the wild look in her eyes—usually the Indian girls were sullen when they first came to the ranch. He liked her small, pointed teeth, feeling them already against his flesh. She would probably attempt to run away, as they all did in the beginning. The thought of riding out on his stallion in search of her filled him with deep pleasure.

He smiled to himself, dismissed her with a wave of his hand and returned to his food. He ate half of the beans and then pulled the bowl of *trepes de leche* toward him. Cut from twelve or fifteen feet of marrow gut, in sections the size and length of a finger, the slender tubes were crisp on the outside and exuded a sweet, creamy fluid. They were his favorite dish—scarcely a day passed that they were not prepared for him. A delight to the palate, they were also, he was certain, largely responsible for his virility. He was a man past fifty, and yet within the last year he had fathered seven children and, except for the mysterious laws of nature and chance, should have begotten ten times that number.

He finished the *trepes,* and turned to Tiburcio who had come back empty-handed. "Now food for Águila."

The golden eagle sat in the sun at the edge of the well. It was a male bird, with a wing spread of nine feet and a broad, powerfully curved beak. Saturnino had brought him down one morning with a broken wing above the timber belt on the peak of San Antonio. Now at the sound of his name, he opened his hooded eyes. His yellow toes spread slowly, the black talons gripped the ground, and he came forward to the length of his silver chain. There he crouched, a couple of paces from Saturnino, with his black-banded tail raised, his clipped wings folded, turning his head from side to side, awaiting his breakfast as he had every morning for three years.

"Patience, friend," Saturnino said. He was very fond of Águila, and it was a great disappointment to him that the eagle, besides responding to his name and accepting food, showed no other signs of friendship. He had, in fact, several months before sunk a talon in Saturnino's leg. "In a moment, my friend, we eat."

From the small willow cage brought by Tiburcio, he lifted out a fat field mouse and tossed it to the bird. With a flash of claws faster than the eye, Águila caught the mouse in the air, tore it methodically and gorged the bloody pulp. He cocked his head for the next one and caught it this time in his beak. This was a fairly recent piece of dexterity that delighted Saturnino. With patience, the eagle might be taught other tricks; even, in time, to permit his feathers to be caressed. For some reason, next to his palomino stallion, he was fonder of Águila than anything else on the ranch. He looked forward to the day when they would be friends.

Saturnino stood up, emptied the remaining six mice on the ground, within the radius of the chain, laughed as the eagle snatched each one up before it could scurry away, and walked toward the forge. He must not forget to tell Vicente, whose sole duty it was to gather food for Águila, that he would be gone overnight, and to feed him promptly in the morning. Once when he had gone to the pueblo his beautiful golden bird had not been fed for three days. Rudolfo had earned twenty lashes for this dereliction and had been sent away into the hills with a flock of sheep, but Águila had sulked for a week, refusing all food.

As he drew near the forge, Saturnino saw his daughter hurrying along the *portale* on the morning inspection of the house. He had had great fun last night, when he returned home from Vejar's, recounting the story of how she had sent the gringo riding off with a flea in his ear. The servants were still talking about it in the kitchen; it was only Doña Carlota who out of everyone on the ranch failed to find the story amusing. Like Juan Mayorga, she had pulled a long face. Bad enough, he thought, to have a man in the valley whose sympathies were with the gringos. To have one in the house, under his very roof, and his own mother to boot, was something hard to endure.

*"Hola, hombre,"* he called out. "Ho there, man!"

Before he could say anything more, Luz closed the storehouse door behind her. She was still in a state—over the black stallion, he supposed, which had slipped its hitch when she was leading it in yesterday, the fruitless hours she had spent searching the hills. A careless mistake, true enough, and one which he had never known her to commit, but it was no reason for her not to eat supper or to get up this morning in a bad humor, without so much as answering his greeting. She could wait now for the good news until he had talked to Mitla.

The forge was filled with a ruddy glow. Mitla, with his black hair hanging in his eyes, was pumping the bellows. He stopped, as Saturnino came in, and bowed.

"On with your work!" Saturnino said. "No time exists for bows."

He walked over to the bench and examined the previous day's work. The rumors which had been circulating through the valley about the delay in Governor Pico's plans had not caused any slackening of preparations on the Hawk. When the call came, tomorrow or next week or the week following, Don Saturnino de Zubaran and his men would be ready. He had given strict orders for the utmost industry in fashioning the materials of war.

Musket balls had already been molded, carefully rounded and stored in leather pouches, one pouch for each of the men who would accompany him. The only thing now lacking was an extra supply of lance heads. It was always possible to cut a willow and make a shaft in the field, but extra heads had to be carried along. The supply of iron had been exhausted. He was forced now to resort to old files and rasps. These implements made good heads, because they took a keener edge than iron; unfortunately, they required additional labor.

Saturnino took a final glance at the forge, the glowing iron on the anvil, the finished lances leaning against the wall, and went outside and along the *portale* to the storehouse. Luz was standing on a stool with her back to him. She did not look around as he came in, but reached up, untied a string of peppers from the rafter and tossed them on the floor.

Grinning, he stooped and picked up the peppers. "You're still in a mood, I see, over the stallion."

In reply she tossed a string of dried onions on the floor.

"Well," he said, adding them to the peppers, "it's time to cheer up, *hombre*. I have news." He waited for her to turn around; he was disappointed when she didn't, but went on anyway. "Vicente found the stallion early this morning down by the river. It's now in the corral, waiting to be branded and broken. What do you think of that for luck!"

She looked at him and smiled, but the smile was so strained he was forced to the conclusion that the injury to her pride at having been careless was greater than her pleasure at getting the stallion back.

He knew her well enough not to pursue the subject farther. "I am going to the pueblo this morning. Is there anything I can buy you there—a length of ribbon, a cask of chocolate?"

"Nothing, thank you."

He tried something else to improve her mood. "If the gringo rides past again, give him some more of your good advice." Laughter boomed out of his great chest and he leaned against the wall for support. "They're still talking about what you told him."

Luz was filling a bowl with maize, and as he recovered himself sufficiently to glance at her, he saw her pause and stand erect. There was a curious light in her eyes.

"I don't wish to hear any more about the gringo," she said.

"All right, *hombre,* but it remains good." Puzzled by the rebuff, he frowned and then, struck by an inspiration, said, "It's time that you had a servant for your personal needs—someone to comb your hair, bathe and serve you in various ways. This new girl Guadalupe——"

"I would find of no use," Luz interrupted him. "I can comb my own hair and also bathe myself." She paused and looked at him steadily. "And if I were you I'd send her back to the Santa Rosas."

Don Saturnino clamped his jaws shut and quitted the room.

Luz reached down a haunch of smoked venison from the rafter, gathered up the other things on the table and took them to the kitchen. The kitchen was filled with girls giggling over their morning chores; they fell quiet when she came in and after a moment one of them asked her to tell the story about the gringo. She answered all of them with a flaring glance and gave Merced, the cook, curt orders for the two remaining meals of the day. Then she went out on the *portale* and continued with her morning inspection of the house.

The hour was late—usually she was through with the house by this time, off riding in the hills, or with the men at the corrals. This morning she had planned to go with Jorge to the Vejar ranch to finish the roping of the *mesteños,* which had begun two days ago. But she had overslept. She had lain awake for hours. She had seen the moon set and the sun gild the crests of San Gorgonio, the dawn advance westward through the mountain passes; heard Merced starting the fires in the ovens. At the moment when she should have risen, she had fallen asleep and dreamed the horrible dream which still disturbed her.

Luz opened the door of the saddlery. The small room was in its usual clutter, with saddles, *reatas,* bits, bridles and spurs strewn about the floor, wherever it had suited Don Saturnino's fancy to drop them. There were pegs along the wall to hang them on, but Saturnino wanted everything where he could find it—on the floor. So she touched nothing and made her way, a careful step at a time, to the desk beside the window, dusted the big leather-bound ledger and filled the inkhorn. The quill had been used only once, but she sharpened it, for though Don Saturnino did not write, he was insistent that it should be in good order.

When she had finished with the quill, she walked to the window and looked out at the small cloud of dust rising on the rim of the mesa and, closer at hand, the sun on the black coat of the stallion as he galloped around in the corral. She was glad that the *mesteño* had been recovered, particularly since she had let him go deliberately, as an excuse to visit Wolfe's. She couldn't wait until he was broken and ready to ride. It was not considered proper for a girl to ride a stallion, but she would ride him anyway—the valley could talk, if it pleased!

The weaving room was next to the saddlery. Through the open door the sun shone on the lime-washed walls, the piles of foamy yellow wool, the dark skins of the girls. The room was full of morning chatter, the click of the looms, the hiss of the carding sticks searching out the wool, the hum of the spindles—all the sounds which were usually pleasing to her ear. This morning they made her head ache, and she paused only long enough to correct an error Delfina was making in the woof of a blanket.

The ten rooms comprising the Indians' quarters received no more than a glance, even Consuelo's room, which was always in disorder. She passed the armory where powder and ball, muskets and lances were stored—no woman was permitted to enter here—without turning her eyes.

Beyond the armory was a naked three-year-old. He was standing on the edge of the *portale,* braced, his toes gripping the edge of the tiles, with a faraway look on his face. He was curving a stream into the courtyard. She slipped quietly up behind him and gave him a resounding whack on his bare rear. When he turned and she saw that he was Consuelo's child and had yellow eyes, she gave him another whack.

In answer the boy lifted a sullen face and stuck out his tongue. Luz picked him up and smacked his coffee-colored behind until it was red, set him down hard on his feet and left him with the threat that if she caught him again she would cut it off with the shears. As she went through the door of the chapel, his tongue was still sticking out. The blood of the De Zubarans, she thought, covering her head and walking down the aisle between the wooden benches. No tears, nothing but defiance.

The votive candles shed a rosy light over the Virgin and the wooden crucifix. Kneeling before the altar, she began to pray. The words came slowly, mixed up with the thoughts of the night and the dream she had had at dawn. Holy Mother full of grace . . .

Luz said the words over twice, but the dream came back, more vivid than ever now that she was trying not to remember it. She was in the hills. It was dusk and the hills were lion-colored in the failing light. Suddenly from an oak thicket she heard the sound of hoofs, after that the breaking of branches. From the thicket, treading proudly, came a dark *mesteño*. The sun was down, but his coat glistened like sun on metal. He snorted deep in his chest at sight of her and broke into a gallop.

Uncoiling the *reata,* she started in pursuit. The horse was fleet. His sharp hoofs struck fire from the rocks. But she gained on him; the *reata* sailed true; it circled his arched neck. She pulled up her mount, feeling the jar as the snubbed rope threw the *mesteño* to the earth. He rose and she threw him again. Three times she threw him and then he lay still, breathing hard from the falls. She dismounted and came near him, and as she did he raised his head and looked at her. Then she saw with a start that his eyes were gray.

She tried to step backward, but her legs had turned to water. She could not move. While she gazed at him, in the taking of a breath, the horse changed into the figure of a young man. The man rose and came toward her, his gray eyes on fire. She still could not move. She screamed, but no sound issued from her mouth. He came and put his hands on her, and his hands were hot and burned through her dress. She screamed again. There was no sound on the hills except the sound of the wind.

His arms were around her, lifting her from the earth, against the beating of her fists, lifting her up and away into the oak thickets, where a spring flowed and ferns were growing. He said nothing, but there was a smile on his mouth, and in his eyes a cruel questing light as he pinned and held her to the earth, bending above her. He placed his hands beneath her jerkin, sought and found her breasts. His breath was hot on her neck, like a wind blowing from the desert. His mouth bruised her lips, muffling the cry that rose in her throat.

As she lay there, breathing and yet not breathing, crying out but no sound coming from her lips, slowly and then swiftly as a hawk hovers above a field and plunges downward through the air, her strength came back.

It was at this moment that the strange thing happened. Thinking of it, Luz raised her eyes to the Virgin. Strangely, with her returning strength, she suddenly had no wish to use it. She cried out, but the cries were cries of endearment. She raised her hands, but only to hold and draw him closer. . . .

She was lying among the ferns, smelling their musty fragrance, hearing the sound of the spring flowing from the rocks. He was gone. Rising, she saw the *mesteño* beyond her at a short distance. On his back was the young man. He waved to her and started off through the thickets. She mounted her horse and followed him, but as she drew close she saw that it was no longer a young man and a *mesteño* she was following. The two figures had changed into one—a figure half man, half beast, a centaur. The centaur broke into a gallop, and though she rode hard, he easily outdistanced her. Beyond the next hill she heard the beast calling, and the call became one with her father's voice in the courtyard calling Tiburcio.

Luz rose suddenly, her prayers unfinished, and went outside. The sun shone against the walls of the courtyard with a blinding light. The three-year-old was standing in her path as she strode along the *portale.* He had one finger of each hand stuck in his nose. She reached down and gave him another smack.

In her room she slipped out of her dress and into a jerkin, boots and leather breeches. She combed her hair and pinned it on top of her head and put on a wide-brimmed hat. She sat on the bed and strapped on her heavy rowels. It would be noon before she could reach the Vejar ranch. There would be few mustangs to rope by the time she arrived, but some would be left, and the ride there and back was long. Her work in the house was not yet finished, not half finished really, but she had to get away from the ranch, away into the hills, to ride until neither she nor the horse could ride any longer.

Through the window she could see Jorge down by the corral throwing the saddle on her mare. When she got there she would change saddles to the gelding—she would require a strong horse today.

Luz raised the lid of the chest to take out her quirt. The quirt was not there. She looked around the room, on the floor, the chairs, on the peg behind the door. Then she remembered—she must be losing her mind to have forgotten. She stood holding the lid of the chest; the blood mounted to her face. How stupid she had been so much as to look in his direction when she was roping the mustang, or to give him the directions to Wolfe's ranch! Or to go there, if only to express her hatred of all Americans! Or to be driven to anger by his arrogance! She felt like swearing; instead, she slammed the lid of the chest and stared angrily around her.

There was the sound of hoofs on the mesa. She supposed that it was Don Saturnino on his way to the pueblo, but the sound, in place of growing fainter, increased in volume, separated into two horses, one being ridden, both trotting toward the house. She went to the window, bent down and looked out. The first horse was a pinto. The man astride it was dressed in a gray coat and gray trousers. The sun shone on his black boots and his gold watch chain.

Luz stepped back from the window. Her hand went to her mouth. She stood there in the middle of the room as if touched to stone, but though she didn't move or breathe for a long moment, her mind raced faster than the hoofs approaching the gate. One of the servants would open the gate and send for Don Saturnino. If that happened, if Saturnino was called and found the American there, she would never get to talk to him, because her father would never permit it.

The sound of hoofs drew closer. Luz did not move. It was only her quirt that she wanted. This and to repay him for the way he had humiliated her, and then laughed at her humiliation. She had lain awake and invented biting things to say to him, things she hadn't thought of yesterday. She had not imagined then that she would ever have the chance to say them. The horses were slowing from a trot; they were nearing the gate.

She whirled and ran outside. She saw before she reached it that the door of her father's room was open. Had he already heard the horses and gone to the gate? No, she could hear him walking around. She quit running. I must pass the door quietly, she thought, so as not to be seen, and if I'm seen, I'll give the impression that I am on my way to the kitchen.

But as she reached the door, her father saw her and called out. The room he was in, one of the three he used, had no window. It was possible that he had not heard the horses on the mesa.

"I am busy," she said.

"It is only for a moment," he explained. "Do you think this is a proper hat in which to appear before Governor Pico?"

He stood just inside the door, studying himself in a mirror. The hat was made of black leather, with a high conical crown, like a candy drop, the underside worked with silver. He had it placed on the back of his head, so as to display the handkerchief knotted behind, and had tucked the braided antelope strap under his chin. It was the most becoming hat he owned.

"I like the other one, that of the vicuña. It's in the sleeping room, in the chest," she said, though she didn't know where it was.

Luz waited, making certain that he was going to take her advice, then she hurried on past her grandmother's room—she hoped that Carlota was sleeping—and reached the gate. Should she open the gate before he knocked and thus let him know that he had already been observed? If she did, would he think, with his usual arrogance, that she was so anxious to see him she couldn't wait until he knocked? Should she wait and take the chance that his summons would not be heard by a servant or her father?

The clink of a bit sounded outside the walls, a low snort from one of the horses—the pinto, for it was the sound made by a horse which has been ridden hard and anticipates rest.

She lifted the iron bar from its keepers, pulled the massive gate toward her, not to the point where it always began to squeak, but just far enough so that she could slip through. The American had raised his rifle, held by the barrel, and was on the point of striking the gate when it opened and she stepped outside. He gave her a look of utter surprise, the rifle still gripped in his hand. It was the first time he had looked at her with anything but self-assurance. It was the look of a small boy surprised in some nefarious act.

She put her shoulders against the gate and closed it noiselessly after her. She enjoyed his moment of embarrassment. She looked up at him and said good morning in a cool voice, without the smallest trace of interest.

"It's early to be around beating upon gates with the butt of a rifle."

He slipped the rifle into its sheath. He fixed his cravat. When he looked at her again there was no trace of confusion on his thin face or in his eyes. He regarded her as he had yesterday, as if she were some casual object encountered on the trail. She felt the slow fires of anger begin to glow and run along her veins.

"It is eight o'clock," he announced, as if only Spaniards would think this hour early. "I have already ridden two leagues." As if this were some great feat!

She didn't bother to answer him, though she thought of several sharp things to say. She looked up at him, sitting astride his scrawny spotted horse, and wondered why she deigned to talk to him at all, why she had come here in the first place. She ought to leave him sitting there and call Don Saturnino. And she would as soon as she got back her quirt.

"What do you wish?" she said. Doña Carlota's rooms were next to the gate, so she spoke quietly and admonished him to do the same. "My grandmother's asleep."

He was not looking at her as she spoke. His glance was fixed on the roof, then on the flankers at the corner of the wall, then on the gate. Finally it drifted back to her.

He smiled. "I came to bring something you left yesterday at Wolfe's." He reached behind the cantle, drew out the quirt and, turning his horse, handed it down to her. When she grasped the quirt, he did not release his grip. "I presume that it's safe to give it back to you," he said.

She snatched it away from him. For an instant she was again seized with an overpowering desire to strike him, to belabor the horse, to drive them both away. Instead, she held the quirt behind her, tight in her hands, and pressed her shoulders hard against the gate. She felt the gate give a little with the pressure. There was no reason, she thought, to remain here longer.

It was then, for the first time, that he looked at her as though she were a woman and not some casual object. It was the briefest of glances, swift, felt rather than seen, but it seemed to travel over her slowly and palpably, not a glance so much as sentient fingers running over her hair, her face and throat—she was suddenly conscious of the wind molding her blouse—over her body. She stood away from the gate, dropping her hands to her sides.

He met her gaze. She felt the blood mounting to her throat. His eyes were gray. They were the eyes of the *mesteño* on the hill, of the one who had changed from a *mesteño* to a man, of the man who had carried her into the oak thicket, among the ferns and the flowing spring. . . .

"I'd like to talk to your father," he said.

He was still looking at her. She gripped the quirt until her hand ached. Could he see beyond her eyes, inside of her, into her thoughts and what was written there?

Slowly her voice came back to her and, with it, anger. "My father's busy. We have no hides to sell."

"I'd like to talk to him anyway." He leaned his arms confidently on the pommel. "I can wait until he isn't busy."

"He won't see you," she answered. "The reason should be clear." She glanced critically at his pinto pony. "Did you ride this over the mountains from Santa Fe?"

He nodded.

"I thought so."

"Why?"

"Because," she said with all the scorn she could muster, "in California we breed *real* horses."

He laughed at this and made a quick reply which she didn't hear, for behind her on the hard earth of the courtyard were steps, the sudden rattle of spurs. She leaned back on the heavy gate but before she could open it a hand pulled from the inside.

The gate swung and in the opening was her father. He stood with his feet apart, his head lowered and his long chin jutting out. He looked at the man on the horse and then at her. The veins in his neck began to swell.

"Go inside," he told her quietly.

She did not move; she heard herself say, "He wants to know if we have hides to sell."

"Go inside," Saturnino repeated.

For a moment she hesitated, then, meeting his gaze, she walked through the gate and stood behind him. Over his shoulder she could see the American sitting easily in the saddle, the reins loose against his thigh. He was looking steadily at Saturnino, but before he could speak, her father grasped the gate and, twisting his powerful body, without a sound passing his lips, sent it crashing shut.

Saturnino turned and glanced at her, a long, curious, searching look that said more than any words he might have spoken. Hunching his shoulders, he stalked away.

# 14

In the *sala* which adjoined her bedroom Doña Carlota was finishing her breakfast. She sat in a high-backed, high-seated chair, with her small feet, shod in finely stitched vicuña skin, resting on the back of her servant Rosario, who, complacent and half-asleep, lay prone on the floor, serving his mistress as a convenient footstool. On one broad arm of the chair was a plate of *bunuelos* and on the other a silver bowl of chocolate.

The chair was placed beside the window so she could enjoy the morning sun, as well as observe the activities at the corrals and any travelers who might be passing beyond the mesa along the King's Highway. She had seen the spotted horse on the hillside, the two horses start across the mesa, and as they drew closer and approached the gate, she had recognized the young man as the one she had seen several mornings before. She had also, with her lynxlike ears, heard her granddaughter whisk past the door, the bar slip from the gate, an interval of silence and then the sound of voices. She had heard some of the conversation. By rising and sitting on the deep embrasure of the window, she could have heard more, but it wasn't necessary to go to this trouble. Understanding her granddaughter, she knew what she would say and how she would say it.

Now, at the crashing sound of the gate, as Saturnino stamped through the courtyard muttering curses, she gave Rosario a sharp dig with the pointed toe of her shoe. The Indian, relieved of his burden, roused himself and stood up, rubbing his eyes.

"Tell my granddaughter I wish to see her," she said.

Doña Carlota dipped her small silver cup into the bowl of chocolate and helped herself to a sugared cooky. She had not been surprised at Saturnino's slamming of the gate in the face of the American. From the way he had been behaving of late, creating a din in the armory far into the night, so that it was impossible to sleep, and then beginning again at dawn, throwing all manner of stinking ungodly refuse in the pit behind the house in the making of powder, so that every breath of air was befouled, it surprised her that he had contented himself with this mild expression of his hatred.

The old lady wiped her mouth, fixed her gaze on the mesa and, picking up her silver-headed cane, began to tap lightly on the floor. She had said nothing to Saturnino about all the racket and stench he was creating, nor about the message from the governor, which was the reason for it, but her silence did not mean assent. She was not reconciled either to the wisdom or the necessity of fighting the Americans. Like her husband before her, she believed that the wisest policy was to do nothing which would incite reprisals. If the Americans took over California, their government could be no worse than that of the Mexicans. It was foolhardy, in her opinion, to meet force with force when your antagonist was superior in arms and numbers. Only in the event of an attack upon the ranch was there any reason for resistance.

She had said nothing to Saturnino because his mind was closed to all arguments, but she had not yet given up the idea of circumventing him in every way she could devise. She already had thought of a plan—and a very logical one it was too—which would keep Roque, her grandson, out of any trouble that might arise. The next thing was to begin on her granddaughter, whose hatred of the Americans, fostered and kept alive by Saturnino, had reached the point where it matched his own.

Carlota leaned the cane against her knee, reached into the small silver box which sat on the table beside her, and took out her tobacco. Slowly and methodically she began to roll a cornhusk cigarette.

When Luz came into the room she thought at first that her grandmother had fallen asleep, but as she walked quietly to the chair, she saw a wisp of smoke curling upward toward the ceiling.

"Here," Carlota said, "on the window." She waited until Luz had sat down. "And do not sit as though you were going to fly off at any moment. Make yourself comfortable, for I have much to say." She puffed on her cigarette and blew the smoke through her thin nostrils. "The Americans are going to overrun California. Nothing you can do, or Saturnino or Roque or anyone else can do, will prevent it."

Luz looked at the old lady, at her stony mouth and her sharp eyes half hidden behind parchmentlike lids. She closed her mind and said nothing.

"The time has come for you to know and understand this," Carlota said, "and to act accordingly."

Luz remained silent.

"By acting accordingly I refer to your conversation with the American this morning, part of which I overheard, the rest of which I readily imagined. In the old days the Hill of the Hawk prided itself on its hospitality—a night's lodging, a doubloon if one were required, food, at least and in all circumstances, politeness. One or all, as it seemed fitting, to whomever came, friend or enemy, Spaniard or American. But now that this fever has seized upon Saturnino and, because of him, upon you and your brother, travelers are treated with disrespect, if not insulted, and gates are shut in their faces."

"They receive what they deserve," Luz said, in spite of her vow to keep silent.

Carlota went on as if she hadn't spoken. "And as if this were not sufficient, it has been found necessary to go outside the ranch into the highway, to the houses of others, and there carry on this feud."

Luz sat forward, clasping her hands together in her lap, but her face showed no emotion. "I don't know what you're talking about."

Carlota snorted, scattering a noseful of smoke. "Oh, yes you do, *hombre*. I thought that you had been up to something when you came in late last night to supper, with nothing to say and your eyes smoldering in your head. I took the trouble to investigate."

Luz jumped to her feet. *"Maldito!"* she cried.

"Sit down," the old lady commanded, and paused until her command had been complied with. "Your brother Jorge is not to blame. I may be doddering and simple in the head about some things, but I am also a woman of resources and persistence. What information I drew out of him came only after they both were at the point of exhaustion."

"I did nothing which I wouldn't do again," Luz said.

Carlota puffed calmly on her cigarette. "That is why I am speaking now, so that it will not be done again, though with this young man, after your actions, I doubt that you will ever have another opportunity."

"That will be good."

"Perhaps, perhaps not," Carlota said, a faint smile at the corners of her lips. "But this is not what interests me at the moment. It is that you are wrong in taking on yourself a fever, a blindness, a feud, which is not your concern. With Saturnino, it is understandable."

Carlota paused to relight her cigarette. "When your stepmother left here to run away with the captain of a sailing ship, it was natural that Saturnino should be seized with a frenzy. He was never friendly toward Americans before this, and afterward it was only hatred he felt, and a desire for revenge. It was natural but also foolish, for what else could be expected of a girl barely seventeen, who married a man almost old enough to be her grandfather? And this girl in particular, raised as she was in the pueblo, pleasure-loving and bird-witted in the bargain? I warned Saturnino against her in the first place, and later when they were married; if she had not run off with an American ship captain, it would have been a Spanish adventurer or an unfrocked priest or the chief of the Santa Rosas, or all of them, one after the other."

The old lady sat up a little straighter, tapping her cane softly on the tiles, and fastened her clear cold eyes on the girl sitting in the window. "Your father's actions can be excused," she said, "though they remain dangerous to us on the Hawk. Yours cannot, my fine young lady, and they likewise will be dangerous to us if they do not cease."

Luz lifted her chin, and opened her lips, but before she had a chance to speak, Carlota said, "Save your breath. I am in no mood for arguments. There is only one thing of importance. It is the Hawk—these hills and pastures and the river which runs through them, the springs and cattle and the mesa and the house which stands on it. This and nothing else."

Luz turned and looked through the window and Doña Carlota followed her gaze out along the mesa where ropes of sun-infused dust marked the progress of the young man on the spotted pony.

"It comes before emotions or prejudices or feuds, before Saturnino and you and me," Carlota said finally.

Rosario entered the room, and the old lady, weary of her own talk, aware that she had made a slight impression on the spoiled willful half-savage girl, afraid of pushing the matter too far, dismissed her with a tap of the cane and a jerk of the head. When her granddaughter had gone, Rosario refilled the silver bowl with chocolate and resumed his position on the floor. Carlota placed her trim little feet on his back—there was always a cold draft along the floor since Don Cristóbal had changed the beaten earth to tiles—and sank her strong teeth into a sugared cake.

She leaned back in the chair, the lobes of her ears stretched a little by the weight of the heavy amethyst rings, swinging as her jaws moved, and watched the dust rising far out on the mesa.

Grady Dunavant rode down the slope which slanted toward the river, still hearing the crash of the iron-banded gate, seeing the last fierce probing look from the eyes of old De Zubaran. He threw one final glance over his shoulder, before the trees shut off his view, in the direction of the mesa.

The glance was instinctive rather than deliberate. There was nothing now to fear from the De Zubaran clan. He had bearded them in their lair and come away with nothing worse than ringing ears and the memory, galling though it was, of a hostile look. They would not follow him; the only precautions he would have to take would be against the possibility of soldiers from the pueblo. And as he rode even his anger faded out before the memory of Luz de Zubaran. Haughty as ever, and determined not to let him forget that he was a trespasser and a gringo, she still was speaking to him. That fact was significant. The excursion, he reflected, had been successful.

A mile below the point where the King's Highway crossed the river, he made a fording and, avoiding the traveled trail, angled south. He had ridden for ten minutes or so through rolling brushy country when he heard hoofs a short distance to his left. For a moment he thought that the sound came from a mustang heading toward the river to drink. The hoofs changed direction and were suddenly immediately behind him. The brush was heavy but low and there was no chance of concealment; the nature of the terrain made any attempt at flight useless.

He wheeled his horse and waited, his hand on the stock of the rifle. The man came riding up from a ravine, the top of his peaked hat barely visible, and careened through the brush in front of him. It was Joe, the servant, grinning and sweating, on a lathered horse.

"Good day, señor," Joe said, as casually as if they were meeting at Kate Howland's.

"In the name of God where did you come from?" Dunavant exploded.

"Come pueblo. Come slow. Lose track first river. Second river find track. Here."

Dunavant, gathering his wits, stared at him for a full minute. If the Indian had been able to follow his trail out of Los Angeles, then others might have done the same. "How about the soldiers—did you meet any when you left the pueblo?"

Joe shook his head. "All in pueblo. No find track. Ride up street. Ride down. Look." Joe made a dramatic gesture with one hand shading his eyes. "No find him."

"You passed no soldiers on the trail or none passed you?"

Joe shook his head again.

Grady relaxed in the saddle and gave the Indian a grudging look of admiration—he should have known after his experience in the fight that Joe was a man of resources as well as superhuman strength. It was no accident that he had found his tracks where the others had failed; the only wonder was that he hadn't tracked him down before now.

Dunavant turned his horse and for the first time took a good look at the Indian, his flat, mahogany-colored face, the eyes like black pebbles, the bang of thick coarse hair which hung in a black curtain across his forehead.

He said, "Well, as long as you've come this far, you might as well go the rest of the way."

"Where go?"

"To San Diego."

"Good," said Joe. "Got girl San Diego."

It was just before dusk and they were riding along the main trail, coming into a meadow covered with live oaks and grazing cattle. Joe was riding behind and Dunavant was suddenly aware that he had stopped. When he turned around, Joe was kneeling on all fours, one ear pressed hard against the earth.

The Indian stood up after a moment and pointed back in the direction they had left. "Two horses," he announced. "Maybe four. Not sure."

The nearest clump of trees was too close to the trail. So they rode deeper into the glade, behind the main herd of cattle, putting a manzanita thicket between them and anyone who would pass. Minutes went by, and Dunavant, thinking that the Indian might have made a mistake and worrying about the distance yet to travel, was beginning to get restless. Then he heard the horses himself.

Before they came in sight, Joe said, "Three. Make mistake."

There were three horses all right, and they came out of the west at a Spanish trot with the level sun shining on bridles and silver headstalls, twirling metal crickets on their tongues. The crickets, which made a louder sound than the beat of hoofs, were usually the equipment of ranchers out on some sort of a foray, Dunavant knew. But as he heard the soft thud of hoofs and the shrilling of the crickets and saw the flash of sun on silver, he saw also that of the three riders, two wore the blue and scarlet uniforms of the military. The other, dressed in a brown frock coat, was not a rancher.

They passed from sight and when they appeared again along the curving trail they were closer to the manzanita thicket, riding at an angle which gave him a good view of two of the men's faces. In the lead on a sorrel gelding was Julio de Zubaran. Behind him was Cesaire Curel. The third man was partly hidden by Curel, and disappeared with the others before he could catch a glimpse of his face. But there was no mistaking the clothes or the figure of Mr. Fraser.

Dunavant did not move from where he stood until the sound of the metal crickets died out on the quiet air. Then, motioning to the Indian, he mounted, crossed the meadow and started out on the trail. Keeping his horse to a walk, he rode in silence, pondering the sudden turn of events. Mr. Fraser's presence made it obvious that they were not searching for him. But what were they doing on the trail to San Diego? Why was Fraser the Englishman, of all people, in a party composed of Curel and Major de Zubaran? Were they, after all, going to San Diego and if they were, for what reason?

He shifted in the saddle and looked back at Joe—the Indian could do everything, perhaps he knew everything. "Do you know Señor Curel?" Joe nodded in reply. "Did you see him just now?" Joe nodded again. "Where is he going?"

"San Diego," Joe said.

"Major de Zubaran?"

"San Diego."

"Señor Fraser?"

"All go San Diego."

"Why?"

Joe shrugged, twice for emphasis.

Well, Grady thought, he at least knew where they were headed. The problem now was to beat them there, transact his business with Juan Bandini, and before they arrived, leave the town, for if he were discovered in San Diego it would be the same as being discovered in Los Angeles, except that the *calabozo* in the former, he remembered, was smaller and dirtier.

"Is there any other trail besides the Camino Real? A short cut?"

"Come other trail soon," Joe said.

"Before night?"

"Soon."

"You're a good man, Joe," Dunavant said and grinned. "You should be riding up front here instead of me."

"Ride here. Like dust," said Tepeyollotl.

# 15

When they reached the stream where the short trail to San Diego forked off, Joe found signs that the three men had taken it ahead of them; there was nothing to do except to go by the longer way. They camped at midnight and started again at dawn and rode hard all day. It was night as they topped the last hill above San Diego, passed the ruined breastworks of the old Spanish fort and rode down toward the town. Off to their right were the shadowy headlands of Point Loma. The great curving sandspit which enclosed the harbor lay below them and beyond was the sea, scaled with the silver and jet of a rising moon.

The moon had not yet touched the few scattered houses of the town, and on the outskirts, a short distance from a group of brush jacales where a central fire was burning, at Joe's suggestion they stopped. A pack of yelping dogs rushed to meet them, followed by several men carrying bludgeons. The figures around the fire rose and vanished into the huts. But at the first word from Tepeyollotl the men lowered their weapons; the dogs quieted down, contenting themselves with desultory barks and quick sniffs at the horses' hocks; the women came out of the huts and stood chattering in the doorways. It was clear that Joe was well known in the village.

Dunavant prompted him. "Ask your friends if they've seen three white men on horses."

Joe asked the question and translated the answer. "Sun overhead. Come. Go."

This meant that Curel and his party had reached the town some six or seven hours before.

"Chief say stay, eat," Joe said.

Grady was hungry but one breath of the sweet odor which welled up from the pots simmering over the fire was enough to satisfy him. The southern Indians were fond of dog, and this was the odor he smelled—fat puppies stewing with ground corn.

"Give the chief my thanks," he said.

They left the village and rode slowly down the trail past a corral filled with sheep, another cluster of Indian huts, and tethered their horses in the brush. On foot and by a roundabout way, they came to the plaza. There in the shadows of a hide warehouse, Dunavant stopped and reconnoitered. He had passed no one since leaving the village; he saw no one now except a single sentry walking his post, the light from the barracks putting a gleam on the barrel of his musket. The town was silent except for a commotion of some sort in one of the dives along the water front.

The moon tipped the hills and he saw across from him a huge, square, one-storied abode, surrounded on the two sides visible to him by a *portale* supported on slender, wooden pillars. From the brief glimpse he had caught of the house back in '42 while he was being led in chains aboard the ship bound for Tepic, he recognized the home of Don Juan Bandini, the one influential friend the Americans could claim among the California Spaniards. This was his destination. But he would be asking for trouble if he went over and knocked on the door without making certain who was inside. If De Zubaran hadn't been there, or wasn't there now, he would surely come.

"Do you know any of the Indians at Bandini's?" he asked Joe.

"Cruz—Chico—María——"

"Go around to the kitchen then and find out if any of our friends are in the house."

"When eat?" Joe asked.

"Later," Dunavant said.

Since midafternoon when the *Pilgrim* had furled her sails and dropped anchor in the harbor, Juan Bandini had waited for Mr. Teal to put in his appearance. He had twice sent a servant on a tour of the water front in search of the captain and at dusk had even made a trip through the town himself. Now that Teal had been announced, the Spaniard took his time over the glass of pisco he was drinking with his wife. His desire to talk to the captain had been whetted by the hours of delay, but he finished the liqueur and poured himself another glass before he permitted himself to enter the *sala* where the captain was sitting.

During the ten years and more he had been selling hides to Mr. Teal, he had found the agate-eyed, tight-lipped New Englander a hard man to do business with. No harder perhaps than with the rest of the ship captains who plied the coast, and in certain respects less hard, but there were qualities which he shared with them that puzzled and at times frankly annoyed Bandini.

For one thing Teal was a great haggler over prices, thinking nothing of spending an entire afternoon in an attempt to gain a few centavos, even going so far as to up anchor and sail off because of the difference of a single centavo. He had done this on the last visit. In the beginning Bandini had accepted the captain's terms without bargaining, used as he was to the code of a country where bargaining was held in contempt. But over the years his attitude had undergone a change. His first feelings of indignity had given way to amusement and this in turn, as he came to understand Teal's motives, to a hardheadedness which matched the captain's own.

This final change had taken place when he saw that, unlike the peons, who haggled simply for the fun of haggling, Teal was in deadly earnest. It was no mere desire to have the better of the bargain that made him sail off in a huff or to offer half of the customary price or to examine each hide as it came aboard ship, subtracting from the total every one which was damaged in the least, but loading them in the hold nevertheless. It was instead an undisguised avarice so ingrained and natural to Mr. Teal and his countrymen of Boston and Salem that nothing was considered wrong, no practice too sharp if it managed to turn up a profit.

Bandini had often wondered about this New England country from which these men came and returned. Having neither seen it nor read about it, he was thrown back, in trying to picture it, on the character of the men themselves, the meager details of their conversation, and upon his own imagination. From the rich cargoes they carried back not only from California but also from China and the Indies, it seemed to him that the country must be wealthy indeed, a place of splendid cities and sybaritic living where, if the avenues were not paved with gold, they were at least paved with silver. And yet, studying these various men, and Mr. Teal in particular, noting their frugal habits, their unsmiling faces, in which there was not the smallest trace of humor, and observing that they looked on the easy, unhurried life of the California ranchers as something shiftless and even immoral, he had doubts about the cities and the life he had pictured there. It was possible, he had thought, that the women were of a different stripe, gaily dressed and pleasure-loving and exotic, in contrast to their men, and, therefore, that his picture in part was correct. But with the advent into Los Angeles of Señora Howland—that female gryphon who was sharper than the sharpest ship captain—he had been forced to revise the picture again.

In the end he had come to the conclusion that this New England country was a bleak and unhappy place, washed by cold seas and chilled by searching winds, inhabited by cheerless people in cheerless towns. But he still did not understand men to whom avarice was a virtue, who scoured the coast for hides and tallow, sailed the oceans to haul away the treasures of China and the Indies, who lived uncomfortably month after month in the stinking cubbyholes of rolling ships, eating weevily bread and salty meat, enduring storms and privations and monotony in order to store up wealth they did not use.

And now as he entered the room and Captain Teal rose to shake hands, he was as far from understanding them as ever. In the frosty blue glance was the same unyielding, predatory gleam he had always seen before. It was even more intense than in the past, for behind it was the rancor of a man who had sworn on his last visit that he would never come again.

The Spaniard marveled at the force which could drive a man beyond the limits of pride, and smiled to himself. Having few hides to sell and not caring whether he sold them or not, he was in a good position to bargain. He was, in fact, not interested in discussing them at all.

Only one thing really concerned him at the moment, and, as soon as the formalities were over, he lost no time in coming to it. "The Mexican brig *Rosa* arrived last week from Mazatlán with the news that both the British and American fleets are in the harbor. Tell me, captain," Bandini said, "what did you find at Mazatlán? Are the ships still there? What is the news?"

The American, plainly not interested in the questions, crossed one leg over the other, leaned back in his chair and took his time about answering. "I don't know what goes on at Mazatlán. I didn't visit the port."

"San Blas then?" Bandini said.

"Nor there. But I can tell you this from what I heard in Panama—war is coming. There was talk of it when I left Boston in February. There were rumors at Panama that an American squadron was about to start a blockade of the gulf, and that the Mexicans were mobilizing along the Rio Grande. I sailed directly here, half expecting to be arrested when I came ashore. I wasn't, but judging from the general look of things, I will be if I remain, which, I am frank to say, I don't intend to do." The captain fixed his eyes on Bandini. "I leave in the morning with the tide. I'll pick up any hides you have at Guadalupe, at the price I offered last year. If the price is still not acceptable, then I am sailing for the Sandwich Islands."

"There are few hides at the Guadalupe ranch," Bandini said.

"How many?"

"Less than a thousand. We have had alarms here too, and consequently the *vaqueros* have had to be employed in other things than slaughtering."

Captain Asaph Teal cleared his throat. "Not many," he said. "In truth, scarcely enough to be worth the trip. But considering the fact that in event of war you stand the danger of having the ranch looted, I will make the trip. Out of consideration, you might say, for an old friend."

"I deeply appreciate your kindness, but it is too much of a sacrifice to ask of you in the circumstances." Bandini paused as a servant came to the door to announce Major de Zubaran, and then, frowning, said, "As for the looting you speak of, I have always supported the American cause. Therefore I have no fear of reprisals."

"I trust that your confidence has not been misplaced," Captain Teal said shortly. "But I wouldn't bank on it too much." He stood up, took a couple of rolling strides into the room and turned. "In case you reconsider, I can be reached aboard ship until five o'clock tomorrow morning."

Bandini, wishing the captain a safe voyage, watched him disappear through the door. In spite of the penurious unenviable qualities of the man, and against his will, he found himself, as always, moved by a curious respect, a feeling almost of admiration for this breed of men who it seemed were about to assume control of California, for their hardness and enterprise and stubborn pride, even for that force which drove them relentlessly over the oceans of the world.

He preferred them, in all frankness, to the man who now stood in the doorway, his hand resting lightly on the hilt of his sword, all the faults of the Spaniards written on his face.

Dunavant had not moved from where he was standing in the shadow of the warehouse. Ten minutes after the Indian had disappeared through the rear entrance of Bandini's, and just as he was on the point of following him, he had seen Major de Zubaran come out of the barracks, cross the plaza and enter the house.

The moon, tipping the hills now, gave him a good view of the house and its central door opening on the plaza, and the plaza itself. Horses were tied to a rack at one side of the barracks and he recognized them in the clear light as those belonging to the three men. The sentry was still walking up and down, his boots squeaking at each step. Grady saw nothing else. He heard nothing else except the breathing of the Indian behind him.

He did not move from where he stood until, after a short time, De Zubaran reappeared, walked briskly across the plaza and entered the barracks. Grady waited until the sentry had come to a halt, turned and started back. He instructed the Indian to keep an eye on the barracks and quickly reached the opposite side of the street. There he stopped for an instant to make sure that he had not been seen, and then went on along the *portale* to the door of Bandini's house.

Two light knocks brought a servant, who, apparently expecting him, without any inquiry led the way through a series of rooms to a small office in the rear of the house, furnished with two chairs and a mahogany desk. Behind the desk, with a quill in his hand and a ledger opened in front of him, sat Juan Bandini. Dunavant had met him six years before in Los Angeles, but as the Spaniard laid the quill aside and looked up, he realized that Bandini had forgotten the occasion. There was no point in attempting to remind him; instead, he placed Kroll's letter on the desk and sat down in the chair Bandini pushed toward him.

As the Spaniard broke the seal on the letter and adjusted his steel-rimmed spectacles, Dunavant studied the face bent forward into the light. It was thinner than he remembered, the wrinkles around the eyes and those bracketing the full mouth more pronounced, and he noticed that beneath the tight-drawn, olive skin was a flood of color. It was likely, he thought, that the meeting between Bandini and Major de Zubaran, though brief, had been acrimonious.

Halfway through the letter, the Spaniard shoved his spectacles up on his forehead and looked at Dunavant. "Does De Zubaran know that you are in San Diego?" he asked.

Dunavant answered him by giving a short account of the happenings in Los Angeles and the events preceding his entry into San Diego. "De Zubaran may suspect that I am here but he doesn't know it," Dunavant concluded.

"You are aware that De Zubaran has just left?" When Dunavant nodded, Bandini continued, saying, "Earlier I had a visit from Captain Teal of the *Pilgrim* who arrived this afternoon, having sailed here directly from Panama. He brought no news, consequently, from Mazatlán, but he did have the rumors current in Panama. These rumors, if I am any judge add up to one simple fact: it may be a week in coming or a month, but it is inevitably war."

Grady moved uneasily in his chair. The words and the way they were spoken struck him as familiar. They were, he realized, the echo of what he had heard during his talk with Jim Wolfe. Bandini's position was somewhat different from Wolfe's—according to Jacob Kroll he had given staunch support to the American cause—but as far as any immediate help was concerned the two men were in probable agreement.

His surmise turned out to be correct. Bandini spoke at length about his work at the meeting of the Junta in Monterey, where he had openly favored the annexation of California by the United States against Governor Pico who had espoused the cause of Great Britain. He mentioned the aid he had given to Abel Stearns, his son-in-law, a representative of the United States Consul, Thomas Larkin, in bringing about a peaceful solution of the conflict. He was frank about his desire to see the corrupt Mexican Government deposed, but in the end he refused to take an active part in the struggle.

"You will understand my attitude," he said finally, "when I say that it is one thing to favor a cause and even work for it, and quite another to take part openly in an armed attack on a garrison."

Dunavant agreed to himself that it was, but he didn't say so; he spent a half hour trying to change the Spaniard's mind. His efforts, however, resulted in nothing more than a promise of provisions and horses.

"And while you are in San Diego," Bandini said, "I hope that you will consider this house your home."

Dunavant thanked him and picked up his hat. Then, as they were walking toward the door, the Spaniard said something that brought Grady up short in his tracks. Bandini was talking about the men-of-war lying at anchor at Mazatlán, expressing the opinion that Commodore Sloat was only waiting authority to sail for the coast of California, when he asked Dunavant if he knew the Englishman who had come to San Diego with De Zubaran.

"I know him well," Dunavant said. "A Mr. Fraser."

"I believe that is the name," the Spaniard replied. "But how well do you know him?"

"Very well, señor," Dunavant said with an emphasis which was lost on Bandini.

"Do you know that he is an agent of Great Britain?"

It was at this moment that Dunavant stopped and faced Bandini.

"Major de Zubaran came here to warn me against giving aid to the Americans and to threaten me with arrest. I ordered him out of the house, but before leaving he blurted out that I would live to see the British flag flying over the plaza. I laughed in his face. Whereupon he said that an emissary of Great Britain was now across the street, waiting for the *Chubasco* to sail sometime tomorrow for Mazatlán, and that he carried a message from Governor Pico to Admiral Sir George Seymour."

They were standing in front of the door to the *sala*. Before Dunavant could recover his speech, the Spaniard led him into the room and introduced him to his wife and his two daughters. The girls, darkly attractive and voluble, were anxious for news from Los Angeles where their married sister lived, but as he answered their questions his mind was working fast on the matter of Mr. Fraser. By the time he could gracefully leave, he had sorted out the things Bandini had told him and arrived at a plan of action. It was a bold plan and only the greatest luck could bring it off. It depended on a dozen different factors, the failure of any one of which would spell ruin. He rose and said good night to Bandini at the door.

He stood on the *portale* behind the white wooden pillars and faced the barracks, watching and listening. The sentry still moved up and down. The squeak of boots. Voices from the barracks. The three horses at the hitch rail. He stood for a moment and then walked down the *portale* and crossed the plaza to where the Indian was leaning against the wall of the warehouse.

"Has anyone come out of the barracks?" he asked.

The Indian gave a negative grunt.

"Would you know Fraser if you saw him?"

"Know everybody," Joe said.

"Well, if he comes out, follow him and find out where he's going. I'm going down to the beach. I'll meet you here in an hour."

"When eat?"

"Remember, watch for Fraser. No one else."

"When eat?"

Dunavant, walking quickly away, did not answer.

The moon lay across the beach. The tide was high, lapping against the coarse yellow sand. There were no waves and the bay was like silvered glass. A quarter of a mile off shore he saw a two-masted ship, its riding lights washed pale by the moon, and beyond it a sloop lying at anchor. It was impossible to tell which one was the *Pilgrim,* but it didn't matter. Not at the moment, he thought. The problem now was to find a skiff, even a log—any means to get out into the bay.

Off to his right a light showed in an adobe shack, and, as he drew closer, hearing laughter and a woman's screech, he saw behind it a longboat drawn up out of the sweep of the tide. The light came from a window of the shack. He moved cautiously through the deep sand, reached the window and looked in. Along one side of the room was a crude bar and on the bar was a quarter keg fitted with a spigot. The bar was small, but six or seven American sailors stood in front of it, drinking out of gourd dippers and fooling with a couple of half-dressed girls.

The men had likely come ashore in the longboat beached behind the shack. It was possible, he supposed, to hire one of them to row him to the *Pilgrim.* But his appearance, if it weren't actually resented, would at least cause a commotion. The fat woman behind the bar was Mexican, and so were the girls, and he would run the chance of being reported. He therefore decided to row himself. From the sailors' activities, he judged it would be some time before they would need the boat.

The boat dragged hard against the sand but without any sound. Finally afloat, he broke out a pair of oars and headed toward the first ship, the two-master, pulling steady and looking over his shoulder. A short distance from the schooner he shipped the oars and floated noiselessly under the counter. He could hear the voices from the shore but there was no sound on the deck above him. In gilt letters on the black hull, he made out the name *Pilgrim,* and the words Boston, U.S.A.

He poled himself forward along the side of the ship and found the ladder, secured the boat to the bottom rung, climbed to the deck and made his way aft to where a thread of light showed under a door. A voice answered his knock and he found himself, as he opened the door, in a snug cabin filled with smoke and the smell of perique. A wiry little man, dressed in a coat too large for him and frayed at the cuffs, sat under a lamp hanging from a carling, playing solitaire with a pack of greasy cards.

"Captain Neale?" Dunavant said.

"Teal is the name," the man replied, not looking up from the table. "Captain Asaph Teal."

"I've just come from Juan Bandini's," Dunavant said.

"The old man has changed his mind, I take it," Captain Teal said, continuing with his game. "Well, it's no surprise. I thought he'd come around to my offer, considering that I'll be the only buyer on the coast this summer."

Dunavant was prepared for this and, without hesitation or an instant of qualm, said, "I regret to inform you that the offer is still unacceptable."

Captain Teal did not look up. "You're wasting your time, young man, if you've come here to bargain for Bandini. You're barking up the wrong tree. The *Pilgrim* sails with the tide, and for all of me the hides can damn well rot on the beach. Prime hides, one dollar and fifty cents. No more and no less, and if you don't like it, get out."

Ignoring the invitation, Dunavant sat down across the table from the little man in the frayed coat. "I have a proposition, captain, that you should be interested in."

Teal cocked a frigid blue eye in his direction.

"Not about hides," Dunavant said quickly. "Something else. You've heard that the British are at Mazatlán and you know that Governor Pico is anxious for them to take over control of California ahead of the Americans." The eyes fixed on him across the table were getting colder, he noticed, by the moment, but he went on anyway, describing the events which had shaped up in the last month, everything which might have a bearing on the request he was about to make. "Your help is needed," he said. "Tonight."

Teal was laying out cards again, mumbling under his breath. Keeping his eyes on the cards, he said, "Me, I'm a ship captain and I've got my hands full without meddling in a war that's come near to ruining my business already. Seven of hearts, nine—the Navy's hired to fight, so let them fight. I'm sailing in the morning and if I wasn't I still wouldn't get mixed up in it—nine of clubs."

Dunavant, suddenly remembering Kroll's unsuccessful attempts to appeal to his own patriotism, gave up this line of argument and tried another one. "I'm not asking you to meddle in anything. All you have to do is to sail as you're planning to, in the morning. Before then, I'll have a passenger for you."

The captain glanced up from the table. "Where's the passenger bound?"

"The same place you're bound—to the Sandwich Islands."

A suspicious light glittered in Mr. Teal's eyes. "A Spaniard?"

"An Englishman—a gentleman by the name of Fraser."

Mr. Teal lowered his eyes and laid down a card with his stubby fingers, picked it up and put it down again in a different place, tilting his head from one side to the other.

"The fare's one hundred dollars gold," he said, "paid in advance."

The price was high, twice the regular fare, but Dunavant had the coins on the table before the captain had finished speaking.

"I'll need a boat," he said, "and one of your sailors."

Mr. Teal directed him to the forecastle. "Ask for Simpkins, and tell him I sent you—he's a big man with red hair, what's left of it. If he just rows you ashore, there'll be no charge. If you find that you need something further from Simpkins, and he's a handy man—it will be twenty-five dollars all told. You can pay me when you come back and if you don't, then give it to Simpkins."

"I'll be back in an hour or two," Grady said from the doorway. "With a gentleman called Fraser."

And yet, sitting in the thwarts while Simpkins bent his heavy shoulders against the oars, and the longboat trailed after them over the glassy water, Dunavant wasn't certain that he would be back. The easiest part of the plan had been completed. He had a powerful man in Simpkins—he had known that from the first moment when he had opened the door of the forecastle and seen the tall, rawboned sailor lying on the bunk. But the part that was left didn't call for strength; though simple, it was still a matter of intelligence, the ability to walk into the barracks and deliver a convincing message. Joe, the Indian, could do it, he was sure, but Joe was ruled out because he was known. He wasn't sure about Simpkins.

He was even less sure when they ran the boats up the shore and he started to explain what had to be done. "You're to walk in the barracks," he said, "and ask for the man who's sailing on the *Chubasco*—that will be Mr. Fraser, a tall sandy-haired Englishman. Tell him that the ship is sailing in an hour and the captain wants him aboard immediately."

Simpkins rubbed his stubby chin. "I thought we was going to shanghai the gent," he complained.

"Just say what I've told you and be positive when you say it."

"I'd feel better just knocking him over the head. I'm no good at talk."

"The *Chubasco* is a Mexican ship," Dunavant said. "If Fraser wonders why you're not a Mexican, make up a story. He probably won't, but if he does tell him that you're shipping out on the *Chubasco*. Tell him anything to get him aboard."

Simpkins shook his head and grumbled, but finally went trudging off through the sand. Dunavant waited until he was out of sight, and then with another look in the window of the shack, satisfying himself that the sailors were well occupied, he floated the longboat and rowed toward the *Pilgrim*.

His confidence in the scheme was beginning to ebb. Besides his doubts about Simpkins, which were considerable, there were other reasons for his feeling. Fraser might have left the barracks. He might even be aboard the *Chubasco*. The captain of the *Chubasco* might have come ashore and at this moment be sitting in the barracks with Fraser. The chances of success were slim, but there was still a chance, a dim one. He rowed hard and prayed.

An hour had gone by, an hour and ten minutes by his watch. He stood in the doorway of the cabin talking to Captain Teal and watching the shore, the faint silvery line of the tide on the beach, the glow that came through the window of the shack.

Another ten minutes, and he saw a vague shape off the starboard beam. As the shape grew and became a boat, he heard the clear splash of oars and Simpkins' deep bass. Then silence as the boat was obscured by the bulwarks. Then the sound of the boat scraping the side of the ship, a short interval of silence, the creak of the rope ladder as someone stepped on the first rung. Leaving the doorway, Dunavant backed into the cabin and stood in one corner against the bulwarks, as far from the light as he could get.

Teal said, "The cards are running bad. Haven't won a game the last hour."

Dunavant heard steps on the back, and Teal spoke again, to himself, and afterward the steps were nearer and Simpkins was talking, his booming voice drowning out all the other sounds except one, a laugh that he had often heard before and couldn't mistake. He leaned hard against the bulwarks as Fraser stepped into the cabin and said good evening to the captain. He did not look at Fraser. He looked at the man who was now standing behind Fraser in the doorway, who was stepping into the cabin, at Cesaire Curel in his blue and gilt uniform.

Curel, his heels together and holding his sword, bowed to Captain Teal. And then, whether it was from something in Teal's face, or a premonition, or from a sentence begun and left unfinished by a third man, by Major de Zubaran who had just come into the cabin, Curel straightened and slowly turned until he was looking at the Colt held level at Dunavant's hip.

Simpkins said from the doorway, "These buckoes wanted to come along to say good-by to their friend here. I told them I didn't have no time to spend rowing them around, but they was three sheets to the wind and kept saying they'd get one of the government boats if I didn't take them. I didn't want that to happen so I brought them along. If you want, sir, I'll toss them overboard."

"Don't bother, Simpkins," Dunavant said, not looking at him, or at Fraser, but at Cesaire Curel. "They're going to be passengers on that long trip you're taking to the Sandwich Islands."

There was no sound in the cabin for a moment save Teal's stubby fingers shuffling the cards. Recovering his speech, Fraser said something about His Majesty's Government. De Zubaran was pale and silent. Curel looked at Dunavant and did not move, his eyes, red with drink, staring out of a white face.

Dunavant said, "We meet again, Colonel."

"But not for the last time," Curel said.

"It won't be soon," Dunavant said. "The next meeting."

He could feel his heart pounding against his arm held against his side. He could see Curel's brain working behind the staring eyes, figuring not on the future, but on the present—the chances of escape. And he found himself hoping that Curel would seize upon some straw, that he would make some movement out of panic. He preferred to kill him here in the cabin, now, than to send him off on the ship. He looked at Curel and waited.

Teal laid out the five of spades. "Take them below, Simpkins. I can't keep my mind on the game. The sail locker will do for the present."

Simpkins gathered his weight and said from the doorway, "Get movin', my fine buckoes. You heard the captain's orders."

Dunavant saw Curel take his hand from the curved hilt of his sword. Now, he thought, it's coming; any second now it will come—the colonel has made up his mind and all I have to do is to wait. He kept the Colt level; he stood away from the bulkhead. Curel glanced toward the door, at Simpkins standing with a small pistol in the palm of his hand. Then his eyes went slowly around the cabin from Fraser to Major de Zubaran and back at last to Dunavant. They hung there for a long moment, morose, heavy, the pupils distended in the weak light, and Dunavant saw with a bitter pang of disappointment that the chance had gone, that Curel had weighed the odds and found them not to his liking.

Simpkins, stepping aside, spoke again, and without a word Curel walked past him and onto the deck. From there he called back something which was lost in the brief expostulations of Fraser and Major de Zubaran. Dunavant made a motion with his head, inviting them to follow.

"A pleasant voyage to both of you!" he said, and then to the Englishman, "Is there any message you wish to send back to Los Angeles?"

Fraser summoned a stiff smile. "Nothing, thank you very much, Mr. Dunavant."

Smiling in return, Dunavant wondered irrelevantly how long it would be—how many months and after what new experiences—before the Englishman would condescend to address him by his first name.

He followed Fraser on deck and stood at the head of the companionway while the three men and Simpkins went down the ladder. He waited until a door opened and closed somewhere below him and he heard Simpkins singing. Then he went back to the cabin.

Teal glanced up from his game. "That will be two hundred dollars more. And twenty-five for Simpkins makes two hundred and twenty-five. Considering all the bother, it's a bargain at the price."

"A bargain," Dunavant said and laid the gold onzas on the table, "a real bargain, Captain Teal."

# 16

When Grady reached shore the sailors were weaving around at the water's edge, bellowing for the longboat. He looked carefully up and down the beach expecting that the clamor had already aroused the guard, but seeing no one except the sailors and the three women, he left Simpkins to take care of the situation, climbed the beach and, once beyond it, cautiously skirted the town.

Joe was not at the warehouse. He stood there for a few minutes watching the plaza until the guard came piling out of the barracks and started running toward the shore. Then he went up through the brush to where his horses were tethered, mounted and rode toward the north. It was foolish to wait for the Indian and take a chance on being picked up. In another hour, when the ship sailed and De Zubaran and Curel didn't return, the whole town would be turned upside down. Joe might have followed the men to the beach or he might have gone back to the Indian village. Wherever he was, he was capable of taking care of himself.

Dunavant rode until the moon was overhead, and then, having come to a hill that overlooked the bay, he reined in his horse. Point Loma and old Fort Guijarros lay in front of him, and beyond, the low curving sand bar that enclosed the harbor. He saw a ship lying on the moonlit water, but only one—the other, the *Pilgrim,* had slipped through the entrance and was standing out to sea on the larboard tack, hull down under full canvas.

He sat on the hill and watched the ship grow small and finally melt into the brightness of the sea. And after the ship had disappeared he sat looking at the sea, grinning to himself and thinking of Fraser and Major de Zubaran, and then of Cesaire Curel, feeling again his bitter disappointment as Curel had walked through the door.

His luck had run out on Curel—on the chance he had been waiting for since the night at Kate Howland's—but there was still something to be thankful for, a piece of Irish luck. It would be two weeks, according to Captain Teal, before the *Pilgrim* would sight Diamond Head. A longer time, depending on winds and how soon they could find a ship, before the men could get back to the coast. By that time, if Kroll's plans worked out, the American flag would be flying over every town from the border to San Francisco.

And yet, riding on over the hill and down along the cliffs and the breaking surf and along the surf toward the north, he wondered just how it was going to be accomplished. With the exception of the night's luck, the trip so far had borne no fruit. The best possibility, Juan Bandini, had petered out. Of the two possibilities left, an American rancher on the Santa Ana, and Renaldo Chavez near the Mission San Luis Rey where he was now headed, only Chavez could be counted on. Chavez and his wife could be counted on because one of their daughters had married an American, Tom Risk, who had been arrested by the Mexicans and sent to Tepic at the same time Grady had been sent there. He had known Renaldo Chavez for years and was sure of him.

He made camp at the first stream he crossed, watering and tethering his horses on grass that grew along the bank. Suddenly remembering that he hadn't eaten since noon, he took some jerked beef to chew, rolled out a blanket and, masked from the trail by a thicket of oaks, lay down to sleep.

The surf was pounding hard on the beach and the wind whipped spindrift through the thicket. He lay shivering, chewing the jerked beef, and wondered if Captain Frémont had left Sutter's Fort on the Sacramento. Likely not. There would be plenty of smoke on the Sacramento but no fire. He wondered what had happened to Jacob Kroll in Los Angeles. After his escape, it was possible that Kroll had been rounded up and thrown in the *juzgado*—he and Kate Howland both, along with all the members of the small army they had recruited around the pueblo.

It was an unpromising picture, made worse by the cold and fatigue and the dry beef he was chewing. Even the thought of the three men rolling westward on the long Pacific swells did not brighten the picture. Nor, recalling Bandini's news about Commodore Sloat and the American fleet, the prospect of help from this quarter. Sloat was at Mazatlán, and Mazatlán was in Mexico, fifteen hundred miles to the south.

I wish to hell I was out of the whole thing, he thought, chewing hard on the strip of beef. And then, recalling Cesaire Curel and for some reason Luz de Zubaran and her ancient musket, he thought,

Whatever happens—whether the whole thing blows up—not until then.

The next thing he knew the sun was shining hot through the oak thicket.

In the port of Mazatlán, Commodore Sloat stood in the cabin of the flagship *Savannah.* A mirror was propped on a bulkhead in front of him. His steward had brought him a freshly honed razor and a bowl of lather. It was his custom to shave upon rising, immediately after having given the weather a careful scrutiny through the stern window. But he had spent a restless night and had delayed this chore until after he had eaten breakfast and taken a turn on deck. The morning was now well-advanced, and being a person of punctual habits and strong conscience, he condemned himself for the lapse from routine.

Braced against the awkward movement of the anchored ship—a stocky man with white hair and a sallow morose face—he looked at himself in the mirror, noting the circles under his eyes, the lines of strain around his mouth, the color of his skin. The truth is, he thought, I am sick and long since should have left the rigors and responsibilities of the sea. Instead, I am far from home, out of contact with my superiors in Washington, from whom I have received no direct communication for a year. In the harbor of a country which for all I know is at this very moment at war with the United States. Spied on at every turn by the hostile British Navy, whose ships are not a hundred miles away, in numbers and with guns vastly more powerful than my own.

After hours of indecision, the trivial action of shaving had the power to lighten his depression. And as he progressed from one side of his face to the other, he became aware of things outside himself. The creaking of chains when the ship surged. The steady rhythm of the pumps working at the bilge. A bell tolling in the church across the water. Finally, the sound of voices and feet moving rapidly on the quarter-deck.

The door of the main cabin was open to permit a circulation of air, and as he looked in the mirror, he saw Mr. Bolton, the acting consul in Mazatlán, regarding him from the quarter-deck. He went on with his shaving, embarrassed to be found at his ablutions at this hour of the day, and pretended to be unaware of the other's presence, though it was apparent that the consul was in a state of agitation. Not until he had finished and had drawn on his shirt and carefully buttoned his coat did he ask Mr. Bolton to come in.

The young man held a letter in his hand. "This," he said, "has just arrived from Mexico City. It's from Mr. Parrott, our secret agent, and it's addressed to me, but since it contains news which may be vital to you, I've brought it here without delay."

Sloat asked the young man to sit down, but Bolton stood where he was and began, in a singsong voice that greatly irritated the commodore, to read from the letter. Then the consul paused, and as if all which had gone before was a preamble, began again, now reading deliberately, stopping to look up after each sentence.

"It is clear that Mexican troops, six or seven thousand strong, have by order of the Mexican Government invaded the territory of the United States north of the Rio Grande and have attacked the forces under General Zachary Taylor. It is clear also that the United States Navy has set up a blockade of the Mexican gulf ports." Here young Bolton paused and read the remainder with exaggerated emphasis. "You can tell the commodore, if he is with you, that I did not write to him because there is too much risk, that he has a field open to signalize himself, and I wish him a crown of laurels."

"Is there any question of the letter's validity?" Sloat asked.

"None at all, sir. It arrived by a courier in whom we have absolute trust, and it is, as you can see, in the practically illegible handwriting of Mr. Parrott."

Commodore Sloat looked at Bolton who was nervously folding and unfolding the letter. "If you were to sit down," he said, "we could discuss the matter to better advantage." When the consul seated himself, Sloat began to pace up and down the small cabin. "This certainly appears to be more than a skirmish," he said, to himself rather than to the young man. "It may be said to have very grave aspects. It might even be looked on as war."

Mr. Bolton, who had been sitting on the edge of his seat while the commodore paced the cabin, jumped to his feet. "My God, sir, it *is* war!"

Startled more by the consul's abrupt manner and the tone of his voice than by what he said, Sloat came to a halt. "This is a moment for calmness," he said in rebuke, and then resumed his jerky pacing.

"The Mexicans have invaded the United States," Mr. Bolton said, remaining on his feet. "We have retaliated by blockading their ports. Both are acts of war. No formal announcement is needed, nor is it likely that you will receive one soon."

The commodore was silent.

Mr. Bolton said, "You are well within your instructions to act immediately."

Sloat stopped and looked at the young man, his lips suddenly tight. "The nature of my instructions is unknown to you," he said. "Therefore you cannot advise me."

Mr. Bolton gave no ground. He returned Sloat's angry stare and said, "On the contrary, your instructions are known to me and they are extremely simple. In the event of war you are to proceed north and seize San Francisco and blockade all other California ports."

Sloat's sallow face grew mottled. "My instructions I shall interpret in my own way and in my own time," he said. "When I have made a decision I shall inform you. If you receive any further communications from Mr. Parrott you will please send them to me without delay."

The consul picked up his hat. "You will receive no further word from Mr. Parrott. His letter indicates that. He is in Mexico City, watched and surrounded by the enemy." The young man thrust the letter toward Commodore Sloat. "This is all you will receive. And it is all you need." Outside the door of the cabin he stopped and turned. "I wish to remind you, sir, that Admiral Seymour will be in possession of this information, if he is not already, and that the British intelligence has been consistently better than ours. Furthermore, a British sloop has arrived from San Blas within the hour. I will leave you to interpret what its presence here means."

The commodore, as soon as Mr. Bolton had gone over the side, put on his hat, and with his spyglass went on deck. He should have been informed of the arrival of the British sloop, a dereliction that he would look into later. The sloop lay at anchor about a mile off his starboard beam, and, bringing his glass to bear on her, he saw that she was the twenty-four-gun *Minerva.* A boat had put out from her and was heading across the bay toward the town; a glint of gold braid showed in the stern sheets. It was quite possible, as the brash Mr. Bolton had suggested, that Admiral Seymour had already received the news of hostilities, and that he had sent the sloop here to ascertain if it was also known to the American fleet. At least, it was true that the sloop had come here to spy on him.

He began to pace the quarter-deck, nervously opening and closing the glass, pausing to watch the progress of the boat, then to cast a glance at the *Minerva.* The sun blazed over the swampy shore and there was no air, only the hot stench of tide flats and the lush steaming jungle. There was a canopy over the quarter-deck, but his exertions soon started the sweat rolling down his cheeks. His heart began to race. He decided to return to his cabin, and here he sat through the morning, refusing lunch, getting up every half hour to observe the *Minerva,* making a decision only to change it.

Finally, in mid-afternoon, he sat down at his desk and wrote to Secretary Bancroft in Washington:

*I have, upon mature reflections, come to the conclusion that your instructions of the 24th of June last, and every subsequent order, will not justify my taking possession of any part of California, or any hostile measure against Mexico (notwithstanding their attack upon our troops), as neither party have declared war. I shall therefore, in conformity with those instructions, be careful to avoid any act of aggression until I am certain one or the other party have done so, or until I find that our squadron in the gulf have commenced offensive operations....*

When he had finished with the letter he gave it to his steward and went on deck. The sun was low. The breeze had shifted around from the land and was blowing out of the west. The *Minerva* lay at anchor; the small boat had returned from the town and bobbed alongside. He wished now that he had asked for Mr. Parrott's letter; he remembered the wording, but somehow he felt that if it were in his hands he could better make up his mind. He considered sending ashore for it but decided against giving Bolton the satisfaction of such a request. Then, while he stood grasping the rail of the quarter-deck, the *Minerva's* boat was taken aboard, anchors were weighed, the sloop bore out to sea, turned south around the headland and disappeared.

This action puzzled him and he dwelt on it for the rest of the afternoon and during dinner, which he ate alone and without hunger. At no time since he had sailed from the east coast had he confided in any of his officers. No one aboard the *Savannah* knew why the fleet had been sent to Mexican waters or of the existence of secret instructions. It had been a wise policy, he was sure, but standing again on the quarter-deck, he regretted that there was no one with whom he could talk.

The British sloop had come from San Blas, had stayed for a few hours and had returned. Why had she come? What had she learned while she was in port? What information had she taken back to the powerful British fleet at San Blas, to the seventy-four-gun frigate *Collingwood,* which mounted twenty guns more than the *Savannah?* If the

English admiral had learned of the hostilities on the Rio Grande and now felt certain that the American fleet contemplated no action, would he sail forthwith to the coast of California? Time alone held the answers to these questions.

Of equal importance was the possibility of war with Great Britain over the Oregon issue. Congress and the people had clamored for action throughout the fall of '45. President Polk had expressed his willingness to fight for 54° 40′. The American press had supported the clamor, and the British press had roared back. That was almost a year ago, and since then he had received no further information. No additional resources had been placed at his command, while the British fleet had been vastly strengthened.

But more pressing at the moment was his own course in the light of Parrott's letter. Should he sail north immediately, capture San Francisco, according to the instructions given him by Secretary Bancroft in the event of war, and blockade the ports of San Diego, San Pedro, Santa Barbara and Monterery? If he carried out these orders, and then found that Parrott's letter was in error and no state of war existed, he would be in the position of a filibuster, his actions disowned by his government, himself dishonored and relieved of his command. If he left for California and did nothing more than patrol offshore, he would be completely out of touch with any new information that might arrive in Mazatlán during his absence. On the other hand, if he did nothing—and waited here for additional information, while the British fleet, with information possibly superior to his own, sailed north—he would, if war now existed, be accused of the crime of inaction.

The heavy tropical night settled down on him. He stood looking out across the dark water and the fitful lights of the town.

The ranch house of Renaldo Chavez lay in a fold of the hills, on high ground beside a bend in the Río San Luis Rey, and when Grady Dunavant rode up to it, after twelve hours in the saddle, evening smoke was curling through the sycamores, lights showed in the windows, and the smell of fresh beef cooking hung heavy in the air.

Don Renaldo, a fat little man, grown fatter in the three years since Grady had seen him, with bright, black eyes hidden in folds of flesh, and a wide, bushy mustache turned up at the ends, embraced him at the door and led him into the *placita*, where Doña Petra, as fat and friendly as her husband, also pressed him against the ample shelf of her bosom. They both remarked on how thin he looked, and Doña

Petra said, "You must stay for many days . . . a month, perhaps. Then you'll be able to sit in the saddle comfortably, like Don Renaldo." And her husband said, "No, señora doña, he will stay for the summer. Then he will be able to ride without a saddle." They were delighted that he had come just as they were about to sit down to supper.

Putting his long legs under the table set up on trestles under a big sycamore in the *placita,* Grady's delight more than matched theirs, for the table was spread with mounds of food. Steaming *tortillas* of fine ground corn, paper thin. Bowls of pink and calico frijoles. A great earthen crock filled with stewed quail and wild pigeon. Succulent vegetables from the milpa he had passed as he crossed the river. A haunch of beef, crisp and smoky from an open fire, garnished with chili. And as quickly as one dish was emptied, an Indian trotted over from the outdoor oven and replaced it. Another Indian did nothing but move around the table with a wineskin, filling the cups as soon as they were drained.

At the head of the table sat the host, with his broad hat on the back of his head and his feet dangling short of the earthen floor, eating with a long-bladed knife, eating and drinking and urging everyone else to do the same, in between times tossing morsels over his shoulder to the pack of dogs crouching behind his chair. When her husband wasn't urging him to eat more, Doña Petra, sitting next to him, took up the matter. Only she was more direct, helping him every time she helped herself, which was often. Farther down the table were the four Chavez daughters, Lisa, Sarita, Narcisa and Beatriz, ranging in age from fifteen to eighteen. And in their midst, keeping an eye upon their manners, were two withered crones, aunts or cousins, Grady didn't know which.

As he sat there making up for two days of short rations, he kept thinking about Don Renaldo. Here the Spaniard was, happy in the bosom of his family and surrounded by the fruits of his labor. He began to wonder if, after all, he should ask for his help. Don Renaldo had responsibilities, a ranch of more than twenty thousand acres, a wife and four unmarried daughters. He enjoyed a settled happy life of good food and wine and simple pleasures. He would give his help freely in the struggle, but should it be asked for or accepted?

After supper when the pine torches died out and the air grew cool, they all went into the house, to the big *sala* lighted with deer-tallow candles. Don Renaldo maneuvered him off into a corner, and began to question him, evidently suspicious that there was some reason for his visit. But before he was well started, the girls came up laughing and chattering and insisted that they both join the games. It seemed like a good idea to Dunavant, loosened up as he was by the wine he had drunk at supper.

Everyone joined in, except the elderly aunts, and played Indian *tekersie,* with wooden rings, looping them over wickets, and a game where they chose up sides and with curved sticks each side tried to keep the other from pushing a flat wooden disc to the wall. They played at bullfighting, with a grand formal entrance of the toreador and his entourage, with Don Renaldo, the bull, decked out in a hide and real horns, and each of the others taking turns at being the toreador.

The crones sat in stiff-backed chairs through all this, Dunavant noticed, smoking cornhusk cigarettes, their sharp eyes watching every move the girls made, calling attention if too much ankle showed or a hand unnecessarily touched his hand or laughter was too bold or a glance too lingering. Don Renaldo and his wife, in contrast, were very jolly about everything, urging the girls to be livelier if they paused for a moment to catch their breath, and even thinking it great fun when Beatriz, the youngest, fell back in his arms in pretended fright at the charging bull. They could afford to be indifferent to the actions of their four marriageable daughters, while the old women sat and watched, like a pair of dragons guarding a treasure.

After the games everyone had cakes stuffed with piñon nuts and wine in little gourd cups. Don Renaldo cracked jokes that apparently the family had heard before, and Dunavant added a few of his own, which caused great merriment from all the girls except the oldest, Lisa. During the games she had preserved a quiet demeanor and a faintly superior air as if she found them too childish for her taste, and now while her sisters laughed at everything he said, she kept her gaze averted most of the time, her hands folded in her lap. But when she did look at him her eyes were warm and appealing. He thought of the contrast between her and the De Zubaran girl—one quiet and demure, the other riding around the country, haughty and untamed and wild as a mustang.

The evening ended late. When the women went off to bed, Don Renaldo tried to question him again. Dunavant put him off with a concocted story, but in the morning when he rode away from the ranch, the Spaniard rode with him to the river.

"I have news of trouble in Los Angeles," Don Renaldo said as they parted. "What have you heard?"

"Rumors," Dunavant replied.

"I hear the Americans are plotting to depose Governor Pico. This is something I would like to lend a hand to."

"Rumors," Dunavant said. "Nothing more. But if anything happens I'll let you know."

*"Hasta luego,"* Don Ricardo said.

*"Hasta luego,"* Grady answered.

He climbed out of the valley, through stands of buckthorn and lilac, to a ridge fringed with pines. On the ridge he stopped to breathe his horses. He looked back at the winding river, at the green hills and the ranch of Renaldo Chavez. Smoke was rising through the trees; the sun shone on white adobe walls and the flanks of cattle feeding on the June grass.

It was a peaceful scene that lay below him in the morning light. It was different from the country of the Cajon, but as he looked at it, turning in the saddle and resting one hand on the horn, he saw both things, this and the other—the Santa Ana winding to the sea, and the Río San Luis Rey, the hills and the mountains and the meadows, the red grazing cattle. And in this moment he knew that the vow he had made was not one that he would break. It was stronger than ever it had been. Once—it seemed a long time past—Camilla Howland was a part of the vow. It had seemed then that she was most of it. But now he realized that his love for her had been a dream born of loneliness, a chance meeting, a pretty face, his own imagination. This—the river and the mountains and the hills, the springing grass and the untouched earth—lay deep within him. It was neither a dream nor something that he imagined. It was a part of him—his very fiber and blood.

He made the vow again, sitting there in the saddle, and, cocking his hat back on his head, rode north along the ridge toward the ranch of Tom Risk.

# 17

In the early dawn with his workers gathered around him, Don Saturnino stood on the killing ground. The best cattle had been brought in from the hills and driven into the corrals. Stones had been gathered from the riverbank and arranged to support the big trying pots; oak fagots had been cut; the hardwood stakes for pegging out the hides had been sharpened; the many long-bladed knives shone bright from the whetstone; *botas,* shaped and sewn from green hides, sat in handy rows.

The sun was showing above San Gorgonio. Morning dew rose mistily from the grass, and mist lay across the wide-flowing river. Lowering his head between his massive shoulders and speaking in a loud voice, as if to make sure that God would hear him, Saturnino asked a blessing on the work to be done. There was no sound in the meadow while he spoke; even the fat red cattle looked out quietly from the bars of the corral. Then he gave the signal and the workers ran to their horses.

The first steer, prodded through the gate of the corral, paused for only an instant before it bolted off through the meadow. To Saturnino fell the honor of the first killing. When the animal moved off, he spurred his stallion, overtook it and, with one expert blow, plunged the sharp knife into its throat. Roque rode next. Saturnino, scowling from the saddle, watched his son start after the steer. This was the young man's fifth matanza but he still rode without dash, carrying the knife like a club, spurring his horse when he shouldn't, hanging back when the moment came to strike, as if he were about to slit the throat of his best friend, and though the steer fell at last, a *vaquero* had to ride in to finish it off.

*"Jesús María y todos de los Santos!"* Saturnino ground out between his teeth, motioning for Jorge to take his turn. The boy did well, though it was only his second experience, which made up in some measure for Roque's failure. But it was Luz whom he counted on to take the bitter taste from his mouth. He watched her standing ready at the

gate, the reins held firmly, the short-handled, long-bladed knife held properly so that the blade was pointed backward. She sat erect in the saddle, her eyes tense and shining beneath the shadow of her hat.

The steer came out of the gate swinging its wide horns. It set its sharp yellow hoofs deliberately and blinked angrily at the rising sun. A rangy, powerful beast, he saw, proud that she had not chosen a smaller one. The beast swung its lean skull from side to side and then someone shouted and it started away slowly and began to gather speed. Luz waited. She waited until it was well out into the meadow before she rode in pursuit.

He saw the steer swerve as she came up and the girl swerve with it, keeping the steer on the side where she carried the knife. With one foot out of the stirrup and her knee braced against the heavy pommel, her weight in the other stirrup, he saw her swing down and out. This was the moment. He sat forward in the saddle, saying, "Steady . . . steady," feeling the excitement, the surge of the beast and its hot, moist breath, the danger and dignity of the instant. Then he saw her reach out, bring the blade back in a swift, thrusting blow under the lowered head, being careful to avoid the sharp, down-tilted horns, backward and with all her strength into the soft, unprotected flesh of the neck.

As the steer plunged on for half a dozen strides, stumbled at last and fell upon the grass, Saturnino gave out a mighty shout. *"Ole, ole!"* he cried. "I do no better myself. Mother of God, it is something to see!" And he rode, beaming, toward the corral, having forgotten his son's failure.

The introduction to the matanza and the solemn ceremony of the killing was over. The rest of the slaughtering would be done simply in one of the corrals; what was left was long, tedious, sweaty work for which he had little stomach. He supervised the killing of ten more steers and then, riding among his *vaqueros,* the flaying of the carcasses, the stretching and pegging of the hides for drying, and the trying out of the tallow.

By midmorning, when the knives flashed steadily in the sun and the big pots were filled with bubbling tallow, he left the business to Mitla and Roque, and rode back to the house. Luz rode beside him.

"I am going to the pueblo tomorrow," he said. "How would you like to go with me? We will stop at Vejar's and Cervantes' on the way and we will stay all night with Governor Pico, perhaps. We will have a fine time, I can tell you, *hombre.*"

"I would like to go to Señora Howland's."

"*Ole*, to the señora's. We will go there also—I to sell hides—but what is it that you wish?"

"A dress. Can it be afforded?"

"Anything can be afforded by a De Zubaran," he said largely. "A dress? *Demonio!* You are becoming a grand lady."

"A silk dress," Luz said.

The next afternoon the two De Zubarans rode up from the river toward the town, Don Saturnino on his big stallion and Luz on her palomino, with the hot sun shining on the wet coats of the horses, the heavy silver mountings and the silver chains that dangled from the stirrups. They were countrypeople coming to town, but in their postures and faces there was no hint of awe or uncertainty. They rode shoulder to shoulder at a brisk Spanish trot, their legs long in the hooded stirrups, sitting firmly and confident against the high Moorish cantles.

Unlike his daughter who was dressed in sober buckskin and a plain black broad-brimmed hat, Saturnino was resplendent in his best, saved for just such an occasion. His jacket was dark velvet, fastened with many silver buttons, and under it was a white ruffled shirt held at the waist with two belts of red and green silk. His breeches were of gray cloth, the breeches flap showing buttons made of Mexican pesetas, and his leggings were whole antelope skins, rolled down to his knees and tied there with woven cords that ended in tassels. He wore a green, high-crowned hat with a braided strap under his chin. His boots were yellow and curled up at the toes. Over the back of the saddle was a covering, a *sobre jalma* of tiger skin, and in front of him, on the saddle horn, a silver mirror the size of a soup plate.

Now, as they rode into the plaza, he glanced down at himself in the mirror and, satisfied with what he saw, surveyed the passing throng of carts and riders and shuffling peons. A week ago when he had visited Governor Pico, the town had been pretty well deserted, with people standing around in frightened groups discussing the prospects of war. But since then, the next day in fact, good news had come from the North. General Castro had sent a courier to the governor with a message that everything on the Sacramento was quiet. Frémont had left California and taken his army of bandits into the wilds of Oregon. It was General Castro's opinion that he never again would set foot in California. Skirmishes between Californians and gringos had ceased along the river, as well as the Indian forays instigated by the gringos.

The news had wrought a big change in the town; on every side as he rode toward Señora Howland's, he heard talk of herds and flocks, the height and quality of the grass, the yield of milpas—but nothing, nothing at all of war. Well, perhaps that was good, he thought. Yet he still wished that Frémont had not taken to his heels. He had looked forward to killing a few gringos and he found it disappointing now as he realized that he must forgo the pleasure. What made his disappointment greater was the knowledge that he had missed the chance to capture the gringo who had come to the gate the morning he had left for the pueblo. He had not learned until he saw the governor that the man was being hunted. And there he had stood at the gate looking at the gringo, six paces away. Mother of God, but it was a bitter pill to swallow!

They tied their horses at the hitch rail in front of Señora Howland's and went into the store. Saturnino, thinking of the gringo who had escaped and Frémont who had turned tail and run away, felt the need of a drink, but it was better, he decided, to wait until he was through with the señora—he would require all of his wits, since she was a hard woman.

"You look around, *hombre,*" he said to his daughter, "and select anything you want. Silk, satin, it makes no difference. I will be back in a short time with a jacket full of money."

He left Luz at the counter and went to the rear of the store where Señora Howland sat on a stool in front of an open ledger. He bowed and greeted her with a hearty bluffness he did not feel. In the ten years and more the De Zubarans had been doing business with her, the relationship had not varied from one year to the next—it was a polite but wary affair in which no favors were asked or given.

The long-jawed, sharp-eyed woman looked up from the ledger and gave him a greeting as bluff as his own, but the gaze, as customary, was cautious and frosty.

"Damn my eyes, if it isn't Don Saturnino de Zubaran dressed up like the governor himself!" She laid down her pen and closed the ledger. "You're getting handsomer by the year, Don Saturnino. It's a wonder to me how you stay single. Now if I was younger . . ." She gave him a wink and a bawdy smile, and then her lips froze up and she said suddenly, "Hides to sell?"

"One thousand and eight hundred, more or less. We started slaughtering yesterday and will be through by next week."

The señora hummed a tune in her nose. "Prices aren't much this year," she said. "Twenty-five cents less than last season, but with things the way they are, it's a God's wonder I'm able to offer anything. You heard about me being hauled off to jail?"

He knew about it, but he said he had not.

"Yes, they came about a week ago—that Morales and his soldiers—and put me into the *calabozo* on a trumped-up charge. But I didn't stay long. I raised billy-hell till they were glad to let me out."

Offering his regrets, he refrained from questioning her version of the arrest or the reason why she was released. He could well imagine the hell she had raised, but it wasn't this which had led the governor to pardon her; it was the news General Castro had sent from the North.

"It's scared off all the ships," she said indignantly. "Brought the price of hides down, because there's no use buying them if they're going to be confiscated. As it is, there's no telling when Morales will be popping in here again. It's really nonsense for me to offer you anything."

Demons! he thought. There is always some reason why the prices are less than last year. But this year the reason is real enough. I would have given my right ear to have seen the señora in the jailhouse.

"And I'll give you nothing," she said, ducking behind the counter and coming up with a heavy sack, "if that nuisance of a Morales tries any more of his monkeyshines." She counted out eight stacks of gold, and, after glancing in the ledger, subtracted two stacks and returned them to the leather sack. "I was sorry to learn of your father's death. A fine man, Don Cristóbal, and very prompt in his payments." She looked in the ledger again and then looked up at him over the top of her spectacles. "You know there's a loan of four thousand dollars which I made to Don Cristóbal the year of the drought?"

"Yes, I remember, and wish to have the sale of the tallow applied against it."

The señora closed the ledger. "There's no hurry, none at all. I just mentioned it so as to keep things straight. I like everything straight—especially money matters." She scribbled a receipt and passed it and the coins across the counter. "I've already taken out seven hundred and twenty dollars for a year's interest. That's at the regular rate of eighteen percent. And there's the deduction for goods you've bought during the year, which comes to two hundred and sixteen dollars. But we'll forget the extra amount and make it a round figure—two hundred."

"Thanks," Saturnino said, though he was sure she was not cheating herself. Deeming it beneath his dignity to count the money in front of him, he shoveled it into his pocket.

"I hope our dealings will be friendly," the señora said. "Like those between Don Cristóbal and myself."

Saturnino, thinking of his parched throat, bowed.

"And if you happen to talk to that Morales, you might mention that there'll be no market for hides or tallow either one if he doesn't mind his business."

"Doña señora, I will see this Morales before the day is finished and put a large flea in his ear."

Saturnino bowed again and left for the tavern, laughing already at the fun he would have when he saw Morales and learned all the details of her arrest. As he stood in the tavern drinking a cup of brandy, his thoughts still dwelt on it. He wondered what would happen to the loan if Señora Howland were put in jail again and kept there.

In the store Luz was looking at the shelves stacked with bolts of cloth when Kate Howland came sidling along the counter.

"What will it be, dearie? Gingham or Indian silk or Irish linen or flannel? Perhaps a nice length of lace bobbinet? Or bayeta, bishop's lawn, velveteen or cambric muslin?"

"A dress," Luz said.

"Oh!"

"A silk dress."

"A silk one, well, well. Now let's see. . . ."

Luz, watching her disappear toward the rear of the store, could well understand the señora's surprise. It had been two years since she had had a new dress, and never a silk one. Everyone at the ranch, as a matter of fact, had been surprised when she had told them that she was going to the pueblo to buy a silk dress, especially Carlota, who had paused with a cup of chocolate halfway to her mouth and sat there for a full minute before she said, "*Sancta Trinidad,* it is time!" Afterward, openly suspicious, Carlota had tried to ferret out her reasons for suddenly wanting a dress. But her grandmother had failed, everyone had failed—even Don Saturnino who had brought up the subject several times during the trip to the pueblo.

The dress Señora Howland brought back was pink and very ugly. Moreover, Luz realized suddenly, she had seen one like it before.

"It's not of the latest mode," she said.

"From Boston this very year, dearie."

"Dorotea Bustamente wore one just like it when she came to the ranch last summer."

The señora looked puzzled for an instant, and then she gave her thigh a resounding slap. "I clean forgot. I was thinking of another dress. Just a moment and I'll fetch it."

It was ruffled and prettier than the other, but of a style that had been popular the year before. Besides, it was green. Luz shook her head. She had not bought a new dress for two years, but she still knew what was becoming and what was not.

Mrs. Howland, retreating to the cupboard in the rear of the store, decided that there was no further use in trying to palm off the last of the three dresses which had been left over from the previous year—Luz de Zubaran was a hotheaded piece who might end up by flouncing out of the store. She hung up the green creation and ran her eye over the two dresses that remained from the six that Grady Dunavant had brought in from Santa Fe. One, a prize of apricot-colored silk, she was saving for Camilla. She took down the other dress, laid it over her arm, and closed the cupboard.

As she turned away, she stopped, and her jaws snapped shut. Even now, after everyone in the pueblo knew that Mr. Fraser had gone to Mazatlán as an emissary of the British government, Camilla still pretended that she was in love with him. That very morning her daughter had defied her, vowing that she would marry the Englishman as soon as he came back. Kate Howland's jaws clamped tighter; she opened the cupboard. Camilla might marry Mr. Fraser—over her dead body—but she wouldn't marry him in the apricot-colored dress.

Luz gasped. It was the most beautiful thing she had ever seen, shimmering as she held it to the light, changing colors like a chameleon in the sun. She stood and looked at it and said nothing.

"Direct from St. Louis, señorita. Mr. Dunavant brought it in last week. I've been saving it for myself, but it'll be better on you. Mr. Dunavant said he bought it off a man who had just come from St. Louis, so it's the latest style."

"Who is Mr. Dunavant?" Luz said. She felt her heart beat in her throat, as she had felt it beat when his name was first spoken. The name was familiar and yet unfamiliar on her lips.

"A Santa Fe trader, dearie. Now let's try it on and see if it fits. Over there. . . ."

Luz took the dress. She was starting toward the row of barrels Kate Howland had indicated, when someone spoke behind her—a young woman, fashionably dressed, with diamonds in her ears, tall and slender and beautiful. At the moment Luz turned and looked at her, she thought, This is the woman Julio told me about—Yris Llorente. She is the one who let the American escape from the garden. This is the woman who is in love with him!

Yris Llorente had said something to Mrs. Howland, who now replied, "When you were here yesterday, the dress was spoken for. Since then the party has changed her mind."

"You might have let me know," Señora Llorente said. "You could have sent a servant."

"I didn't know until a moment ago, just before this young lady came in."

Señora Llorente glanced at Luz. It was a slow calculated glance which started at her boots and ended with the braided strap under her chin and her broad hat.

Then she said, "It's a shame to waste a beautiful dress on a person who obviously is unable to appreciate it," and turned away.

Luz' eyes flashed after her, but out of pride she did not answer. That is the woman, she thought again, and slipped into the dress.

Mrs. Howland stood off a pace and surveyed her. "Hold still now while I see how the waist fits and how it is for length." She clucked to herself and said, "A little shorter in the skirt. You have such nice ankles—they're like mine. Ankles are important. That's how I came to marry Mr. Howland. Saturday afternoon and I was coming down the steps of the conservatory. Raining cats and dogs, and I had my dress lifted a mite to keep it out of the slosh. Just a mite, and along came the mister. Of course, it could have been on account of the way I played the piano. But the mister always said not. He said he just looked up and saw a pair of fine ankles coming down the steps and decided right then and there."

Her back was turned to Yris Llorente but she could feel the other's eyes examining her.

Mrs. Howland said, "The waist will have to be taken in. You have a small one, dearie. Small as mine used to be. That's a mark of beauty, almost as important as ankles." Cluck, cluck. "The hips need a wee bit, too. You haven't any more than a snake. Riding around all the time like you do, you should have more."

Yris Llorente said, "It obviously doesn't fit. And the color is bilious. It's the Mexican blood, I am afraid, and too much sun."

"Is anyone at the ranch clever at sewing?" Mrs. Howland asked.

"My grandmother," Luz said, as if she had not heard Yris Llorente's insult.

"It doesn't need much, just a snip here and there. Now for the bust.

Uh-huh, it needs letting out—a gusset on each side. You can steal the material from the skirt. You're big for your age, dearie. But that's not against you. There's nothing like a good bust to catch the eye. Important as ankles, I always say. Men place a great store by them, though I could never understand why."

Luz heard the click of heels on the wooden floor and, turning as the door opened, she saw Yris Llorente, silhouetted briefly against the hot light in the lane, lift her slender arms to raise a white parasol between her and the sun, a graceful, deliberate motion full of beauty and disdain. The door closed. Luz smelled the odor of the woman, a sweet cloying scent which hung in the room long after she had gone.

She is beautiful, Luz thought standing there with the perfume heavy around her. She is beautiful, Luz thought as she rode homeward. She is beautiful and she is in love with him!

Sitting at the table eating her supper, with the spicy odors of food sharp in the room, and the strong smell of horses and cattle her brothers had brought in from the killing grounds, Luz could still smell the scent Yris Llorente had left behind her in the store. She could see her standing at the counter, her cheeks the creamy paleness of a yucca bloom and the wide mouth curved and red, pausing in the doorway to open her parasol before she stepped into the sun. She heard again the insults the woman had spoken: they were more galling now than when she had heard them first.

She ate in silence, feeling her cheeks burn and her throat fill with anger. And then she heard herself say, in a voice that surprised her with its coldness and intensity, "Why doesn't Governor Pico arrest Yris Llorente, the traitress, and place her against a wall and shoot her as she deserves?"

Saturnino had been talking about the American and the efforts Lieutenant Morales was still making to track him down. "*Ay María!*" he was saying, "to think that the gringo was at the gate, six paces away, and I did not know." He shook his head in despair and then, hearing her words, glanced up from his plate. "A fine suggestion, *hombre.* It is something Morales would like to do and would, believe me, if it were not for Governor Pico."

"Why waste words on a woman," Roque broke in, "when a gringo is loose in the country seeking to do us harm?"

Saturnino grunted. "You encountered him at the San Gabriel and did little but pass the time of day."

"You likewise, in the business of the gate."

"I did not know then what I know now," Saturnino defended himself.

"Nor did I," Roque answered. "But the time will come. . . . "

"And All Saints' Day."

"It will come," Roque repeated and smiled a curious smile to himself.

Doña Carlota made a sound in her thin nose. "We have enough, both of you, without seeking trouble. There is no time to cavort around the valley with slaughtering half finished and the rodeo yet to take place, as well as other things." She looked sharply at Luz. "And for you, there are things also. In the morning if the day is fair, we will wash. It will occupy your thoughts, I hope, so that you will have less time to worry about this woman being placed before a wall."

Afterward, when she started off across the courtyard to her room, Luz heard Roque walking along behind her. She stopped and waited for him.

He did not speak until they had reached the door of her room. Then he lowered his voice and said, "Can you keep a secret? Say nothing to Don Saturnino or anyone about what I will tell you?" Luz nodded. "Then listen to this. It came this evening as we were leaving the killing grounds, from Cisneros. The gringo is now at the ranch of Tomás Risk!"

"Are you certain?" she said in a level voice.

"Cisneros saw him there this morning—him and the spotted pony."

She spoke calmly, though her throat seemed too tight for words. "What is it?"

"That I cannot tell you, because I have yet to decide. But of whatever nature it will be an honor to the De Zubarans." He clutched her arm. "Speak to no one. It is something which belongs to me. I do it alone, without help or advice."

She felt the trembling of his hand and knew suddenly that there was nothing she could say to deter him. For many years he had suffered the lash of Saturnino's tongue, been taunted and cursed for his timidity, and now, at last, he had discovered the means to vindicate himself. He had built up his courage to a point where any antagonism from her would only increase it.

"The gringo rides past here tomorrow or the next day or the day which follows. If not, then I will go to the ranch of Tomás Risk." He again demanded secrecy of her. "Say nothing to anyone."

"To no one," she said, and left him.

When the day came up clear, with a hot wind suited for drying blowing in from the desert, Carlota ordered preparations for the wash. By the time the sun was two hours high, the carts had been loaded, baskets of food prepared, and the cavalcade was rumbling down the trail to the river. Luz, on her black *mesteño,* rode ahead, followed by Carlota in a cart by herself—one larger than the others, with a girl walking beside the oxen; then came two carts filled with chattering Indian women. Bringing up the rear were three carts filled with wash, mountain-high, since the last washing had been done in the spring, three months before.

All the Indians wore their best dresses, but only for the ride to the river and back. At the river they would change into slips, and then at the end of the day, again into their dresses for the trip home, where the men, back from the matanza, would be waiting, as delighted to see them as if they were returning from a hundred-mile journey. Luz also wore her best dress, though there were yet several things left to do to it, and Carlota had made a great fuss when she had appeared with it on. "To go washing!" she had grumbled. "An eagle does not catch flies. Neither does one wear a silk dress to the river."

Jolting along in the cart, Carlota was still grumbling, but Luz did not hear her. She heard nothing and her eyes looked at the mountains, rayed now with the sun, the sun shining on the snow fields, without seeing them. This was always a holiday on the ranch—sunny hours on the river and the water flowing by, working and gossiping and consuming baskets of food, lying in the warm grass thinking.

Not these things today, she thought. Today it will be different.

She had lain through the night, sleeping and waking up with the question never out of her mind. She could not tell Saturnino, because he would encourage Roque to go in pursuit of the American, and would probably go himself. Carlota would make an effort to stop both of them, but she would not succeed. Only one thing was clear—it had been clear from the instant Roque had told her and sworn her to secrecy; it had been clear even before that, when Julio de Zubaran had come to the ranch just after the American had left and she had said, in answer to his inquiry, that she had not seen the American. She knew then and she knew now, and last night, when out of anger and jealousy she had wished for the death of Yris Llorente.

"They will not find him," she said aloud. "If they do, they will not harm him. This I swear." And then as she rode into the river, holding the dress high out of the water, she thought again of the woman with the creamy pale cheeks and red mouth. She is in love with the American. She is beautiful and knows all the graces of the city. All the arts of love-making are in her face. But she will never have him. Never, never in her life.

Doña Carlota sat in the grass with her back against a fallen tree, her thin legs thrust out in front and her shoes off. She had waded in the river, but the water which came out of the mountains from the melting snow was icy cold, even though the day was warm, and her feet had become so chilled she thought they would drop off. They were beginning to thaw out now, with the hot sun pouring down into the meadow, but she had been a fool nonetheless, trying to act like a filly when she was really an old bell mare of seventy.

She would know better the next time—or would she? People never seemed to acquire sense with the passing years; the longer they lived the more like themselves they became—foolish at the start, then they were always foolish. Really, she thought, she should not have come at all. It would have been much more comfortable in bed, instead of rousing herself at dawn, bouncing her old bones apart on the long trip to the river, wading in cold water, sitting propped up against a log, on ground which in spite of the grass was as hard as stone. And this was not all. She would have to sit for many hours listening to the silly chatter of the Indians, eat the concoctions which they had brought and which would give her indigestion, and then after a long day bounce back up the trail to the ranch.

And all for what reason? Not because she didn't know better; except for the business of wading, she did. It was simply that Saturnino had insisted she come along in the role of chaperon. To chaperon what? she had asked him. Certainly not his daughter, who had been flying around the countryside since she was old enough to ride, and who had suffered no visible harm. Nor the Indian girls, who had experienced everything which could conceivably befall them, and that went for each of them—for Lupe, Consuelo, Encarnación, Violante and Nieves, for Gertrudes, Sarita and Raquel, for the oldest, Merced, as well as her offspring, Juanita.

She raised her eyes now and fixed them on Juanita, who was soaping a shirt spread out on a rock beside the stream. Eighteen years ago Don Cristóbal had brought the girl's mother to the ranch, having purchased her from the Ute who on one of their raids had stolen her from the mission. Merced was a San Gabriel Indian, a *chichinabro,* which meant, in their language, a reasonable being, and in the ensuing years, though she had not strictly lived up to the name, she had been a prolific getter of children, seasonally carrying one, with another hanging onto her skirts. Juanita's father had been a Sonoran, a trader in horses, who had ridden to the ranch one evening and departed the next. How he had become the father of Juanita was somewhat of a mystery, for in those days the unmarried girls were carefully watched in the daytime and locked up at night.

But it had happened and it continued to happen with such regularity, despite all surveillance, to Merced and also the others, that Don Cristóbal had finally given up and thrown the lock away. It was nature or the climate, he did not know which, but he was not going to spend his days worrying about something that could not be helped. Thereafter they confined themselves to a periodic accounting. When Father Expeleta came out from Los Angeles every two or three months, they would round up all the unmarried girls, marry them off to any unattached males that chanced to be available, and if none was, the children were given good resounding names and solemnly baptized. It had been a fine arrangement and everyone was happy, even Father Expeleta and the dragooned males.

Carlota's gaze shifted from Merced's daughter to a girl standing well out in the stream, rinsing a dress. Unlike the other Indians who were bandy-legged and black as pots, this one was handsome, light-skinned, with straight nicely rounded limbs. She had never seen the girl before —someone, she supposed, who had come from an adjoining ranch to enjoy the holiday. Or could it be a stray who had wandered into the herd?

She called the girl and asked her to fetch the bag and parasol from the cart. When the girl had brought them, the old lady asked her to remain, rummaged in the bag for the silver box, poured tobacco from the box into a cornhusk and lighted the cigarette. Then she adjusted her parasol and leaned back against the log.

"Who are you?" she asked.

"My name is Guadalupe."

"Where do you live?"

The girl raised her arm and pointed into the east, toward a chain of mountains twenty leagues away. "In the Santa Rosas," Guadalupe said.

"What are you doing here, so far from home?"

The girl was puzzled. "I am here because of your son."

Carlota fell silent, suddenly remembering that Don Saturnino had spoken several weeks ago about purchasing a servant from the Santa

Rosas, despite the fact that the ranch was already overrun with Indians. She had supposed at the time that he had a *vaquero* in mind. So it was not this after all! The suspicion came to her that Saturnino's insistence on her coming along as chaperon might have been dictated by his concern over the girl.

"Do you wish anything more?" Guadalupe asked.

Carlota gave a jump, having forgotten that the girl was standing beside her. "Get on with your work," she said. "And quit lurking around to scare people."

As Guadalupe started toward the river, Carlota called her back. She glanced up at the girl, and noting the sensuous mouth, the wild deep-set eyes, and again the light-colored skin, thinking that she probably had a Spanish father, she felt the suspicion of a moment before grow into a conviction. With the conviction came a sudden resolve.

"You have been here on the Hawk then for two weeks."

"Since the last moon," the girl corrected her.

"Since the last moon then, and have you made friends . . . among the men?"

"None."

"Not Mitla?"

"Who is Mitla?"

"He works in the blacksmith shop."

"He has gray hairs."

"And sense, which sometimes goes with them," Carlota said. "And he is neither married nor spoken for."

"If he is neither one nor the other, then there is something wrong with him."

Carlota smiled. This one is independent, she thought, and no fool, a circumstance that would make her plans more difficult than they might otherwise have been. "Speak to him tonight," she said, "and tell me in the morning if you are not wrong."

She dismissed Guadalupe and when the girl had gone, sat puffing on her cornhusk. She marveled at the brazenness of her son in bringing an unneeded girl to the ranch—an attractive one in the bargain who would surely stir up jealousy among the others; she marveled also at her own acceptance of the role of chaperon—how she had been forced to jump into her clothes, hurry up her breakfast and make the weary, bone-jolting trip to the river. And for what? Of all things, to keep an eye on a girl she had never seen before, Saturnino's latest prize. Well, she would keep her eye on the girl, and on Saturnino also, who would live to regret the insult he had inflicted upon his unsuspecting mother.

Carlota gazed out at the river flowing past her, broad and shallow and quiet here where it ran over a sandy bottom. The Indians stood knee-deep in the water that swirled around their legs like water around rooted trees; the clothes they were rinsing, trailed out in colored banners on the swift clear current. Her eyes drifted over the meadow, already dotted with drying clothes, and came to rest on her granddaughter.

Luz was standing at the edge of the river, soaping and beating out a blanket. Her movements, usually quick, were now, Carlota noticed, absent-minded; every few minutes she would pause to look out across the meadow, up the river or down, and when she waded into the stream to rinse the blanket, she continued to dawdle. Finally the blanket swept out of her grasp; only then did she bestir herself to retrieve it, glancing over her shoulder to see if she had been noticed.

She had, and from under the parasol, which conveniently gave the illusion of sleep, the old lady watched her throughout the morning. Carlota wondered what in the world had come over her. For the past three or four days Luz had been acting strangely, picking at her food when usually she had a healthy appetite, forgetting tasks she was supposed to do, and, being reprimanded, quick to think of a short answer. And there was the scene this morning over the silk dress when she had flared up like tinder in dry grass.

Could Julio de Zubaran's recent visit have something to do with it? He had stopped at the ranch four days ago, which coincided with the beginning of the girl's strange actions, but somehow she doubted that her granddaughter would be concerned over whatever he might have said or done, for the simple truth was, though engaged to him, Luz was not in love with him.

"And how could she be?" Carlota asked herself.

There was a young man for you, she thought, with his passion for cockfights and cards, his conceit and his silky mustaches that hung down on each side of his mouth like mice tails, too dressed up in his gaudy uniforms to do any work if it came along and too lazy if it did. Not that he didn't have a certain charm or was any worse than the rest of the young men she had seen around. But compared with the men who had settled the country, with his own father for instance, he was a pretty poor excuse. Don Felipe, like her husband, had traveled over land thousands of miles from Mexico City, contending with hunger and thirst on the way. He had taken a wilderness and built a home out of material dug from the earth, raised cattle and corn and a family. He was a man of resource and industry. His son, like the sons of other men, was a lazy seeker after pleasure, who soon would not be worth houseroom.

Julio was admired for his prowess with the ladies. But there was little doubt that once married he would forsake his nocturnal prowlings and settle down, with only occasional relapses, into the customary role of a husband—by turns indulgent and arrogant, jealous and indifferent. Inevitably, once his wife had grown fat and had many children tugging at her skirts, he would find a slimmer and more congenial pillow for his passions.

This was the cycle as she had seen and lived it—certain as the turning of the earth and the coming of the seasons and the rising of the sun—but when she thought of her granddaughter, something in her rebelled against it. She wanted to break the familiar pattern and the accepted custom. She wanted more for the girl than she herself had been able to wrest from life. She wanted it for Luz, who, despite her faults, had a spirit which was worthy of a better fate than this, and for herself, in revenge against the humiliations she had been forced to suffer.

At noon while they ate their lunch, Carlota studied her granddaughter, leading the conversation into paths that she thought might reveal some small clue from which the whole might be unraveled. But Luz was reticent or sly, she couldn't decide which, and by the time the girl had gone off to put out the last of the clothes, she remained as puzzled as ever. She made another cigarette and sat smoking and thinking until at last, her brain weary, lulled by the heat of the day, she fell asleep. When she woke the sun was across the river, slanting under her shade, and the washing had already been gathered.

It was then, as she folded her parasol and walked toward the cart, that the answer to the problem presented itself. On the trail that ran parallel to the river, at a distance of a half mile, was a lone horseman. He was riding a spotted pony and leading another. She could tell at a glance from the way he rode and the character of the horses that he was not a Spaniard. She thought nothing of this at first, but a moment later as she climbed into the cart and turned to sit down, everything became clear.

Luz was standing in the meadow, with her hand on the picket rope, facing toward the south. She was looking at a point where the King's Highway looped around the hills and the sun lay along it in a level yellow swath, beyond the horseman. Her attitude, Carlota noticed, was no other than it had been during the day. But then, as Luz shifted her gaze to take in the trail where it ran beside the river, in the act of turning away she suddenly stopped, transfixed. The picket rope fell from her hand.

With a bemused smile, Carlota seated herself and waited for the rest of the story to unfold. She did not have long to wait. As soon as Luz had mounted her horse, she rode up to the cart. Her face was composed but there was color in her cheeks, and when she spoke, making an effort to be casual, her words were tense with excitement.

"I have lost a *reata* somewhere," she said. "Probably on the other side of the river."

Carlota's lips drew together. Her granddaughter apparently took her for a fool. "It is likely at the ranch," she said.

"I looked for it there this morning."

"Look again," Carlota said, still disgusted with herself for having spent most of the day dwelling on a false scent. "You were in such a state this morning that you would not have seen the *reata* even if it had been hanging around your neck."

"But I looked, Doña Carlota. With your permission, I will cross the river here and meet you at the house."

The old lady made a wry face. "Since when have you found it necessary to ask my permission about anything?" Let the girl fret and stew, she thought; it will teach her not to trifle with her grandmother. "Why all this sudden concern about what I will think?"

Luz, whether she had heard these questions or not, didn't answer. She had turned in the saddle and was looking again into the south. Carlota followed her gaze. The horseman had left the King's Highway where it approached the river and, instead of taking the trail which wound past them and on through the Hill of the Hawk, had made a crossing upstream. He was heading west through the hills.

"He has good cause to avoid us," Carlota said.

Luz started in the saddle. The color on her cheeks deepened. She looked quickly around the meadow and finally at Carlota.

"Out with it, *hombre,*" Carlota said, "and do not speak like a Catalonian, from both sides of your mouth at once."

The old lady was not prepared for it when it came. She expected the obvious, a repetition of the business about the *reata* or a guarded admission perhaps, but not that Roque, her grandson, was mixed up in a plot against the American. She sat with her mouth agape until the girl had finished.

"I will attend to the young señor," she said then, motioning the Indian to start the oxen. She looked up at Luz erect and motionless in the saddle. "Why do you sit there?" she burst out. "Bestir yourself!"

# 18

Grady Dunavant, having crossed the Santa Ana and halted on the far bank to water his horses, debated whether to ride on or to camp. For several minutes he sat there in the gathering dusk and then swung down, tethered his horses and started a fire in the grassy tree-protected swale that lay between the brow of a hill and the river.

He had ridden since early morning without rest or food; Jim Wolfe's ranch was still better than three hours away—a difficult trip until the moon came up, since he would no longer be traveling a well-marked trail. He was a safe distance from the Hill of the Hawk, with two lines of hills between him and the De Zubarans. Night was coming on.

In his rucksack were only a few stale *tortillas* and a slab of goat cheese, which a sheepherder had given him that morning, but, crossing the river, he had seen trout lying on the sandy bed, their green backs and pink-mottled sides showing bright in the clear water. He took a fishline from his rucksack and caught hoppers in the grass, tracking them down and trapping them under his hat. The water was fast, sucking the line out and then eddying it back where the current ran deep beneath the undercut bank. Before all the line had run out on the wood bobbin, a trout began to mince at the bait. He gave it a chance to swallow the hopper and then struck. With the bite of the hook the fish swung from under the bank in a wide swift arc that made the line slice the water. Stepping downstream to a sandy beach, he brought it in.

He caught five trout without moving upstream, and cut five green branches, skewered each fish and slanted them over the fire. Then he spread his blanket in the grass, unwrapped the *tortillas* and goat cheese and squatted by the fire, turning the spits deliberately as the trout browned and the skins began to break and show rich white meat.

The wind had died down. In the quiet dusk a calf was bawling by the river and cattle were moving through the trees to drink. Farther off, along the main trail, he heard the rumbling of carts, and beyond this the crying of the carrion birds he had seen before he had crossed the river, a dark cloud hovering over what he had presumed was the De Zubaran killing ground. It annoyed him to think of all the good beef, the hundreds of carcasses lying there untouched to rot and be fed on by the birds, while he had to be satisfied with fish. He glanced at the fat cattle moving down to the river. In the old days when he had first come to California, he wouldn't have hesitated to kill one of them and leave the hide staked out to dry as evidence of his thanks. But he didn't dare to do it now; in fact, he was taking a chance sitting here broiling a mess of fish.

It's a hell of a thing, he thought bitterly, when an American has to go skulking around the countryside. He turned the fish and thought of the ranch he was going to own when the fighting was over. There'll be beef then—haunches and shoulders and thick steaks—and no squatting over a fire, listening to every sound, in fear of your life.

A moment later he heard brush breaking and the rustle of leaves. More cattle, he thought, on the way to the river, or deer. The fire was between him and the sounds, and he didn't see that it was a horse and rider until they were on the swale, less than fifty paces from him. He stood up out of the glare and smoke, his hand moving to his Colt.

*"Hola,"* he said.

It was a girl. She came riding up from the river through the trees, with the firelight shining on her yellow dress, sitting stiff in the saddle and the reins held loosely in her lap. He had seen a group of women at the river, as he came down the trail; this, undoubtedly, was one of them. His hands fell to his side, and again he said, *"Hola."*

"I saw the fire," the girl said.

She had ridden up within a dozen steps of him and pulled in her horse, but it was not until he heard these words that he recognized her. He looked at the silk dress and the laced shoes, without spurs, and the slender ankles and the feminine posture. She was bareheaded and her hair was braided and wound high on her head. She spoke again before he answered.

"I saw you as you came along the trail," she said.

Even her voice had changed, he noticed. It was no longer haughty and condescending; the words were softer, more feminine, the vowels accented in a manner he had never heard except in Santa Fe. He couldn't help thinking of the first time they had met, and as he did, he remembered also his anger, the single contemptuous word she had flung in his face.

"You're in time for supper," he said.

She looked at the fire and the spitted fish and then at him. "You must know that soldiers are searching for you in the pueblo."

"I'm a long way from there," he answered indifferently. "There are enough trout for two."

"And that others are searching for you."

"No doubt," he said casually to cover his surprise. "From here to San Diego." He looked at her sitting stiffly in the saddle and was silent. He shouldn't be surprised, he thought. There was no reason why everyone in the valley should not be out searching for him—the news had had more than a week to spread around. Then he said, "Apparently *you're* not, or you'd be carrying a musket."

She ignored his jibe. "My brother is one of them," she said.

"I've encountered him before."

"You will again if you stay here."

"I'm not staying any longer than it takes me to eat."

"That is good," she said. "For both of you."

He understood what she meant. "Yes, for both," he replied.

The trout were burning and he stooped and took them off the skewers and laid them on a flat rock. When he looked up she was standing beside the fire, watching him. He smiled to himself and set the rock with the trout on it in the middle of the blanket and with his knife divided the cheese, hammering the knife with his hand, and spread out the *tortillas*.

"Sit down," he said.

She sat down across the blanket from him. "I am not hungry," she said, but she took one of the trout nonetheless, and a *tortilla*. He offered her a piece of the goat cheese. "It's too hard," she objected.

"You have strong teeth."

"It's my wish to keep them."

She sat with her dress spread out around her. Threads of firelight ran over it, shifting and changing color as she moved, and as the flames moved in a faint wind. There was something familiar about the dress, but he didn't know what it was. It had puffs at the shoulders and long sleeves, which fitted tight around the wrists, and a row of small buttons down the bodice.

She saw him looking at the dress and said, "I bought it at Señora Howland's."

"It's becoming. More so than what I've seen you wearing before." His eyes ran over her slowly. "You look like a woman now."

She was silent, and he saw that she was embarrassed by what he had said, especially the way he had looked at her when he had said it. He was certain that the embarrassment was pretended, for no girl who ran around the country as she did could be so innocent.

"You don't even recognize it," she said after a moment. "It's a dress you brought from Santa Fe."

He reached across the blanket and touched the skirt, felt it between his fingers, realizing that it was the dress he had bought for Camilla.

"I like it," she said.

"I was hoping that someone like you would get it," he said. He looked at her again and thought that she filled the dress better than Camilla ever would. "After a thousand miles of desert and rivers, you like to know that it's appreciated. That it's being worn by a beautiful girl and not some fat old woman."

The girl was eating now; and as far as he could tell, not listening to him. She ate as if she were hungry. She made small noises with her mouth and tossed the trout bones, of which there were plenty, into the grass. Her head was lowered a little, but he could see the curve of her chin, the hollows in her cheeks and at the temples, the full breasts straining at the bodice. He noticed her fingers, the strong wrists, square yet delicately formed, and the turn of her arms as they disappeared into the tight sleeves. He tried to imagine Camilla Howland sitting in the grass in a silk dress, eating fish with her fingers, sitting with a stranger and night coming on. As a matter of fact, it was hard enough to imagine Luz de Zubaran doing so, everything considered.

When she had finished, she left him and went down to the river and washed her hands. He threw another stick on the fire and, to fortify himself, took a drink from a skin of wine he had picked up at Pala. Luz came back and stood by the fire but refused his offer of wine. She stood very primly with her hands at her sides, watching the light that shone across the swale, over the wet sand and the river, her head turned to one side in an attitude of thoughtful innocence. He looked at her and frowned. The other girl, the one in the leather jacket and breeches and roweled boots, with the musket and the wild, half-savage eyes, was more to his liking. The silk dress had worked a change with her, and with him also. He could cope with the girl who insulted him on the trail, give her as good as she asked for, but the guilelessness of this one, even though it were put on, gave him pause.

He looked at the faint streak of light that still showed along the crest of the mountains, forgetting her for the moment, and thought of the long trip which lay ahead of him. As he stood there making up his mind, he heard running hoofs, the sound muffled and intermittent. He saw a gray stallion come to the far bank and pause, his neck arched and his flowing tail extended.

A herd of horses appeared slowly and quietly from the brush and stood behind the stallion, waiting for him to move into the stream or turn back. The sound of their breathing carried across the swale. The stallion lowered his head and picked his way daintily into the river, thrust his muzzle into the water and drank. Then he lifted his head, moved deliberately for a few steps and broke into a gallop. The herd poured down over the bank and followed him, running in a compact group up the stream, spray rising around them, and disappeared.

"They'll be back," the girl said, a sudden note of excitement in her voice. "It's love play."

And as she spoke, the stallion *did* come into view, still running hard, his mane and tail flowing out in the wind. The herd was behind him but he was moving away. He increased the distance and then, as if he had proved he could and was satisfied, drew up and began to nuzzle the water again. When the herd came up and ranged around him, he bared his teeth and swung his head, nipping at their flanks.

Grady rolled up his blanket, fastened the straps of his rucksack, walked to his horse and tied them behind the cantle. When he came back to the fire, the girl was still standing there watching the stallion shouldering the mares away from the water.

"A greedy beast," he said.

The girl said nothing. Her eyes shone in the firelight.

The stallion began to drink again. Then, led by a black mare, the rest of the herd moved downstream. The stallion turned his head, the muscles gathering under his wet coat, waiting. The black mare pulled up and started to drink, and when the others were also drinking, she slipped quietly away from them and doubled back to the stallion, trotting by him, but finally, making a circle, she returned to brush his flank.

Grady grinned and then, tired of the game he had been playing, with all the bitterness he had been nursing since the morning on the trail, more than a week ago, said, "They always come back."

The girl turned away from the horses and looked at him. She stood motionless and silent for a moment. The fire had died down but he could see the defiant set of her shoulders against the darkening river. He could imagine, though her face was now shadowed, the glitter in her eyes and the old look of contempt.

"I am sorry that I bothered to warn you," she said, raising her voice.

"It was nothing that I didn't already know," he replied.

"You may learn differently."

"I may learn that your coming here was for another reason." The suspicion had been with him when she had first appeared, while they were eating, during the time they had been watching the horses, and now looking at her and hearing the ring of her words, he held it back no longer. "Your brother probably knew that you were coming. He's likely waiting over the next hill."

She said nothing in reply, but suddenly she walked toward him and, before he was aware of her intentions, struck him across the mouth. It was a stinging blow that made the blood leap in his veins. He seized her hand as she drew it back to strike him again, and the other as she raised it, and holding them, feeling the blood pounding in his throat, drew her to him. She fought fiercely, in a quick movement sank her teeth in his hand, but he broke away and held her so that she could not move.

He held her, wondering how she could manage to breathe. He was aware that she was no longer struggling against him. She was limp in his arms, her hair falling around her shoulders. He released her, half expecting her to fall to the ground, but she didn't. She clung to him and together they sank in the grass. In the flickering light her eyes were closed. She lay for a moment with her hands raised beside her head, as if in fear. Then suddenly and swiftly she began to fumble with the buttons of her bodice.

The horses had left the river and there were no sounds in the swale save the wind in the trees and the noise of the river flowing past. In the east he saw a glow where the moon was rising. Luz stood against a trees, with her head resting against it. She was looking at him but her face was indistinct in the darkness. He held the reins in one hand, sitting relaxed in the saddle. She seemed small there against the tree in the light of the dying fire, small and lost and defenseless, the fierce ardency gone, changed again to a girl in a yellow silk dress.

He looked at her and thought, She made the challenge that first morning on the trail. Then, and at the corral, and on the hill with the *mesteño,* and later at Jim Wolfe's. The next day at the gate of the ranch she flung the challenge again. She laid down the gage and it was accepted and now her defiance is gone.

He had said good-by to her; there was no point in saying anything more. Quickly he moved off through the trees and along the hillside, gained the top of the hill as the moon rose, got his bearings there and headed straight into the west. Below and off to his right he saw the sprawling outlines of the ranch house, the orange reflections of the outdoor ovens, the line of corrals zigzagging along the mesa and, dimly, carts winding upward from the river.

The brush was heavy but he decided not to take the chances involved in following the main trail which skirted the mesa. Though it would mean another three hours or more of travel and possibly delay his reaching Jim Wolfe's until dawn, it was the wiser of the two courses. Her information had made that clear. Whether or not her brother was out searching for him, it seemed fairly certain that others were. Major de Zubaran, on his way to San Diego, would have seen to that.

About Roque de Zubaran, the thin narrow-shouldered youth who had stopped him at the San Gabriel, he wasn't so certain. It was possible, as Luz had said, that he and the rest of his gang with their high-peaked hats and battered muskets were on the prowl. It was also possible that Luz de Zubaran was lying, that she had invented the story and used it as an excuse to explain her visit. For some reason he no longer harbored the suspicion, which he had openly expressed to her, that the whole thing—the story as well as her presence—was a ruse.

He looked down at the moon on the mesa and beyond at the glimmering walls of the ranch house. By now she would be riding up from the river, taking the long trail which led to the house. She was probably there on the mesa now, with the moon shining on the yellow silk dress he had brought from Santa Fe, sitting with one foot in the stirrup, her wide skirts billowing around her, erect in the saddle as she had sat when she rode through the trees and into the swale. But not as confident as then, for things had not turned out the way she had planned.

He remembered her standing by the tree in the light of the dying fire, and thought, She got what she deserved. But the memory, no more than had the moment itself, brought neither pleasure nor a sense of triumph. Curiously, his feeling was one of sadness, as if he had committed some shameful act. It was a feeling which was strange to him, strange and disturbing, and suddenly, seeking to deny it, he thought, To hell with her! I will never see her again!

The hill sloped off to a narrow shelf, and as he rode along it, he put Luz de Zubaran, all the De Zubarans, out of his mind. But a moment later, riding down toward a shallow arroyo, his gaze strayed back to the mesa. She was there again, with her black braided hair and the yellow dress—odd that he had brought it for her—and her wrists that were strong and square, yet delicately formed, the hollowed temples and cheeks and the smell of sunlight about her. He saw her as plainly as though she were riding along beside him.

And then, looking downward through the moon-washed night, feeling the pounding of his heart, he thought, Since the morning on the trail this thing has been growing, changing from what in the beginning was hatred and a wish for revenge, until now it is something else. Those things are gone. Left behind there on the river. Dead as the ashes of the fire. He pulled up his horse and sat motionless, overcome with a sudden realization. By God, he thought, I'm in love with her. And as he repeated the words, aloud this time, he was seized with an overpowering impulse to turn back, to seek her out and take her with him.

But where? Where, since the pueblo was closed to him and every trail was watched, could they find safety? How was he to find her except by going to the ranch—she would certainly be there by the time he could reach the mesa—and so take the chance of capture or ambush?

Besides these objections there was still another. Tom Risk, with eight of his men, would leave the lower Santa Ana in the morning and arrive at Wolfe's by tomorrow night. The next day, according to plans already made, they would all ride toward Los Angeles and a rendezvous with the forces that Jacob Kroll had organized.

The sensible thing was to wait until the fighting was finished, when he was no longer in danger of arrest. But he was not in a sensible mood; the objections which flashed through his mind served only as a spur to action. Wryly he recalled an admonition from the book packed away in his rucksack: "The only victory in love is flight." And still another of Napoleon's pieces of advice: "Love . . . is destruction to the warrior."

But even this had an opposite effect, and abruptly, his chin stubborn, he wheeled his horse and rode out of the arroyo, over the low ridge where he had stood a week before reconnoitering the house. The moon threw his shadow. The desert wind, sweeping free here in the open, beat against his face.

He rode at a fast trot and would have ridden faster except for brush and thickets of buckthorn, impatient at the slowness of his pace, his thoughts racing ahead of him. Had she reached home? And if she had, how was he to see her without arousing the family, her brother and bull-necked father? Joe would be useful, he thought. But Joe was not here. He would have to find one of the Indian women and bribe her to deliver a message, which wouldn't be difficult because an Indian was always amenable to a bribe and invariably attracted by the role of Cupid. Then he was struck by something that had never occurred to him. After he had found an Indian to take the message and the message had been delivered, would Luz go with him? Would she, against the traditions of a lifetime, leave her family to face certain ostracism and an uncertain future?

The King's Highway lay in front of him, and as he crossed it, reflecting on this problem, he noticed a horseman riding along the trail from the direction of the river. For an instant he thought it might be Luz de Zubaran. His heart began to pound. He slackened his pace, but a moment later the figure came into better view and he saw that it was a man, a young man with high, narrow shoulders, riding with one hand on the shaft of a lance held upright in the stirrup. There was a small triangular-shaped pennon fastened near the head of the lance. The head, black and shining, was clear against the pale sky.

His first instinct was to turn before he reached the trail and take the direction from which Roque de Zubaran was approaching, a parallel course that would pass the rider at a sufficient distance to make an encounter unnecessary. Then, moved as much by the fact that the young Spaniard had seen him as by an unreasoning distaste for retreat, he continued on.

The rider passed in front of him and did not speak, but though there was not the slightest movement of the head or slackening of pace, Dunavant was sure he had been recognized. Keeping his eyes on the Spaniard, he came to the trail and was about to turn east along it, away from the mesa and toward the river, when he saw the rider wheel his mount in a slow circle.

He knew, during the moment that the circle was being completed, while he saw the lance lowered and before the cry of "*Santiago!*" broke hoarsely upon the night, that this was trouble.

The young Spaniard came at a gallop, leaning down and forward in the saddle, the lance gripped far back and held hard against his forearm. But in the brief interval Dunavant managed to untie the horse he was leading, slip his pistol from the holder and cock it. The click of the hammer was lost in the rush of hoofs. His horse responded to the bit. And yet as he reared backward and to one side, and the rider bore past him, he realized that it was not possible to cope with the man, any Spaniard, on horseback. He had evaded the lance this time and might again, but in the end he would be ridden down.

The youth brought the stallion to a pounding halt, at a distance of a hundred feet. Grady saw him wheel for the return, and though now there was no possibility of argument or retreat for either of them, he shouted, "Stop, you fool! Stop!" The words were answered by a flash of spurs, the lowering of the long lance, the swift, oncoming thud of hoofs.

Dunavant raised the Colt, held it level and, with sudden clarity, knowing that he could not kill the young Spaniard, aimed at the stallion. Once unhorsed, Luz de Zubaran's brother could be taken care of, tied up and sent back to the ranch on the extra mount. The shot was accurate; the heavy slug struck the broad chest. The horse faltered and veered away from the sound and the burst of flame. In a blinding instant, Dunavant felt the impact of the lance head against his shoulder, the grinding shock of iron and bone.

He fell backward from the saddle and struck the earth. The night exploded around him and then settled into darkness.

# 19

Sitting in his big chair beside the hearth, Don Saturnino watched the Indian crouched at the fire and the roasting kid held on a long iron skewer. The table was set for supper but the candles had not yet been lighted. The roots of manzanita were cherry-red. Ruddy flames streamed up the chimney. A steady glow fell on the face of the Indian and over the white walls of the room.

"Turn the iron with less rapidity," Saturnino said. "Give the fire a chance to accomplish its purpose."

He greatly relished roasted kid and enjoyed the preparation of it almost as much as the eating. Two days ago he had slaughtered and skinned the goat, split it down the middle and hung it in the cool-house. This afternoon he had taken the kid down and carefully arranged it for roasting, twisting the hind legs and folding them over the back, the front legs over the head which was tucked in on the shoulder. Then the whole thing, solid and flat, was worked down firmly on the skewer. The gnarled dense root of the manzanita, which burned hot and gave off little smoke, was the proper wood for the fire. This part of the preparation he also attended to himself, heaping up the roots and lighting them an hour before the roasting began. The only part of the ritual that he did not enjoy was the part now taking place—the dull period when the kid was being slowly turned. An Indian could do this as well as he; besides, the stooping posture cramped his legs.

Fat began to drip from the kid, falling into the coals with bright spurts of flame, and a rich odor began to well out from the fire. Saturnino got to his feet, took the skewer from the Indian and examined the roasting meat. He squatted down at one side of the hearth, thrust the end into an iron ring in the masonry at the back of the fireplace and began to turn the skewer.

"Light the candles," he said to the waiting Indian. It would be some time before the kid was ready but he enjoyed having everyone present for this portion of the ceremony. "Call the De Zubarans to supper."

Jorge came in first, as he usually did when kid was being prepared, and knelt down beside his father on the hearth, his yellow eyes bright with excitement.

"It is already done," he said.

"You will never make a roaster of kid," his father replied, as he always did to this same remark from his son. "You have not the proper eye or nose."

"Test it, Don Saturnino."

"It is not time for testing," Saturnino said. But this was part of the ritual too, and he took the knife from his belt, withdrew the skewer and pressed the point of the knife into the meat. "See, as I told you. It is not yet done."

The boy was waiting to turn the skewer. Saturnino fixed the end securely into the ring and handed it over to him.

"Turn with some speed," he said, "and keep your mind on it. Do not drop it into the ashes as before."

Saturnino rearranged the coals and threw on another root. His mother had come in while he was doing this. She sat now at the table, holding her knife and fork.

"When supper is late I know for a certainty what the reason will be," she said.

"If it were on time," he answered, "you would not be here to eat it."

"Then you could eat it all yourself, which would please you," she said.

He laughed and turned around to give her a wink. She was a greedy old woman, his mother, and he enjoyed making her wait for her food.

"Did you have a good day at the river?" he asked. "Did you blacken many names and clean many clothes?"

"Many clothes and many names, including yours," Doña Carlota said.

"What was said concerning me?"

"That you are a man who is cruel to his mother."

"Nothing of more novelty?"

"Yes, many things in that category."

He looked at her, sitting at the table with her hair pulled back from her bony forehead, her long upper lip seeming longer than usual, and decided not to press the matter. He took a ball of fat from an earthen crock, thrust a skewer through it and held it to the fire until it caught and blazed. He held the fat over the revolving kid, letting the flames dribble and spread.

"Will the kid be burned again, as last time?" Carlota asked.

"As last time, in not the remotest degree."

Carlota came over to the hearth and stood looking down at the turning kid that crackled and gave off little spurts of flame. He waited, smiling to himself, for her to speak.

When she could contain herself no longer, she said, "Give me a piece now, so I may judge."

"Wait, woman. This is no time to interrupt."

"I have a name."

"Wait, Señora Doña Carlota, if that suits better. And since when have you been a judge of these matters?"

"Since you were an infant lacking teeth to chew with."

"I was born with teeth, as you well know."

"I know many things about you, but not that one," she said. "Many unique things."

He kept his eyes on the kid, noting its color and texture and that no place was burned, knowing all the while what his mother was alluding to. It was Guadalupe. She had found out about the girl and was itching to berate him. Well, let her; the deed was accomplished. He wished, however, that she had chosen a more propitious moment.

"Turn slowly now," he said to his son, "and with great deliberation."

Carlota edged closer to the fire. "I observe that we have a new servant—a very comely girl and a good worker besides."

Saturnino did not betray any emotion at his mother's conciliatory tone.

"She will make a good wife for one of the men," Carlota continued. "Likely it will be Mitla, for they already seem friendly."

Saturnino frowned but made no reply. The supreme moment of the ritual, begun two days ago, had arrived; this was no time to discuss such matters. He would attend to the business of Mitla tomorrow. "Hand over the kid," he said to his son, and then, raising his voice, he shouted, "Where is Luz?"

"At the table, waiting for you," Carlota said.

Saturnino turned in surprise. "What happens, man? Why are you not helping here at the fire, as customary?"

"I am tired," Luz replied.

Grunting, he glanced back at the kid. "And Roque? Where is that young man? Riding around the valley in his green hat?" No one answered his question. "Well, the wearer of the green hat can consume cold food. We eat without him."

He took the skewer from his son, lifted it out of the ring and held the kid close upon the glowing coals until it turned crisp and brown. Sweating from the heat of the fire, he rose to his feet, paused dramatically, and with a flourish withdrew the roasted kid and bore it triumphantly, crackling and glowing with thin, bluish flames, to the table. The Indian, who had been standing at the door, ran to the courtyard and shouted. In a moment two girls came into the room with steaming bowls of frijoles and lentils.

Saturnino, his feet braced and his sleeves rolled up, sank the sharp knife into the kid. The skin crunched and the pale, milk-colored flesh was revealed. A breath-taking odor engulfed the table. Never had he smelled such richness nor gazed on meat so surpassingly cooked. In an expansive mood, a fine dew of anticipation covering his upper lip, he began to fill the plates, spooning up the clear, savory juice which had gathered on the platter.

The task completed, he sat down and looked at his mother. "Señora Doña, I pause for your opinion."

"I find it possible to eat," Carlota said. "But it is only because I have considerable hunger."

Saturnino beamed. "Then I am satisfied that it is of a surpassing nature."

He attacked his plate with great relish and finished it off before the others were well started, but as he commenced on the second helping, his thoughts turned to Mitla. Now there was something for you—Mitla and Guadalupe. Something he had not reckoned with. He recalled that he had seen them talking together in the forge less than an hour ago, also that Mitla had shown considerable interest in the girl when she had first arrived at the ranch.

I will have a talk with Mitla, he thought, the keen edge of his appetite suddenly dulled. I will talk to him after supper.

Carlota watched her son from the far end of the table. She observed this sudden lack of appetite and correctly guessed the cause. The plan she had worked out during the afternoon was beginning to bear fruit It was the first step in a larger plan which had occupied her mind for days, ever since the morning of the burial when Major de Zubaran had come with a message from the governor. There was much more to accomplish, and now with this initial advantage, she had no intention of putting it off.

"From young Cisneros," she said, "whom I spoke to several days ago,

I learn of a drought in Santa Fe. His uncle has just returned and reports that sheep are dying by the thousands for want of grass. It is further reported by the uncle of Cisneros that both the Spaniards and Navajo are willing to dispose of their animals at low prices."

Saturnino looked up from his plate. "We possess no money for sheep."

"We possess what you brought back from Señora Howland, gold sufficient for two thousand sheep."

"We require the gold."

"Not if you refrain from purchasing things that cannot be afforded—like lead for bullets and silk dresses. Furthermore, we will receive additional money in a few weeks from the sale of tallow."

Saturnino helped himself to another plate of meat.

"It is a unique opportunity," Carlota went on. "Cheap prices in Santa Fe. A breed superior to our own. More and richer grass here than any time within memory."

Saturnino filled his mouth and spoke. "Who takes part in this operation?" he asked. "Not me, now that the gringo threatens."

"The danger has passed," Carlota said, although she thought differently.

"Not me, woman, needed as I am in the valley, whatever the gringo does or does not."

"You are needed for other things, but not this. It is Roque, however, about whom I was thinking."

Saturnino glanced down the table and laughed. "That is a good one. *Ole*, what you will devise next! Roque? Why that young man would become lost before he reached the Cajon. It would take him five years to find Santa Fe and as long to return. Woman, you furnish me with great amusement. Continue so that I may be further amused."

Carlota, well satisfied with the way things were moving, kept her temper and said calmly, "He would go, of course, with someone of experience. With Chico or Miguel. Better than either of these, perhaps, would be Mitla, who has made the journey twice."

Saturnino's laughter ceased abruptly, but he made no reply. He went on with his eating, wielding his knife as if he would never eat again. She was not deceived, however, by his silence or preoccupation, nor was she surprised when he paused, glanced around the table and brought his fist down with a mighty smash which set the plates jumping.

"Where is Roque?" he shouted. "Where is this wearer of a green hat and carrier of a musket which is never used? Why is he not here? Whom does one ask, where does one go to find him?"

He glanced at Carlota and from her to Luz. Neither of them answered him, but Jorge, looking sidewise, said, "He came home late from the killing ground."

"That I know. Then what?"

"He talked to Doña Carlota in the kitchen."

Saturnino waited for his mother to speak.

"From there he went to his room to change his clothes," she said. "He is there now."

"No," Jorge said with an air of mystery, enjoying the attention of everyone at the table. "He is not in his room."

Saturnino struck the table again. "Where then? Speak up!"

"He left the house," Jorge said, caught the menacing look his father threw at him and quickly added, "He took a lance from the saddlery, the best one—of filbert wood with the design of oak leaves stamped on the head. When he was sure no one was watching, he slipped out the gate. I ran there and saw him gallop across the mesa."

A moment of silence fell over the room. Carlota sat straight in her high-backed chair and dropped her fork on the table. Her lips drew together. Roque did not heed me, she thought, and looked at her granddaughter.

Luz had not come home until she herself was here in the room; there had been no chance to learn anything about the American. She had not even thought of asking, confident that the talk she had had with Roque in the kitchen would suffice. And as she looked at Luz now, she saw no answer to the question. Luz' face was pale—it had been pale when she came in and sat down to supper. This meant nothing, for she had been pale all day—nothing, Carlota thought.

"Galloping off with my best lance," Saturnino was saying, his voice hoarse with anger. "The one of the filbert shaft and the oak leaves. What more will I be asked to endure?"

Carlota did not take her eyes from her granddaughter. At last Luz looked up. Their gazes met briefly, but in that instant she read everything as clearly as if the girl had spoken.

Saturnino rose and walked to the fire, kicked the coals with the toe of his boot, threw another root on, turned and stood with his feet widespread.

"*Jesús María,*" he groaned, glaring around the room. "Without so much as a word, he rides off with my finest lance. No 'by your leave.'

Nor 'with your permission, sir.' Gallops away, bearing a lance presented to me by the governor himself, on some hairbrained impulse, at the hour of supper. What sin have I committed to deserve this indignity?"

Luz did not look at her father, standing there in front of the fire with his face lifted in mock helplessness, nor did she hear his words. Her eyes were fixed on the window which gave on the courtyard. She was listening to the big gate creaking open, the gate closing, the heavy iron bar being thrust into place. It is Roque, she thought. He has come back and soon I will know.

She sat, her food untouched, trying to breathe against the tightness of her throat, listening to the sounds in the courtyard, the tap of boot heels, the rattle of spurs.

"Is it not enough to father a milksop," Saturnino said. "One must also be a father to a purloiner of weapons, who lacks both courtesy and the rudiments of respect."

"You are not the inventor of gunpowder," Carlota said.

"No, I am a humble man, without pretenses. But I am still one who deserves a consideration which I do not receive."

The steps were nearer now, on the *portale*. She should never have returned until there was no longer any danger. She should have followed him out of the valley, as far as Wolfe's ranch where he was surely going. It was foolish of her, knowing Roque's determination, ever to have trusted in Carlota.

"I wash my hands of this," Saturnino said. "I present this one, past and future, to you, woman."

Luz saw a shadow pass the window. Others saw it too and suddenly there was a long silence. Please God, she thought, may no harm have come to him!

Saturnino left the fire and, leaning his fists on the table, fastening his angry eyes on the door, said, "The warrior returns. Be ready with flowers and wine. Pluck the violins."

Now, she thought, not moving, now I will know.

The door opened and Roque stood in the doorway. He turned, closed the door behind him and faced the room again, his eyes blinking in the light of the candles. But before he faced them for the second time, before she saw the broken lance held in his hand, before she saw the blood smearing the green jacket, she knew that the two men had met on the trail. Even then she did not move; unable to rise, she watched him leave the door and walk around the table to where Saturnino stood, now erect and menacing.

"I observe that the lance is broken," Saturnino said. "*Diantre!* My mind recoils from the gory encounter. Was it a spavined bull lacking sight and the means to run? A mountain lion without teeth? A bear caught in a trap? But perhaps it was something else. A skunk more likely, giving suck to nine little ones." He paused ominously and then reached forward and grasped the broken lance. "Speak, before I break the rest of this over your ears."

Roque, with his shoulders thrust back, had remained silent during Saturnino's outburst. There was a curious smile at the corners of his mouth which deepened as he relinquished the lance. There was an instant of quiet after Saturnino had finished. Still her brother did not answer. He is enjoying his moment of triumph, she thought, and rose though her legs were stone. The American has been killed! She opened her lips to speak but no words came.

Saturnino took a step toward his son; only then did Roque answer, saying in a voice quiet with pride, "It was none of these, neither a spavined bull nor a toothless lion, nor yet a skunk giving suck." He paused and, at last losing the air of a man, blurted out, "It was a gringo. The one we met on the trail. The one who came to the gate."

Saturnino had raised the lance to strike; he stood now, clutching the shaft in his great hand, holding it poised above his head. "The gringo!" he croaked. Slowly he lowered the lance and then raised it again. His face darkened. "If this is a joke you are presenting, I will give you the lash, strip the hide from your bones."

"It is the gringo," Roque said, taking a step backward at his father's glowering stare. "I found him on the trail, where the road crosses from the mesa. He is there now. He lies in the dust where he belongs."

She had picked up the knife from beside her plate. The bone handle was smooth and cold against her burning flesh. The candlelight falling on it was reflected against the wall beyond her, a tiny sliver of light which trembled with the trembling of her hand. She waited. If he is dead, she thought, then . . .

Her father asked the question.

"He breathes, unfortunately," Roque said. "But he breathes little. The wound is deep. I beg your forgiveness, sir, for having broken the lance. It struck a bone of the shoulder."

She heard the shaft strike the floor and saw her father step forward, tears starting from his eyes, and clasp Roque to his chest. She heard Saturnino shout to the servants, "Bring wine! Heat the food!" And looking once at Doña Carlota, meeting her gaze and seeing there in the glittering hooded eyes the command to do what she would have done without it, she slipped out of the room.

She found Mitla in the kitchen. She did not stop to change her dress, but kilted it up, mounted astride and rode away from the gate. She gave the horse its head. The moon lay clear on the mesa. The night was still. The hoofs of her horse and the horse Mitla was riding echoed back from the hills. She had no spurs, but she dug the heels of her satin shoes into the *mesteño's* flanks.

"Holy Virgin," she said, "let him live!"

She said the words over and over to the streaming wind.

He lay beyond Roque's dead horse, beside a scrub oak, the print of his body in the dust where he had been dragged. There was blood in the dust where he had fallen and beneath and beside him. He was breathing, but his breath was light, barely passing his lips, so light she could scarcely feel it against her face.

Mitla knelt beside her. "He will never live if we take him to Wolfe's," she said.

"Wherever he is taken, it will be the same."

She did not answer him. Crouching on her knees, she thought of her father and Roque at the ranch, the scene if he were brought into the house, the danger to both the American and to her. It went through her mind in a flash and was gone.

"We will take him home," she said. "They will not harm him. Never while I live."

Mitla glanced at her. She could see the surprise on his stolid face, but she was beyond caring what he thought, or anyone.

"When we have him on the horse," she said, "you will ride ahead and prepare for us—start the fires and heat water. . . . "

"But what of Don Saturnino?" Mitla said, standing up.

"It does not matter."

"But . . ."

"You will do as I say," she answered.

Then she rose from her knees and ran toward the pinto horse grazing beside the trail.

# 20

Carlota sat silent at the table. The two men were standing in front of the fire, passing a big silver mug of wine back and forth between them. On the back of Saturnino's chair was a skin of wine, and when the mug was drained, he walked over, slung the skin over his arm and filled it again.

"Ho there, woman," he said, turning his gaze on her and shoving the mug down the table. "I had forgotten you were with us. A thousand pardons, señora doña."

She looked at him, his face flushed and beaming, his powerful shoulders bent toward her and straining with pride.

"I take no wine," she replied.

"Drink, woman. It will improve your digestion. Likewise your disposition."

"Neither requires improvement."

Saturnino laughed. "It is not every day that you can celebrate an occasion of this magnificence."

She made no move to pick up the mug. Since Luz left, she thought, this is the first time that he has spoken to me. He has not yet missed her.

"Your grandson, Roque de Zubaran, has reached manhood," Saturnino said. "He has accomplished what all the soldiers of the governor have failed in. He has found the gringo they all seek, met him in battle and after an unequal struggle, in which pistol was pitted against lance, has vanquished him. Still you sit with a long face. *Ole,* woman! It would depress me if I were one to depress."

His tone was light and chiding. He was too carried away with the moment to know that she did not share his pride and excitement, or that she was not really listening to him, that her ears were alert for every sound which came from the courtyard. It was just as well.

He reached out and picked up the mug. "Well, then, old woman, we drink without you." With the mug held in front of him, he suddenly paused and glanced around the table, at Jorge and then at his daughter's empty place. "Where is Luz? She will share the honor." He turned and peered through the murky, smoke-filled room. "Where is she?"

"In her room," Carlota said. "In her room with a headache caused by your shouting."

He laughed and took a long draught of wine. "More likely her nose is out of joint from jealousy," he replied, wiping his mouth on the back of his hand. "She does not like it because she is not now the one of importance." He drank deeply again and strode back to the fire. "We share the bowl alone," he said, handing the bowl to his son. "Which is fortunate, since the wine is our best and not plentiful. Drink up! We have not yet begun to honor the event. And do not permit sulking women to tarnish your pleasure."

Carlota held her tongue. She sat, outwardly calm, in her high-backed chair, looking through the window into the courtyard. She would have liked to leave the room, but Luz had not yet had time to reach the trail and return. Until she did, until the American was here in the house, it was not safe for her to leave Saturnino. There was already some excitement among the servants in the kitchen, and if she were to go and in some way he got wind of what was happening, he would close the gate on his daughter and the American, one with the other, equally.

She strained her ears, above the noise of drinking and the second recounting of the story—interrupted by frequent, boisterous remarks by Saturnino—for every sound from outside. Then Saturnino returned to the table, again filled the mug and decanted what was left in the skin into his gaping mouth.

He dropped the skin on the floor and gave her a sly wink. "I can see that you have changed your mind, old woman. There is a dusty glitter to your eyes and a dry smirk around the mouth which bespeaks thirst." With exaggerated steadiness, he came around the table and held out the mug. "Let no one say that I am lacking in filial respect."

Roque left the fire, sat down at the table and, though he was pale from the quantity of wine he had consumed, managed to add his voice to that of his father. As he spoke, she heard the gate open and the sound of hoofs in the courtyard, a low exclamation from one of the Indians.

"I grow tired holding the wine," Saturnino said, making a show of shifting his weight.

"I do not drink," she answered. "Then or now."

"Listen, Roque. Do you hear?" Saturnino laughed and turned to regard his son, who now lay forward with his head sunk on the table. Receiving no answer from him, he looked at Carlota. His eyes narrowed. "Then or now, is it? Am I to understand from this that you do not take pleasure in the event?"

Carlota remained silent.

"Perhaps you wish that your grandson had been killed instead of the gringo, and that the gringo should be free to roam the valley unmolested?"

Rising from the chair, Carlota said, "With your permission we will leave the subject. Drink and permit me to refrain. Also permit me to think what I choose."

*"No faltaba mas."*

"It may cap the climax or not," she said, hearing the gate close. Saturnino heard the sound, too, but apparently thought it of no importance. "One or the other, I do not drink."

For a moment he looked at her uncertainly, and it seemed as if he had relented. The next instant, however, he grasped her arm and thrust the wine to her mouth.

*"Ea,* woman," he said. "To the occasion!"

She tried to wrench herself free, but he tightened his grip and pushed the wine closer. Suddenly her nostrils flared in anger, and with a backward swipe of her hand, she sent the mug spinning to the floor.

"Cowards!" she cried, goaded beyond caution. "You and your son, and you more than he, for this would not have happened except for you. It is a stench in the nose. It is something which possesses neither honor nor dignity."

Saturnino, stepping back, pawed at the wine stain on his shirt; his mouth hung open. Beyond him, Roque raised himself up, stared at her weakly and buried his head once more in his arms. Saying nothing further, she took her silver-headed cane, walked to the door, where she told the Indian to fetch more wine, and went outside to the *portale.* Hurrying along it, she looked in as she passed the window. Saturnino still stood where she had left him, but he was beginning now to rend the air with curses.

Bellow! she thought as she hobbled along, jabbing her cane viciously against the tiles. The more noise, the less you will hear.

Chattering Indians were clustered in the doorway of the kitchen. She made a pathway with her cane and commanded silence. Fires were going. The room was hot and filled with steam from the bubbling caldrons. A blanket had been spread in the middle of the floor; on it her granddaughter was kneeling. The American lay sprawled in front of her, his head turned to one side, his eyes closed, a torn and bloody jacket beside him.

"Stand aside," Carlota told the girl. "You have accomplished your part. The rest belongs to me." She turned to Merced, who was supervising the heating of water. "Bank all the fires save one—we are not attending the birth of seven babies. And dispose of all the caldrons except the largest. The place is like the steam hut of a *chichinabro*."

Luz got to her feet. In answer to the unspoken question in the girl's eyes, the old lady said, "He occupies himself with bellowing. At length he will become tired and then we can expect a visit. *Pues, veremos quien puede más*. Then we will see who is the most powerful. Bring me now a cup of brandy—a large one."

She knelt down and stripped away the young man's shirt. The wound was massive, running diagonally, with the course of the lance, through the muscles of the upper chest and into the shoulder, where the tip of the lance, she saw, had been broken off and imbedded. The American had bled greatly, he was drained of color; his skin was the white of the wall behind him.

The Indian women at the door began to moan at sight of the wound, and Carlota turned on them, saying, "To your rooms! Close the doors and remain silent."

She had extracted many arrowheads in her time, but never the head of a lance. It is bad, she thought, taking the cup of brandy Luz had brought. She managed to force a little of the fiery liquid past the young man's lips, the rest she drank herself, blinking as it sped down her throat. Then she motioned for a steaming cloth.

With the cloth she cleansed the blood from the chest and from around the wound. "It is red," she said to herself. "The blood of an American is red like the blood of a Spaniard." Somehow this seemed unique to the old woman. Luz was standing at the door, her hands tense at her sides. "Bring another cup of brandy and drink this one yourself."

"I require nothing," the girl answered.

Carlota mumbled at this reply. She settled her weight firmly on both knees and again looked at the lance head. It is like an arrow, she told herself, only larger. To Mitla, backed against the wall too frightened to move, thinking of the possible consequences of his part in the affair, she said, "Do not act like one from the land of those whose heads are shaped like gourds. Lend me a hand."

The Indian slouched forward and held the American's shoulder as she directed. Together, Mitla holding and the old lady exerting a steady pressure, they worked at the lance head. The iron gave slowly, the man groaned, but the pressure was not relaxed. She was surprised when the iron came loose that the wound did not bleed more.

"It is because he has already bled so much," she said. "He is without blood and it is a miracle if he lives."

She took the cup of hot water and powdered chilicote root which Merced had prepared, and forced the drug little by little into the young man's mouth. Then she placed the herb poultice over the wound and tied it there.

"Fetch a litter," she instructed Mitla. "We take him to the room which is next to mine." When Mitla returned, she summoned Tiburcio, and the two men lifted the American on the litter. "Walk carefully now," she said.

At this moment, as she spoke and the Indians raised the litter, she heard steps outside. They were light and for an instant she thought it was Roque, but looking at her granddaughter in the doorway, she saw by the girl's expression, the stiffening of her body, the sudden defensive attitude of one who expects a blow, that it was Saturnino instead.

He brushed past Luz, apparently not seeing her, and stepped unsteadily into the room. He halted just inside the door to stare around him with red-rimmed eyes, first at Merced, then at his mother, and finally at the two men. It was a full minute before he spoke, and then not until he had looked at everyone a second time, at the cauldron of water over the fire, the torn coat lying on the floor, and lastly at the figure on the litter.

His face changed slowly; the eyes and mouth and long chin seemed to grow smaller in the shifting light of the candles and then to enlarge. Carlota could see the color visibly fade under his swarthy skin and after a moment return, leaving his face congested. She saw his great chest heave as he gulped a deep breath of air. The hissing of the indrawn breath was the only sound in the room.

He is not going to say anything, she thought, placing herself between him and Mitla, who stood with his arms outspread, holding the handles of the litter. He will strike Mitla down without speaking.

She knotted her hands on the head of the cane. She looked at Saturnino. He was motionless there in the center of the room. He was not breathing now, his shoulders hunched forward, hands clenched and feet planted squarely, barring the way to the door.

"We have tended the American," she said. "We now take him to bed."

She still expected violent action from him, and if not that, then a violence of words, but he said in a curiously quiet voice, "Who brought him into this house?"

"It does not matter who. He is here and here he stays until he dies or is well. It is a debt thrust upon us by your folly." She spoke as quietly as he had spoken, and then, not changing her tone, said, "With your permission we go."

He did not look at Mitla or Tiburcio as the two men passed him carrying the litter, nor at her when she walked toward the door. He was looking through and beyond all of them, his eyes small and staring in his head. He said nothing, but in the look, in his silence, was an ominous quality that chilled her blood.

"Go," she whispered to her granddaughter. "Go to my room and remain there."

Saturnino was conscious that the kitchen was empty, that his lungs were aching for want of air. He stumbled to the door, crossed the *portale,* and, on reaching the courtyard, stopped and raised his face to the wind. Still blowing from the desert, the wind was hot, with a dry gritty edge which burned his lungs.

He lowered his head and looked straight in front of him, like an enraged bull who, having smelled the enemy, gathers his strength for the charge. The courtyard was filled with dense shadows and a long bright strip of moonlight. The leaves of the blue ash rattled above him. On its perch among the branches of the tree, he saw the golden eyes of the eagle watching him.

"There are things to do this night, Águila."

The eagle ruffled its feathers.

"But we must think first . . . choose one step at a time . . . make certain inquiries."

Candles were burning in the room which adjoined the rooms of his mother. He could hear voices but he made no effort to decipher them. His gaze was fixed on the man who came out of the room and was now scuttling along toward the Indians' quarters, making an effort to conceal himself in the shadows.

He permitted the figure to reach the far side of the courtyard, to open the door softly. Then he shouted, putting all the force of his lungs into the words, "Mitla, here by the tree!"

It was Mitla who would have the information he wished to know. A stubborn man, Mitla, but there were ways to loosen his tongue if he chose to remain silent. Saturnino thought, I will strip the flesh from his bones or learn that which I wish to learn. I . . . The Indian was standing in front of him. "Mitla, you are a young man and therefore value life. There is a question which I ask and I ask it only once. Who brought the gringo to this house?"

The Indian opened his mouth.

"Speak," Saturnino said softly.

"He was brought by . . ."

"By whom?" Saturnino asked with deadly patience. "Not by you, Mitla, for you are a young man wiser than this."

"By . . ."

"Yes."

"By your daughter."

Saturnino said nothing. He doubled his fist, struck the Indian on the skull, watched him fall, and then turned and went into the saddlery. He lighted the candles on his desk and walked over to the rack which held his muskets and lances. From a peg he took down a lash. It had a bone handle and the thongs were made of bull hide, braided and tipped with silver wires. He looped the strap over his hand, secured it around his wrist and went outside.

"She is in her room," he said aloud, "or with the gringo. Either one pleases me, but the latter more than the other."

As he spoke, passing the chapel, he noticed that the door was ajar. He walked on, but moved by a vague suspicion, he retraced his steps, stopped at the door and looked in. Votive candles were burning on the altar; the chapel was dim with smoke. The smell of incense and burning wax came to his nostrils. Through the smoke he saw a figure kneeling in front of the altar, shrouded in a black *manta*. The Indians often appeared here at this time of night, and he was on the point of turning away when something about the posture of the body struck him as familiar. Opening the door and drawing closer, he recognized his daughter.

He closed the door behind him and walked down the aisle between the rough-hewn benches, moving as softly as his spurs allowed. Luz did not hear him or if she did she showed no sign. She was praying audibly, her face lifted to the Virgin above the altar, and she continued to pray when he was only a step behind her. He stopped, listening, trying to catch the meaning of her words, but there was a great ringing in his head which turned everything into a meaningless jumble. He made a rasping sound in his throat; still the girl did not pause or show any sign that she knew he was standing behind her.

He cleared his throat again. In a voice which was meant to be quiet, but which boomed through the silent chapel, he said, "You think by coming here to avoid me. Repentant, you flee, thinking to find a sanctuary. Yet there is no place within these walls or without them where retribution will not overtake you."

Luz stopped praying, but she did not turn. He saw a faint movement of her shoulders under the *manta.* "The sin of disobedience is a black one," he said. "It is the blackest of all because it has no roots in passion. Woe to the father whose lot it is to endure this sin!"

He paused, waiting for a reply, but none came. The silence beat with the thunder of a thousand hammers against his eardrums. He expected entreaties and repentance. Instead there was this hammering silence. Through a mist like a red curtain he saw the calm face of the Virgin above the altar. Its very calmness increased the thunder in his brain, and his fury.

Then he heard something which he could not believe—his daughter, her face still lifted, was again praying. God pardon me, he thought, and almost at once, the storm of his anger breaking at this final act, he raised the lash and brought it down across the shrouded shoulders.

The girl gasped, but after an instant the prayers went on, louder now than before. Again he wielded the lash; and three times more the silver-tipped thongs slashed the air before she turned, shuddering, and rose to her feet.

Dropping the lash at his side, he said, "I am ready to consider your repentance, though I am far from forgiveness. You leave the table without permission, not to go to your room as your grandmother said, but to ride across the mesa to the King's Highway, there to give succor to the enemy, to transport him, of all places, to this house, to dress his wounds and, with your grandmother's connivance, to place him in the bed of a De Zubaran. You do this against all the traditions of your race, against my teachings, without pride or shame, and now without remorse. The time has come to speak so that I may properly weigh the punishment. What is there in mitigation?"

She looked at him, standing with her *manta* held tightly around her shoulders, and said, "There is nothing in mitigation."

It was not her tone or her words or the way she looked at him which aroused his suspicions, which gave him the first clue that she had not come here to seek sanctuary from his wrath. It was something compounded of all of them, and of no single one; something as intangible as the incense drifting around him, which he sensed rather than heard or saw.

His hand clamped shut on the handle of the lash. "You encountered the gringo on the trail the morning of the burial. Again at Vejar's by the corral. Again at the gate of this house. Where else have you encountered him, unknown to me?" Remembering back, bits of the puzzle began to fall into place. His grip tightened on the lash. "The day at Vejar's, when you went off looking for the lost stallion, did you encounter him? And today at the river, in your new silk dress?"

She looked at him and made no reply.

"Speak!" he cried.

He did not need her silence, the level look in her eyes, to tell him what he wanted to know. He knew it in a moment of clear intuition which made everything that had gone before superfluous, and as the enormity of her sin dawned upon him with the swift impact of a bludgeon, he struck out in all his fury.

She sank to her knees at the cut of the lash, but in a frenzy of self-pity that this enormity should happen to him, and in torment at the pride of the De Zubarans now trampled in the dust, he struck again and again, until he realized that his daughter was no longer on her knees, but lying prone on the floor, and that the lash was wet in his hand.

He stepped back, gasping for breath, and dropped the lash. He looked up at the Virgin and said, "God forgive me." Then, feeling the first touch of remorse and fighting it back as something unworthy, he lifted the girl and bore her out of the chapel. He strode toward the windowless cell in the armory, where unruly Indians were sometimes imprisoned. He carried her inside and placed her on a straw pallet in the corner. Closing his mind to her sobs, he shut the door behind him, turned the key in the heavy lock, put the key in his jacket and made his way toward the lights burning on the far side of the courtyard.

He passed the blue ash tree, which was struggling now with the increased wind, bending and recovering, the clash of its leaves filling the night with a roaring metallic clamor. The sounds throbbed and ran through his veins. Among the branches the eagle, clinging grimly to its swaying perch, ruffled its feathers and screamed. The cry rose high and challenging above the clamor of the wind.

Between clenched teeth Saturnino repeated the challenge, giving the cry of the eagle a meaning of his own. "Beware!" he said. "Beware the wrath of a dishonored man!"

The room was lighted with a single candle burning on the table. Beyond the table was Merced. The gringo lay on the bed only a few steps from him. For a moment he stood in the doorway, not speaking, listening to the labored breathing, smelling the strong sweet odor of chilicote root. The man had his head thrown back and his neck exposed. Saturnino could see the faint quick movement of the chest. It was broad but the slightest pressure against the gringo's throat would end that movement.

"You may go," he said to the Indian.

The woman walked toward the door and he moved aside to let her pass. He took a step into the room, his hands working at his sides.

"Now," he cried. "Now, gringo!"

But as his voice sounded in the room another voice spoke beside him. It was the voice of his mother. She was sitting against the wall, outside the radius of the candle.

She said, "There is sufficient clamor in the night without adding your voice."

Saturnino hunched his shoulders and glowered, not looking at her or speaking. He had forgotten about her; he had not expected to find her here. She was the last person he wanted to see, this witchlike old woman who, because she was his mother, had always exercised in the past a final power over him, and would attempt to exercise it now. In silence he stared at the figure on the bed.

The candle was guttering, and she rose and lighted another, forced it down in the ring of grease. She did not go back to the chair. "You come for no other reason than to leave," she said, facing him. "Neither to act nor to talk, but to leave."

A half-dozen steps, he thought, and he could reach out and grasp the exposed throat, with one swift gesture finish the task so well begun. But there in front of him she stood, as she had stood in the kitchen, leaning on her cane, watching him with her hooded gaze.

"If he dies," she said, "it will not be with your assistance or to the sound of your curses."

A cunning light came into his eyes. "I am here to learn how the gringo fares," he said, "and to give you respite. It is beyond your time to sleep. Go to your bed, señora doña, and permit me to keep the vigil."

"I will keep it until I tire," she said, sitting down. "It is for you to sleep since tomorrow you occupy yourself with the journey to Santa Fe."

Saturnino did not move toward the door, nor yet did he go past her to the bed. He stood for a long moment, his hand opening and closing in frustration. The Devil take her, he thought, and the earth rest heavily on her! Then, struck by another thought, he muttered good night and left.

In his room he flung himself on the bed fully clothed. He lay there listening to the wind, grinding his teeth while he marked the lengthening of the moon shadows. When the courtyard was in darkness and only the topmost leaves of the ash showed the touch of the moon, he rose and quietly made his way back toward the room.

The candle on the table, flickering in a pool of grease, had almost burned out. He could hear the breathing of the man on the bed, the softer breath of his mother. He took off his rowels and stepped into the room. His mother sat in the darkness; he could not see her face but he could still hear her breathing, the soft regular sounds produced by sleep.

A half-dozen steps and it would be done. He took the first one with great care, for the floor in this room was wood and gave under his weight. There was a sharp creak at the second step. He stopped and waited. The sound of breathing continued. The third and fourth steps brought him in front of his mother. It was then that the blow fell heavily across his shoulder. At first, in his surprise, he thought that it had come from behind him. But at the same instant, like a ghost in a black shawl, the old lady rose up beside him and spoke three words, one phrase which was the ultimate in Spanish venom. Another blow of the cane sent him reeling toward the doorway.

"Come back in one hour," she shouted after him as he staggered toward his room, "or at the hour that follows. Or at dawn. You will encounter the same."

He sat on his bed and held his head in his hands and cursed. He cursed and fell asleep, sprawled half on the bed and half on the floor, and woke up with the sun shining in a yellow sky, the wind whining among the tule bundles of the roof, and with a definite plan, now that his head had cleared, for the disposal of the gringo. Before the day was out, if the man still lived, he would send Roque to Los Angeles to bring back the governor's soldiers.

His mind had cleared but his wrath had not diminished. As soon as he had sloshed a bucketful of water on his head and taken a copious draught of the water that was left, he went to the room where he had placed his daughter. Sand had collected in the lock and it responded slowly to the key.

Luz, who had been lying down, jumped up when he came in. He was certain that by this time, having had the night to ponder her sin, she would be ready to ask forgiveness. The suddenness with which she rose to her feet confirmed this belief, and he steeled himself against being too precipitate in granting clemency.

He stood with his brows knit in thought, trying to think of a suitable penance. Almost at once an idea struck him. "I send your brother to the pueblo to inform the governor of what has taken place. Since you have obviously seen the error of your ways and therefore desire to atone for what you have done, it is fitting that you accompany him, so that the governor may hear the information from your own lips. . . ." It was a suitable penance and he savored the cleverness of it as he spoke.

"Then he lives," Luz said.

With these words, simple though they were and spoken in a flat voice, he should have known, but while a faint suspicion entered his mind, the thought was so preposterous, his pleasure at the cleverness of the plan so intense, that it quickly passed. "Wait," he said, "until I finish. Having told the governor, then you may lead the soldiers back to the Hawk and supervise the task, undo what you have already done."

She said nothing. Little light fell into the windowless room and he could not see her expression clearly, but from the set of her shoulders and, more than this, from her continued silence, the suspicion came to him again that she did not intend to ask his forgiveness. A hard look came into his eyes and he took a step toward her. "The idea does not please you?" he said.

Even now he expected her to relent, to fall to her knees, at least to implore his mercy, but she did none of these. She stood facing him, her shoulders unyielding. Quietly she said, "I will never take this information to the pueblo."

# 21

IT WAS not yet night but the room was growing dark. Someone had just closed the door and Dunavant could hear steps in the courtyard. The shutters on the window moved against their fastenings, rasping and straining in the wind, and the wind was working at the walls of the house and along the roof.

Slowly he moved his head on the pillow; when he could move it no farther he shifted his eyes toward the window. Through a crack in the shutters he saw a segment of earth and sky, both indistinct and joined together in a yellow flowing haze. He looked toward the door where yellow light showed also along the sill. A shadow fell across the light, passed on, and then another shadow which did not move.

His gaze drifted around the room. It was small and meagerly furnished, with a chest and table against the opposite wall, a rawhide chair, the bed on which he lay, which was not a bed but a pallet of straw suspended from strips of leather. The window was low and narrow and barred with iron. There was a wooden crucifix over the chest, but this could be disregarded. The room was a cell, a cell in a prison. Not in Tepic as he had thought when he had first gained consciousness, not there below the ground with water dropping from the ceiling and green scum crawling over the stone walls, yet a cell nevertheless.

The shadow was still at the door and now someone was talking. He had heard many voices since he had been here in bed—was it last night or the night before he had come?—and he was beginning to recognize them. This one belonged to the old woman who wore a rusty black dress, a black shawl around her head, and loops of black wooden beads that rattled when she walked.

She was talking quietly, but he realized that it would be possible to hear what she was saying; by concentration he could separate her voice from the confusion of the wind. The effort, however, would require more strength than he had, and besides, he already knew. He had heard it before, from her and from the man with the long bony face and hair braided like a cap on top of his head, the same one he had seen at the gate—De Zubaran himself. They had said it in many ways without saying it. He, Grady Dunavant, was going to die, if not today then tomorrow.

Well, they were wrong, he thought. He was not going to die in this cell, either today or tomorrow. He was going to get up and get the hell out of here.

The room was in darkness now and the old lady was no longer outside the door. He moved one elbow under him, secured a leverage and turned his body slightly. The ease with which he accomplished the movement surprised and pleased him as much as if it had been some complicated feat. He drew up the leg he was lying on. This was more difficult and when he was finished he was too tired to be pleased. Resting for a moment, his eyes closed, he kept his mind fixed on the next step.

The covers were heavy but he managed to pull them back so as to free the foot he was going to place on the floor. He opened his eyes and looked down; the floor was farther away than it should have been and had a peculiar slant. It began to move a little and he watched it intently until it stopped. Then, seeing that the covers had been pulled back, he eased his leg over the edge of the bed. It was the easiest thing he had done so far.

Grinning, he sat there gathering his strength. He planned what he would do when he was on his feet. A lull came in the wind and during it he heard horses stirring around in the corral below the house, the sound of dogs and coyotes fighting over the remains of the slaughter down by the river. The stench of offal began to seep into the room. The smell turned his stomach. Then the wind came up and he felt better.

All day, lying in bed, he had tried to build up in his mind an accurate picture of the ranch, the position of the gate and corrals, and the location of the whole in relation to the compass. The location he knew from his first sight of the ranch from the hillside. The arrangement of the house had been difficult to construct, for all he had to go on, besides the fact that it was built in the shape of a hollow square, was a restricted view of the courtyard and what lay beyond. The important thing, the position of the gate, he hadn't been able to figure out.

His foot didn't reach the floor and he saw that it would be necessary to lift himself from the pillow. This was hard because the arm he needed for the movement was the one which was numb, but he shifted his weight from his elbow and gradually lifted and transferred it to his clenched hand. At the same time he started to turn his body, using his hand as a lever. There was an instant of tension and he pushed harder to overcome it. Then, as if a chain had snapped, the tension ceased. An icy knife ran through his shoulder; his throat was filled with suffocating pain. A cry escaped him. He closed his teeth on it and sank back on the bed.

When he opened his eyes, small points of light were flickering over the dark beams of the ceiling. A candle was burning on the table and beside it stood the old woman. Instantly he closed his eyes and pretended sleep. He didn't open them again until she had gone, leaving the door ajar behind her.

He would have to wait for a while because she would come back, wait until everyone had gone to bed. He realized now that his efforts to get up had been senseless—if he had managed it, even got as far as putting on his clothes, she would have found him when she came in. An hour or two and he would try it again.

The thought of the effort and pain that lay ahead of him, the simple struggle to get to his feet, threw him into a cold sweat, but it didn't lessen his resolve. Tom Risk and his men were waiting for him at Wolfe's. Jacob Kroll was waiting in Los Angeles. Undoubtedly De Zubaran had sent word of his capture to the garrison there and at any hour Pico's soldiers could be expected to come bursting through the door.

Bitterly he damned himself for a fool. If only he had shot Roque de Zubaran instead of the youth's horse! That tender quixotic impulse had brought him to the pass he was now in, wounded, in the house of a Spaniard, in imminent danger of being captured. And all for what? Love for a girl who had not so much as bothered to enter the room. Everyone else had been here at some time—De Zubaran, his sons, the old woman in the black dress, a dozen servants—but not Luz. She had not even taken the trouble to send a message. He had looked for her throughout the day, listening for her footsteps, thinking each time someone came into the room that it was she. But now as he lay there and waited for time to pass and tried to brace himself for the ordeal in front of him, the whole thing was borne in upon him for what it was—a ridiculous piece of folly. Only a fool, and the vainest of the breed, would have thought anything else from the start, from the moment on the river when she came riding through the trees, than that both her warning and her surrender were a calculated plan to betray him—the warning an excuse for coming and the surrender a means by which to delay him.

Presently the old woman appeared with a bowl of gruel and, when she saw that he was apparently asleep, put the bowl on the table and left. His clothes lay on the chest next to the bed and by effort he found his watch. In the dim light he made out the dial and the hands stopped at ten minutes after eight—the time, likely, he had been knocked to the ground.

He put the watch back in his jacket. The time did not matter or, as far as that went, the day. The thing that mattered was that he was in a tight spot. Curiously he felt no panic. He had been in tight spots before and had always got out of them. And I'll get out of this one, he thought. Dead or alive, I'll get out. He wondered if they had taken his Colt. Probably. He would have no trouble finding a horse—if not his own, another. It was about three hours to Jim Wolfe's. What he would do when he got there, he didn't know; he would have to work that out later.

As he lay listening to the wind, waiting for time to pass, a strange feeling came over him, as if this weren't happening to him but to someone else, as if he were living in a different time and place, in another century. The house with its thick walls and barred windows, the heavy iron-banded gate, the shot tower—everything save a moat—could be a castle in feudal England. And within the house, the clan fiercely resentful of all strangers, arrogant in the strength of their lances. It might all be from a story of Sir Walter Scott, and he himself an actor in the story, a prisoner waiting for an uncertain fate, in a feudal dungeon.

For an instant he grinned, but as he thought of the girl, a wave of anger swept over him. "Damn her!" he said deliberately. And then, putting her out of his mind, he began to plan how he was to get his clothes on and out of the gate. The very thought of the effort which he faced made him sweat.

Leaning against the wind and clutching her shawl tight against her breast, Carlota hobbled down the *portale*. In her free hand she carried her cane and under her arm a worn copy of the *Spanish Herbalist*. The book had been printed years before in Cádiz, changed and reprinted here in California by General Vallejo. She had read it many times and knew most of it by heart, but there were several points she wished to clear up when she got to her room. For one thing the matter of wounds which have begun to fester. She remembered the exact wording of the book, "Weave a tiny cage of twigs. Place bluebottle flies inside it. Then tie the cage to the wound . . ." It was a sovereign remedy, which she had used many times with arrow wounds, but with the santana blowing, none of the servants had been able to catch bluebottles, not so much as one. Therefore she was in need of a different cure.

Governor Pico's soldiers would probably appear tonight, since Saturnino had left for the pueblo late yesterday afternoon. It was unlikely, however, that they would depart before morning, and with luck, she might delay their return for another day. In that time she should be able to get the American in shape to travel.

She had made an effort to detain Saturnino, to induce him to wait until after the caravan had been outfitted and started off for Santa Fe before making the trip to Los Angeles, but while his first wrath had cooled somewhat after he had slept on it, nothing she could say or do had succeeded. Even another reference to Mitla and the Indian girl had been of no avail. Saturnino had answered this by taking Mitla with him.

In the end, she realized now, it was better the way everything had developed. Once in the pueblo, the American would have the services of a surgeon, not a good one, yet someone more skilled than she was. There never had been any chance of keeping him out of the hands of the military, in view of Saturnino's attitude. The one important thing was the saving of his life, of getting him to Los Angeles safely. When he had arrived there, she would have done all she was capable of doing in the circumstances. She had held her own against her son; Governor Pico and his soldiers were another matter.

In only one thing had she failed, and this failure rankled as she made her way through the courtyard. All of her entreaties and threats had been of no avail when it came to freeing her granddaughter from the noisome hole where she now had lain for two days, without proper care for her wounds, subsisting since yesterday on the meager rations of corn and water Saturnino had placed there before he left. The house had been searched for another key, but Saturnino had taken the only one with him, as well as Mitla, the one person capable of fashioning another. He had gone, she was certain, out of fear that her threats would finally wear him down. For in the beginning, before she had commenced to work on him, he had planned to send Roque with the message. It was well for him, she thought bitterly, that he had gone.

With the head of her cane Carlota tapped on the door. *"Hola, hombre!"* she shouted. "One thing you may be thankful for. You do not have to live in this wind. And furthermore you still eat as well as any on the Hawk." As soon as Saturnino had ridden away she had given orders that no food was to be cooked and nothing eaten except gruel in order that the shame of the deed would be impressed upon everyone. "The soldiers arrive shortly and then the door opens," she said.

The girl's voice came clear and strong through the iron-banded planks. "What has happened since you were here?"

"Nothing. He sleeps. I have just come from there and he sleeps so soundly I did not attempt to give him food."

"Then you didn't say what I told you."

Carlota snorted. "How does one speak to those who sleep?"

"He has been here for two days!"

"Be patient. I will talk to him before he is taken to the pueblo."

After a moment Luz said, "Isn't it possible to take him to Wolfe's?"

"I have thought of it. But what happens then? Pico's soldiers will search for him, there at Wolfe's among the first. They will find him. Then what transpires? He will be taken off to Los Angeles. Nothing would be accomplished and much would be risked. He is mending. Another day or two and he will be in shape to travel. It is a time for patience."

"Patience!" the scornful reply came back. "Have you searched again for the key? There *is* another. I have seen it in the saddlery."

"It does not exist. We have looked."

"A file?"

"They have been hidden."

"Then a stout post from the corral and two men."

"The *vaqueros* are not here. They left this morning at dawn, undoubtedly at the request of your father, and they will not return until he does." The door began to rattle on its hinges, the heavy lock creaked. "Again, patience!" Carlota said.

The sounds stopped. "You will give the message?" Luz shouted above the wind. "Now?"

"Now," Carlota replied, drawing her shawl across her mouth.

At the door of the room she paused and looked in. The American, lying beneath the heavy sheepskin covers, was still asleep. She went on past the room to her own, sat down in her high-backed chair, lighted a fat, deer-tallow candle and opened the pages of the *Spanish Herbalist*. Little idea did she have, when she had sent her granddaughter chasing off after the American that day by the river, what it would lead to. And now, as she began to read the print which was too fine for her eyes, she wondered where it would end. But somehow, despite all the misfortune, she could not find any regret in her heart. The wheel, she reflected, had not made its full circle.

At the moment the thing which annoyed her the most, besides the fineness of the print, was that her feet were cold. Cold feet in June. *Ay de mi!* If only Rosario, her footstool, had not gone running off with the rest of the men. What a thumping he would inherit upon his return!

Tepeyollotl, the Indian, stood by the corral. Wrapped to the eyes in his great poncho, his back to the wind, his broad hat pulled far down over his forehead, he stood where he could watch the gate. When the time was right she would come to the gate—that was the signal. The horse of Señor Dunavant, of which he did not have a high opinion, for in his life he had never seen a spotted horse worth its grain, was saddled beside his own. Everything was in readiness outside the gates. What, he thought, happens within?

The wind, turning cold, bit through his poncho. He had not eaten since last night, unless a handful of corn could be called eating—on a ranch of these proportions, he mused, a man had a right to expect better fare. Also he was tired. Since the day Don Juan Bandini had secured his release from the *juzgado* in San Diego, where he had been placed the night the ship sailed, he had ridden northward without stopping. Ridden two horses from under him, neither sleeping nor resting, following the trail of the señor, but always a day behind him.

He was, when he thought of it closely, very tired, more tired than he was hungry. For more than a day now he had been at this ranch where the best that could be found was a palmful of corn, and not that until this morning, when after lurking all night in the brush, he had seen the men ride away, and had gone up to the gate and knocked.

It had not been necessary for him to inquire about the señor, and he had not gone to the gate for that reason—he had found pieces of the broken lance, the signs of a struggle in the churned sand, the pool of dried blood there and marks along the trail, likewise on the saddle and the coat of the spotted horse. He had gone to the gate, having brushed his clothes carefully, and rehearsed the manners he had learned in the service of Señora Llorente, to make friends among the Indian girls. With him he carried a ready story about being the servant of a *caballero* who was en route to Sonora and who wished to ask the small favor of a pinch of salt for his breakfast.

The way things turned out, the story was not required. To be more accurate, when the girl came in reply to his summons, smiling as she closed the gate behind her, he completely forgot the story, and it was only now, standing here by the corral, that he recalled it.

In that instant, as she looked at him and smiled, with her hair blowing wildly around her face, he had not only forgotten the tale he had invented, but also his manners. He had stood gawking at her like a lout of a cholo, like one who cuts wood for a living or who has spent his life in a cave and never before has laid eyes on a woman. He had even forgotten to doff his sombrero, he who had lived in the City of Mexico, in a house whose chandeliers were brighter than the sun.

"Good day, señor," she had said. Just this simple greeting, but it had been enough to bring a tightness to his throat. She spoke again, asking what his pleasure was, and he knew then, if he had not known it before, that he must have this woman with the blowing hair, whose voice made drums beat in his blood.

Her name was Guadalupe. She came from a village beyond the first tall mountains, on the trail to San Diego. For three weeks she had been here and was unhappy and wanted to return to the mountains. He had learned these things from her when late in the afternoon she had slipped away and met him in the barranca. It was not until the sun was going down and the time came for her to leave that he remembered to ask about the señor.

Tepeyollotl drew the poncho closer around him. He had lost track of the hours he had been waiting here at the corral. He looked overhead—the stars were obscured by the driven sand—and back again toward the house. The señor was wounded and would need help. When Guadalupe appeared, he would lead the horses to the gate, and she would take him to the room, where between them they would clothe and carry him to his horse.

The wind grew sharper, the minutes passed, the lights in the two windows he could see from his vantage point went out, and then as he began to think of finding a place to sleep for the night, the gate opened.

Quietly, the stirrups looped over the pommels to keep them from making a noise, he led the horses in a wide circle to avoid being seen from the windows, and slowly approached the house.

Guadalupe came running to meet him. She was excited, and he thought at first that something had gone wrong with their plans, but as she spoke, saying that the American had left the room, that she had been unable to find him within the house, he saw the American beyond her. He appeared out of the courtyard and stood an instant leaning there against the gate, his head on his chest. Looking up and seeing the spotted pony, he started toward it, stumbled and fell.

He was heavy and of little help, but working together they managed to get him into the saddle and his feet in the stirrups.

"Where do you go?" Guadalupe asked.

The man in the saddle said nothing, and Tepeyollotl answered for him. "We ride from here."

Suddenly Guadalupe said, coming close to him, "Take me with you. I will cook your food and watch over you both."

Her voice made the drums beat again in his blood, and not trusting himself, he did not reply until he had climbed into the stirrups. "I come back," he said then, and moved off, leading the spotted pony.

She ran forward beside his horse. "When?" she cried.

"Soon," he answered her.

"I wait," she said and fell behind. "Go with God!"

Tepeyollotl rode across the mesa. He did not know where he was going; it was of no importance at the moment. His thoughts were concerned only with the girl. Wherever it was, when the time came, he would leave the señor and return to the pueblo and there inform Doña Yris, his mistress, that he had fulfilled his obligations—she could not ask him to spend the rest of his days chasing after a man whose actions were unfathomable and of no special concern to him, who went from one trouble to another. In due course, with her permission or without, he would ride again to the gate he had just left.

As they reached the King's Highway he said, "Where, señor?"

Sitting upright and grasping the pommel in one hand, feeling a recoil of pain at each step of his horse, Grady Dunavant gave the directions. He gnawed on his dry lips, but his mind was clear. He had got over his surprise at seeing Joe and his fear when he came through the gate that Joe was one of the De Zubaran *vaqueros*. It was a long ride to Jim Wolfe's, but he would get there, for the anger, which kept him in the saddle, was greater and more enduring than his pain.

# 22

The sun was a red ball in the west. Outside the barred window, chickens stood in a patch of cottonwood shade, their beaks open, tipsy with the heat. Somewhere beyond the thick walls he could hear the wheezing of bullocks. Drops of pitch hung from the roof, slowly lengthened out in thin shining black ribbons and fell into the hot dust. Above all the sounds was the soft tread of the sentries, moving along the walls.

From his bunk, Grady Dunavant looked down on the crooked lanes of the pueblo, at the smoke turned yellow by the blazing sun, and the plaza where a regiment was drawn up for inspection, two ragged lines which seemed from the distance like gaudily painted toy soldiers. He sat hunched forward on the bunk, favoring his wounded shoulder, trying to piece together the succession of events since the night he and the Indian had ridden down from the mesa. For the first time in the three days he had been here his mind was clear.

His head throbbed more than his shoulder, but he could think clearly and consecutively. He now knew where he was and why and what lay ahead of him. And little by little, with the exception of the last hour before they reached Jim Wolfe's and the five or six hours afterward, he had pieced together what had happened there at the ranch. He remembered the next morning lying in the great four-poster bed which Wolfe had brought around the Horn, and hearing the faint shrill of metal crickets. The sound came from the east over the rolling hills, and long before they rode past the window—six men in long blue capes with scarlet facings—he was certain that they were soldiers from the Los Angeles garrison, and that they were coming for him.

Jim Wolfe knew it too, for at the first thin piping he rose, picked up the buffalo gun leaning against the wall, and by the time the soldiers were at the gate he was there to meet them. He had closed the door when he went out, but Dunavant could hear snatches of the conversation through the open window. It started with everyone exchanging pleasantries in the politest Spanish fashion, and then a period of silence followed in which he heard Tom Risk and his men whispering in the courtyard. Then the voices began to rise and two of the Spaniards and Wolfe were talking at once. In the midst of the shouting the gate crashed shut.

He heard horses moving away, the sound of crickets growing fainter toward the west, and a moment later Jim Wolfe came into the room, red in the face and swearing.

"I damned well gave them something to think about," he said, striding up and down the room, clutching the heavy buffalo gun. "They wanted to come in and nose around. As much as called me a liar when I said you wasn't here. No man living does that to Jim Wolfe. When I lie I don't like to be told about it. Leastways not by a bunch of coyotes." He paused at the window and looked out. "Got a good notion to take Risk and his men—they're spoiling for a ruckus—and shag them all the way to the pueblo."

While Jim Wolfe paced the floor uttering his threats, Grady fell asleep. Out of exhaustion and relief he had slept the clock around and would have slept longer except for the arrival of Phelps from Los Angeles. The man rode up in midmorning, and Wolfe brought him immediately to the room. Phelps was a wiry young trapper whom he had met at Jacob Kroll's, one of the eleven men Kroll had recruited for the attack on the garrison. Staring from dirt-rimmed eyes, he stood at the foot of the bed and poured out a story of a long running fight with Governor Pico's soldiers which had begun in the pueblo and had ended before dawn when he had eluded them at the San Gabriel.

But it was not this that had brought Dunavant upright in bed. When Phelps had finished his story and taken a swig of *aguardiente* furnished by his host, the young trapper said in a calm voice, as if it were an unimportant incident which had slipped his mind, "Captain Frémont has struck in the North."

By stages, between swigs from the jug of *aguardiente* Phelps supplied the rest of the details as they had come by courier from General Castro, Pico's commander at Monterey. The attack had been made on the Sonoma fortress, at dawn eight days before, and after a bloody battle General Vallejo was forced to surrender. A flag had been raised, the California Republic proclaimed. General Vallejo had been placed in irons and carted off to Sutter's Fort.

But the vital part of the story came later, just before Phelps sat down and gave his whole attention to the jug of *aguardiente*. It seemed that when the courier, spurring a lathered horse and discharging his musket, had galloped into the plaza the previous afternoon, the news had upset a hornet's nest. The garrison was turned out, cannons unlimbered, proclamations issued, calling on the citizenry to rally to the defense of the motherland, parties were sent out to search the homes of all foreigners, and by nightfall several arrests had been made, Jacob Kroll and Kate Howland among them.

Grady knew then that the jig was up, that sooner or later, likely before another day had gone, Governor Pico would send the soldiers back to the ranch, their numbers increased, to arrest him.

They didn't come the next day but they did come the day following—thirty this time instead of six. His first reaction to the arrest of Kroll and Kate Howland had been to flee, to take his horse and hide out in the mountains, although the chances were small that he wouldn't be captured eventually. He had found, however, as soon as he tried to get on his feet, that he was in no condition to travel far, let alone to undergo the rigors of living indefinitely in the mountains. There was nothing to do, therefore, except to wait and hope.

When the soldiers had ridden up, Jim Wolfe, passing carbines around among his *vaqueros,* had proposed to make a fight out of it. Tom Risk was still there with his men and, like Wolfe, still spoiling for a ruckus, but it was plain to Dunavant that they would lose in the end; furthermore, that he had no right to involve others in something which was really his own affair. And so, while Wolfe was exchanging insults with Lieutenant Morales through the gate, he had walked out and given himself up.

Down in the plaza a bugle sounded, the two lines of soldiers wheeled off and disappeared. A few minutes later he saw two men on horses leave the Governor's Mansion and cross the plaza. They started up the winding trail that led to the house, now converted into a jail, in which he and Kroll and Kate Howland had been held for five days, waiting the convening of the military junta. They moved at a leisurely pace, the sun hot on the gilt and scarlet of their uniforms, laughing as they rode—after five days still in no hurry.

Grady got to his feet and went into the next room where Kroll and Kate Howland were talking. They had already discussed their coming appearance before the junta, having had little else to do during the period of their imprisonment, but he wanted to be sure that they were in final agreement. From hour to hour Mrs. Howland had changed her proposed defense. At first she had been too outraged either to discuss it or even to admit that Don Pío Pico would have the nerve to bring her to trial, since he as well as many of the influential ranchers who supported him were in her debt. Didn't she hold mortgages on five of the largest ranches in the south, and hadn't she lent Pico himself the sum of two thousand dollars? Certainly he would never have the temerity to make her stand trial before a military tribunal!

The first two days of her arrest had been spent in her own house. She had expected to be released hourly either by the intervention of Pico or by Abel Stearns, the Los Angeles agent of the United States Consul Thomas Larkin. At the end of the second day she had sent letters to both men, but Pico ignored the letter and Stearns was out of town. Consul Larkin was in Monterey, four hundred miles to the north.

And then when Dunavant had been brought in, and she and Jacob Kroll were removed from their homes and the three of them placed in the servants' quarters of the old Bustamente house, which in her estimation was only fit for cattle, she had fallen into a determined and silent rage. But as the days passed and it became clear from the news leaking out of the garrison, relayed along by the sentries, that the junta was preparing evidence for their trial, and that neither Don Pío Pico nor Stearns had any intention of coming to her aid, she began to concoct fantastic plans for escape. Finally, after this was poorly received by Kroll and Dunavant and by Monsieur Malibran, a Frenchman who was likewise sharing the house, she commenced to take interest in what was to be said when they appeared for trial.

She had a fertile but changeable mind, and as Dunavant now entered the room he was certain from the gleam in her eyes that she had cooked up something new. "A couple of Lieutenant Morales' men riding up the hill," he said, and with an attempt at humor; "they should be here by dark."

Kate Howland jumped to her feet. If she had any new proposal, it left her as he spoke. Casting about her, as if looking for her long-barreled musket, she snapped, "I'll not go, not a step. You can tell them that for me." Then a hopeful light broke over her leathery face. "I'll stay right here until Captain Frémont comes."

The Frenchman, a neat little man and a botanist, who spent his time arranging a collection of wild flowers, said, "It is this—to wait for *monsieur le capitaine*—which I prefer also."

"And it won't be long before you'll see him," Kate Howland said.

When everything else failed, she invariably fell back on Captain Frémont. To Dunavant this was a forlorn hope, although he had never bothered to say so and didn't now. From pieces of information he had been able to pick up, the version of the battle at Sonoma which Phelps had brought to the ranch was incorrect in every important detail. In the first place, the attack was not made by Frémont and his men, but by a handful of freebooters led by a trapper named Merritt. In the second place, the battle was not bloody; in fact it was not a battle. The commander of the fort, General Vallejo, surprised while asleep, had responded to the interruption by offering the attackers a jug of his best brandy. Moreover, Merritt and his men and the California Republic, which they proclaimed, had been promptly repudiated by the American Consul Thomas Larkin. About the only correct detail of Phelps's story was that Vallejo had been seized and placed in custody at Sutter's Fort. Where Captain Frémont was, no one seemed to know. It was unlikely, Dunavant thought, that he was on his way to Los Angeles to rescue Monsieur Malibran and Kate Howland. More probably, he was at Sutter's on the Sacramento, mulling over Consul Larkin's repudiation of the newly organized Republic.

Jacob Kroll was of the same opinion, and blunt about expressing it. "Let's forget this business of being rescued. If by any remote chance Frémont does come, do you suppose for one minute that Governor Pico will not have advance warning, and if he abandons the town, he'll not take us along as hostages?" Kroll pulled his waistcoat down over his paunch and fixed a cold eye on Kate Howland. "What have you decided to say when you meet Lieutenant Morales?"

"I'll not say anything because I'll not leave the house," she replied, rising. She shut herself in her room.

As it turned out no one was called on to say anything at the moment—no one save Monsieur Malibran—for when the soldiers appeared it was the Frenchman whom they took away. From his bunk Dunavant watched the prim little man stumbling down the hill between the two horsemen, running to keep up, his collection of wild flowers grasped tightly in his hand. Where, he wondered, had Morales found the inoffensive Frenchman? What possible case could they have against him? Why were they bothering with him when there were bigger fish in the net?

And pondering this as he watched Monsieur Malibran disappear, and the night fall swiftly over the town, he wondered if, after all, the influence of Yris Llorente was not behind the delay in bringing him and the others to trial. It certainly was not any of Camilla Howland's doing. For the last three days Yris had been making a nuisance of herself in the town. According to the reports of the guards, she had threatened Governor Pico and accosted Morales on the street. She would probably end by being carted up the hill. It might be, he thought suddenly, that this was her plan!

Yes, the delay of the trial was due to Yris Llorente. Twice each day food was carted up the hill by an old woman on a donkey. On the first day, along with an unsavory pot of mashed beans and tough meat, she had brought him a note from Doña Yris, in which he was advised that there were forces working for his release. No word had come from her the following day and nothing so far today, though the old woman had not yet arrived with their supper.

She came later than usual, with the same cold pot of beans and meat, with another note which she slipped into his hand when the sentry was not looking. He had said nothing to either Kate Howland or Kroll about the first note. He said nothing about this one. Reading it after supper in his room, he learned to his dismay why Monsieur Malibran had been arrested and quartered with them, and why he had left. The note said, besides the news that events were progressing satisfactorily in town, ". . . Do not take Malibran into your confidence. I learn that he has been placed among you in the role of an informer."

"The little flower-picking sonofabitch," Dunavant said to the empty room.

The rest of the evening he spent reading his book of military maxims—though the way things were shaping up he would never have any use for them—between pages trying to remember what had been said in the presence of Monsieur Malibran. When his head ached too much to read—it was always his head that hurt more than the wound in his shoulder—he sat in the dark and looked down at the lights of the town and wondered what the Frenchman was telling Lieutenant Morales there behind the closed doors of the *cuartel.*

Whatever it was, whether it was true or not, it would put a new complexion on his situation. Whatever Doña Yris had done for him before, her chances now of bringing about his release were considerably lessened. One fortunate thing was that the soldier he had clubbed over the head outside the gate had suffered nothing more than a headache. But he was still a conspirator, subject to any punishment the Spaniards wished to inflict—continued imprisonment, the *baqueta,* deportation, one or all of them.

And so, as he sat watching the pine torches burning in front of the *cuartel,* he found himself in the end pinning his hopes, like Kate Howland, on the possibility of the American forces laying siege to the town. Not the forces under Captain Frémont, he thought, managing a grin at the irony of himself, the intrepid liberator, now called on to seek liberation. But perhaps Commodore Sloat. For a month or more, according to rumor, Sloat had been maneuvering his squadron at Mazatlán. There was a chance that he had already sailed. A chance that he was off the Port of San Diego. Even as far north as San Pedro, making ready to send marines ashore! . . .

Dunavant sat in the dark elaborating the dream and thought, I'm as bad as Kate Howland. I'm getting to be an old woman. A tiresome one at that.

Captain Frémont, as Grady Dunavant had supposed, was still on the Sacramento, weighing Merritt's success at Sonoma against Larkin's repudiation of the attack. But things were more promising with Commodore Sloat. Although he was not yet off the coast, he *was* on his way northward in the 54-gun *Savannah,* racing along the shore of Baja California toward the Port of Monterey.

On the morning following his talk with Mr. Bolton, after a sleepless night spent going over every detail of the letter Secret Agent Parrott had sent from Mexico City, Sloat left his cabin and went forward to the quarter-deck. Across the glassy waters of the estuary the roofs of Mazatlán shimmered in a sticky haze. The hot breath of the jungle and the reek of tide flats, borne to him on the light land breeze, sat heavily on his stomach. The hammering of sailors chipping rust in the forward chains jangled his nerves. He turned and fixed a bilious eye on the first luff.

"We'll see the ship at six bells," he said. "Battle stations, Mr. Long."

He returned to his cabin, squinted at the weatherglass, opened the logbook and closed it, and sat looking out through the stern ports. He had inspected the ship yesterday afternoon, and the day before, and there was no reason for another inspection except that it would serve to ease his taut nerves, to allay perhaps the grumbling of the afterguard and some of the officers, who were beginning to chafe after weeks of inaction.

Long before the hour of inspection he was on the quarter-deck, and as the ship's bell struck six times, marking eleven o'clock, he was making his way below. The steerage was in good shape—as good shape as could be expected after a month in a tropical port—but he succeeded in finding enough wrong to occupy the attention of the second luff, Mr.

Leimert, one of the more restless of the officers. After the steerage he visited the sick bay, the berth deck and wardrooms. He took his time about each, and gave the purser a bad five minutes over the ship's provisions, likewise the surgeon and the loblolly boys in the cockpit, criticizing the way the instruments were laid out and even the sand buckets. He climbed the main ladder to the gun deck, where the ports were open, the guns run out, and the serving crews stood at attention. He first inspected the marine on guard at the grog tub, and then passed on to the batteries, giving each as close a scrutiny as if they were going into an engagement the next hour.

He paused to query the purser, Dangerfield Fauntleroy, a dour-faced Vermonter who looked like a purser and was the best rifle shot in the United States.

He had reached the quarter-deck ladder when he heard above him the cry "Sail ho!" from the mainmast lookout. He scrambled to the quarter-deck, feeling the sudden pumping of his heart, in time to see Captain Mervine, who had left him a moment before, looking toward the southwest. There, under topsails alone, a British sloop of war was bearing in from the sea. On the making tide she slipped past the gray sandspits that lay like sleeping lizards on the harbor's entrance. She came so quietly across the water, her canvas barely holding the sultry air, with no show of white along her forefoot, that she seemed to be borne onward solely by the tide. She came so quietly that he could clearly make out the chanting of the leadsman.

"The *Minerva,*" Captain Mervine said.

The finality of the statement irked Sloat. He took the captain's glass and counted the guns—twenty-four in number, not including a brace of deck carronades—and scanned the yards. It was not the same ship that had entered the harbor yesterday and left with the tide, but it was a ship from Admiral Sir George Seymour's fleet, on the identical mission of spying out his movements.

"By the deep nine," came the chant of the leadsman.

Sloat without comment handed the glass to Captain Mervine. He kept his eyes on the approaching sloop. For weeks he had been subjected to this almost daily scrutiny and his patience was beginning to run thin.

"And a half eight," the leadsman chanted.

The sloop was on the broad starboard tack which had brought her through the entrance, but, now well inside, she suddenly came up on a course that set her bearing down directly on the *Savannah.*

"By the mark seven," said the leadsman.

Sloat watched the ship in heavy silence, expecting to see her luff or go over on the larboard tack. She did neither. Under a steady helm, though losing headway, she bore down on him to the faint flutter of canvas and the chanting of the leadsman in the chains.

"My God, sir!" Mr. Long said behind him.

Sloat said nothing. The sloop, as the lieutenant feared, was not going to double the *Savannah's* quarter, but the calculated insult was too apparent to mistake. Her course had been set deliberately to give them all a good view of British seamanship. He turned on his heel and, speaking to Mervine, led the way into his cabin. There, out of sight of the British captain and the sailors that lined the sloop's bulwarks, he waited until the ship had passed close under the *Savannah's* counter and come up into the wind at a distance of a half mile.

When he again emerged on deck, the sloop's cables had been run out, men were in the rigging furling the sails, and awnings were being stretched fore and aft. She lay broadside to the *Savannah,* and for a moment Sloat was seized with the impulse to order a beat to quarters, the guns again run out, the powder monkeys sent scurrying to the magazines, loggerheads to the braziers—a show of action in return for the lesson in seamanship.

But as he stood embracing the idea, spots of livid color burning on his pale cheeks, he saw a string of signals run up on the sloop. A quick glance told him that they were not meant for him. For whom, then? The British consul across the water in Mazatlán? One of their numerous Mexican sympathizers? A moment later a boat put out from the sloop and made for the shore under the sweep of four oarsmen. In the stern sheets were two gold-braided officers.

He turned to Mervine. "Go ashore, captain, find Mr. Bolton and learn if any additional word has come from Mexico City." Walking to the break of the quarter-deck as the captain lowered himself to the waiting boat, he said, "If you can, find out what the two Britishers are up to."

He stood at the rail and trained the glass on the two officers now stepping ashore, watching them while they got into a carriage and set off toward the plaza, a band of barefooted urchins running at the wheels. With instructions to Mr. Long, who had the deck, to report any unusual activities aboard the sloop, he returned to his cabin and began a frugal lunch of fruit and weak coffee. The brazenness of the British captain in bearing down upon him, with the whole estuary to maneuver in, was still a hard lump in his stomach. He puzzled over the signals that had been run up and the departure of the two officers, presumably on an urgent mission for they had debarked as soon as the ship had anchored. And then, tormented anew by the problems raised by Parrott's letter and Bolton's advice, neither of which he had acted on, he rose and with his lunch half finished went to the open stern port.

The sloop lay quietly at anchor in the steaming heat, the string of signals no longer flying at her masthead. Beside the boat pulled up on shore, the sailors stood waiting in the shade of a palm clump. The two officers might have gone into the town on a routine visit, but the fact of their haste was against it. Were they, like him, seeking fresh instructions? Or had they already received the news of war and were here simply to inform the British consul? And if this were true, if war had been declared, was it possible that Admiral Seymour had already sailed for the coast of California? Could it be, he thought, that the arrival of the sloop, the mysterious signals, the hasty departure of the officers, were parts of a plan devised by Seymour to deceive him and mask his own movements?

In a state of nerves he again sat down to eat. He had finished his lunch when Captain Mervine appeared at the door and reported that nothing new had been heard from Mr. Parrott. "But," said Mervine, "Mr. Bolton has learned that an emissary from Governor Pico, José Covarrubias, who was sent to Mexico City last January and is now on his way home, stopped in San Blas four days ago and asked Seymour to assume a protectorate over California."

Sloat stood up. "What would you do, Captain Mervine?" At no time during the weeks at Mazatlán had he asked Mervine's advice or the advice of any of his officers, and now as he spoke he was aware of the other's surprise. "Would you sail, captain?"

Mervine, who had long concealed his impatience, concealed it at this moment. "I would, sir," he said, as if he had just made up his mind.

"Then give the order," Sloat said, and feeling suddenly twenty years younger, finished his coffee, glanced at the weather gauge, walked to the door and reached the deck as the pipes twittered and the first command was shouted.

While the flags came down, winches groaned and chains rattled in the hawsepipes and men scrambled up the ratlines, Commodore Sloat, though he was aware of every movement and sound on the ship, kept his eyes on the British sloop and the four sailors still standing on shore.

At the instant the first reefs shook out of their courses and the topsails cascaded above him, he saw a puff of smoke at the sloop's bow. A second later the boom of the recall gun came over the water. The *Savannah* was moving slowly under her topsails before the carriage and the two officers, with the driver beating his horses, pulled up at the shore.

"They'll have a good chance to show their seamanship," Sloat said to Captain Mervine, and gave orders for more sail.

Under royals and skysails the ship trembled and surged forward through the harbor entrance, met the long swells of the Pacific and, raising a school of porpoises, headed west across the sun-bright sea. Astern, the sun shone on the roofs of Mazatlán; the shore and the white line of the breakers grew faint. And yet no sail showed at the entrance of the harbor. Nor, as he swept all the horizons with his glass, was there any sign of the *Collingwood.*

In his cabin he sat down at his desk, opened the logbook and wrote in it with a steady hand, "June 8th at 2 P.M. got under way for Monterey." Then, sanding the entry, he lay down on his bunk. The telltale compass, placed in the carlings so as to be visible from where he lay, was steady on the ship's course. Exhausted, he closed his eyes and fell into a light sleep, from which he was awakened by the long, descending wail of the lookout, "Sail ho!"

He was on deck in an instant. "Where away?" he shouted.

"Close on the larboard quarter" came the reply from aloft.

He was certain that it wasn't the sloop from that quarter. "What do you make?"

"She's British, sir. A frigate."

The *Collingwood!* Seymour had been lying off the harbor and had seen him come out. "At what distance?" he shouted through cupped hands.

A pause and then the answer, "Fourteen miles, sir."

Sloat turned to Captain Mervine. "If Seymour has later news than we have, why should he follow us? If war has actually been declared, and he has the news and intends to protect California at the request of the Mexicans, why should he wait on our movements?"

Mervine said promptly, "Either he hasn't the news or he's running a bluff."

Sloat returned to his cabin and sat alone, puzzling over the appearance of the *Collingwood.* He was not satisfied with the captain's reply.

The thought flashed through his mind that war had been declared between the United States and Great Britain—that Oregon issue which had long been a bone of contention. The truculent attitude of the sloop when she entered the harbor could be taken in support of this theory. But why, if this were true, had Seymour not attacked him there in the estuary? The observance of the neutrality of a port had never since the earliest days been a British virtue.

It might be wiser to return to the harbor, raise the *Warren,* which he had left there to bring any dispatches that might come, and together with their combined guns await the intentions of Admiral Seymour. This plan he dismissed, however, as soon as he thought of it. Whatever the situation, it would be better to sail for Monterey where he would have the support, if need be, of the *Cyane* and *Levant.*

He glanced overhead at the telltale. The ship was on course, headed for the Sandwich Islands, an instinctive precaution he had taken at the outset. From the reported position of the *Collingwood* and allowing for her superior speed, she could not overtake the *Savannah* before nightfall. At that time, in the darkness, he could alter his course for Monterey.

Throughout the afternoon the ship crept closer, and when he went to the quarter-deck just before sunset, she was visible through the glass, hull down dead astern. The *Savannah* was logging fourteen knots, but though this was approaching her limit, and she was already carrying top and topgallant stuns'les, he ordered further trimming of the sails. As the command, "All hands the watch!" rang out he kept the glass on the *Collingwood.* When the sails were trimmed he ordered the ship log cast, and found to his pleasure that they had picked up a half knot.

Darkness fell swiftly, and with it he altered course to the northwest. For an hour they ran over a black sea, moving with a fine limber motion for which he silently thanked the New England builders and their sturdy oak. Then the moon came up. He looked astern and saw that the sea was empty.

He ate his supper alone, indulging himself in a small glass of wine, but every few minutes he went to the deck for a report from the lookout, and when he lay down in his bunk he left orders to be called at midnight. Sleep came slowly, for he found himself again thinking of his position if he took Monterey and then discovered that war had not been declared on Mexico. When he did sleep, it was fitfully. He would have slept sounder if he had known that on May 13, almost a month before, President Polk had signed a declaration of war.

In the cool dawn a rider forded the upper reaches of the Santa Ana and, turning south on the trail that followed the river, spurred his horse toward the Hill of the Hawk.

The cattle had been slaughtered, the hides pegged out to dry; on this morning Don Saturnino was supervising the trying out of the last of the tallow. Striding up and down between the two rows of iron pots, testing each batch and making certain that the bubbling scum was properly drained off, for the Hawk prided itself on the quality of its tallow, he wore a heavy expression of disgust. He had been around this work every season for twenty years and more, but the smell of cooking fat was still repulsive to him. It was a job that he would gladly have given to someone else if there had been anyone who could do it satisfactorily. To Juan Mitla, for instance, but Mitla and Don Roque were now three days along the trail on their journey to Santa Fe. It was unfortunate, the matter of Guadalupe, and that Mitla was not here this morning.

He missed the Indian greatly; he missed him even more a short time later, when walking down to the river for a breath of fresh air, he saw a horseman break through the brush at the upper end of the meadow and come galloping toward him. Before the man had covered a quarter of the distance he recognized Don Ricardo Haro from the Two Brothers, a ranch situated at the mouth of the Cajon. His big roach-maned bay was lathered with sweat. Don Ricardo himself was in a lather, his peaked hat bobbing on his shoulder, held there by his chin strap. Cajon was the pass through which marauding Indians, Ute, Piute and Shoshone, rode silently into the valley. He knew before Haro drew up at the corral in a shower of dirt why he had come. Haro might appear at the ranch twice during the year, or again not for two years. But whenever he came it was for only one reason.

He was a man of immense girth, with no neck and a broad powerful chin, furrowed along the jaw with the white scar of an Indian arrow.

"*Hola*, Don Ricardo," Saturnino said.

Haro sat in the saddle, catching his wind, and did not speak for several minutes.

"You have ridden hard and far," Saturnino said.

"I never encounter you except with news of Indians," Haro said.

"When you rode through the meadow I thought that. I thought of Indians and of Don Ricardo."

"Likewise, Don Saturnino, Indians and Don Saturnino de Zubaran. Never the one without the other." He wiped the ring of dirt from his mouth and set his hat on his head and apologized for his appearance. "I have ridden in a hurry."

Saturnino, remembering that Haro was a man of much politeness, even at a time like this, and anxious for the news he had brought, said, "I will inquire later after your health and the health of your family."

The big man smiled, showing yellow teeth streaked with dirt. "I likewise shall inquire later, for I have come on a mission of great urgency. But I trust that you and your family enjoy good health."

"Yes and you also."

"The rodeo has been to your satisfaction."

"To my satisfaction."

"Then with your permission I will speak," Haro said, looping the reins over the pommel. "Yesterday late in the afternoon two of my *vaqueros*, who had gone up the Cajon in search of cattle, saw Indian fires burning in a valley at the head of the pass. It was the time of dusk, but they could make out horses to the number of fifty, and though it was too dark to ascertain for certain, it is their opinion that the Indians were of the tribe of the Utah, with whom you are familiar."

Saturnino nodded, remembering that it was in this month three years ago that a band of the same Indians had raided the valley ranches and driven off more than two hundred head of horses. "But proceed, Don Ricardo."

"Immediately upon the return of my *vaqueros*, shortly before midnight, I dispatched men through the valley to the south, and departed myself, stopping at all ranches between here and the Two Brothers. I regret that I find you occupied in such an important work. I am pleased to learn, however, that you and your family are in good health."

"It is not a cause for regret," Saturnino said. "It is for me to regret that I will be able to furnish not more than ten men. My son and two *vaqueros* have departed for Santa Fe, and I deem it wise to leave three men here at the ranch."

"I have heard of the departure. I trust that they enjoy a safe journey."

Saturnino thanked him. "The rest of us are at your service," he said;

he was impatient to be off. "We will equip with lances and shields—we now carry muskets—and three days' provisions." He doubted that he owned a horse sufficiently strong to support Haro, but he said, "Do you wish a fresh mount?"

Don Ricardo expressed his thanks at some length but refused the offer. "Do you think it advisable to inform Señor Wolfe? We could send a man to summon the gringo."

"The emergency is great, but not of that greatness."

"Your opinion is mine." Don Ricardo picked up the reins. "With your permission we will ride."

It was midday as Saturnino, with his own men and sixty others collected on the trail, rode out from the walls of the Two Brothers and started up the winding Cajon. They rode two abreast, all well-armed and provisioned, in their jackets of antelope hide, with heavy leather shields fastened to the cantles and long lances in their hands. Saturnino brought up the rear, his men in front of him singing and laughing like the rest. Also like the rest, he noticed, they were beginning to dip into their provisions, as they always did on these Indian expeditions. He had already cautioned them against it, but they would persist, with the result that if the fighting lasted more than a day it would be done on empty stomachs. He wished that sometime he could go out to fight Indians when the men rode in silence, as was sensible, though he knew that he would never live to see the day. Noise, like the consuming of provisions, was one of the pleasures of Indian fighting—without both there would be little or no spirit among the men.

The pass narrowed and above him on the ridges where pines showed dark, broad fields of snow flashed in the sun. He had no taste for fighting in the snow. In the spring of '43 he had been through two nights of this snow fighting. It was now past the middle of June and the nights would be warmer, with less wind, but he still lacked enthusiasm for the snow. In fact, thinking of the task he had left unfinished at the ranch, he lacked enthusiasm for any kind of fighting.

Riding down to meet them before they had gone far into the pass, the three scouts that Don Ricardo had sent out brought news that the Utah were not more than a mile away, dropping leisurely down the canyon without flankers or an advance guard. There were upward of forty men in the party, and, what was of extreme importance, an equal number of women. Don Ricardo immediately deployed his forces, fanning them out across the canyon and leaving them to find what cover they could. Then he sought shelter behind an oak and called a counsel of the three leaders.

"If they travel with their women," Don Miguel of the gray hair said, "it is not a raiding party."

Saturnino, much relieved by this turn of events, agreed, but Don Ricardo said that he had never seen Indians in this number who did not come to raid. Don Andrés said nothing, drew his musket from its sheath and faced up the pass.

Where they stood behind the low-growing oak, the canyon floor was strewn with boulders and among them in a series of curves the stream fell rushing out of the mountains. Off to the right against the canyon wall there were fewer boulders. Along this defile the Indians came one by one, the women in front, riding with a clatter that reminded Saturnino of his own men. They even had dogs and the dogs were barking.

Just beyond the range of a musket ball, the column halted, the dogs ceased barking, and a man on a white pony rode out toward them, holding his hand above him, the palm turned outward in greeting. He rode in leather trousers and moccasins, without saddle or bit, with a horsehair rope secured in a half hitch around his pony's muzzle. He was deep through the chest and the color of weathered bronze, with a large head and long, bladelike nose.

Don Miguel, who understood Shoshone and some words of Utah, returned his greeting. The Indian rode up to the tree, his powerful odor making the four men wince, looked at each of them in turn and finally spoke, pointing toward the Indians and toward the west and the sun. Then he stopped and, scratching his stomach, waited for Don Miguel to translate what he had said.

"His name is Wak," Don Miguel explained. "He is chief of a large tribe. He has brought a small number of his people to barter in California. He has objects to trade, mostly blankets, which he has from the Tao-Utah, who have them from the Navajo, which means that they are Navajo blankets. He comes as a friend, in proof of which he points to the many women."

"For my part he can barter," Don Andrés said, "if it is not accomplished near my ranch. The odor cannot be endured closer than a league."

Don Miguel agreed with him, but Don Ricardo was of the opposite opinion and voted against allowing them to pass. For the moment Saturnino was silent. He was familiar with the Pah-ute, who, related to the Utah, were a mild though pilfering tribe forever engaged in stealing horses. This was the first Utah he had encountered and he could detect little difference between the two tribes, except that this man had more bearing. Also a certain devious look in his black eyes which he did not trust.

As he stood there trying to make up his mind, the Indian women had come up and ranged themselves on the far side of the oak, unseen and unheard by the four men. The first knowledge Saturnino had of their presence was when he was smitten by an overpowering smell compounded of many ingredients.

*"Diantre!"* Don Ricardo exploded.

Saturnino did not favor the smell either, but his discomfort was lessened by the fact that the women were the best-looking Indians he had ever seen. Dressed in soft moccasins and hareskin skirts, and naked above the waist save for brief hareskin capes, they would have been handsome if it were not for the red mastic which covered their stomachs and breasts. He did not trust the look in Chief Wak's eyes, but it suddenly occurred to him that in the event of a raid there would be a good chance to capture some of the women. Though squaw catching was a dangerous sport—he still carried on his thigh the teeth marks of a Mojave—one or two of these handsome Utah would be an addition to the ranch, as well as a means by which to remove the proud Guadalupe from the tall horse she was riding. Particularly the one with breasts like ripe melons.

*"Diantre!"* Don Ricardo said again. "What is your disposition, Don Saturnino?"

"That they pass."

"It is three against one," Don Ricardo said to Don Miguel. "Tell him he can enter, providing he and his party take a bath in the stream. And let us depart before we are overcome."

Reaching the Two Brothers at dusk, the Indian fighters found six horses, lathered and bearing the brand of the military, tied to the rack outside the gate. In the kitchen they found six soldiers seated at a table laden with food, surrounded by an admiring circle of Indian girls. One of the soldiers, a corporal, stood up and asked for Don Ricardo Haro.

"I carry a proclamation from Governor Pico," the corporal said. He swallowed the *tortilla* he was eating, composed his features and began to read. " 'On the fourteenth day of this month, at dawn while General Vallejo was sleeping, a band of Americans treacherously attacked and overthrew the fortress of Sonoma. With considered insolence they proclaimed the existence of what is termed the California Republic; with equal insolence they raised a flag, which contains a figure resembling a hog but which they call a bear, and throwing General Vallejo in irons, transported him to Sutter's Fort.' "

The corporal's words were received in stunned silence, and while he paused, having spoken in one breath, the silence deepened. Leaning closer to the candle, he continued with the proclamation, but before he was well started, Saturnino interrupted him with a violent oath. The corporal waited a moment, stuffed another *tortilla* into his mouth, and went on.

" '. . . Fly, Californians, in all haste in pursuit of the treacherous foe; follow him to the farthest wilderness; and in case we fail, let us form a cemetery where posterity may remember to the glory of Mexican history the heroism of her sons.' "

The words stopped Saturnino's breath in his throat. They hung before him there in the crowded room as if they had been written in letters of fire. Suddenly, blood racing through his veins, he struck the table a mighty blow with his fist.

"What does the governor demand?" he cried.

The corporal wiped his mouth. "All able-bodied men are to go to Los Angeles without delay, provisioned and armed."

Saturnino glanced at the three Spaniards and, noting a look of hesitancy on the face of Don Miguel, did not wait for him to speak. "Tell the governor that all the men on the frontier are at his service. Tell him that we will fill the pueblo with the thunder of hoofs and that the flash of our lances will dim the sun." He looked pointedly at Don Miguel of the gray hair. "Tell him that there are no traitors in our midst."

# 23

THE east was graying when he and his *vaqueros* rode into the Hawk, but Saturnino did not go to bed. As the sun came up and throughout the morning, while the ovens glowed in the courtyard, he worked feverishly completing the preparations begun several weeks before. At that time musket balls had been packed in leather pouches, an adequate supply of lances had been fashioned. All that remained now was the gathering of provisions, the baking of the hard yucca cakes whose strength-giving qualities were an indispensable part of every campaign, and the apportioning of powder.

Powder, unfortunately, was short. The pit he had dug and filled with refuse was not yet ready to yield niter crystals; therefore he was forced to do with what he had, which was of an inferior quality purchased at Mission San Gabriel. Into each of the eleven horn flasks, a flask for each man including one for himself, he mixed finely ground charcoal, sulphur and saltpeter, enough for six charges. His father had always insisted on mixing the ingredients at the time they were to be used, since combining them in advance and then carrying them around jolted the heavier saltpeter to the bottom and the fluffy charcoal to the top, which resulted in a faulty mixture, if it did not explode accidentally. The nature of a campaign, however, where he might become separated from his men, overruled the better method.

By noon, everything being in readiness and the men from the eastern ranches not having arrived, he went to his room and flung himself on the bed. He slept for an hour, woke refreshed and, as he had trained himself during many years of Indian fighting, instantly alert. From the chest he took the heaviest of his jackets, a *cuera* made of seven thicknesses of cowhide, heavy as iron, laced up the front with thongs. From its peg on the wall he took down the finest of his shields, which, oval in shape and of two pieces of untanned hide, was a good three feet in diameter. In his *cuera* and carrying his shield he then went to the chapel and prayed, resting on both knees before the altar, to both Santiago and Saint Christopher.

Under the ash tree he stopped for a moment to say good-by to his golden eagle, throwing it a quail which Jorge had snared that morning. As feathers fluttered down around him he spied Guadalupe on her way into the storehouse. He followed her and closed the door behind him. He found her, unluckily, with a long-bladed knife in her hand, carving a haunch of beef.

"I leave for the wars," he said, "to protect you and the ranch from destruction."

"It is an act of bravery," Guadalupe replied, surprising him with the warmth of her tone.

"I go with a heavy heart," he said, "knowing that I leave you behind."

"Other hearts will be heavy also," she said.

She looked at him boldly and, for an instant, in spite of the ironlike *cuera,* he was overcome with a desire to crush her in his arms. But beneath the boldness of her glance was a glint he did not wholly trust, and, remembering the knife, he confined himself to the remark, "I return soon. May you go with God," and backed out of the door.

He sought out his son and came upon him leaning against a pillar in front of the kitchen, amusing himself by tossing his *reata* at the Indian girls who were passing back and forth to the ovens.

"You are the man of the ranch now that I go," he said. "You are the only male De Zubaran on the Hawk, so take care to conduct yourself with this position in mind. No shooting of the cannon. No trips to other ranches with or without fighting cocks."

"Do I heed my grandmother?" Jorge asked.

"That is a matter of discretion. But in other things recall what I have said. No cannon. No jaunts. And do not molest the Indian girls."

"What happens, sir, if they molest me?"

"In that event you are big enough to resist."

Jorge wound up his *reata.*

"Father Expeleta will be at the ranch within the month. I do not wish to embarrass him with tales of rape."

"If I am molested?"

"It is the same."

"Yes, sir."

There were other things to attend to at the last minute, but since one of the Indians had sighted Don Ricardo and his men coming up from the river, he was forced to leave them to the care of Carlota. He had taken pains to avoid her during the morning, and it was now with some trepidation that he walked into the room where she was eating her dinner. For several moments after he spoke, informing her that he was leaving three *vaqueros* behind and to have the tallow carted up from the killing ground before nightfall, she sat munching in silence. Then for the first time she raised her eyes from the plate and ran them slowly over him from head to foot.

"The warrior departs," she said. "But this time not to engage Indians or a band of politicians who wish to do nothing more than parley. This time there will be musket balls fired by men who have never heard of the prowess of Saturnino de Zubaran, to whom you will be just another Spaniard in a leather jacket. Take care that you do not permit yourself to be killed."

Saturnino grunted. It was this sort of thing that he had been evading all morning. "I return as I depart."

"You depart from here," Carlota said, "and likewise from your wits. It is senseless. For weeks and for months the Spaniard exists in a dream, acquiescing in all forms of corruption, indifferent as one who walks in his sleep. Then at some small thing—a stolen horse which was of no value in the beginning, the flogging of a scoundrel who should be hanged, a violated woman who possessed no virtue to violate—he of a sudden arouses from his slumber and sets about himself, killing friend and foe regardless, like a maddened bull, and in the end, for the small thing of small importance, being killed himself."

Saturnino shifted his feet. "This is not a stolen horse," he said.

"It is less. It is someone else's horse. In this case the horse belongs to Governor Pico. Take the advice of one who has seen much fighting, who has lost a father and two brothers in battle. Add nothing to the fire that rages. Remain here until it passes, where you or the ranch will not be harmed. There is no reason why these two peoples cannot exist in peace. In the end they must and will."

"Do not forget the tallow," he said to escape further argument.

"You go?"

"I go."

"Then may you go with God!" his mother said.

Once outside, he took a deep breath, casting a final glance at the courtyard, the well, the blue ash tree, his golden eagle preening its feathers in the sun, and walked toward the open gate. There beside the saddled horses stood all the women saying good-by to their men. Luz also was there and he embraced her, though her sin still sat heavily on his heart. He advised her to devote herself in his absence to the preparations for the wedding which he would arrange before he returned from the pueblo, and to daily penance. Then he mounted his stallion, thrust his feet home in the stirrups and at the head of his men rode out to meet Don Ricardo.

From the rendezvous he rode in the lead, for this was an honor that properly belonged to him. Don Ricardo, Don Miguel and Don Andrés, with their sixty men, followed. They headed toward the King's Highway. Metal crickets clacked in the hot air. Green pennons, which tipped the lances, floated in the wind. Hoofs thudded and dust rose against the sun.

At the rim of the mesa Saturnino looked back at the ranch, one final glance that included everything he owned, and then shut it all from his mind, and with it the regret that he lacked the services of Mitla and his son Don Roque. He fixed his thoughts on the enemy, on Kate Howland who, according to the corporal he had talked to last night, was now in jail—he would not have to pay her the loan after all—on the gringos who were there with her, and all the other gringos wherever they might be.

"The life of a gringo," he swore, "for every day I am gone!"

From her high-backed chair beside the window Carlota watched the cloud of dust grow smaller in the west and at last disappear. She had never had much faith in her ability to change her son's deep-grained obsession, and when he had ridden in at dawn with staring eyes and announced the news from Sonoma and the summons he had received from Governor Pico, she had resigned herself to the inevitable. In one thing, however, she had not failed—Roque was safely on the trail to Santa Fe. By the time he returned the fighting would be over.

As the sun shifted and poured through the window, she dozed in the heat, awoke to give the orders Saturnino had left with her, and during the rest of the afternoon, while the carts lumbered up from the river loaded with *botas* of tallow, she turned her thoughts to the young American who was now imprisoned in Los Angeles. At first she confined herself to worrying about his wounds and if he was receiving proper care. But after a time, visited by a curious impulse which exceeded and took the place of her maternal feeling, she began to think along bolder lines. She was not without friends in the pueblo. She was related, if distantly, to the high-placed Peraltas, and she was on good terms with Governor Pico himself. Was there not some way, either direct or clandestine, by which she could use this influence in the American's behalf?

She pursued the subject until supper, and there, as she sat at the table with Luz and Jorge, the solution came to her, at least a plan which had possibilities of success. It was something that she could do herself, without exciting suspicion. It had been a long time, nearly a year, since she had been to the pueblo; it was only natural, now that fine weather had come and the danger of rain was passed, that she should go again.

Quietly the next day she set about making preparations for the journey, mending the rent in her best dress, packing the few things she would need, arranging small presents of food for the Peraltas and the Vicente de Zubarans. She said nothing to anyone about her trip and did not propose to until word came that Pico's army had ridden north, for there was no point in her going to the pueblo until the army had left, and Saturnino with it. Word came sooner than she had expected. The next morning one of the *vaqueros* who had gone with Saturnino showed up at the ranch. Sick with dysentery, he had been sent home with instructions for her to dispatch another man in his place. The army had departed and would camp at Santa Barbara for two days, recruiting additional forces; the substitute was to be sent there in all haste. She did not send the substitute, and by noon she was on the trail.

She traveled in the lightest cart with a pair of the best oxen, accompanied by two Indian girls, one to attend to her needs and the other to mind the beasts, a willow basket of food, a jug of *aguardiente,* a generous supply of tobacco—she was determined to make the journey in comfort—and a musket primed and loaded beneath the seat. The day was fine, with a nice wind blowing in from the sea and the long grass shimmering on the hills.

She had planned to spend the night at Vejar's, but there were still several hours of daylight when she reached the ranch, so she decided to continue on to the home of Don Roberto Gil, some two leagues distant. At dusk, as she came within sight of the house, she heard hoofs behind her on the trail, and a few moments later, her hair streaming in the wind, Luz galloped up on her black *mesteño.*

Carlota's first thought was that something had gone wrong at the Hawk, and she ordered the oxen halted. But at once, as the girl brought her horse up to the cart and their gazes met, she knew differently. Luz had been on the river when she left the ranch; when the girl returned and learned of her departure from Merced, she had set out to overtake her.

"Where do you go in trousers, with your hair streaming?" Carlota asked, though she knew the answer to the question.

"To the pueblo."

"And what of the ranch? Who stays in your absence?"

"Jorge and four *vaqueros* and fifteen girls, not including Merced, who is dependable."

Carlota jabbed the oxen with her cane. "We are now at Don Roberto's, where you will eat and then return."

They traveled on in silence, across the stream and up the slope which led to the house. At the gate, Luz said, "In the morning, if you leave the cart here and ride a horse, we can reach the pueblo before noon."

Carlota gathered herself and stood up. *"Ay de mi,"* she said, puffing out her thin cheeks, "it is not enough that I go. I must also break my bones in the bargain."

# 24

Early the next morning they started out from the ranch, Luz on her *mesteño,* and Carlota, still adamant about riding a horse, seated in the cart. They came to the San Gabriel in midmorning, and since the river was high and the footing insecure with quicksand, Luz had to snub her *reata* on the pommel, fasten the other end to the cart and help drag the cart through the river.

It was a long operation and by the time they had gained the far bank, after Carlota had changed her wet shoes and stockings for dry ones, taken a nip from the jug, and they were again on the trail, Luz had despaired of ever reaching Los Angeles. Ahead of her the trail seemed to stretch endlessly, looping and twisting through the hills, disappearing and then appearing far out on the horizon. Behind her the cart creaked and groaned, the oxen swung their ponderous horns, set their feet down precisely—one . . . two . . . three . . . four—and no matter how fast she rode could not be enticed into anything quicker than a measured walk. Once she had to stop while Carlota got out to pick wild flowers; another time to talk with friends they met on the trail.

She watched the sun swing overhead and past; they rode it halfway down the sky, stopping again, this time to eat the lunch Don Roberto had sent along, which could just as well have been eaten while they were riding. Then against the low hills she saw the roofs and the thin wood smoke of the pueblo. There it was, the trees along the irrigation ditches, the white houses and the blue smoke and the hills beyond where the deep grass was now turning yellow. Her heart began to race.

What if he is not there? she thought, unconsciously increasing the gait of her horse. What if they have taken him away? To Santa Barbara or in irons on a ship to Tepic as they did before?

But there hadn't been time for that, she told herself, for it was only a week since he had left the ranch, only a few days since he was first imprisoned in Los Angeles. Sailings from the coast were infrequent, and in these few days it was unlikely that a ship had been available. And yet, riding through the shallow river and up toward the town, the thought persisted that she shouldn't have waited. She should have gone the morning her father brought the news back from the Two Brothers. She had intended to; she had even saddled her horse for the journey. But at the last moment caution had stopped her, the fear that she would encounter her father in the pueblo, as it did the next day while she waited for word that he had ridden north, not knowing that her grandmother was waiting for the same word.

And now, two whole days after she first learned that he had been imprisoned, she was creeping at a snail's pace toward the town. In desperation at the slowness she began to count the Indian huts she passed. One in which old Fernando lived. The next belonged to the widow Ochoa. Then the hut of Carlos Medina. He was out in the field, a short distance from her, grubbing weeds from a ditch where water was running. She reined in her horse.

"What happens, old man?" she called to him. He left his patch of corn and beans and hobbled toward her. She did not wait for him to reach the trail. "What happens in the town? The troops have left?"

"Gone," he said, pointing north, "in great numbers."

"What of the gringos Don Pío has captured?"

"In the house of Bustamente and guarded heavily, which is wise, for they are like the eel in slipperiness."

Luz said nothing for a moment, feeling her heart stop and then start again. "Your crops grow well," she said. "You will have a good harvest."

"If I can kill more crows. They are very troublesome, and I lack powder now that Don Pío has scoured the town."

The Indian, rolling a cigarette, was fixing himself for a good chat, but before he had a chance to ask about her family and all the various servants at the ranch, she promised to drop by on her way home and turned her horse up the trail.

He has not gone! she thought, looking ahead, beyond the plaza and the church, where the Bustamente house stood out against the hill. He is there behind those walls. Suddenly she felt weak with relief, and then almost at once she was seized with a new fear. What if he is in need of care? she thought. The house is not filthy like the *calabozo*, the one near the Campo Santo, but he is wounded and there will be no one who cares whether he lives or dies.

She heard a screech behind her and, turning in the saddle, saw that she had left her grandmother far down the trail. Another screech rent the air and the cane was brandished aloft. She pulled in and waited until Carlota overtook her.

"Listen, *hombre*," her grandmother said, standing up in the cart. "Against my better sense I permit you to come. But having committed this first folly, I am in no mood for more, thank you. The rest of the way you will ride beside the cart, slow or fast as the case may be. And when we reach the home of Don Lorenzo de Zubaran you will comport yourself as his son's betrothed. What can be done, if anything, I will do. Is it understood?"

"It is," Luz replied, although her mind was a half league away.

Ten minutes later they rumbled into the big corral in the rear of Don Lorenzo's, just as the family was coming to life after the day's siesta, and a sleepy-eyed servant rose up from a pile of straw in time to take charge of the horse and oxen. She had hoped that Don Lorenzo, her father's cousin, a thick-set pompous man, would have departed with the troops, and that his wife Doña Sol would be away on one of her numerous visits. But both were in the patio to meet them—he to launch into a long greeting, though scarcely two weeks had elapsed since they were all together; she to take each of them in turn to her breast, to plant on their faces a series of moist kisses.

Afterward, when the flurry of excitement was over and she and Carlota sat stiffly on red plush chairs in the *sala*, Doña Sol began to dab at her eyes with a lacy handkerchief. They both had heard the tale of Julio's abduction before, but they were now forced to hear it again—the endless details of how he had been set upon by brigands, overpowered and carried aboard a gringo ship, which had then sailed for no one knew where, perhaps to the Sandwich Islands, perhaps to San Francisco.

Luz squirmed in her chair and in spite of Doña Sol's distress, as the story went on and on, found herself wishing that wherever Julio was it would be a long time until he came back. She sat with a determined look of sympathy on her face, from time to time casting a glance toward her grandmother which she hoped would spur her to say something. But Carlota smoked her cigarette in silence, and when Doña Sol paused for breath, Don Lorenzo, his face flushed with anger, began to damn the gringos responsible for the outrage on their son.

"All of them!" he said, bouncing to his feet. "The moment has come to do away with all of them. Otherwise, we will live to see greater outrages than this. We will see the very soil, inherited from our fathers, snatched from under us. Our families made the victims of the most barbarous servitude. Our women violated, our innocent children beaten by the gringo lash, our temples profaned, and we ourselves forced to drag out a life of shame and disgrace."

Luz said nothing. Both she and Carlota expected little in the way of help from Don Lorenzo, but this outburst, delivered in a loud voice while he paced the room as if he were addressing a meeting of the junta, put an end to any hope they may have had. They looked at each other and remained silent.

Doña Sol said, "We will yet have revenge for the harm done to our poor Julio!"

"And quite soon," Don Lorenzo added, placing his paunchy figure in a chair. "It is tomorrow that they try the gringos who have conspired against us. Señor Kroll and Señora Howland and this other whose name I forget."

Doña Sol's large eyes narrowed. "It would be no surprise to me if it were these three who are responsible for Julio."

"They or their fellow brigands," Don Lorenzo announced with an air of finality. "The truth may have to be pried from them, but it shall be—Lieutenant Morales is adept in these matters, my dear—and then you will find that I am right."

Luz was no longer listening. As Don Lorenzo went on, rousing himself to another tirade, her eyes were fixed on the window. Outside in the plaza, shadows had lengthened. A company of soldiers marched past, smart in new uniforms, circled the square and halted in front of the *cuartel*. Now, she thought, feeling cold with anger, now before he says anything more, I'll stand up and stop the words in his throat. She looked at him then, pacing the room once more, but at that moment Carlota must have read her thoughts for she clambered to her feet.

"You speak for me also, Don Lorenzo," she said, with a quick warning look at Luz. "For both of us. And now with your permission since I have things to do before dark—various sundries to purchase for the ranch—I depart. My granddaughter has been indisposed for several days and will wish to lie down."

Luz took the cue. She went to her room, and when she finally got rid of Doña Sol and the last of the servants had trooped in and out, she did lie down. She must have dozed, for the next thing she knew Carlota was standing by the bed. She was out of breath and her nostrils flared.

"*Ay!*" she said. "One would think that the town has been bereft of its wits. Everywhere one goes nothing is heard except talk of the trial—the clerks in the stores, urchins in the lanes, beggars, peons with loads of wood on their backs, women in the doorways, all talk of nothing else. I did not go into the Calle de Los Negros among the *putas* and cutthroats, but it would be the same there. . . ."

Luz jumped out of bed. "Where *did* you go?" she cried. "Whom did you see?"

"*Chist,*" Carlota said, cautioning her to lower her voice. "I do not wish to sleep in the street, which we will do if we are heard." Wearily she lowered herself in a chair. "I went to see the Peraltas, and the first thing asked of me was if I had come to the pueblo for the trial. Needless to relate I said that I had come for no other reason."

"Why didn't you speak the truth?"

"Because the Peraltas, I saw at once, were of the same mind as these in the house. One uses powder and ball with the lion and treacle with insects. I therefore listened and said nothing."

"Governor Pico?"

"Tomorrow I go to talk with His Eminence."

"But that is too late. There is time now."

"It is not wisdom to talk to a man who waits for supper with an empty stomach. I go in the morning, after breakfast, when the stomach is full."

"But the trial is tomorrow!"

"We cannot prevent the trial. No one can, not even Governor Pico himself, for the populace demands it and will take matters into their own hands if they are denied. It is afterward, when the trial is over and the sentence pronounced, that there is a chance for intercession, a delay or two, which will give time for many things—who knows what?"

"Surely something can be done."

"Perhaps it was not your father who invented gunpowder but you yourself," Carlota muttered under her breath. "You who seem to possess the stubbornness for such an undertaking."

Luz threw herself on the bed and lay there gazing at the ceiling. It was clear to her now that nothing was to be gained by arguing with Carlota or, at this late hour with the trial only a day off, by talking to Governor Pico or Father Expeleta or anyone else. But there was still something she could do and must do, while it was yet light, as soon as she could leave the house without being seen. Feigning sleep, she lay until Carlota left the room, and then, moving as quietly as her high-heeled boots permitted, she let herself into the patio, crossed it to the corrals—if anyone saw her they would think that she was on her way to tend her horse—opened the gate into the side lane and, as the bell in the church struck the first note of *Ave Maria,* set out for the Bustamente house.

When she came to an open space behind the church she had a good view of the house above her on the hill, nestled among a grove of cottonwoods, a faint reflected glow at its windows. At first she saw no evidence of guards, but a moment later, two soldiers with muskets on their shoulders appeared at once from opposite corners, passed each other and disappeared, to be followed after a brief time by two others.

As she reached the path that led upward to the house, a guard she hadn't noticed before stepped out from behind a tree and stopped her with the command to halt. He was young, neatly dressed in a tight-fitting uniform, obviously impressed with his authority.

With a flourish he grounded his musket. "You have a pass, señorita?"

Luz shook her head.

"Then you are not allowed beyond this point."

She was not prepared for this, but her mind was working. "I live in the house beyond the one of Bustamente," she said quickly. "I don't need a pass to go there."

"At Castanares'?"

"Yes."

The soldier examined her a moment in silence. "You are not a Castanares—I am acquainted with the family."

"A servant," she said.

"Nor a servant. I know them all and you are not one."

She looked at him coolly. "I'm new. I've just been engaged and I'm going there for the first time. I'm also late and fearful of losing my place if you continue to detain me."

"You are not dressed as a servant."

Did Castanares, she wondered, have children?

"Nor are you an Indian," the soldier said.

"I've been hired as a governess."

With the toe of his boot he traced a pattern in the dust, and for an instant, her heart beating wildly, she thought he had accepted her story.

But the next instant he said, "Señor Castanares has just passed on his way to the church. It is his habit to return promptly. If you wait a few minutes you can go with him." He gave her a level glance. "You can wait here with me."

In the failing light she saw the half-smile, half-sneer on the full lips, a look which told her plainly that he not only didn't believe what she had said, but also that he took her for one of the *putas* from the Calle de los Negros.

"I'll not wait," she said. "I'll go to the church."

Her cheeks flaming, she left him there with the sneering smile on his mouth, and strode down the path. Out of his sight, she ran and did not stop until she came to the plaza. Vespers were not yet over; it occurred to her to enter the church and pray. Suddenly she thought, If I can talk to Father Expeleta he will help me. He may be able to get a pass for me, and if not, perhaps he will take a message to the house. She retraced her steps as far as the sacristy and let herself in. There were two other women in the dark room waiting for the priest, but when he came, she forgot them in her excitement and, stepping in front of them, followed him into his study.

Father Expeleta lighted a brace of candles on the table and motioned her to sit down, showing only a small hint of disapproval at her garb. "What brings you to the pueblo, daughter—the same thing that brings everyone?"

She was tempted for a moment to unburden her heart, to tell him everything from the beginning, but a certain caution restrained her. She stood in front of him, refusing the chair he had offered, and said, "I've come for another reason—to ask your help in getting a pass to visit the house where the Americans are held."

The priest showed no surprise at the request. He regarded her casually, almost wearily, as if nothing she could say or anyone could say would surprise him. He did not even ask her why she wanted to visit the house.

"You ask the impossible," he said. "Since this frenzy has seized the town, everything is impossible—to find anyone who wishes to work, to buy provisions at the store, to enter the door of the Governor's Mansion, unless, of course, one belongs to the Military."

"Then will you take a message there for me?"

"I would gladly if I were permitted. But all of my efforts have so far met with a refusal. I tried on the day the wounded American was brought in. I have tried since. It is a state of affairs without precedent, but it is a fact that I can neither arrange for you to go nor go myself."

She stood in silence, drained of all emotion, unable to think anything except the simple thought, There must be a way. And this, meeting the pale eyes of the priest, she repeated over and over as if by repetition she hoped to make it true. She was aware that his eyes had taken on a new light and were looking through her, past the candles behind her, and beyond the walls of the room.

He rose. "One possibility exists," he said, "although I am frank to say that it is only a possibility—one which you may not wish to explore. Perhaps it is . . ." He paused, then walked to the table and set the candles deeper in their holders, and for an instant, watching him, she was afraid that he had changed his mind about speaking. But presently he turned and faced her. "Do you know Yris Llorente?" he asked.

Luz did not answer him immediately; her throat was dry. She closed her hands to keep them from trembling. She said, "Why, yes. That is, I've met her—once at Kate Howland's."

"Yris Llorente is in a position to aid you. She is the only person I know who has access to Governor Pico and the Military. And while she cannot arrange for you to go to the Bustamente house, she can have a message sent there for you. I am certain of this because I have learned, not from her but from someone else, that she has had messages delivered there herself."

Her whole body was trembling now. She picked up her hat from the table and held it tight in both hands, thinking, She is in love with him too or she wouldn't run the risk of sending him messages. She remembered the incident in the garden when Yris Llorente had helped him to escape from Morales' men, and thought, She is trying to help him again. A wave of fury seized her.

Father Expeleta was saying, "She *can* aid you, as I have already said. Whether she will or not is another matter which depends entirely on whom the message is for."

Luz looked at the priest. Did he know? she wondered. Had he guessed who it was and what she wanted to send in the letter? The caution that had kept her from telling him in the beginning—the fear that for some reason he might receive her confession with disfavor and refuse his assistance—again prompted her to be evasive. She was about to say that the word was for Kate Howland when the priest, running the beads through his thin fingers, interrupted her.

"I suggest that the letter be addressed to Kate Howland. It is more plausible that you would send a letter to the señora than to Jacob Kroll."

Her cheeks flamed. The evasion was useless after all, she thought. He knows.

There was a moment of uncomfortable silence, and then the priest opened a drawer of the table and set out a quill, a sheet of paper and an inkhorn. "While you are writing I will talk to my parishioners," he said.

When he had left the study she sat down at the table and wrote quickly, not pausing to choose her words but putting them down as they came flooding out of her heart. And by the time Father Expeleta returned the letter was finished, folded and tied with the ribbon he had furnished.

"Do you know where she lives?" he asked. "It is the house which . . ."

"Wouldn't it be better if you sent the letter to her?" Luz broke in. "She'd be more apt to see that it got there if she knew it was a favor you were asking."

"Less," the priest said promptly. "For two or three weeks now we have not enjoyed each other's confidence . . . a certain incident. Since that time she has not been near the church."

"You can send it by one of the Indians."

"None is here—all of them are playing truant in the excitement over the trial. But if anyone were available, she would still know that I had sent him."

Her hand tightened on the letter. How was she to walk into the house of a stranger, give it into the hands of a woman whose very name filled her with fury? And dressed as she was, with an angry welt from the lash still showing on her neck. What was she to say? How would she ever disguise her desperation, a desperation so overwhelming that it forced her to ask a favor of a woman she hated? And, finally, how ingenuous of her to think that Yris Llorente would help her!

"There is not much time," the priest said, "if you want the letter delivered tonight. The woman who will take it leaves shortly."

Luz put the letter in her jacket. "Where does Yris Llorente live?"

Father Expeleta gave the directions, walking with her to the door of the sacristy, and as she started off toward the plaza, he stood in the doorway and watched her hasten on into the darkness. A heavy frown knit his brow. He was not one to review a decision once it was made, but tonight, thinking of how he had chosen to flout the wishes of her father, how Don Saturnino had come to him with the story of his daughter's dereliction, he was visited by a moment of doubt.

It was not that he sympathized with Don Saturnino's attitude and the punishment inflicted on the girl; it was simply that instead of cautioning her to be certain of her heart and of the young man—a foreigner whom he did not know, and perhaps an infidel—he had, without so much as a word of counsel, sent her off on a mission whose consequences no one could foresee.

The darkness had swallowed her, but he could hear the rapid steps hurrying on. Why had he chosen to send her to Yris Llorente? Was it, he wondered, that he wished to see this wicked and godless woman chastened, finally defeated in the one thing she had set her heart on? (Quickly, thinking of her and her voice as he had heard it in confession, sinful, unrepentant, harsh with passion, and smelling again the perfume she wore, he thrust his fingers outward in a swift movement of excoriation and said the word, "Go!") Was it, he wondered, that as usual he could not resist the role of matchmaker? Or had he taken this means to even the score with Governor Pico for not allowing him to visit the prisoners?

The steps were lost now in a surge of voices from the plaza, where throughout the afternoon crowds had been banked in front of the Governor's Mansion. His frown deepened. And suddenly perplexed by a greater concern, hearing the increasing clamor and aware that it was the forerunner of the storm which would soon sweep over the land and against the very walls of the church, he closed the heavy door behind him.

Seated at her writing table in the pink and gold boudoir, Yris Llorente dipped the quill twice in the silver inkhorn, once to wet the tip and once, being superstitious, for good fortune, and began to ponder over the letter to Grady Dunavant.

It was a difficult letter to write, because in it she must confess that her efforts to bring about his release had not been successful. She was unused to failure, and this, almost as much as the fact that he would have to stand trial, was galling to her. She had started, of course, with a handicap. The night in the garden when she had aided him to elude Lieutenant Morales and his men had placed her in an embarrassing position, with Governor Pico as well as Morales and Cesaire Curel, and though she steadfastly contended that she had not known he was hiding in the garden at the time of the search, suspicions had died slowly. Not, in fact, until she was instrumental in unearthing the cache of arms, collected and hidden by Kate Howland and Jacob Kroll, beneath a pile of hides in a warehouse at San Pedro, did the suspicions die. (How convenient it was and helpful that they should be suspicious of the wrong things; that they—Pico and Morales and the others—did not have the slightest knowledge that she had been sent to California by President Paredes to spy upon them.)

The thing which made the letter doubly difficult was that she had almost succeeded in effecting his release. As late as this morning Governor Pico had considered setting him free, but at the last moment chose to take the counsel of Lieutenant Morales. Morales, the hulking perfumed pig, had finally won out because she couldn't ask for Grady Dunavant's freedom without asking the same for the other two. Kate Howland and Jacob Kroll were guilty. The finding of the cache at San Pedro proved it. But nothing was proved against Grady Dunavant, except that he had eluded the efforts of Morales to arrest him on a charge trumped up by Major de Zubaran, and that another pig, a little French *puerco,* Monsieur Malibran, had reported a few things said at the Bustamente house. In spite of this, she couldn't press his case too far, show too much interest in it, without rousing old suspicions.

Still hesitating over the letter, Yris nibbled the end of the quill with her small white teeth. There was no doubt in her mind that he was as deeply involved in the conspiracy as Kate Howland and Jacob Kroll. She hadn't thought so at first, when she met him at the dance, or later that night when she had invited him here and done her best to surprise him into making some incriminating remark, or the next night when, curiously, she had helped him escape Morales. But she was certain now—and she was not alone in believing it—that he was the one responsible for the disappearance of the three men at San Diego.

As far as she was concerned, his guilt had been proved this afternoon with the arrival of Lieutenant del Rio of the San Diego garrison. Del Rio brought the news that a servant of Juan Bandini's had admitted under questioning to having seen a tall gray-eyed American at the house on the night the men were abducted. Morales had scoffed at the idea. He said it was the work of the captain of the ship in connivance with Juan Bandini. In support of his theory he cited the fact that Bandini had left the next day for his ranch in Baja California, that the foreman of the ranch, a John Tremaine, was a tall gray-eyed American, one of several Americans who worked for Bandini, that Captain Teal of the *Pilgrim* had long been a troublemaker on the Coast, and finally that Grady Dunavant could not have ridden the forty leagues to San Diego in time to place him there on the night in question.

She hadn't argued with Lieutenant Morales as he and Del Rio sat sipping brandy in the courtyard only an hour ago. She hadn't pointed out the fact that the presence of Bandini and Captain Teal in the plot did not necessarily exclude Grady Dunavant. Nor did she remind him that the American was used to long journeys on horseback. She did neither for obvious reasons, and because she knew that Morales himself was sure of Grady Dunavant's part in the plot. He wouldn't admit it, the perfumed pig, for by doing so the American would then become a resourceful young man, and Morales, who had allowed him to escape, the fool he was.

She again dipped the quill in the silver inkhorn and began to write. The woman who carried her letters up the hill each evening was waiting in the kitchen, but she took her time, choosing her words and forming them carefully in her small and precise script. As she wrote she was not aware of the faintest twinge of conscience. Although she was betraying a trust, certain as she now was of his guilt, the fact to her astonishment added a thrill to each word she set down.

Halfway through the letter, Tepeyollotl appeared at the door to announce that a young lady wished to see her.

"Who is it?" she asked, not looking up.

The Indian was slow to answer, and finally she raised her eyes. He was leaning in the doorway, staring off into space, with a blank expression on his dark countenance. It was the same expression she had seen when he returned to the pueblo more than a week ago, and every day since. She had questioned him about it several times, but to this, as well as to what he had done in his absence and where he had gone, the Indian was the soul of vagueness—for all she could learn he might have been sitting under a tree somewhere braiding a *reata*.

"Who is it?" she shouted.

"Señorita de Zubaran" was the reply.

Yris went on with the letter. Señorita de Zuzaran was probably some relative of Julio de Zubaran, the inquisitive youth whom she had chased from the house, who in the first place had started the rumors about Grady Dunavant and later reported him to Lieutenant Morales.

The young lady, she decided, could cool her heels. But almost at once she remembered that the American had been ambushed on a ranch owned by one of the De Zubarans. Could the señorita, she thought, belong to this branch of the family? She put down the pen and stood up. She looked at herself in the gilt-framed mirror, touched her lips with rouge and walked quickly toward the *sala,* her pale cheeks glowing with color.

The girl rose as she came in. It was a moment before Yris recognized her, and then, seeing that it was the same person she had met in Kate Howland's store, she took another moment to appraise her, casting a slow glance at her boots, the leather jacket opened deep at the throat which was darkened by the sun, at the sun-streaked hair falling thickly around her shoulders.

"Well, my dear, you didn't buy the yellow dress, after all," Yris said. "And it's just as well."

The girl hesitated an instant as if she were going to answer, but she didn't. She said, "I've come to ask a favor of you." Reaching into her jacket she drew out a paper folded and tied with a ribbon. "It is this—a message for Kate Howland."

Yris, though her face betrayed no sign of emotion, froze. Swiftly she thought, This is something planned by Morales. And then, covering her confusion by a look of surprise, They've found out about the letters.

"I don't understand," she said. "I have no connection with Kate Howland. As a matter of fact I haven't seen her since the day in the store."

The girl looked at her steadily. "The message is really from my father," she said. "He has gone north with the troops and before he left he asked me to see that it was delivered. It's very important."

"I'm sorry I can't help you," Yris said, managing a tone of concern. "But you know how things are—with the place under heavy guard, and no possibility of getting a pass. I'd like to go there myself, or at least send word, also to Kate Howland. Perhaps when the trial is over things will be easier."

Yris fell silent, amazed at the clumsiness of the ruse. It was so clumsy that she began to doubt that it was a ruse. If they had learned about the letters, surely they wouldn't go to all this trouble. If they hadn't, and were only suspicious, it would be simpler to search the few who entered the Bustamente house.

"It's very important," the girl repeated.

Her voice was low-pitched and intense. Moved by its intensity as much as by the manner in which she stood twisting the paper in her hand, her amber-colored eyes fixed and unwavering, Yris abandoned the idea that she had come here for any other reason than the one she had stated. This girl, freshly arrived from the frontier, with her hair tumbling over her shoulders and the very smell of horses about her, was not artful enough to pretend to a sincerity she didn't feel.

"It's very important," Luz said again. "My father Don Saturnino owes a sum of money to Kate Howland—it's about this money the letter speaks."

At the name Saturnino, something stirred in Yris' memory. She recalled that it was this man Don Saturnino de Zubaran who had ridden into town with the news of the ambush. The anger she had felt when she first entered the room once more flushed her cheeks.

"It was your father," she said, attempting to control her voice, "who lanced the American."

The girl was silent. Then she said, "No, it was my brother Don Roque."

"Your brother is very brave. To vanquish one who is armed with pistol and carbine, by the use of a lance, requires courage."

Yris spoke lightly, but in spite of herself a strained note had crept into her voice, a tinge of anger, which the De Zubaran girl was quick to detect.

"There are those on the Hawk who regret the deed," Luz said. She paused and a curious look flashed across her eyes. "Who think of it without pride."

"This is nothing to regret," Yris said. She resented the fact that she had betrayed her feelings, resented it more than the other's efforts to placate her. "We're all proud of your brother here in the pueblo," she said, thinking, The girl is more clever than she seems. And then, Perhaps not so clever after all, for the story of the American's escape from the garden gained wide circulation.

Luz de Zubaran was talking about something else now, running a sun-darkened hand under the fall of her hair, the candles shining on her young throat and the pulse that beat there visibly, standing tall and wide-shouldered and long-legged in the light-brown, leather trousers like a boy, with the stammering fervor of a boy, explaining why she had come, her eyes behind the heavy, straight lashes looking at Yris not with a boy's glance, but direct and unfaltering, with a look so intense that it might have sprung from hatred.

"Who told you to come to me?" Yris said.

"No one."

"The priest?"

"No."

"It sounds like the priest."

"I had heard that you have influence with Governor Pico, and so because I failed elsewhere I turned to you."

Yris studied her. She noticed again the intent, unwavering gaze, and now something more pronounced than this as the girl stood twisting the letter in her hands. It was a look of desperation she saw in the amber-colored eyes.

"I am sorry that I am powerless," she said, and then on a sudden inexplicable impulse, forgetting her anger, she added, "However, Lieutenant Morales will be here later in the evening, and if you care to leave it I'll ask his assistance."

For an instant the girl hesitated, holding the letter at her side. Then she thrust it into Yris' hand. "Thank you," she said as if it were an effort to speak, or to do what she had done.

"Where may I reach you?" Yris said.

"At Don Lorenzo de Zubaran's—the house with the four pillars on the far side of the plaza."

"If I have no luck with Lieutenant Morales—and I doubt that I will—I'll return the letter there."

Anxious to be rid of the girl, she led the way to the courtyard, said good night, and went back to her boudoir. The manservant came in every few minutes while she was finishing the message to tell her that Señora Gomez was waiting, but she wrote slowly, and when she was through, she folded the message and sealed it with a drop of wax, which she pressed down neatly with her finger. She also sealed the letter she had taken from the De Zubaran girl, and gave both of them to the Indian with orders to move lively.

She rose from the writing table, crossed the room and looked at herself in the gilt-framed mirror, at the pale oval face, the wide red mouth and the glistening black hair coiled on her head. Then she walked to the open window. The courtyard was dark but beyond it, above the high wall, she saw a glow in the direction of the plaza and heard the confused babble of voices. For the last two nights fires had burned in the square, fed by a singing and shouting populace.

There was no way of knowing what the military tribunal would do tomorrow, how severe the penalty would be, whether Morales would ask for the *novenario* as he said he would do, or whether it would be the *carreras de baqueta,* favored by the other officers. Whatever it was, Grady Dunavant would be prepared by her letter. He would also know, no matter what the punishment, that he was to be held as a hostage. The only thing she hadn't told him in the message was that she would manage somehow to arrange for his escape, as she had already arranged for their passage on the Mexican brig which was sailing for Callao within the next two weeks.

Closing her ears to the shouts, she lowered her gaze from the red glow in the sky. The night was warm. The dark mass of the vines beside the gate, hung with clusters of white bloom, gave off a fragrance that set her senses to reeling. Callao, she thought. "*Sancta Trinidad!* Never to see the great bore Cesaire Curel again in her life! To be in Lima beside the winding Rimac, in the city of La Perricholi, the famed actress whose protector, Viceroy de Amat, had changed the course of the river so that it would flow in front of her house. To be in the City of the Kings, and in love, if love lasted only a month—it had lasted three months when she was there before. Perhaps this would endure as long. Perhaps longer.

Señora Gomez, with a basket of food on her head and the letters hidden away in her shawl, padded out of the darkness and across the courtyard toward the burro waiting in the lane.

"Bring me word back," Yris called from the window.

The señora halted. "Each night you ask this and each night I say the same thing—it is impossible."

"For a gold onza?"

"For a dozen." Señora Gomez drew closer to the window. "I do not like the burden of two letters—one is care enough."

"You will be paid."

"But think of the danger."

"You will be paid in proportion," Yris said, and to put an end to the nightly haggling before it was well begun, she made a gesture of dismissal. Señora Gomez greeted the gesture with a grunt, steadied the basket on her head and started off for the gate. She had gone only a few steps when Yris called after her. The woman, grumbling about the delays she had been caused and the excitement she was missing in the plaza, took her time coming back. "Give me the letter," Yris said. "The one tied with a ribbon."

When it was passed through the iron bars of the window, she told Señora Gomez to wait, turned and crossed to the candles burning on the writing table. From the moment she accepted the letter from the De Zubaran girl she had been increasingly uneasy, increasingly critical of the impulsiveness which had led her to say even what she had about Lieutenant Morales. Did she really know that the girl was speaking the truth? And after all, why did she care whether the message was delivered or not?

She stood for a moment looking at it, the name Kate Howland formed in bold flourishes. And then, taking the paper knife from the table, she slit the ribbon, unfolded the paper and began to read. She read the first sentence through before she was aware that she was not reading a letter to Kate Howland. She finished the second long sentence before she knew whom the letter was for. Then she turned and looked at Señora Gomez, who was watching through the window.

"Go!" she said to the face pressed against the iron bars. "Go!"

She did not move until she heard the gate close and the burro's hoofs in the lane. Then she sat down, spread the paper out on the table and went on from where she had stopped, reading quickly, her wide mouth twisted in a grimace of fury and disbelief.

*. . . and when we brought you back to the house you were still scarcely breathing and no one thought you would live through the night except me, and I only because of faith that the Virgin in Her compassion would not permit us to be parted. I thought so even as I knelt at the altar and prayed.*

*This I write because no one has told you. Nor do you know that while I knelt asking intercession for you my father found me there and lashed me and locked me away so that I could not be with you or communicate with you, though my grandmother tried and failed because you were always, always sleeping. I was not freed until the next day after you left and then it was too late, for the news came that you had been taken to Los Angeles, where I could not follow you because my father was called there by the governor.*

*I lived in torment for the next two days and nights, knowing how you must feel toward me. And then, the word coming that my father had gone north with the troops, I left with my grandmother and reached here this afternoon. I will not go into the details of how she tried and is trying to help you, or how I tried to reach you, only to be turned back by the guard, or how I went to Father Expeleta to ask his advice, and how I have taken his advice and am sending this word to you, which, if it is received, will be through the kindness of Señora Llorente.*

There was more to the letter, several paragraphs more, but Yris read no farther. Blinded by jealousy and a fierce explosive rage, she leaped to her feet, sending the chair clattering to the floor, and snatched the letter from the table. With trembling hands she held it to the candle; not until the flames licked at her fingers did she drop it. As the final flame died, she ground the ashes to powder beneath her foot.

# 25

Grady Dunavant stood upright, a step between him and the table, hot in his tight-fitting gray coat and ruffled shirt, breathing the stale hot odor of the room through tight nostrils. The red velvet curtains were drawn shut against the curious throng that filled the plaza, and though it was afternoon and pulsing light slanted out of the west, a row of candles burned on the table. At the far end of the table sat Governor Pico, flanked by members of the tribunal—two lieutenants and two ensigns—and two guards behind him at the closed door.

One of the lieutenants was Morales, and as Grady stood here breathing the stale air of the room and listening to the clamor beyond the curtains, he looked at the big, dark-complexioned, sheepfaced officer. Morales was not talking now, but leaning forward with his arms on the table, elbows clasped in his hands, and his head with its low-curving brow swiveled toward Governor Pico.

Lieutenant Morales had declared for a *novenario de cincuenta azotes,* fifty lashes delivered on each succeeding day of nine days. He had made his declaration in a bright small voice, a voice surprising small for his bulk, nibbling the words with his sheep's teeth. He was waiting now for the governor to speak. One of the ensigns had voted for the *carreras de baqueta*; the other lieutenant, although it was his opinion that the punishment was one which should properly be reserved for the Military and the *baqueta* therefore irregular, had voted likewise. The tribunal was consequently tied, and Morales was waiting for Governor Pico to decide the issue, leaning forward and moving his protruding teeth up and down over his pale and fleshless lips.

Dunavant looked at Lieutenant Morales but he was thinking about the ensign, a young dandy with black short-cut hair brushed upward over his forehead, who had said that the punishment was irregular. The whole thing is irregular, Dunavant thought, remembering that he had said the same thing at the beginning of the trial in plain words to Governor Pico. Properly, as the ensign had said afterward, running a finger along the pomaded sweep of his short-cut hair, it was a matter for the civil court and a decision of the alcalde. Morales had laughed at this, nervously in his hoarse small animal voice.

He was not laughing now as he sat there moving his lips up and down; he was worried lest the governor would choose the lesser of the two punishments, the *carreras de baqueta.* It would be the fault of Lieutenant Morales, Dunavant thought, if Don Pío Pico, slouched at the moment in his chair and studying the silver rings on his fat blunt-ended fingers, decided for the gantlet. For it was Morales himself who had derided the testimony of the witness, Lieutenant del Rio; when the officer had repeated the words of Bandini's servant, Morales had gone to considerable pains to show that Grady Dunavant could not have been in San Diego. On direct questioning Dunavant had agreed with him, having been instructed in this by the letter from Yris Llorente.

And yet his guilt, Grady knew, did not depend on this, or on the testimony of the Frenchman, Monsieur Malibran, but entirely on the fact that he had eluded arrest, and in doing so had struck a soldier of the garrison; worst of all, though it had not appeared in the trial, that he had embarrassed Lieutenant Morales. And the severity of his punishment, whether the lash or the gantlet, did not hinge on his guilt: it hinged, he thought, watching the sheeplike head of Morales, on the governor's final evaluation of something else.

At breakfast yesterday morning a rumor had leaked past the guards that a Mexican brig sailing in from the Sandwich Islands had sighted off the lower coast what it took to be an American man-of-war, headed full-rigged to the north. As he sat there, with the velvet curtains stirring at his back, and studied his fat silver-ringed hands, it was the man-of-war that Governor Pico weighed. The man-of-war was American and not British. It carried, he was thinking behind the swarthy brow, sailors and marines who would be landed somewhere along the coast. He was thinking about Frémont and his men already reported to be active on the Sacramento. He was thinking also about General Castro in command of the Northern Frontier, a man whom he did not trust. He was weighing the punishment of Grady Dunavant against these things, the secretive Spanish mind aware that leniency would bear favorably for him in the scales of an unfavorable future.

Beyond the gently moving curtains, one voice rose suddenly above the background of voices in the sun-smitten plaza. A single word came clearly into the room, as if it were spoken there. The word was *andale,* move, and when its meaning, plain as a hurled stone, dawned on Don Pío Pico, a shadow crossed his face. In the fleeting look Grady read more than he had thought was behind the swart and secretive brow. Pico, weighing the punishment, had also considered setting him free. It was there in his face, this thought, fixed and then erased by the one shouted word of impatience.

Governor Pico glanced again at his silver-ringed hands, and again the four officers, leaning from their hips against the black table in the motionless smoke of the candles, watched him. Then the governor looked up, down the long table, rose slowly to his feet, coughed once and spoke the sentence, in a voice touched faintly with weariness.

Grady did not look at the men standing at the head of the table, or at Morales smiling his sheepfaced smile. The guards had opened the door and without a word he walked through it, through the dark hallway and into the blazing light of the plaza. Sweat poured across his chest and gathered in his knotted fists. He swallowed hard on the anger that rose in his throat. He looked over the heads of the crowd at the crows wheeling down the sky.

The troop was drawn up at the lower end of the plaza, three slouching lines of men leaning on their muskets. A bayonet prodded him from behind, and as the crowd made way the shrill notes of a bugle brought the straggling troop to attention. The sun was bright on the brass of their muskets. The crowd closed in at his heels. He walked straight, with one arm stiff at his side, toward the troop that had stacked arms and stood in two wooden lines, facing each other, with their long greasy oaken ramrods held like flails.

The *carreras de baqueta!* Governor Pico had spoken the sentence in his harassed and weary voice; the sentence had been carried to the commander of the troop by Morales, who stood there in the sun, balanced on the balls of his feet, his sheepshead raised and pointed toward him.

Across the hundred yards that remained he saw the pale ovine eyes in memory, as they had looked moments ago in the candlelight. He saw them now, out of this memory, at the far end of the plaza beside the waiting troop. They were not the eyes of Cesaire Curel in any outward characteristic, but in them was the bland cruelty that marked the murderer of San Saba, and as he strode through the yellow dust, with the birds wheeling overhead and the crowd hooting at his heels, and people leaning from the windows of the houses that rimmed the square, it was not about Morales that he was thinking but of Cesaire Curel. He had stood before the tribunal and looked at Morales and thought about

Curel. Now as he came to a halt and met the pale shifting eyes, he thought about Curel again, and then about the girl Luz de Zubaran.

The taste of hatred was bitter in his mouth. He looked at Morales, at the narrow alleyway formed by the two lines of soldiers through which he was to pass, then at the gaping crowds beyond it. He settled the front of his ruffled, soiled shirt and put his heavy watch in a trouser pocket where it would be protected from the blows of the ramrods. Holding his hat in his hand, he did not wait for the officer to speak but stepped forward between the first two men of the long corridor of grinning faces and ramrods held like flails.

Someone behind him said, "Run, gringo!"

He walked deliberately, his injured arm tight at his side, hand clenched in his coat pocket, and as the first blow fell across his shoulder, he said, "Damn you all to hell! You with the grinning faces, and you Governor Pico, and you Morales, and every damn Spaniard in California, and wherever you are, you—Luz de Zubaran!"

The next blow glanced along his neck and then there were two blows in quick succession, but it was only the first blow that he felt. The sun was in his eyes and he blinked, and one of the soldiers, raising his ramrod, taking the movement of his eyes for a sign of pain, said, wine breath spraying out into Dunavant's face, "You do not care for the *baqueta,* señor? It is not to your liking?"

It is not to my liking, Grady thought, receiving the man's blow.

A wave of catcalls rolled out from the crowd and down from the flat roof tops, filling his ears. He lost count of the blows, and after a few steps he no longer heard the crowd or the jeers and grunts of the soldiers as they used the ramrods or the swish of the ramrods themselves. The sun blinded him and it was difficult to walk straight. And then he realized that there was blood in his eyes, and looking down, he saw flecks of blood on the soiled ruffles of his shirt.

The dust was thick; he thought for a moment that it was this that made it hard to walk. Then he was aware that it was not the dust that caused it but his legs. They did not belong to him and when he moved them they did not do what he wanted. He was sure, though, that he was walking. He was walking down the alleyway and not running, as the crowd and the soldiers and Morales wished him to do. He didn't know whether he were walking fast or slow, but he was walking.

The end of the bitter lane was farther away than it had seemed when he started. For a moment in a confusion of weariness and pain he was seized with the fear that he would never reach the open square, that it was receding cunningly away from him at each step, like a mirage. Against his will, as if his body were independent of his mind, he felt that he must run, gather his strength and run.

He wasn't running, he realized. But he could no longer see the opening at the far end. He could see the yellow powdery dust and his shirt front that was now covered with blood, and the blood that ran along the hard gray fabric of his trousers, and the blood that dropped and made pockmarks on his dusty boots.

He saw the leg thrust out to trip him. He tried to step over it. He was certain he had until he was lying on the earth, with the flails falling on him. He got to his knees. He was rising when he heard through the thunder in his ears a sound that seemed to come from beyond the plaza. And then he realized that it was near and that it came from one of the houses, a woman's scream. It was a curious sound, he thought, to come from a crowd concerned only with his destruction, and the thought persisted, even as he sank again under the blows and lay watching the sun-washed sky during another moment of consciousness.

The sun fell, broken by the shape of the iron bars, on the plump figure of Doña Sol. In the last hour she had been to the window a dozen times, peering down at the crowded plaza through her nearsighted eyes, dabbing at her perspiring face, giving out angry squeals of impatience, and then returning to her chair to rock and to berate Governor Pico.

She was rocking now, fanning herself with a small ivory and silk fan and tipping the chair back and forth in little angry bursts. "*He* won't dare to free the gringo," she said, casting her eyes upward at her husband. "He might do anything but he simply won't do that."

Don Lorenzo stood at the window. He had already explained that there were certain procedures to a trial, unavoidable delays to be expected, even where a gringo was concerned, and had counseled his wife to be patient. Therefore, weary of her chatter, he did not offer a reply. He stood with his back to the room, his hands behind him, and watched the square in silence.

Luz looked at his hands opening and closing at his back, and then at Doña Sol rocking and fanning herself, dressed for the occasion in a white silk dress and heavy gold earrings. The sun sparkled on the gold mountings and, shining through the amethyst stones, cast violet shadows on the floor. She looked at Carlota sitting against the wall, her lips clamped tight on a dead cigarette, and then back at Don Lorenzo and then to the patch of blue sky beyond him. The room was hot and she loosened the throat of her jacket.

Doña Sol said, "You are very calm, my dear. If I were one of your years, I would be outside in the plaza."

Luz looked at the dark crescents of perspiration on the white dress, the silk slipper tapping the floor, at Don Lorenzo's corded hands opening and closing, and thought, If she says these words again—it is now the third time—I will choke her with my hands. She thought this, looking again at the dark stains of apprehension, and said nothing. In her ears, like an angry surf, beat the sound of the crowd below the window, no voice distinct, only a vast murmuring, rising and falling away to a whisper and rising again.

For an instant there was no sound at all, and then as she saw Don Lorenzo lean suddenly forward and heard the surf of voices break and roll through the plaza once more, she knew that *he* had appeared. Without a word from her husband, Doña Sol knew it too. She stood up quickly, upsetting the chair, tottered on her small feet to the window and craned her fat neck so that she could see the Governor's Mansion.

"It's the gringo!" she shrieked. "There he is. He's walking this way. He's walking fast, with a bayonet at his back."

"The *baqueta,*" Don Lorenzo said. "The troops are stacking arms."

"Only that," Doña Sol said bitterly. "Just ramrods. That is because we have a weak-kneed governor—a swine . . ."

"The ramrods will suffice," Don Lorenzo said. "I have faith in Lieutenant Morales and the ramrods."

Luz did not move; she was cold. She buttoned her jacket and looked across the room at her grandmother lighting a cigarette. The smoke curled up straight in the still air. Carlota watched her through the smoke and said with her eyes, "Be quiet. It will soon be over."

Doña Sol had stopped gabbling, and there was no sound below, except a dog barking and the crying of a child. Then, clearly as if the blows were struck in the room, she heard the sound of the ramrods, the sound repeated, and the rising surge of voices once more, beating against her ears and echoing through her body as if it were fleshless and hollow.

The heavy gold earrings swung violently, spraying the room with tiny points of violet light, and Doña Sol said, *"Otra vez, otra vez,"* in a frenzy of excitement.

Another time, another time, Luz thought, standing up. The eyes of her grandmother still spoke to her across the half-dark room, but she went over slowly and stood behind the two figures in the window.

"Here, my dear," Doña Sol said, making way for her. "Stand here so you can see."

He was walking between the soldiers, holding his hat, his head turned a little against the sun, his shoulders straightened. His hair was very bright in the sun and it had not been cut since she had been with him on the river. It lay heavy and bright and curled up against the collar of his gray coat that was now flecked with blood. She counted the ramrods that remained, held aloft and waiting, the soldiers bending forward, shifting and jostling one another for advantage. There were fifteen. And then there were twelve. And then, counting no longer, she thought, Why doesn't he run? Why must he permit them this advantage? Run! she wanted to cry, but the word would not come.

Doña Sol breathed heavily, sweating beside her. "This is Julio's revenge," she gasped. "Our dear son is revenged."

Then she saw a soldier, who had been crowded and could not wield the ramrod, thrust out a leg. She saw it and wondered, even as he fell in the dust, if he would see it. There was the sudden taste of blood beneath her teeth. He was moving now from under the flailing sticks, moving to his knees. "Run!" she tried to say again, and as the word hung on her lips, he was no longer on his knees. He was in the dust, moving, but in the dust, with the ramrods beating upon him.

The scream filled the plaza. It cut through the other noises like a blade, and for a moment she did not know that the sound came from her own throat—not until the faces below turned upward toward the window as if they had been moved by one impulse, and Doña Sol stopped breathing beside her. Don Lorenzo stepped back, his face frozen in disbelief, and then she was past him, and her grandmother, past them all and out of the room, and down the stairs, through the door.

As she ran across the *portale,* raised slightly above the level of the plaza, she could see that someone had thrown a jug of water on him, and that he was on his feet, walking.

She pulled away from the hand that grasped her, but the hand reached out and grasped her again. Furiously she turned and saw through a red haze the blanched face of Yris Llorente.

"You fool!" the woman said. "You utter little fool! Everyone is gaping at you. Do you wish to make him a laughing stock?" She increased the grip on Luz' arm. "See," she said, "he is through the line. It is over. Calm yourself."

Luz brushed the hair out of her eyes. The crowd swirled around them. Wiping their ramrods, the soldiers walked toward their muskets standing in shocks, like corn. She looked at Yris, the red mouth and the white face and the hot heavy-lashed eyes. She loves him, she thought, the sharp knife of jealousy turning in her heart, and now she knows that I love him too. She knows it and this is why she is barring my way.

She flung herself out of the woman's grip. "I don't need you to tell me what to do," she spat out.

Yris smiled slowly. "You can do as you wish. But you can see that he is gone. He is already out of the plaza, under guard."

It was true; he was moving along the lane that led past the Campo Santo, a guard of six men marching at his heels. He carried his hat in his hand and the sun shone on his sun-streaked hair. Then he was out of sight, lost in the crowd that pushed out from the plaza into the narrow lane.

Yris said, "I am on my way home. If you like, come with me. There are things we can discuss."

Luz looked at the woman, her eyes naked with hate. "Did you send the letter?" she demanded.

Yris' gaze was veiled. "Of course it was sent. I knew that it wasn't from your father, so I made a special effort to see that it reached Mr. Dunavant." She opened her parasol and lifted her skirts out of the dust. "And I have a message for you in return. If you wish to hear it, come."

Luz looked straight ahead, her eyes burning. If the letter was not sent, I'll kill her, she thought, walking beside Yris Llorente. I swear it.

Rain had fallen all afternoon, a misty drizzle with distant thunder and lightning that showed under the crack of the door, and now water was beginning to run down the walls and collect in puddles on the hard earthen floor.

A week had gone by. He sat on a rawhide bed in a shack not far from the church. There was no window in the small room, but he knew that he was near the church, for when the bell was rung morning and evening the sounds beat down on the roof and vibrated through the adobe walls.

It was not the season for rain—the Mexican sentry, who had to stand outside under the meager shelter of the eaves, had called on all the saints to witness the unholy happening, swearing that in twenty years he had never seen the like, except once, on the day he was born—and yet it was raining and water was oozing down the walls.

Dunavant sat propped up in the bed, his feet out of the lake forming on the floor. He had stuck a candle in a hole that someone before him had scooped out in the wall. He was reading the book of Napoleon's maxims, the one thing he had managed to save from his belongings. His Colt had disappeared at the Hill of the Hawk; the rucksack had been taken from him the morning of the trial and not returned, but he had the book—not that it was going to do him much good, he thought, sitting here in an adobe shack.

The thought twisted his mouth into a bitter smile. The smile, pulling the unhealed flesh of his cheek, made him wince, and he said aloud for the hundredth time since he had been here in the Spanish stink hole, "Damn them all to hell!"

Through the wall he heard the sentry mutter something in reply. He repeated the words, louder this time and in Spanish, so there wouldn't be any mistake about how he felt. Feeling better for the moment, he went on reading the book, thumbing through the pages, only half aware of what he was reading. "It is necessary in war to profit by every occasion, for fortune is a woman; if you let her slip today, do not expect to find her tomorrow." Someday when he had more time he could think about this passage in detail—there were more than a few observations he could add to it. "Bold men should not be sought for among those who have anything to lose." That was a good one too, he thought, well worth his attention, and he would store it away for the future, alongside the other.

The thunder was rolling away toward the Sierra Madres, but rain was still falling. He closed the book and put it in the pocket of his coat. From his waistcoat he took his watch, ran a finger along the dent made by a ramrod, clicked open the scrolled lid and marked the hour. He put the watch away and stood up and began to pace the room. He forgot the puddles under his feet.

It was after nine o'clock, an hour past the time when the message had instructed him to be in readiness. He had found the note when he got up to dress that morning, tucked in the top of his boot. It had been placed there while he slept, probably by one of the sentries, and although he wasn't certain he was content to leave it at that. The message was in an unfamiliar hand, and he had thought at first that it had been scrawled by Jacob Kroll. Later he had learned from the sentry who had come on at noon that Kroll and Kate Howland were still imprisoned on the hill. That seemed to leave only one person who could have written the message—Yris.

And yet, as he paced back and forth, six steps one way and six the other, he was struck by a thought which had occurred to him before and which he had dismissed. It was possible that the note had been written by Morales or one of his men. The oldest of Spanish tricks, and one which appealed to the singular Spanish mind, was the *ley del fuego.* The door was opened, the prisoner released, and then in the act of leaving he was shot down from behind; a report was made that the prisoner had been shot while attempting to escape.

Grady walked to the door and tried it. The door was locked. Almost at once, as he turned back into the room, he heard hoofs, muffled in the mud and at a distance, but unmistakable, moving at a walk. The sounds ceased; he heard the sentry give the challenge; a period of silence, the steps of the sentry walking forward, away from the shack, and then voices that he couldn't distinguish in the soft falling of the rain.

He was sure that it was a ruse of Morales, the *ley del fuego.* All the letters he had received from Yris while he had been on the hill had been written in her hand and signed with her name; there was no reason now for the writing to be disguised. He had heard nothing from her during the week he had been here in the shack, and furthermore, three days ago, in answer to his direct question, one of the sentries had given him the information that she had gone to San Pedro, accompanied by Morales and Governor Pico.

When the key grated in the lock, he was still certain. Even when the door opened and closed and she stood in front of him, dressed in a long riding cloak with a hood that partially concealed her face, it was several moments before he spoke in recognition, and then it was against the damp hood of her cloak, for she ran forward across the muddy floor and was quickly in his arms.

Her face was white, whiter than he had ever seen it, with splotches of rain on her cheeks, and rain on her heavy lashes. He brushed her face with his hands, feeling the texture of her skin beneath his fingers, and the beating of his blood as he had felt it the night in the garden. She stepped back but with her hand tight on his wrist.

"I was afraid you wouldn't get the message," she said, not lowering her voice and shrugging off his warning about the sentry.

"I got it this morning, but I thought it was one of Morales'. And he might have written it, judging from the scrawl."

She smiled. "Tepeyollotl," she said. "I sent him back from San Pedro yesterday afternoon. He was to give you the message as I had told it to him, but he decided to try out what I've been teaching him the last few months, and wrote it down."

"It was only one line—'Be ready tonight at eight o'clock.'"

"I wonder that you could read it."

"I still didn't know who wrote it."

"Who else except me?" she said, the rain shining on her lashes, as she turned her head toward the door. She looked up at him again. Her eyes clouded, and she said, "Are you in the habit of getting messages from someone else?"

He had to laugh. "By every mail, from three different girls—all of them beautiful."

She was silent, pressing her nails into his wrist. Her tone changed. "We are wasting time that we could use on the trail. Are you ready? Have you everything you wish to take?"

He looked at her and tried to collect his wits. "My coat has gone to the tailor for repairs," he said. "It won't be delivered until morning."

"It is no time for jokes," she said softly between her teeth, her nails biting harder into his wrist. "It is time to leave."

"But where? What is it all about? I get a message of one line. You appear . . ."

She took a step away from him, releasing the grip on his wrist. "Is it that you don't trust me? Is it because you are so secure that you can afford to ask questions? Do you desire the *baqueta* again?"

He interrupted her. "None of these things, but I would like to know——"

She answered him in a rush of words, unfolding the plan in one swift minute. There was a Mexican brig in the harbor at San Pedro. She had already spoken to the captain; passage had been arranged for the two of them to Panama. The sentry had been bribed. Tepeyollotl and three horses were waiting now a hundred yards down the lane.

"The ship sails in the morning," she said. "It will take six hours at least to reach the harbor. Six hours and we debate!"

He saw the whole thing as she spoke, and all its implications—the voyage, Panama, his obligations when he reached there, the wandering life with a woman who sought and wanted nothing except pleasure, who excited him but whom he did not love. He saw it all in swift appraisal, and when she had finished, he had made his decision.

"I came here," he said, "for a reason."

"Reason!" she cried. "The talk of a child whose mother still must need to change his pants!" She paused, and said then, lowering her voice. "It's because you do not love me. That is the only reason. Why don't you say it—'I do not love you and therefore I talk like a priest'? Say it and have done."

"It is as I've said." He was aware that his words were inadequate. "There is nothing else."

She was close to him now. He could smell the odor of her cloak drying in the warm room, this odor and the smell of her perfume, and he could feel her breath hot and musky on his face as she answered him.

"Do you know what will happen?" she said quietly, in cold measured anger. "You will be taken out again and beaten till you are unconscious. Water will be thrown on you to revive you. And you will be beaten again. And you will lie nursing your wounds until they are almost healed. Then you will be taken out once more. I know this and I say it . . . "

"That's the way it will be," he said. "They will grow tired before I do. And if not, there are American troops in the North: Commodore Sloat and his marines."

She laughed coolly in his face. "You have great faith in yourself. Even more faith in your Americans. Where are they? There is much talk, but where are they now? They are where they were two months ago, far to the north, and you are here, hundreds of miles away, with the troops of General Castro and Governor Pico between them and you."

He reached out and took her hand. Instantly, she snatched it away.

"Be beaten," she cried to him. "Be beaten into a bloody pulp and rot here forever in this hole. It is what you deserve and what I desire for you!"

She backed away from him across the muddy floor. She put her hand on the latch. A last faint roll of thunder drowned out the rest of her words. She was silent for a moment, looking at him with her head raised in pride and anger.

Suddenly she was running toward him. Her cloak opened and swirled around him, enclosing them in its folds. Her lips found his. Her long curving body, breast and thigh, pressed against him. Her hot scent rose and filled his nostrils, turned his legs to water beneath him. The fire from her lips ran through his veins, and he thought, Why not? Why not drain this cup of fury and passion? Panama, Havana and the endless night of the tropics.

The sentry stirred beyond the wall.

Her lips ran over his, her breasts besought him in a final entreaty. Then, through the pain of his wounds and the blood pounding in his ears, out of bitterness and an unfulfilled dream, and, even more than these, thinking curiously of Luz de Zubaran with hate and love both, he rejected it.

She drew her cloak about her and went to the door. She left him without speaking or looking back. He watched her, conscious of the sentry's stare, until she was lost in the thin rain. He closed the door on himself, cursing Grady Dunavant for a fool. He heard the sentry bar the door. "An utter, damnable fool!" he said aloud.

They came for him, as Yris had warned him they would, on the next afternoon. There was no crowd this time; they didn't bother to take him to the plaza. The lines were formed along one side of the Campo Santo. There were fewer soldiers in the line than before, not more than half the first number; he gathered from what he overheard that a call had come for reinforcements, that the rest of the troop had been sent north to join Governor Pico in Santa Barbara.

But there were still enough of them left, along with Lieutenant Morales, to reopen his old wounds. When he walked out of the line and past Morales and down through the lane of trees to the shack, blood was oozing in his shoes. He lay on the rawhide bed for days in a delirium, not knowing dark from light or who it was that came into the room, except that once he recognized Father Expeleta, and once Yris.

Then his wounds were healing again and he was able to move about, to eat and read his book, to watch the sun come up and shine through the crack under the door, and go down, to lie in the dark and quietly nurse his hatred. Morales came in one morning and examined his wounds, smiled at what he saw, and left. That day Grady suspected Morales would send for him again.

The next morning when the sentry brought breakfast, his hands shook as he laid the food on the floor, and he departed hastily. At noon he did not appear. When he didn't come that night and there was no evidence that he had been relieved, as was the custom, Dunavant beat on the door and shouted. His shouts weren't answered and as the night wore on he became certain that something was afoot—what, he didn't know, unless it was that the American forces were approaching the town.

With this thought he got up from the bed and walked to the door, his heart pounding. He held his breath and listened at the crack. He heard nothing. Usually there were sounds of revelry from the Calle de los Negros, the creak of a cart moving through the plaza. But he heard nothing, nothing save the barking of dogs, a sound that never ceased night or day. He shouted again and kicked at the heavy door. No answer came from outside.

Suddenly he thought, Everyone has gone away. The town is deserted.

The door was made of two thicknesses of oak, banded with iron, swung on enormous hinges. He wrenched a leg from the bed and wielded it with all his strength against the oak panels. He broke the latch loose, but the door would not give, and he realized that it never would with the means he had. Sweating and weak with exertion, he began to dig under the wall. The ground was hard as flint and after an hour of clawing he had to rest, with a hole no larger than his hand and not more than a foot deep to show for his work.

He listened at the door again and shouted. While he stood there he heard horses trotting up the lane. He shouted again. This time he was answered. The horses pulled up in front of the shack, and after a moment Kroll spoke to him through the door, out of breath with excitement, wanting to know if he were all right.

"I'll feel a lot better when I get out," Grady Dunavant said. "Can you find a ram—a trunk of a tree and someone to help swing it?"

"I have an Indian," Kroll called back, "and one of the pillars from the Governor's Mansion. Stand away from the door."

At the sixth blow the frame came loose from the adobe walls, fell inward in a shower of dirt. Dunavant stepped over it, took a deep breath of the night air and climbed into the saddle.

Kroll handed him a cigar and a flint. "When did you hear the news?"

Dunavant took a long draw on the cigar before he answered. "I haven't heard any news. But I imagined there was something going on when I missed two meals."

Kroll's cigar glowed in the dark. "Commodore Stockton has landed in San Pedro. He's been there for three days, sending demands for Pico and Castro to surrender or take the consequences. When the first demand came, Castro sent word down to the harbor that he would never surrender. But yesterday he lit out for the Colorado. Pico has gone too—some say to San Juan Capistrano. The *ricos* have fled to the country and the poor are hiding in their hovels."

Dunavant sat up straight in the saddle, puffing on his cigar. He took the news calmly. He looked at the scattered winking lights of the town, at the deserted lane, and thought, The war is over. I am alive and the war is over. This is the end of the Spaniards in California. Then almost at once, he thought, feeling a sudden, bitter disappointment, This is the end of Curel too. I'll never see him again, or Morales either. Luz de Zubaran, but not Curel.

Kroll nudged his horse and they started off toward the town. Kroll said, "Frémont is in San Diego. He'll meet with Stockton somewhere along the coast and they'll march on the town. From all reports, tomorrow."

Dunavant rode along the lane in silence; his thoughts were deep in the future.

It was the middle of the afternoon when the final word of the Americans came, and then almost as the rider pulled up in front of the inn, Dunavant heard the brassy notes, sweetened by distance, of a military band.

He had been standing at Kate Howland's bar, drinking with Jacob Kroll, when the horseman rode up the street shooting off a pistol, and together they went outside, with Kate hard on their heels. Her leathery face was pale, but she had dabbed it with rouge, and she was dressed as if she were going to a dance. In one hand she clutched a bouquet of roses picked from her own garden, mixed with ferns she had found somewhere; in the other hand she carried a short-barreled carbine. She was prepared for any contingency.

"Had to walk more than a mile to get the ferns," she said. Dunavant eyed the carbine. "Just in case there's any looting," she explained. "We're going to have an orderly town."

The day was cloudless. The shutters had been drawn in all the houses along the lane, and in the houses around the plaza. A cart, piled with household goods, was lumbering away on the North Trail. Otherwise the town was deserted. Even the dogs had slunk off. The rich, as Kroll had told him the night before, had disappeared into the country, to seek refuge among friends on the various ranches. The poor had stayed behind, but had left their hovels that morning when the first word arrived that the American troops were on their way. They had fled to the hill back of the pueblo, and Grady could see them clearly now, a crowd of men, women and children, huddled above him among the stones and brush.

The blare of the band grew suddenly louder, coming up from the south. While his gaze rested on the hill, he saw the huddled figures shift. A movement, almost imperceptible, ran like a slow wave through the crowd. A man detached himself from the others, ran forward and, raising his hand, pointed to the south. A woman screamed. The sound hung in the quiet air for a time, and was followed by another scream. There was a moment of utter silence on the hill. Then, as though the wind were blowing across a forest, he heard wailing rise and fall away, grow again in volume until it dimmed the sound of music.

The flag came into view first, with the band striding along behind it, and flanking riders a little in front.

Kate Howland dabbed at her eyes. She covered her emotion by asking where Captain Frémont was. Dunavant's reply was swept away in the flood of music that came pouring down the lane. The band went past. An officer on a Spanish horse raised a glove to them. Then soldiers four abreast in glossy caps and blue, gilt-buttoned coats. Then the marines and the webfeet, and four carts, each drawn by four oxen, with cannon secured to the floor by their breechings, followed by carts filled with provisions and ammunition.

Kit Carson and his Indians came next. Behind them were Captain Frémont and thirty or more bearded men in buckskin, black as Indians, holding carbines across their pommels. In a flash, skirts flying around her skinny legs, Kate Howland was in their midst and running along beside Frémont, holding aloft the bouquet of roses.

Grady's eyes were fixed on an officer riding beyond Frémont—a short thick-set man with his campaign hat pulled forward over his eyes, the brim rolled up rakishly on both sides. He had known on the night he had walked into the gambling room and seen Cesaire Curel that sooner or later, before the fighting was over, he would see Major Gilson. There before him, riding a white horse, his dusty hair rounded and dense on his neck, his heavy-jawed, red face set in a frown, was his man. Only Gilson was no longer a major and an irregular. He now wore the insignia of a captain in the regular army.

Gilson passed out of sight, his broad back lost in the dust. Dunavant left Kroll and made his way through the plaza, where the army was now deploying, and down the lane to Yris' gate. He had gone there early that morning and received no answer to his summons. He knocked again, beating on the heavy gate with the butt of the pistol he had borrowed from Kate Howland. He heard someone stirring inside, the sound of wood moving against wood, as if a shutter had been opened and closed, but no one appeared at the gate. He went down the lane and along the wall to the small gate in the garden. It also was barred. He heard the noise again and shouted, but no one came.

The band was playing in the square. The peons on the hillside had ceased their wailing, and most of them, seeing that they weren't to be murdered, had started to drift down the hill toward the music. It wouldn't be so easy, he thought, to tame the *ricos.*

In front of the Governor's Mansion Carson was talking to Captain Frémont. The commanding officer, neat in a blue uniform, his shoes and buttons glittering in the sun, his stiff black mustache cropped with military precision, looked more impressive than he did on a horse, though he was not much over five feet. Grady waited until he had left.

Carson held out a horny hand. "I'll be dogged!" he drawled.

"How are you, Bub?" Dunavant said, using the Taos name. "How's your wife?"

"Don't rightly know—being I laid nary an eye on her for months."

"Still pretty," Dunavant said, thinking of the beautiful Josefa, fourteen when she married Carson, and a head taller than he was. "Is Sloat in charge?"

"Stockton took over in Monterey. Things have been happenin' since."

"Who's under Stockton?"

"Gillespie."

"How about Gilson?"

"Can't say as I know the name."

"He's under Gillespie then," Dunavant said, relieved.

He found Gilson in the Governor's Mansion, sitting back with his boots on the table, the same table Grady had stood in front of before the tribunal.

The captain recognized him instantly, without surprise and without getting to his feet. "I thought about you, Dunavant," he said in his Mississippi drawl, "coming up from the ship. I was sure you'd be here. I understand you've been in trouble with the greasers. By the looks of the scar on your face, quite a bit of trouble, I'd say. You were always unlucky with the greasers, weren't you, Dunavant?"

Grady said deliberately, "I have a friend here. Her name is Yris Llorente. She's helped me out when I needed help. You'll probably start rounding up all the Spaniards. When you come to her, remember, captain, that she's my friend."

Gilson shifted his stogy, rolled it back into a corner of his mouth and looked at Dunavant with his pale-blue eyes, undecided whether to comment on the friendship or not.

"We'll examine them all," he said. "She can take her chances with the rest."

Dunavant quietly put a fist on the table. "I'm not in the army now, Gilson. I'm not serving under you any longer," he said. "So remember what I've told you." He walked out of the room.

# 26

Wak, Chief of the Utah, lay in the grass by the willows. He could scarcely hear the stream flowing past him, but he could feel its coolness on his bare skin. The day had been hot, and though the sun had gone down, the hills still threw off heat. The coolness of the stream felt good; after a while he might even go into the stream and bathe to please his favorite wife Tolewah, who was now plucking hairs from his face with bone tweezers. He would not see Tolewah again for a while, so it would be good, he thought, to send her away with a feeling of pleasure—many moons had passed since he had done anything to please her, or so she had just told him.

He looked up at the sky ruddy with the last glow of the sun and gave a deep sigh. Tolewah's hands were soft as the wind at dawn and the stars at dusk, as well-chewed deerskin was soft. She was not so pretty as Naik, or so resourceful in the dark of night as Solai whom he had bought from the Cocopa, but she was the finest wife he had ever owned for the plucking out of hairs. The little tweezers snipped here and there over his face so lightly that he did not feel the smallest pain. Her hands moved swiftly like wild horses before the wind, like the fine horses he had come to California to steal from the Spaniards.

Bats were veering through the darkening air, and in the rushes by the river frogs started to talk. It was the hour when gods take shape and walk among the people, when monsters come forth from their lairs, lifting awesome heads to sniff the coming night. But Chief Wak did not think of gods or monsters. He thought, as he had been thinking all afternoon, about the fine Spanish horses. His plans were now complete.

Before he had left the far mountains and traveled across the desert and down the Cajon, he had heard many stories of strife between the Spaniards and the men who came out of the east. He had never raided in California, but it had seemed to him then, with the Spaniards too busy with other things to keep a close watch on their herds, that this would be a good time to start.

His ruse of bringing along his women had fooled the Spaniards, and though the tales he had heard about warfare had appeared untrue at first, within the last two suns he had received news that soldiers were on the march from the coast. At dawn he had sent three of his men to reconnoiter the pueblo. Before long they would return. Then, having spent the day in preparation, he would send the women up the Cajon and out of the country, under the cover of night.

Fires began to burn in the camp. Light rippled over the willows by the river. Tolewah, finished with his beard, went off to help with the meal. But Wak lay there in the grass thinking about the envy of the other tribes when they saw him riding back after many moons with a herd of Spanish horses. This thought made his broad paunch swell upward with pride. And then, beneath his ear, he felt the vibration of the earth. The movement came from far off. It was the vibration of running hoofs.

He rose and walked to the ring of fires burning in the oak grove, and waited for his men to ride up. When they came, everyone ate, and, sitting in the grass, Wak digested the news they had brought back from the pueblo. When the meal was over, he passed around a bowl of *pispibata,* a brew of ground sea shells, tobacco and wild cherries. Each man stuck his finger into the bowl and placed a small portion of the *pispibata* on his tongue. Then they rose and went to their horses. The women were already waiting.

They traveled for many miles, until they came to a river. There they said good-by to the women, who left them and rode north, following the riverbank, toward the mountains. Wak and his men lay in the grass and waited. They waited until an hour had passed and another. A coyote barked in a near-by thicket. An owl hooted twice. It was a good sign, Wak thought. He stood up and divided his men into two bands. With both bands he then rode out of the bottom, up the hillside to the mesa, and with the hoofs of the horses muffled in deerskin shoes, across the mesa to the corrals.

There he left one band and rode slowly toward the house where small lights showed in the windows. The arrows had been prepared that afternoon, the heads wound with sheep's wool and soaked in fat. He stopped within a hundred yards of the house and deployed his men in a half circle, and then struck flint and lighted an arrow, which was passed from man to man until every arrow was burning. Making certain that the signal had been seen and that the other band had opened the gates to the corrals, he gave the order to pull the bows.

The arrows went out from the half circle of men in a great plunging arc, dripping streamers of fire. They lighted up the sky. They fell at the end of their course on the thick, dry roof of the house, fell almost at the same time so that there was but a single sound. The horses wheeled and raced past the corrals that were now empty, following the thunder of the driven herd.

At the rim of the mesa Wak looked over his shoulder. The sky was already aglow.

No one in the *sala* saw the flight of arrows or heard them when they curved silently out of the night and struck the roof. No one saw them because only a small window opened on the courtyard. No one heard the arrows because the sound of their falling was drowned by the heavy tread of Don Saturnino.

Since supper Luz had been sitting at the long table, with the breeze shifting the taper flames, shuffling and dealing the red and yellow cards. She had played such a bad game that Jorge, poor at it as he was, finally grew disgusted and took himself off to bed.

When he had gone she put the cards away in the chest and walked to the window. She had stood with the seawind blowing cool on her face, her thoughts in turmoil, looking out across the mesa to the hills that rose up dark between her and the pueblo. It was then, while she faced the west, that she saw the horsemen coming up out of the dark, the moon pale on their lathered horses.

At suppertime one of the *vaqueros* had brought word of the capture of Los Angeles. He had ridden in out of breath, shouting the news through the courtyard. Above the cries of the Indians the word had come softly into the room. Carlota had looked up from her plate in silence. Her face was still but there were tears in her eyes. Luz' own throat had tightened, but stronger than the taste of defeat, deeper than the loss of her country, was something else. She looked at the tears coursing down her grandmother's cheeks and thought, He is safe now. That is all that matters. Our city has been taken, but he is safe at last. Nothing matters except that.

As she stood at the window the horsemen rode up to the gate, and a moment later the three came into the room. Her father's eyes were red-rimmed, and his clothes, like the clothes of the other men, were caked with dirt. They lurched as they walked, as men walk in their sleep.

She stood now, with her back against the table, looking at them. They had been in the room for several minutes and she had heard the story. When the word had reached them in the North that Stockton had landed at San Pedro, they had left the rest of the army, which was already beginning to disperse, and ridden two days without stopping, skirting the pueblo when they learned that it had been taken, and finding their way to the ranch by a roundabout trail.

Saturnino, striding back and forth through the room, ground a dirty fist into the palm of his hand and cursed.

Malaspina said, "There is nothing left for us but to wait."

Saturnino whirled and glared at the man, his head lowered. "Angels of Christ!" he thundered. "Wait for what? Wait for the raping of our women, the driving off of our herds, the destruction of our homes?"

Ricardo Haro of the Two Brothers leaned his exhausted bulk against the wall. "Our forces are scattered to the winds and our leaders with them. Three men, and two dozen *vaqueros,* cannot ride out to meet an army equipped with cannon."

The muscles tightened in Saturnino's jaws. He swung his lowered head aimlessly, like a bull mortally wounded, and his bloodshot eyes swept the room, the muskets ranged against the wall, the unused lances, his two friends, and finally rested on her.

Meeting his gaze, she thought, A curse on the Americans, who have done this to us! But again, stronger than the bitterness and the love of her father, was the other, uncontrollable thought. He is safe, she said to herself, her lips moving under her father's gaze, and marveled, though she saw his distress, how nothing mattered save this one thing.

"You have what you wish," Saturnino said to her.

She had read his thoughts. She knew what he was going to say in his extremity, but she met his eyes without flinching.

He took a step forward and raised his fist and then, out of exhaustion, dropped it to his side.

"I'll get food for you," she said, walking past him.

He gathered his strength and shouted, "I vomit at the thought of food, and at everything else."

She opened the door on the courtyard. The air that struck her face was hot, and at once, looking upward, she saw the flames. They were running along the roof of the storehouse, bent slightly by the wind. The men were past her before she could speak, and as she ran after them her thought was that it was the Americans. Then she heard the pounding of hoofs by the river, the neighing of horses, and Tiburcio, coming in by the gate, shouted the alarm. She ran across the courtyard, roused Carlota and Jorge and, still running, reached the well where the leather sacks were being passed.

The flames had risen shoulder-high, but the wind was herding them away from the main part of the house. Her father and three men had gained the roof and were braced there to receive the buckets which were now starting down the line, passed from hand to hand.

Above her, as Tiburcio lowered and raised the water from the well and poured it into the leather sacks, the eagle clawed at his chains and screamed. The sound of the flames rose above his cries and the cries of the men on the roof. She saw her father, clear against the sky, a lurid, demon figure, plunge forward to the edge of the fire, then back to grasp another burden of water.

The fire was being driven back, back toward the earthen roof of the watchtower and, sure that it was beaten, Tiburcio said that it was time to go in pursuit of the Indians. But at the moment he spoke, the roof of the storehouse crashed in. It fell at a slant and in an instant the stored tallow had caught.

The walls of the house were suddenly red with the conflagration. She saw her father and the three *vaqueros* leap to the ground. The heat was so intense that they and everyone at the well had to retreat to the far end of the courtyard. Saturnino went back once, crouched against the flames, to get the eagle, and then they all stood on the *portale* and watched the flames roar upward between the earthen walls, like fire out of a great pit. Oily smoke engulfed the courtyard, but the sparks, driven by the wind, stretched away to the east, away from the rest of the house, in a red angry banner.

The fire lasted until dawn. In the first gray light they crossed the courtyard and looked into the gutted storehouse.

Carlota said, "We have lost the tallow, but saved the house." She left them and disappeared into the chapel.

Saturnino stood in the dawn, his shoulders sagged forward, his face black with smoke. He looked at the empty storehouse for a long time in silence. Then he looked at her.

"This transpires," he said, "because of your friends, the gringos, for without them the Indians would not have attacked. If we had not been in the North, the Indians would not have had a chance to plan our destruction."

She said nothing in reply. She looked at the blackened pit where the tallow had been stored and thought, It *is* the fault of the Americans.

Damn them for this thing which they have caused! But he is safe. He is safe and the letter that I sent was delivered.

She gazed at the last wisps of smoke curling away in the dawn wind and remembered the message Yris Llorente had given her the afternoon of the *baqueta,* when they had sat sipping chocolate. He had received her word and sent word to her in return. He was safe now and somehow, before long, she would see him. And thinking of him, looking at the destruction of the storehouse, seeing the cold fury on her father's smoke-blackened face, she marveled again at the pounding of her heart.

Grady Dunavant was leaning against the counter in the rear of Mrs. Howland's store when the great buckskin stallion and its rider pulled up at the hitching rack. Kate sat on a high stool, with a leather-bound ledger opened in front of her. The afternoon was hot, and she had her sleeves folded back from her bony wrists.

Only two days had passed since the Americans had ridden in, but the town already had undergone a change. Although the houses of the *ricos* were still deserted, the peons, lured by the band concerts in the plaza every afternoon, were again living happily in their hovels. Again a heavy pall of wood smoke hung over the roofs. There were not many people abroad in the lanes, but in the Calle de los Negros a bevy of *putas* were plying their ancient trade, and soldiers and marines crowded Kate Howland's bar.

Dunavant had been talking to Mrs. Howland for an hour. Together they had pored over the ledger, discussing the details of the three ranches she had for sale. One was situated on the upper reaches of the Río Porciuncula—some eighteen thousand acres of level land and hills, with an abundance of water, without cattle or buildings. The second was a smaller ranch, near the ocean, and well stocked. The third was beyond the Santa Ana. The prices varied from thirty cents an acre to forty cents. They all sounded good to Dunavant, and he had written down the price and location of each one, with the intention of spending the next week riding around to look at them.

The appearance of the buckskin stallion and its rider brought an abrupt end to their talk. When Grady turned and looked through the open door and saw the Spaniard tying his horse to the rack, he put on his wide-brimmed gray hat.

"De Zubaran," Kate Howland said, following his gaze.

"I've seen him before," Dunavant answered.

The Spaniard came to the door, and paused there for a moment staring at two soldiers who were making a purchase, as if uncertain whether or not to enter.

"They're not so high and mighty these days," said Kate Howland. "The last time this one was here you could hear him coming a mile away, galloping down the street and making more clatter than an army, swinging from his horse, and stomping through the store with his spurs clanking, like he owned the place." She showed her teeth in a wry smile.

Dunavant said, "I'm going to have a drink. I'll be back."

He turned away from the man walking down the aisle and went next door. The gambling room was filled with soldiers playing monte; they stood two deep at the bar. He sat down at a table and ordered a bottle of wine, noticing that there wasn't a Spaniard or Mexican in the place except the two bartenders. He drank the bottle of wine and then went in and played ten hands of monte.

His mind wasn't on the game, but he won every hand. He stood and held his cards and raked in the money, thinking all the time about Cesaire Curel. About him and Joe the Indian and the fight in which he had come close to being choked to death. And about Yris who had apparently left the pueblo with the rest of the *ricos*. (He had been back four times to knock on the gate in the lane and the one that opened on the vineyard. It was just as well that she had disappeared, with Captain Gilson throwing his weight around, itching to arrest the first Spaniard who crossed his path.) And Camilla who, now that she knew that he was responsible for the disappearance of Peter Pomeroy Fraser, passed him without speaking!

When he got tired of winning, with his pockets full of silver he walked out and down the passageway to the store. The Spaniard had gone, and Kate Howland was sitting on her high stool chewing on the end of the quill pen. She made a notation in the ledger, closed the ledger with a bang and looked up, peering over the rims of her silver-mounted glasses. There was a curious gleeful light in her eyes.

"Mr. Dunavant," she said, smiling her tight thin-lipped smile, "there's nothing warms the bones like retribution. Wait long enough and Fate will even the score for you." She thrust the pen into a cup of buckshot, took off her glasses and slowly lifted her gaze across the counter. "You know why I got thrown into that smelly house up there on the hill?"

Grady shook his head.

"Well, I'll tell you, young man. And listen carefully, because you'll enjoy it." She leaned her elbows on the slanting desk. "You saw De Zubaran when he came in here a moment ago meek as Moses. Well, he's the one who had me put up there on the hill. He went to Morales and Pico and told them that when you were at the ranch, about dead and out of your mind, you kept talking about me and how we were going to run the Spaniards out of the country."

"How do you know that he went to Morales?"

"Because it all came out at the trial," she said. "And that's why I got arrested and had to spend weeks living like a pig, with my business going to pot and everything. There were other reasons—the Llorente woman was mixed up in part of it—but that was the main one."

Grady bit off the end of a cigar. His mind was racing ahead of her. It isn't possible, he thought; things like that just don't happen. He lighted the cigar and waited for her to go on.

"And do you know why he went to Morales and Pico with this lie?" she said, leaning toward him, her eyes narrowed to slits. "Well, I'll tell you, because you'd never guess in a lifetime. He owed me money on a loan I made to his father, three years ago during the drought—four thousand dollars, it was. The loan was due last month, but I gave him an extension. So what does he do? He goes to them with this lie, thinking that if I'm thrown in prison and my business ruined, he won't have to pay the loan."

Grady puffed slowly on the cigar.

"Well, it didn't work, young man. I am here and California belongs to the United States. God bless Captain Frémont!" she said. "He thanked me for the bouquet of roses, tipped his hat, and said, 'Thank you, madam,' just like that, in a deep voice. He has wonderful dark eyes, deep like his voice, and brooding."

Grady studied the end of his cigar and put it back in his mouth. Her reference to Frémont had pulled him up short. It was this, he thought, the taking of California, which proved the point she had made about retribution. It was not the other, the attack upon the Hill of the Hawk.

Kate Howland climbed down from the stool and came around the counter to where he stood.

"You heard yesterday," she said, "about the fire on the Hawk."

"Eight hours after it happened. I was talking with Captain Gillespie when the word came in."

"Well, the Indians set fire to the storehouse and burned up about eight hundred arrobas of tallow." She paused and pressed a bony finger against his shirt front. "Here's where Fate dealt me a hand," she said.

"De Zubaran came in just now to ask me to extend the loan again—he was going to pay it off with the tallow." She looked at him for a long moment. "What do you think I did, Mr. Dunavant?"

"Turned the other cheek."

"Not by a jugful. Hell's blazing fires, young man, nothing of the kind! I told him that the loan was foreclosed. Now. Beginning today. He tried to pawn off another ranch south of the Hawk on me. I told him to get out and go live on it."

Dunavant ground out the cigar on the heel of his boot. "Then you're the new owner of the Hill of the Hawk?"

"From this day on—just as soon as I can get Captain Gillespie to issue the orders—we have a military government now, you know."

"Tomorrow?"

"Maybe."

"What's the price?" Grady asked.

Kate Howland's eyes grew shrewd. "Well, about that, Mr. Dunavant . . ."

He interrupted her. "Whatever the price is," he said quietly, "I'll take it."

Dawn had come and he was riding east from the San Gabriel, riding his pinto pony again, his rucksack bulging with clothes he had bought from the store, a new Colt strapped to his hip, and in the sheath beneath his leg a Spencer rifle which he had won from a soldier. Shaving by candlelight that morning, he had debated about wearing his new clothes (they were the same kind, trousers and jacket and high soft boots, that were worn by the Californians—all that Kate Howland had in stock), but he finally decided to put on his gray coat and gray tight-fitted trousers; after all, he wasn't a Californian, not yet, or a Jim Wolfe married to a Spaniard.

The sun lay hot on the dry grass of the hills and the small drifting wide-horned cattle. The grass was golden with the light and its own color, smooth and golden like the pelt of a young lioness, and it rippled and moved before his eyes under the faint dawn wind, changing as the sea changes. The hills to the right rose irregularly in a rhythm of their own, but the rhythm was pleasing, enclosing little valleys or rolling away one above the other to low wooded crests. They were firm and rounded and feminine, curved like the forms of resting women. But the mountains, the Sierra Madres away to his left, blue even in the golden light, shouldered the sky. In color and contour, in the lift of the granitic peaks and the shaggy belts of pine below them, they were masculine. Across the great running valley, unfurrowed by a single plow, waiting for the seed, the hills and the mountains regarded each other.

He looked at the golden grass and the hills and the iron-blue mountains. He had seen them before but always with the eyes of an outlander, an interloper who comes upon a sleeping girl in a meadow, lying naked in the sun, who looks furtively and passes on. Now, as he rode into the east toward the Hawk, with his hard gray hat at an angle, his eyes rested boldly on earth and sky and everything between. The journey was ended; the dream fulfilled.

And yet as he rode a vague and formless misgiving lay at the bottom of his mind. Eight days had elapsed since the transaction had been made; six days since Kate Howland had sent a Spanish lawyer to the Hawk; it had been four days since his return with reports of a violent reception, and two days now since Gillespie's soldiers, making the round trip, had come back with word that the De Zubarans were moving.

It would have been wiser, he thought, and so had been counseled by Kate Howland, to wait for another week, until it was certain that the ranch was vacated. The chances were good, due to his impatience, that he would run into some member of the family, or all of them. But this was not the source of his misgiving. It lay in the circumstances of his buying the ranch, the act of foreclosure, the rooting up of ordered life and the breaking of ties, though it was plain that if he had not done it, it would have been done by someone else. Still, at the moment the doubt assailed him, it was engulfed in the memory of the lance that had sought his life, the girl's betrayal of him, the trial, the *baqueta* and the pain.

Under the brim of his hat, his gray eyes hardened. He ran a finger over the edges of the scar that ran along his cheekbone. Tightening his mouth, he set spurs to the pony. "Damn all of them!" he said. He said the words again, louder and slower this time, giving the pony its head.

The trail was tinder-dry and he should have seen the dust before he rounded the low hill, but the light was the color of dust and he didn't see them until they were coming up out of the watercourse, De Zubaran himself riding in the lead, the boy behind him and then three carts filled to the top timbers, and finally the girl. It was too late to change his direction, to do anything but ride on, leaving the trail, and pass around them.

De Zubaran had seen and recognized him. On the bank of the

watercourse the Spaniard pulled in his stallion and sat waiting. He did not speak until Dunavant came abreast, with eyes level and narrowed in the sun. Grady's Colt lay firm against his hip, ready to his hand.

Then Don Saturnino said, "Our meeting is fortunate, but not an accident. My *vaqueros* have reported you on the trail." He carried a musket across the pommel and one hand rested on it. "There are things I wish to tell you," he said. "We have left the ranch. Also we have left our curse upon you, which I now repeat. We go into the hills, but we will return, and not while you sleep. We will return in the light of day, a hundred of us, and more, and we will take back what is ours. And you and all your soldiers will not prevail against us. Likewise we will take back this valley, which is now desecrated by the feet of the gringo, and the pueblo."

Dunavant said nothing. He was watching the hand on the musket, the yellow violent eyes in the dark high-cheekboned face. De Zubaran was speaking again, but he did not listen. The girl had ridden up and stood now beside her father, holding a musket along her leg. He took his eyes from the man and looked at her. Her eyes were opaque. They looked back at him without a trace of recognition, hard and level and heavy with hatred, like the eyes of a cornered animal.

He looked at her, at the swell of her breast moving visibly against the leather jerkin, the place where the neckline ended that was a lighter color than the rest of her skin, the sweep of her hair as it fell from under the broad hat, lying wide and shadowed on her wide shoulders, her upper lip turning under at each corner and the lower curved and full, at her fine hands on the musket, at the square, strong delicately turned wrist, and her legs long in the stirrups.

He saw these things in an instant, each separately and yet at once, feeling them with his blood more than with his eyes. They ran along his veins like threads of fire. His throat grew thick with the sense of them, thick almost to bursting, but even as the fire ran through him, anger would not let him speak.

De Zubaran said, "We leave you nothing except our curse, bandit and gringo."

Dunavant looked at the malevolent eyes, the broad heavily muscled hand lying on the musket, and then at Luz. Her expression had not changed. In her gaze he saw repeated the words her father had just spoken, as plainly as if she had spoken them herself.

"This," De Zubaran said, "and the promise to return."

He spurred his stallion, turning in a half circle around Dunavant;

as he came back to the trail Luz rode with him, shoulder to shoulder, her eyes meeting Dunavant's in one final, swift look of hatred. They were well down the trail before he kneed his own horse into a trot.

There were no cattle on the mesa; when he came to the house the gate was open. He tied his horse to the rack and walked into the courtyard, his steps sounding hollow against the walls. No fires burned in the outdoor ovens. He walked along the *portale* and looked into the rooms. They were empty, heaped with debris, and already a thin layer of dust lay over the floors. The saddlery was stripped of everything, but in the blacksmith shop a pile of coals was glowing. A broken lance head lay on the anvil. It was still warm to the touch.

He went outside and stood looking over the low roofs. The moun tains had changed color in the heat, but they rose tall and forbidding into the sky. Suddenly the old misgiving swept over him, and then, lowering his gaze, he saw the room where he had lain close to death. He crossed the courtyard, opened the door, and set his rucksack on the floor, unstrapped his Colt and laid it on the rucksack, and then he walked on along the *portale*.

The door was ajar and he stepped inside. The room was in half darkness, the small windows that opened on the mesa shuttered, but he saw to his surprise that the furniture had not been removed. Against the far wall he saw a point of light. The light glowed for an instant and then paled out, and as he stood looking at it in amazement, smelling the sharp odor of aromatic smoke, a figure rose from a chair and with the click of a cane on the tiles came slowly toward him.

She came to the door where he was standing. On her head was a rusty black shawl held tight along her leathery cheeks. She said, "My name is Doña Carlota Escalante de Zubaran. I know *your* name because I have seen you before, one evening when I took a lance from your shoulder. I liked you then. Now I withhold judgment. This is my home and I do not propose to leave. For you or soldiers or God himself. Remembering this, do as you wish."

Then she reached out and, as he stepped forward onto the *portale*, closed the door in his face.

# 27

Meadows and hills and mesas without cattle—sixteen thousand acres without so much as a knock-kneed yearling. A ranch without *vaqueros.* A servantless house, except for one slow-moving Indian who belonged to the old lady, and who spent most of the day lying on the floor in the capacity of a footstool. A house without furniture, except for the *sala* and the old lady's bedroom. A storeroom bare of provisions; a blacksmith shop without iron; an empty armory and a saddlery that had no leather.

On his first morning at the Hawk, Grady made this rough inventory. He made it leaning against the stone coping of the well in the center of the courtyard. He looked around him at the silent house while he made it, smoking one long rattail stogy, and then he mounted his pinto and rode hell-bent for Los Angeles.

The second morning he was on his way back to the ranch, with three Indians driving three pairs of cream-colored oxen (he wished for a couple of good Tennessee mules) and three big carts filled with all manner of supplies—just about everything that Kate Howland had on her shelves. He stopped by Jim Wolfe's, made a dicker for two Indian girls, one of them in early pregnancy, and at nightfall pulled into the ranch.

By the third morning the place had taken on a different aspect. Fires burned in the ovens; the sound of corn being ground on the metates echoed in the courtyard; the bellows were working in the blacksmith shop; one of the Indians was putting a new roof on the burned-out storehouse, and six of the rooms, including his own, had been furnished, not well but adequately.

At noon he climbed the ladder to the watchtower, frowning when he saw the gaping holes—silent evidence that Saturnino de Zubaran intended to return—where the swivel gun had been wrenched from its moorings. He stood in the blaze of midday and looked at the shimmering sea of grass stretching away in all directions. He still owned a ranch without cattle or horses or growing wheat or even a milpa of corn and beans.

The next day he went in search of cattle, stopping first at the ranch of old Malaspina. He was surprised at the Spaniard's friendly greeting; as he went from ranch to ranch, visiting three during the day, his surprise increased. At each place he was met at the door, welcomed inside, offered food and drink, and at the ranch of Don Anselmo Espinosa he was introduced to the marriageable daughter Lupita, a plump, pretty miss of sixteen, who said nothing but ogled him, all the time he was there, out of big sultry eyes.

Riding homeward in the dusk, counting up the cattle he had bought during the day—six hundred in all, with twelve head of good horses, to be delivered within the week—he continued to marvel at the welcome he had received everywhere. He was prepared for the opposite, for open hostility, but he had been accepted as if he were an old resident of the valley. Whether this was because De Zubaran was disliked, as there was reason to believe, or whether it was an effort on the part of the Spaniards to ingratiate themselves with the gringo conquerors, or both, he didn't know. The result was the same in either case.

It was Doña Carlota who puzzled him most, the old lady who sat all day wrapped in her rusty black shawl, with her tiny feet on the back of her servant. He had seen her only once since the night he came, a wordless meeting, but he had caught glimpses of her as he passed the *sala,* sitting there smoking her cornhusk cigarettes and staring out over the mesa. She never came near the kitchen, but sent her servant to prepare and fetch her meals, and only left the room to sleep.

He was even more puzzled by her that night. When he was on his way to bed, she shouted to him from the *sala;* as he entered she greeted him with a curious smile. Candles were burning on the table. She sat wrapped to the chin in her shawl.

"Señor Grady Dunavant," she said, having trouble with the G in his name, her voice neither friendly nor unfriendly. She looked slowly at his long gray coat and tight trousers and brocaded waistcoat—his American clothes—and said, "Since you are now a ranchero, you should dress like one. Not like one who gambles for a living."

He grinned. "Running a ranch is a gamble, señora. And therefore my clothes are appropriate."

She blew thin streams of smoke from her nostrils, sniffing at his pleasantry. "It is the best ranch in the valley," she said, "or in any other valley. It always has been and so it will continue, providing you are a man of reasonable wits, which I am not sure of." She puffed on her cigarette and studied him through the rising smoke. "What is it that you have been up to since dawn?" she said.

He had the feeling that he was again in knee pants, on the Ohio, being questioned by his mother. "Buying cattle," he said, suppressing a smile. "At Malaspina's and at Don Anselmo's."

"Neither has good cattle—they are raisers of goats and poor ones at that. You should have gone to the ranch of Don Luis Taraval. How many of these goats did you purchase?"

"Six hundred," he said. "Half the number I wanted."

She sucked in her breath. "*Madre de Dios,* you are a man of vast dreams!"

"I am going back to Don Anselmo's in a few days to talk him out of the rest."

"To the ranch of Don Luis Taraval, as I have just advised. Cattle cannot be raised from goats." She gave him a shrewd look out of her black eyes. "You have encountered the Lupita?"

He nodded.

"How were you impressed?"

The feeling that he was being questioned by his mother still persisted. "I was there to buy cattle."

The old lady was not satisfied with this evasion. "I have known her since she was a mewling infant," she said. "She is of an extreme laziness, lightheaded, and a possessor of the Espinosa temper, which is a matter of legend. Why else would she be single at the age of sixteen?"

It occurred to him to remind her that her granddaughter belonged in this category, but he decided against it.

"Don Anselmo's cattle and his Lupita are of the same quality, as you will observe." She rose and dismissed him with a gesture of her bony hand. "Go with God," she said, "and hereafter see that you consult me on matters of importance—it will save you trouble and money."

He lay in bed and wondered how he was going to rid himself of the old harpy; he couldn't very well throw her out bodily. Why, he wondered, was she here? Was it some plan of De Zubaran's to embarrass him, a part of the curse? Was she here in the role of an informer to spy on his every movement and report it to her son? As a part of some longheaded scheme to get the ranch back?

Far into the night he pondered, but no solution presented itself. Nothing occurred to him then or later. The next day she sat smoking her interminable cigarettes, and the day following she was there, still smoking and looking out over the mesa. Fortunately she left him alone; it wasn't until the end of the week when Don Anselmo and his *vaqueros* rode in with the herd that she again approached him.

He stood outside the gate talking to Espinosa, making arrangements to have the herd branded sometime during the next week by Espinosa's men, who would use an iron that one of his Indians had fashioned and which he had taken to the pueblo to have registered. In the midst of the discussion she came hobbling through the gate and inserted herself between him and Don Anselmo. She cast a brief deprecating glance in the direction of the herd which was grazing on the mesa. Then she looked at Don Anselmo.

"These—" she pointed with her cane—"they are a gift?"

Don Anselmo colored. "My best stock," he answered.

"Crow bait," she replied. "Food for lions that have great hunger and many teeth." Turning a deaf ear to Don Anselmo's protests, she shouted to one of his *vaqueros*, "Drive these inhabitants of crags and crevices to the corrals—we will find a dozen perhaps that are fit to eat our grass."

And off she hobbled toward the corrals, kicking up spurts of dust with her cane. Dunavant ground his teeth but fell in behind her, with Don Anselmo furious at his heels.

There were two hundred and fifty cows in the herd. She stood at the first corral, and as each one was cut out and driven toward the gate, she did one of two things. She either permitted it to enter or she signaled with her cane to drive it away. When the first corral was filled she hobbled on to the second. At the end of the morning the task was finished; there were more cows on the mesa than in the corrals.

She gave Don Anselmo a long glance. "Those without differ little from those within—they are all goats or the offspring of goats. On your return remember that you deal with me, who knows one end of a cow from another."

When he had ridden off in a huff with his *vaqueros* and the remainder of the herd, she said, "The Espinosa temper, of which I have spoken. It is shared by his daughter, the Lupita."

Grady never expected to see Don Anselmo again, but he came back the next day, driving a herd of fine cows, so fine in fact that the old lady, standing again at the corral gate, found only a dozen or so that didn't please her.

That afternoon as he and the Indians were hauling cartloads of meadow grass to the corrals (it was her idea that time would be saved by branding the cows before they were turned loose) Doña Carlota again buttonholed him. The herd looked sleek and productive in the bright sun, feeding on the rich grass. In an expansive mood he was forced to remark about it, to go even farther and compute the increase for the coming year.

The old lady snorted. "Do they have cows in the country from which you come?" she asked.

"Of course we have cows," he said. The grudging admiration which had been forced upon him by her handling of Don Anselmo, and which had been wearing thin under the bite of her sharp tongue, now deserted him entirely. "Do you think we live in trees?"

"And the cows have calves?"

He looked at her and said nothing.

"The cows in this country are not so unique," she said. "Here it is necessary to have bulls."

He had one foot in the cart; he left it there and turned, his gaze sweeping the corrals. His ears reddened. He got into the cart and drove away. He could hear her when he was far out on the mesa, leaning there on her cane, laughing her shrill cackle.

"God Almighty!" he said. "More than four hundred cows and not a bull in the lot!"

It was Saturday night and he was fixing his waistcoat. The cows had been branded; he was getting ready to go to a dance at Don Anselmo's. He had laid out his new Spanish clothes on the bed, but now at the last moment he couldn't screw up the courage.

He got into his threadbare gray jacket, put on his gray hat, slipped his Colt in his hip pocket and went outside. Candles were burning in the *sala*, but the old lady wasn't there. At last, for one evening, he was to be spared her tongue. But the gate was ajar and when he walked through it and closed it after him, he saw her sitting in the cart, her servant beside the oxen.

Silently he mounted his horse. Is it possible, he thought, that the old lady has given up? He remembered that she had been in her room clawing around since suppertime. He tipped his hat, holding his breath as he did so, but as he started away his hopes were shattered.

"Ride slowly," she shouted at him. "Remember that you are my escort."

"Escort!" he shouted back. "I am going to Don Anselmo's."

"We go together," she replied. "It is many months since I have been there. He has good food, but very poor music. Since I eat but do not dance it does not matter."

Riding slowly through the dark—slowly because the gait of the cart was slow—he cursed. When he got to Don Anselmo's he was still cursing, and as the evening progressed his temper did not improve. No matter what he did, the old lady wasn't far away. When he danced she sat against the wall, with the other old ladies, chattering and smoking, but always with her black eyes following him. And when he took Lupita into the room where the food was heaped on a long table, she was hard on his heels.

"Neither the food nor the music was good," she said on the way home. "Not enough seasoning in either one. A very dull evening, indeed."

"Dull, all right," he said.

"Then you did not like the Lupita?"

"A very charming girl," he said. "So charming that I may give a dance in her honor."

"At the Hawk!" she said, outdone.

He had spoken in jest, but hearing the tone of her voice, he began to consider the matter seriously, and as he rode onward through the night the idea took another turn. He had been treated well on the horse-buying trip; he had met many people during the evening at Don Anselmo's, most of them interested in his new venture. (Several had privately expressed their opinion that the departure of De Zubaran was a happy event for the valley, and advised him to stand no nonsense from Doña Carlota. Two of the women had told him openly to toss her out bag and baggage.) It was only hospitable, therefore, since this was his home and these people his neighbors, to bury old animosities. What better way than by giving a fandango, a big one, the biggest that had ever been seen in the valley!

He forgot the idea completely in the press of affairs; for one thing it took him the better part of a week to round up twelve bulls and drive them back to the ranch. He had to take time out to show the Indians how to fashion proper yokes for the oxen. It was the custom to fasten the beasts to the carts by their horns, with the result that the weight fell painfully on their necks.

"It is done this way in Spain," an Indian said.

"You're not in Spain," Dunavant replied—if he couldn't run the old lady, he could at least run his Indians—"and you're an American, not a Spaniard."

Then there was ground to clear for a milpa of winter vegetables, a strip of rich soil back from the river. This took two days, with him working alongside the Indians, principally because the plot lay close to the crossing of the King's Highway and everyone who passed had to stop and give advice. On the third day, while they were planting, a group of horsemen trotted by without pulling up. A few moments later, as he came to the end of a row, he straightened up and saw that a man was standing in back of him. The sun was in Grady's eyes; all he could see was that the man was in buckskin and slight of build. But almost at once he realized that there was only one person he knew who could cross the field and approach within five paces of him and not be heard.

He stepped forward and said, "How are you, Bub?"

Carson held out a horny hand. "Heard you was out this way, and thought I recognized you when I went by." He squinted his blue eyes at the beans Dunavant was holding. "Never thought I'd live to see the day when you would be farmin'. Me, I'm still coyotin' around."

"What's happening in Los Angeles?"

"Commodore Stockton's left. Things pretty quiet. I'm on my way to the eastern country. Got a dispatch from the commodore to deliver to Washington and President Polk. You'd best come along."

Dunavant looked at his handful of beans and grinned. "I've got a field to plant."

Kit Carson took off his hat and smoothed his sandy hair. "Hell," he said, "plant it and come along! We're going to Taos and St. Looie. From St. Looie there's boats and stages and steam trains. Travel all the way on government money. Clear to Washington and President Polk. Going to make it in one hundred and twenty days, there and back. Finest trip a man ever took and the fastest."

"When you come back I'll cook you a pot of beans out of my own milpa," Grady said.

Carson put on his hat. "That's a bargain. Mighty sorry, though, you won't come along—we can use a good man." He looked at the beans again, plainly puzzled, and then stumped off.

Up from the river and north toward the Cajon Grady watched him ride away in the lead, with ten white men and his five Delawares. Grady stood there in the bean patch and watched them out of sight, thinking of the blue Wasatch, the Wind River country and the tumbled ranges of the Mogollons. He thought of all the country he would never see again, and for a moment his eyes were shadowed.

Then he looked up at the running shapes of the Sierra Madres and the San Bernardinos, at the brushy Temescals and San Jacinto, the beautiful mountain soaring in the eastern sky, and the great bald peak of San Antonio. He looked at the flowing river, the meadows dotted with cattle, his cattle, the golden hills and the rich silt of the furrowed field. Grinning, he went back to his planting.

He had several other visitors that day—some with advice, all finding it difficult to conceal their disapproval of a *patrón* working in the field beside his Indians—but by night the beans were planted.

Another week passed and he had forgotten about the dance, when something happened that suddenly brought it to mind. He was in the blacksmith shop repairing a yoke. The man who ducked his head to walk through the door he had seen on the afternoon Stockton had ridden into Los Angeles, and later at Kate Howland's. His name was Ezekiel Merritt, and with Ide and Semple he had been one of the band that had taken the fortress at Sonoma.

Merritt was thin and tall, a half head taller than Dunavant's six feet. He was dressed in a buckskin jacket and trousers dark with grease, and walked in moccasins. His face was thin and seamed and he had a long scraggly beard stained brown with tobacco juice. In addition to a rifle he carried a tomahawk strapped to his waist, the handle covered with notches. He lounged forward into the shop, grumbled a greeting and handed Grady a crumpled piece of paper.

Grady opened it, read the first part hurriedly and then paused over the remainder. ". . . and since you are in a position to report any infractions of the regulations contained herein, you are requested to report the same to this command. Signed: Captain Thomas A. Gilson, for Archibald H. Gillespie, Captain, United States Army."

He reread the list of prohibitions. One item particularly held his eye. He looked at Merritt.

"Do you mean to say that no more than two Californians are permitted to assemble at one time, to walk down the street together or gather in a home?"

"Them's orders," Merritt said.

"And they are being enforced?"

"Right to the letter."

"What do the Californians think?"

Merritt spat a stream of juice on the floor. "They don't like it none."

"That's understandable."

Merritt screwed up his little eyes. "You mean you don't favor the regulation?"

"I mean that, and I mean also that I'll not report any so-called infraction of the law." Dunavant put his foot on the treadle and began to pump the bellows, but watched Merritt. "Furthermore," he said, "while I don't know Captain Gillespie, I do know Gilson. So when you go back tell Gilson what I've said."

Merritt bit a twist of tobacco with his long yellow teeth and settled it in his lean jaw. "'Pears like you're sorta high and mighty," he said. "'Pears like I should oughta drop in on my way back from Diego and have a talk with you."

Dunavant disregarded the threat. "How many of you are going to San Diego?"

"Fifteen men all told."

"How many does that leave in the Los Angeles garrison?"

Merritt gave him a cautious look. "That's military information," he said.

"Probably not more than fifty men."

Merritt remained silent, his long jaws working slowly.

"That's not a very big garrison," Dunavant said. "If you try to treat grown-up men like children."

"Big enough. We took Monterey and Frisco and Sonomy with less 'n that. Took 'em with nary a shot. Greasers talk big but they don't have no hankerin' for a fight."

When Ezekiel Merritt had gone, Grady continued to mull over the letter and the list of regulations. They sounded very much like the work of Captain Gilson, and the more he thought of them the more he was convinced that they would lead to trouble. The edge of his bitterness had been dulled; he had what he wanted and he wanted to keep it—he didn't want to be called on to get out of bed some night and start the war over again.

A different slant on the matter was provided in a few days when he was riding home from Jim Wolfe's, driving a pair of oxen before him. He heard horses behind him, but did not turn until the riders were abreast. On a gray mare, sitting a prim sidesaddle, in a blue riding cloak he had brought from Santa Fe, was Camilla Howland.

He spoke her name, and was instantly corrected. "It is now Mrs.

Fraser," she said, lifting a stubborn chin which he was glad he would not have to look at every morning at breakfast. "We were married three days ago."

Beyond her, Grady saw the happy groom, now tanned by his long sea voyage. "How do you do, Mr. Fraser?"

"Fine, thank you very much, Mr. Dunavant. And you?"

"Congratulations, Mr. Fraser."

"Thank you, thank you."

"Did you enjoy the Sandwich Islands?"

There was a trace of a smile around Fraser's mouth. "Pleasant, very pleasant."

"More pleasant and profitable than the trip to Mazatlán, possibly."

"Possibly."

Camilla said, "Mr. Fraser received a grant of land—fifteen thousand acres—just before Governor Pico abdicated. Beyond the Santa Ana."

"The cows on fifteen thousand acres are going to be pretty smelly," Dunavant said, and then asked Fraser, "What's the news from Los Angeles?"

"We would have done a better job of it than you. Americans are not experienced in these matters. You are making a horrible hash of things, if you will pardon me for saying so."

"It's quite all right. I agree. Did Curel come home with you?"

Fraser nodded. "But where he is, I don't know."

Grady bade them good-by. "If you ever need to be pulled out of the river," he said to the Englishman, "just let me know. Or if you ever feel the need of another sea voyage."

Camilla cast a haughty glance in his direction and clucked to her horse. Grinning, he watched them out of sight.

As soon as he reached the Hawk he sought out Carlota. If trouble did come—and both Merritt and Fraser had indicated the possibility—it would be a wise thing to have friends in the valley. The old lady was sitting in her chair by the window, as usual.

"I'm going to give that dance," he said, "the biggest dance that's ever been given in the valley."

Carlota was not interested. She smoked her cigarette and said nothing, letting him talk. He talked until he realized that she was still thinking about Lupita Espinosa.

"A dance in honor of everyone," he said.

Immediately her face brightened. "When?"

"Now, tomorrow."

"It will take a week to prepare. You cannot have a fandango without preparation. You invite people for a day and they stay a month. Food, wine, music—these take time."

She rose. "Not for the Lupita?" she asked, fixing him with her black eyes.

"For everyone," he said.

His decision to let her in on the plans was wise, for she took charge immediately. She made a list of guests, more than sixty altogether, dispatched her servant with the invitations, computed the amount of wine necessary and sent out another Indian to procure it. She told him where to round up four musicians, made plans for the food and set him to cleaning out the barbecue pits and hauling oak wood. A week's work and at the end of it, the night before the fandango, he fell into bed exhausted, regretting that he had ever thought of the damned thing.

The day dawned clear. He had been up for two hours getting the oak fires well started in the pits. He stood now in his room, spread-legged in front of a mirror propped up on a chest, shaving himself and wondering if, after all, anyone would come. He had finished one side of his face and had started on the other when the boy came to the doorway. In the mirror Grady saw him pause there and look, with eyes that held the same guarded curiosity he had seen months before at Jim Wolfe's.

"Come in, Jorge de Zubaran," he said, and thought, God Almighty, certainly the old lady hasn't invited the De Zubaran clan! Jorge took a step into the room and stopped, fingering his hat. "You're the first guest," Grady said.

"I am riding to the Conejo," the boy answered. "I have talked to my grandmother, and now I am riding to the Conejo."

Grady said, "You'll come back, though, señor?"

The boy moved around in front of the chest so he could watch the shaving. He stood, following the movement of the razor, for a time, and then he said, "The De Zubarans were not invited."

Grady was relieved. "I invite you now."

"I am on the way to the Conejo," the boy said stubbornly.

"You can go another day."

Jorge did not answer. He stood stiffly, with his bang of thick black hair falling low on his forehead, and watched the motions of the razor. He did not meet Grady's eyes. On his dark face were the signs of an inner conflict, of curiosity at war with Spanish pride.

Then he said, "Do you like it here on the Hawk? Is it like the country beyond the mountains where you lived before you came here?"

"Unlike," Grady said. "You don't have petrified forests in California."

Jorge stared.

"It was in the winter of '41," Grady said. "That was the winter it snowed for eighty days and eighty nights and the snow in most places was eighty feet deep. I was riding along over the treetops, and after a while I came to a canyon where there wasn't any snow, and when I crossed over to the other side I came to a valley where grass was growing green, and there were green leaves on the trees."

Jorge's face was serious.

"It seemed like a good place to camp," Grady went on, looking as serious as the boy. "I was hungry. Sitting up on the limb of a tree, I saw a fat partridge, so I brought up my gun and shot him right through the eye. The bird fell off the limb and broke into a dozen pieces. Fell in the grass and the grass broke into pieces. I went down to the stream to drink and the water was stone. I saw some raspberries growing, but I broke my teeth when I went to eat them—they were rubies. I thought I would make a fire and got out my ax and chopped on a log. But the log was stone, like the water, and I smashed the ax. I was in the petrified forests, for certain."

Jorge studied him. "Where are the rubies?" he said.

"I had no place to carry them that trip, but I always planned to go back, with a big sack."

"I would like to see the rubies when you get them."

"I'll give you a handful," Grady said, searching his memory for another story.

"That is one thing we do not have—a forest that is made of stone, but I am glad, except for the rubies."

Grady said, "There are other things you don't have. You don't have a trout that can walk. Up at Bent's Fort there was a man by the name of Jake who had a pet trout he called George. Jake kept George in a barrel but after a time the trout got too big for the barrel, so Jake decided that he would train George to live out of water. At first he took the trout out of the water for only a few minutes at a time. Then he found that he could leave George out all night in the wet grass, and then in the grass when it wasn't wet. Finally George got so he did not need water at all, and he began to follow his master wherever he went, down dusty roads or any place."

Grady tilted his chin and shaved underneath. "But George came to a bad end. One day he was following Jake to town and they crossed a bridge. After a moment or two Jake looked back and did not see his friend. Jake went back to the bridge and found a hole where a plank was missing. He looked through the hole and there was George below him, floating bellyside up. He had fallen in the water and drowned."

Jorge ran the back of his hand along his chin. "I think maybe there is a petrified forest, though I would prefer to see the rubies. But I do not think there was a trout by the name of George who could walk."

Grady wiped his face and put away his razor. The boy watched him, and when he turned their eyes met for the first time since he had come into the room.

"I do not believe this story of the trout," Jorge said. "You think because I am a Spaniard and have never been beyond the mountains that I will believe this, but I do not. I think it is a lie."

Grady looked into the yellow eyes, smoldering with anger and outraged pride, and suddenly his blood pounded in his throat.

"How is your sister?" he said, seeing Luz standing there in front of him, her tawny eyes and lifted chin, in the person of her brother. "She will not be coming, of course."

"She will not be coming," the boy said, "and the other question I do not answer. I was told not to discuss this. I was told this by her and by my grandmother." He walked to the door, bowed stiffly and said, "But I would like to see the rubies."

# 28

Jim Wolfe was the first to arrive. Riding up to the gate with his wife and three servants, he sent his voice booming through the courtyard in a Spanish greeting. From his horse he looked at Dunavant's ranchero clothes, the slashed trousers and silver-buttoned jacket, slapped his broad thigh in a fit of glee and vowed that he had never seen anything to match it for elegance.

"Your Santa Fe friends oughta be here, señor."

Dunavant, on his dignity, was glad they weren't.

The guests came fast after that, in droves, and from all directions, in carts with servants, on horseback with dogs at their heels and crying babies in their arms, young and old, dressed within an inch of their lives, the women reeking with perfume, their faces white with powder, and the men's hair shining with bear grease. They poured in until after noon; by that time the hitching rack was filled and he had to rig up another. Carts fanned out over the mesa. The old lady had invited sixty people, but by a rough computation he decided that it was nearer twice that number. The whole valley, apparently, had turned out to see the new owner of the Hawk.

Most of them were countrypeople, ill at ease at meeting someone they did not know, and a gringo at that, not sure that they should have come, but anxious, like Don Anselmo, to be friendly. He stood at the gate, Carlota at his side, and shook hands with each one as she introduced them—Don Arturo Peña and his wife, Don Ricardo Lopez with his wife and two daughters, Doña Margarita Arenas, Don Vicente Sosa y Madera.

After the first dozen had passed through the gate, he was suddenly concerned with the question of food and gave up trying to remember names. Two steers and an ox were roasting over the pits; there were two large twenty-gallon pots filled with beans, meat and vegetables; the Indian girls had been grinding corn since the morning before. But looking around him at the crowd that filled the *sala,* overflowed into the other rooms and out into the courtyard where he had built a square of benches around the well, he knew this would not be enough if they all stayed for supper and the dancing, which Wolfe assured him they would. There was a good chance, Wolfe said, that some of them would stay all night.

"You hold a fandango," he explained, "and it lasts till everyone gets worn down. I held a whopper last November and some of them were still around a week later."

Wolfe obliged by sending his Indians out to bring in another steer, and rounded up two girls to help out in the kitchen with the grinding of more corn and the making of *tortillas*. The six skins of wine would have to last out somehow. They lasted as a matter of fact through the dinner, and then, appalled by the prospect of a wineless fandango, Wolfe sent two of his men to his ranch to fetch more. The *vaqueros* left at a gallop and arrived back at a gallop, riding fresh horses, with the leather *botas* slung across the saddle horns. Fortunately, during the three hours they were gone, there was little need of wine.

A fandango, it seemed, was nothing without racing, feats of horsemanship and jousting with lances; so, prompted by Wolfe and Don Anselmo, Dunavant mounted his horse and led a procession to a likely spot on the mesa. Carts were arranged in a wide semicircle and the women seated themselves to form a gallery, while the men gathered to arrange the tournament. Seated in an oxcart, the orchestra, consisting of two violins and two guitars and a boy with a triangle, struck up a lively tune.

The sun blazed down, the musicians sawed and sweated, the dust rose in clouds, the women waved their colored handkerchiefs and shouted advice to their favorites, and the favorites, with grim good nature, raced one another on horseback, snatched hats from the ground at a gallop, chased cows and threw them by a twist of their tails.

Dunavant wisely refrained from displaying his horsemanship. He was a good rider but no match for these men who, born in the saddle, were the finest horsemen in the world. He stood on the side lines, cheering the victors and the vanquished impartially, and as he cheered he weighed the success of the fiesta. He was not worried about the women or the married men—all of them were friendly; it was the young Spaniards, the bucks who were bent on making an impression on the girls, who eyed him furtively.

The last event of the tournament was jousting, and he tried to remain a spectator of this also, but a youth of twenty or so, one of the band who had been watching him all afternoon, a tall Spaniard with sideburns slanting to the edges of his jaw, swaggered up to him.

"The señor," he said, lisping, "does not participate?"

"I leave that for my guests," Dunavant replied, "who are equipped for such things."

"We will supply you," the youth said, "with a lance, and likewise with shield and *cuera*."

It was a challenge; the young Spaniard looked down his long nose and smiled, waiting. Even then Dunavant would have refused except that the rest of the band stood behind their leader watching, and behind them a group of older men.

They found him a shield made of bull hide, a *cuera* fashioned of six thicknesses of antelope skin, and an oaken lance ten feet long from which the iron head had been removed. They helped him into the heavy coat, fixed the shield on his left arm, assisted him into the saddle and cleared the field.

On his pinto pony he rode for a distance and turned to face his antagonist. At a signal and a fanfare from the musicians, he set his spurs and charged, holding the lance extended, the butt end against his side, leaning forward and braced. It was the first time he had ever had a lance in his hand; it felt heavy and unwieldy.

He heard a shrill cheer from the semicircle of carts, and at the same moment, with the same impact as if he had ridden into the branch of a tree, and before he had really aimed, he felt the Spaniard's lance strike him high on the chest. The blow rocked him in the saddle; in a sickening flash he remembered the encounter on the mesa when he had been wounded. He ground his teeth and by an effort of will remained seated. He made a demivolte for the next pass, and then pulled up as he saw that his antagonist had broken a lance.

A dead silence fell over the mesa. He glanced toward the carts and saw as he started forward that all the women were standing up. He had a firmer grip on his lance this time and a better aim; it struck the Spaniard above the hip, lifted him and threw him to one side, but simultaneously the other lance struck him. He was wrenched backward in the saddle by a blow greater than before, but he would have recovered if it had not been that the girth snapped. The pony sped out from under him and he fell, clasping his lance, heavily, rolling twice his length through the dust.

He picked himself up, dimly aware of gasps and mingled cheers. The young Spaniard was riding back, smiling—the Disinherited Knight from the lists of *Ivanhoe,* and he, the mighty Templar, stood divesting himself of dust, shaken to the teeth and angry, but with no sword to unsheathe upon his conqueror.

When he got back to the house after removing his *cuera* and having a draw from the wineskins that had arrived in the meantime, the courtyard was filled again, and the fiesta continued, with the musicians playing in relays, the boards replenished from the kitchen as fast as they were cleared of the trays heaped with cookies and confections.

The wine raised his spirits and eased the aches in his bones, but he was aware as he stood talking to Jim Wolfe that a subtle change had come over the party. Voices were louder, the glances cast in his direction bolder, the young bucks now looked at him openly, with a trace of contempt. He remarked about it to Wolfe.

"That's the Spanish blood coming out," Wolfe said. "You were one of the conquerors before you got thrown. Now you're just a human being. Some of them will like you more, most of them less. And the ones who like you less will like all gringos less—that's the way they are."

The heat had diminished. In the cooling dusk pine torches were burning, and the courtyard, cleared of the tables, was a sea of figures revolving to the strains of an Arragonese waltz.

Dunavant lighted a thin Havana, left his partner, Lupita Espinosa, and, happy to get away from her chatter and the watchful gaze of Doña Carlota, walked to the gate. The air was fresh, blowing in from the sea; the first star glowed pale above the western hills. He noticed below it the shadowy figures of four or five horsemen moving slowly across the mesa, but thought nothing of it—they had been arriving steadily all afternoon and would continue in all likelihood for the rest of the evening.

He did not look at them until they rode up to the gate, and then, biting down on the end of his cigar, he saw the powerful, one-armed figure of Joe, the Indian, and behind him, with a servant on either side of her, Yris Llorente.

He strode forward and caught her as she slid from the saddle, and held her for a moment, laughing in his arms, before he set her on her feet.

"You've heard about the fandango?" he said.

"Yes, but that is not why I came." She turned and gave the two servants instructions about the baggage strapped to a pack horse.

"From the looks of the panniers," he said, "you have come to stay."

"Overnight is all. In the morning I leave for San Diego and from there on a foul hide ship to Acapulco." She saw his mouth move, and said quickly, "Alone. I shall not ask you to go. I would not go with you if you begged on your knees."

"I looked for you in town. The afternoon the army came, and later. Several times."

"Did you expect to find me?" she chided him. "With the town full of enemy soldiers! I left the night before, when I saw you last, and hid with friends in the country. I have been there until this morning."

Carrying her luggage, he led the way to his room, and left her there to remove the stains of travel. He had a tray of food and a steaming pitcher of chocolate sent to her, and then stood on the *portale* chewing the end of his cigar, watching the dancers and wondering what sort of a scene Carlota would kick up when she laid eyes on Yris.

They were dancing together when the old lady first saw them. She was sitting on a bench beside the well, talking to a group of ancient crones, her rusty shawl hugged tight against the night air, the inevitable smoke seeping from her thin nostrils. Her gaze picked up Yris' flowing white dress and white shoulders before she saw him, and she turned to whisper something to her companions. But when her eyes lighted on him, she stopped in mid-breath, rigid on the pine planking, and twin sparks of fire shot in his direction.

Thereafter, following the routine she had practiced at Don Anselmo's, the old lady never let them out of her sight; wherever they went, she was two steps behind them, listening in silence, coughing at propitious moments, introducing new guests to Yris if he danced with her longer than two minutes. And when the crowd had thinned out to a trickle of dancers and Yris expressed the wish to retire, they found that her things had been moved out of his room. He knew who had done it and started in pursuit, but he had taken no more than a half-dozen steps when he ran head on into Carlota, standing in the shadows.

"The belongings of this woman," she said, "are in my room, where there is a large bed, a bed sufficiently large for two. It is there that she will sleep."

He dropped his cigar and ground it out with his heel. "Listen here," he said, but got no farther.

The old lady poked him with a bony finger, speaking in his face, through clenched teeth. "Man is kindling," she said. "Woman is fire. And the Devil comes and fans."

"She's a friend, an old friend," he sputtered.

"Even between saints, a wall."

She gave him one last poke with her finger and departed in a swish of skirts and a rattle of beads.

He slept until noon as if dead and woke to the sound of strange voices in the courtyard, the tapping of Carlota's cane as she hurried along the *portale*. He jumped up, puzzled, for while three of the guests had been put to bed, being unable to ride home, the rest had departed last night.

He shaved and hurriedly pulled on his clothes. There were some fifteen people in the courtyard when he went out, and more were arriving by the time he had found the old lady standing at the gate, a reception committee of one.

"I thought the affair ended last night," he said. "At least I hoped so."

"Fandangos," she said, "big ones, of the character given at the Hawk, always last two days, frequently longer."

He clasped his brow and swore, gazing out across the mesa where there were now a dozen carts and horsemen wending their way toward the house.

Besides many of the old faces, there were some new ones. He gave up early, before the tournament began, gracefully made his exit on the pretext of having business, which his guests could understand because he was one of these Americans who were perpetually beset by such matters of no importance, and with Yris, who decided to delay her departure until the following morning, rode into the hills.

They rode, having escaped the eye of Doña Carlota and fearful that she might follow, until they were well out of range of the people on the mesa. They tethered their horses on the crest of a grassy slope and sat in the grass and talked, watching the small figures below them, the dust rising under the hoofs of competing rivals . . . talked mostly of one thing.

Yris was certain that before another week had gone the pueblo would be under siege. A band of insurgents, led by a young Mexican, Sérbulo Varela, had organized and were now camped near Los Angeles at a place called Paredón Blanco.

"It is because of the laws," Yris said. "They are an insult."

"I have heard about them and protested. . . ."

"People arrested on the streets for nothing more than talking to one another. Their homes searched for arms which do not exist. But for this, Varela would have no followers."

There were, she told him, several hundred of the insurgents at Paredón, and as he had guessed from what Ezekiel Merritt had said, the American forces did not number more than fifty.

"It is a weak garrison," she said. "And it will be taken. Not only the garrison, but also your ranch. The country will be running with blood before the winter is out."

There was a purpose in her prediction, he was certain—it was plain in her presence here—but he did not discount the truthfulness and wisdom of what she said. He thought of Captain Gilson, as she talked, cursing him for a fool, and made a resolve to ride into the pueblo the next day. It would be a pleasure to talk to the captain; there were many things that had long been left unsaid.

She rose, walked forward on the slope in the lengthening shadows and stood with the wind molding her skirts. He followed her. The mesa was deserted; from afar he heard the thin scraping of violins.

He looked at the rolling acres stretching away, the curving margins of the river lined with willows and sycamore, the grazing red cattle copper-bright in the last of the day's light, the blue mountains, the fortresslike house on the mesa and the wood smoke rising from the pits.

She said nothing—if she were aware of what he saw, she showed no sign of it. He untethered their horses and held his hand to help her to the saddle. Instead, she seized his hand and turned upon him in sort of a fury.

"You are in danger here," she said, the words rushing from her mouth. "And if you are not killed, you will die of loneliness."

"I'll not be lonely," he said.

She looked at him in sudden horror. "This place! This dreary, godforsaken place! With these dreary countrypeople!"

He felt a shudder run through her body. "I prefer both to what you will experience," he said. He helped her into the saddle. He arranged her skirts, mounted his horse, and together, neither of them uttering a word, they rode homeward in the failing light.

He saw her at the end of the courtyard, in the cleared space just inside the gate. A pine torch flamed beside her; it shone on the yellow silk of her dress, her hair piled high on her head and pierced by a comb that showed transparent in the light.

He was standing beside the well, talking to Yris and watching the dancers. For an instant he thought this was something he had dreamed, but the next moment, as she followed the direction of his gaze and moved against his arm, he knew that what he saw was real.

Then, at once, Yris spoke in a low voice, and he saw under the flaming torch, behind Luz de Zubaran in her yellow dress, two figures whom he had not noticed, two men in uniform, one of them Julio de Zubaran, and the other, Cesaire Curel.

The hand on his arm tightened, and as she spoke again he was aware that Yris' fear was not for him but for herself. "Curel," he said, "is here for other reasons." The Colt, he remembered, was in his room.

They had left the gate when he reached it; he heard them behind him, in the *sala,* Luz speaking to her grandmother, and Curel acknowledging the introduction in his precise Castilian. Curel saw him as he came into the room, shifted his feet involuntarily and then, to cover the movement, took a step forward and bowed, holding his sword, a pair of white gloves in the other hand.

His hands were pale, but his face had been tanned by the sea, and when he spoke his teeth showed a startling white. "A very enjoyable voyage, señor. I discovered many things of interest. Palm trees. Lagoons the color of the sky. Girls the color of gold."

"They didn't please you enough to stay," Dunavant said.

Her back was turned to him. The room was crowded, filled with the low hum of voices and the music from the courtyard, but she knew he was here, standing a few short steps from her, for, as he answered Curel, her shoulders straightened, the faintest trace of color showed along the lifted column of her neck.

"There are more important things," Curel said, "than lagoons and girls the color of gold."

He looked at Curel. They looked at each other for a long moment, and he saw there in the thin aristocratic face, with its black short neatly trimmed beard, the answer to his question. There had never been any doubt why Curel had come, but he knew now, meeting his eyes, finally.

"You are late, colonel," he said. "Six weeks late."

"Not as late as you think," Curel said.

Dunavant looked at Luz. She had not moved, but the color was deeper now beneath her skin. Curel, yes, he thought, but why has she come? Why has she come with Curel? Why has she come at all?

Curel was speaking, and then as Dunavant glanced at him, he paused, turned away and swept the room with his dark eyes. Talk had ceased and the only sounds were in the courtyard, the dragging notes of a guitar, the shuffling of feet, a girl's laughter. Everyone in the room, Dunavant saw, was watching them, everyone except Luz, watching him and Curel and Julio de Zubaran, who stood beside her, a smile on his round face, as if he were already aware of what Cesaire Curel was to say.

"Not too late, señor," Curel said, addressing his words to those in the room rather than to him. "It may surprise you to know that I am here in time to be of service, for the pueblo is under siege, surrounded by three hundred men, whom I shall have the pleasure of leading in the annihilation of the American garrison."

At this moment, while Curel fixed him with a look of pure hatred, while a murmur ran through the room and swelled into a confused babble, and a retort froze in his throat, he saw Luz turn quickly. She faced him and, without words, with no other sign than what he could read in her eyes, told him to leave, to flee the ranch, to leave now and ride for his life. He had seen that look before, on the river, and remembered the warning that had gone with it. He remembered them both and thought, It is like the other. He looked at her and, in a surge of anger, rejected all that she had said.

Suddenly Curel was surrounded; in the confusion Grady left the *sala* and went to his room. There he lighted a candle and found his Colt. He tried the mechanism, put the ivory-handled pistol inside his waistcoat and buttoned his jacket over it. In front of the mirror he straightened his neckpiece. He wondered where Jim Wolfe was and in what condition. He pulled the comb through his hair, noted that the bulge of the Colt showed against his jacket, put the comb away and turned to snuff out the candle.

Luz stood inside the door; as he lifted his hand from the candle, she closed the door behind her.

"Why are you here?" he said.

She walked forward into the room.

"Why with Curel?" he said.

The candlelight flamed over her dress. She held it slightly raised, one hand thrown across her skirt, and looked at him. "I came with Julio de Zubaran."

"Why did you come with anyone?"

She did not answer this. "What Curel has said is true. The pueblo is under siege. You are unsafe here—every American in the valley is unsafe. My father is armed and on the trail with a dozen *vaqueros.*

Cesaire Curel is armed and also Julio. They have men posted outside the gate. The pueblo will be taken in a few days. The ranch tonight, before another hour has passed."

"It is possible," he said, "though I don't believe you any more than I do Curel. I've had experience before with your warnings. With both you and Curel."

He stood in front of her with the candlelight outlining his shoulders. She looked at his face in the shadow, tense with anger, his gray eyes dark under his heavy frowning brows, the sinewy hands open at his sides. She knew then, as she looked at him and thought of what he had said, that the letter had never been delivered.

"You may remember these warnings," he said. "I do—I remember them very well. What you want is for me to scramble out of here—into the arms of a dozen men with knives!"

He snuffed the candle and was past her in two strides, past her outflung hand, out of the door and the hearing of her voice. She stood for a moment staring after him. She watched him until he had disappeared among the crowd. Then she closed the door after her and walked to the edge of the courtyard. Her eyes ran swiftly over the dancers, over the people who were grouped around the small floor, the knot of old women sitting by the well. The woman she was looking for was nowhere in the courtyard.

The music stopped; in the interval of silence before the dancers shouted for the musicians to continue, she heard Curel's voice. He was in the *sala*, and as she moved toward it, half running, certain that Yris Llorente was with him, she saw a light under Carlota's door. She stopped and listened, holding her breath, her ear pressed to the door. There were sounds in the room, hurried footsteps, movements that were too quick to be those of her grandmother. The door was bolted. She knocked and when the movements ceased, knocked again. There was no answer. Then the light under the door disappeared. She stepped back against the wall and waited.

Minutes passed. The music had started up. She heard the bolt slide, the creak of the hinges as the door opened. The woman was standing in the doorway looking into the courtyard. She was dressed in a long riding cloak and the light of the lanterns shone faintly on it, and on her hair. With a swift gesture she gathered her cloak about her. The next instant she was running.

Luz, stepping away from the wall, grasped the silken cloak, the arm beneath it. She swung the woman around so that they stood facing each other. They were close in the warm darkness, but she could not see the other's features. She could only feel the woman there and smell the heavy scent. Yris raised her arm to wrench herself free, cursing. Luz grasped both of her hands.

"*Campesina! Rustica!* Country lout!" the woman cried.

Luz said quietly, "Where do you go?"

"It is none of your affair."

Luz increased the pressure on her hands. "Where?" she repeated. There was no answer. Small animal sounds hissed through the woman's teeth.

"Wherever it is," Luz said, "it is away from here and without him. You will go and you will go alone." Yris was straining, twisting her body; Luz could feel the hard length of the blade where it lay against her thigh. Yris was trying to reach it, fighting against the hold.

"I will kill you," she cried.

"Nothing is forgiven," Luz said. "The letter that was not delivered. The lies. The amusement at my expense. Nothing!"

She released her hold and Yris stepped back. She could hear the rustle of the cloak, and for a brief moment as Yris bent forward, she caught a glimpse of her face distorted with rage. "I am not afraid of the knife," Luz said. "If you attempt to use it, it is something that you will regret."

She waited for Yris to straighten. There were people walking toward them. Quietly she said, "He is mine and you will not have him. Go and do not return. I will watch to see that you go. Now!"

Like fire running through grass, the news that Cesaire Curel had brought spread from lip to lip, from the old women by the well to the men drinking wine in the kitchen, to the dancers and the musicians, to everyone on the Hawk.

Wolfe said, "It means trouble sure. The thing to do is to get out quick and ride for my place. You'll be safe there."

"Safe as the last time," Grady Dunavant said. "I'll take my chances here." He was aware of the band of young Spaniards lounging in the darkness of the *portale*. Curel was still in the house. Luz he had not seen since he had left the room. "What I should do is to send everyone home," he said. "Clear out the place and barricade the gate."

But even as the thought came to him he realized that he stood no chance against the odds he would have to face. He was alone—even Jim Wolfe could not be expected to help him. He was a gringo among a hundred and fifty Spaniards, in a country risen in revolt. He put his hand on his Colt where it lay snug against his side.

"You can skin over the roof at the other end there," Wolfe said.

Grady met the glances of those who danced past him, of the young Spaniards lounging on the *portale*. He met them all in stubborn anger. He thought about Curel, planning what he would do, each step at a time. His shoulder was still stiff from the lance wound; he was not Curel's equal with a pistol, but he would have certain advantages in circumstances which he would make for himself.

Several moments passed and he heard his name spoken; turning, he saw Carlota standing behind him. She was hidden from those in the courtyard, on the far side of the crude platform he had erected for the musicians. She motioned him into the shadows.

"Come," she said, leading the way to the far end of the courtyard. Where the dim light from the chapel lay on the tiles she faced him. "I have watched you for many weeks," she said. "I remained here at the Hawk to watch you, though, mind you, I would have remained in any event."

The music had stopped. Above the stir of voices he heard a sudden bucketing report of a musket outside the walls. In the silence that followed the old woman said, "It is I who sent for Luz tonight. That she came with this carrion of the beard is not my doing."

The silence in the courtyard was prolonged, as if everyone awaited the sound of another shot. No sound came, and in the utter quiet he heard the far-off barking of a dog, the wind over his head wandering along the eaves.

"I asked Luz to come," the old lady said, "because while all males are much alike, you are less so. Because—and listen to me while I say it—she is in love with you."

He started to protest, but she silenced him with a sharp tap of her cane. "What you don't know," she said, "is that she had nothing to do with the lancing. She was beaten in the chapel as she knelt in prayer, and locked for days behind these walls."

She paused as hoofs pounded on the mesa, and shoved him toward the door of the storehouse.

"Go," she said. "Do not stand there in a dream."

Grady Dunavant was not dreaming. He could find no words, but he was not in a dream; his mind was clear.

"There are no bars on the window of the storehouse," Carlota said. "Take the first horse you find and do not stop short of the pueblo."

"Tell Luz," he said, and in an excess of joy he stooped and kissed the old lady on the cheek. "Tell her that I'll be back."

He opened the door of the storehouse and closed it after him.

# 29

THE moon had set and the sky was dark, with the stars hidden by a high mist. No light showed yet along the San Gorgonio ridge, but dawn was not far off. He had ridden hard against the dawn, changing horses twice—the last time at the Mission San Gabriel where he had taken a saddled horse tied to the corral—and now as he rode through the river he slackened his pace. A half hour back he had passed through the Spanish lines, close enough to see their campfires; his problem was to get through the American lines without being shot for a Spaniard.

Where a clump of trees grew beside an irrigation ditch he pulled up and waited for the dawn. With the first light, holding his Colt on his thigh, he trotted up the main trail, into the plaza, crossed it at a walk and spoke to the sentry before he was challenged. The sentry, eying his Spanish clothes, brought a rifle to his hip.

Dunavant put his Colt away, got down from the saddle and asked for Captain Gilson, thinking as the gate of the compound opened and he walked through it leading his lathered horse, God help the American cause if Gilson is running things!

A broad-shouldered man with an open tunic and thick red hair sat behind the desk instead of Gilson. There was a crude sketch of the town and surrounding country on the wall behind him, and a map of California, which looked as if it had been done by an army engineer, beside it. The room was stale with last night's cigar smoke, and there was a saucer filled with cigar butts on the desk and a sprinkling of ashes over everything. An officer was looking at the maps; when he turned Grady saw that his eyes were swollen and bloodshot, either from drink or loss of sleep.

Dunavant introduced himself, explained why he had come and asked for Captain Gilson. Gilson was in bed; the way the officer said it, Dunavant knew that there was no love lost between the two men.

"I am in command," the officer said. "My name is Gillespie. Where did you come through the Spanish lines?"

"Northeast about three miles," Dunavant told him. "The Californians are camped on the main trail, with no guards out. I took time to reconnoiter the camp and I would judge from the number of horses that there were about two hundred men. Unless each man has two horses, which is unlikely, since they can pick up horses anywhere."

He had thought that the information would be valuable, but even as he spoke, he saw that the officer's gaze was wandering. He knew then, standing there with the dawn stealing over the deserted town and the yellow light falling through the window, that the garrison was doomed. He looked at the bleary wandering eyes and the desk strewn with ashes and realized that Captain Gillespie knew it too. It was only Gilson, snoring now in the next room, who didn't.

"How many men are here?" Dunavant asked, and had to repeat the question.

"Less than forty," Gillespie said.

"How much ammunition?"

"We're short."

"How about provisions?" Dunavant asked.

"We'll send out foraging parties."

All the main trails, Dunavant learned, were invested by bands of Mexicans, *Sonoreños* under the leadership of Varela. The pueblo, in fact, was besieged, cut off from provisions and an adequate supply of water, with no possibility of relief from any quarter. Ezekiel Merritt was still in San Diego with a dozen of the best riflemen. Commodore Stockton, believing that the war was over, had sailed north in the *Congress* and was presumably at San Francisco, occupied with plans for meeting a threatened attack of the Walla Walla led by Pewpewmoxmox. Frémont was again on the Sacramento.

Gillespie finished in a voice that was scarcely audible. His gaze wandered to the window and the silent streets. Then he stood up and leaned forward, swaying a little, with his hairy fists on the desk.

"Don't misunderstand me. We've got enough of everything—ammunition and men—to whip hell out of them."

His tone was blustering; his young hard sun-burned face was defiant in the harsh light. But now, as Dunavant looked at him, appraising the boast and the man who had made it, he knew finally that in leaving the ranch he had ridden from one trap into another.

"They attacked yesterday morning about three o'clock," Gillespie said, "sixty-five of them. We beat them off with twenty-one rifles, killing and wounding three. At daylight Lieutenant Hensley took several prisoners and drove the rest off. We'll do the same when they make another attack."

The town is doomed, Dunavant thought, looking at Gillespie, the open tunic and the swollen eyes. The knowledge was a lead weight in his stomach. When Lieutenant Hensley came in with a report, he went outside to the compound where he found a pile of straw under a lean-to roof. Shaky with fatigue he lay down on the straw.

In one corner of the compound armorers were drilling out three cannon that the Californians had spiked. The tapping of the hammers sounded inside his head. He lay with his eyes open and watched the shadows shorten, the sun swing up in a molten sky. In midmorning two Americans rode into the compound on spent horses. They brought the news that General Castro's old officers had joined Varela, that many of the rancheros were heading for Paredón Blanco, Varela's headquarters.

Dunavant followed them into Gillespie's office. While he was there Captain Gilson appeared, and a few moments later an elderly Mexican under a flag of truce, with a demand for the surrender of the garrison.

Gilson was freshly shaved and his uniform lay snug on his heavy hips. He had given Dunavant a casual look, but did not speak. He handed the demand for surrender across the table.

Gillespie's gaze ran over it swiftly. He looked at Gilson, and watching the two men, Dunavant saw all of the argument of the night before re-enacted in one long moment. Then Gillespie crumpled the paper in his fist and tossed it on the floor.

"Tell Varela to come and get us," he said to the Mexican.

There was no conviction in the remark or the gesture, but Gilson smiled and, turning toward Dunavant, studied his Spanish clothes.

"What arms did you bring?" he said.

"A Colt. All I had time for," Dunavant said, watching Gilson's eyes traveling over him. "Your revolt came suddenly."

"Mine?" Gilson said.

"Yours," Dunavant answered, with the full force of the anger that had grown in him during the hours he had lain in the straw under the lean-to. "The restrictive laws," he said, "are yours. They're the cause of the revolt."

Gilson pursed his mouth and spoke quietly, looking again at Dunavant's clothes. "It hasn't taken you long to become a greaser. You look like one and talk like one. Your place is with the greasers at Paredón Blanco."

Dunavant said nothing. He walked outside to the low brick porch and stood in the blazing sun. Dust followed the trail of the Mexican riding toward Varela's camp. The sun glittered on the tar roofs of the town and the wings of the buzzards floating in the milky-blue sky. The tap of the armorers' mauls was the only sound in the pueblo, that and the snarling of dogs over carrion.

The garrison could hold its own, he thought, against the muskets of the Californians. But it would be starved out, eventually, probably without a fight, without his having so much as a chance to use his Colt. "Damn Gilson!" he said aloud. And as he said it to the buzzards and the torrid sky, he was aware for the first time that his loyalties were divided. He would fight, but with half of him not fighting.

Another demand to surrender came that afternoon, and at dusk Gillespie sent out a party to scavenger the town. The men came back with a small supply of powder, an oxcart of iron scrap scrounged from the blacksmith shops, a thousand pounds of lead irrigation pipe, which they had procured from a French vineyardist, and four ancient six-pounders.

Night had fallen, and Dunavant was standing beside the fires, where the lead was being melted down for round shot, talking to a young soldier. His name was John Brown—but after that night he would be known as Juan Flaco, because of his first name and the fact that he was thin.

It was Captain Gillespie's voice that broke up their conversation. He strode across the compound shouting for John Brown.

The young soldier shifted his tobacco, but didn't move until Gillespie came up. Then he gave the officer a sketchy salute.

"I understand you're a good horseman," Gillespie said.

"Some say so, captain."

"Can you ride to Monterey?"

"If anybody can."

"In how many days?"

"How far up there?"

"About four hundred and sixty miles."

John Brown pondered. He was tall, a collection of bones loosely held together, with a long ferine hollow-cheeked face, and yellow hair that hung to his shoulders.

"Oughta do it in four days or the like," he said.

Gillespie stared at him. "No man can ride that fast. You've got to change horses, stop to eat and sleep. Can you make it in twice that time?"

"Four days," John Brown said. "I'll sleep when I get there."

"We'll figure on eight days." Gillespie took a bundle of cigarette papers from his pocket and gave them to the young soldier. "Hide these somewhere on your person. All of them bear my seal and the words 'Believe the bearer.' You know the conditions here. When you reach Monterey give the information to Commodore Stockton. If he isn't there, to anyone in authority."

John Brown put the cigarette papers in his hair. "When do I set off, captain?"

"As soon as you can."

Brown rubbed his chin. "I'm ready about now."

"What do you want to take in the way of arms and provisions?"

"Nothing," said John Brown, "except my spurs."

Dunavant, looking at Captain Gillespie, wondered why John Brown was being sent.

John Brown rode quietly out of the compound. The dust softened the sound of hoofs. The houses were dark and he saw no one. Beyond the plaza he increased his pace, and after skirting Fort Hill, where a sentry rose up out of the brush and challenged him, he gained high ground above the pueblo. The moon had not risen and the trail was obscure. A wind was blowing. He spurred his horse to a trot, heading into the northwest.

He had picked the best horse in the corral. It was a California horse and understood nothing except Spanish, but it was a stocky animal, with a deep chest and an easy gait that ate up distance. If his luck held he might be able to ride it all the way to Santa Barbara, where it would be easy to get a fresh horse, unless the Spaniards had taken the town. If that had happened he'd have to find another one somewhere. Five or six good horses ought to get him through to Monterey.

He looked up at the sky. He had told the captain that he'd get there in four days. He had said it without thinking very much. Four days had popped into his mind and he had said it right out, without giving it another thought. Four days. He wished now he had said five. Six would be better, counting bad luck he might run into. But he had said four days and, goddam, it was up to him to make good on it! But he sure wished he'd thought a little before speaking up so brash.

There was a shine in the east and he guessed it was the moon coming. One thing, he had been smart enough to stand out against dragging along a rifle, like the captain kept saying he should. What was the good of a rifle if you were jumped by a dozen Californians, which you would be if you were jumped at all? It was just extra weight to tote. He hadn't wanted to take anything to eat, either, but the captain had given him an order on that one. It didn't amount to much, just jerky, and moldy at that. He'd rather go without.

The trail was clearer now, winding through low hills. They reminded him of the hills around Monterey, except that these were covered with brush instead of pine trees. That was sure a pretty town, Monterey, with the hills coming right down to the sea and the sea blue enough to startle a man, and the waves coming in, and birds flying. And the women were pretty, too, even some of the Indians. . . . He guessed he'd got to thinking of all those things when he told the captain four days. It sure seemed far off now, the more he thought.

The worse thing was that he was going to get lonesome, with no one to talk to, unless he could pick up someone on the way who wanted to ride with him. He couldn't even talk to the horse, since it only understood Spanish. A man could get a lot of company from a horse if it understood what you were saying. But there wasn't any pleasure in talking to a Spanish horse. He hoped that the next one would understand American.

The low hills were behind him and the country was flattening out some. He didn't hear anything, except a coyote far off, and a bear snuffling in the brush, and the sound of his horse breathing steady. He figured he must be through the enemy lines, but it was funny that he hadn't seen anyone or heard a hoof. He was thinking this when he saw off to his right some shapes moving along a shallow draw that ran parallel with him. They would likely be cattle, he thought. But the next moment, while he watched, the shapes changed direction and started toward him. He saw that they were men on horses, about fifteen of them.

His horse leaped under the spurs and he swung down on the far side of his saddle, out of sight. A musket ball hit somewhere close, and the crash came an instant later. The horse wheezed, stumbled and recovered. He straightened in the saddle and held its head up. Something wet was trickling on his leg; he knew then that the horse had been hit, low and back of the saddle, through the belly. He looked over his shoulder and saw the Spaniards about two hundred feet back of him.

Another musket ball plowed the air to one side. They were close now and yelling, but they weren't gaining on him, in spite of the way his horse had been hit. The moon was up and it shone plain on the trail. He bent over the saddle and hoped the horse would hold out until he could make a dash for a brushy slope he spotted ahead.

He didn't see the ravine, and later when he thought about it, he decided that the horse didn't either. It was about thirteen or fourteen feet across, in the middle of the trail and running at right angles. He had no chance to set his spurs, but at that moment another shot struck the horse in the back, and it leaped, cleared the ravine, staggered, but kept galloping. He could hear the Spaniards pulling up, shouting and cursing, as he swerved off to his left into the brush.

The horse didn't slow, though it was beginning to breathe hard, and his leg was wet from blood. The brush petered out on the top of a round hill, but he crossed a narrow arroyo and rode into more brush. When that petered out he couldn't hear the Spaniards any longer. All he could hear was the heavy gasps of his horse. He pulled in on the bit, but the horse did not answer, plunging on. Then, with all feet in the air, it seemed to collapse under him, like a pricked bladder.

The next thing he knew he was lying on the ground. He was skinned up, but in one piece. He got up and went back to the horse. It lay on its side, not even gasping now, its legs all tangled. He waited for a while. Then he unfastened the *reata* from the saddle, undid the cinches and pulled the saddle off the horse. He stood up and looked around. He figured he was about twenty miles from the nearest American ranch, Las Virgenes.

The saddle got heavy; after about two miles he dropped it under a tree. He took off his spurs and put them in his pocket. He took a sight on the North Star and another look at the country. If he walked right smart he should get to the ranch by sunup. Monterey sure seemed far off. He hoped that the next horse would be as good as the last one.

The night was hot, with no breeze stirring here under the brow of the hill. There were no lights showing in the town, but beyond it and the river a faint pulsing glow indicated the campfires at Paredón Blanco. Below Dunavant a few paces was the officers' shelter, a crude arrangement of willow poles and brush. Below the shelter where Gillespie and Gilson were arguing, he could hear the tread of the sentries, and farther down the slope hoofs of a horse striking stone.

Two days had passed. The garrison had moved and was now encamped on Fort Hill, a short distance from the old compound, where there were a small spring and high ground that commanded the town and its approaches. The garrison was short on provisions and powder, but the morale of the men was high nevertheless. They had faith in themselves—the old belief that one American could whip ten Californians—and all of them thought that John Brown would get through to Monterey. Their chief disappointment was the wraithlike enemy who would not stand still and fight, preferring instead to taunt them from a safe distance, appearing on horseback and then fading away after a few wild shots.

Things were different with the officers. Since the night John Brown had ridden out of the compound, Gillespie had gone about with the air of a man who saw no hope of victory or relief for the garrison, short of speech, and openly hostile toward Gilson. Gilson himself had lost some of his cocksureness, but he was still holding out against surrender. This was what he was doing now, as he stood there beside the shelter, his heavy body outlined in the rays of the lantern.

The horseman was climbing the slope, weaving slowly through rocks and brush, and Dunavant, chewing on a cigar butt that was too short to light, walked down to meet him. The man flung himself from the saddle as Dunavant reached the shelter, staggered, caught himself, and then stood for a moment dazed and silent.

When he did talk, his words came out in a confused gabble that was hard to decipher. He was an American, a supercargo from a hide ship. On the way up from his ship, as he came out of the Santa Ana Canyon, he had run into a party of Americans who told him that Los Angeles was besieged and that all the Americans in the valley were gathering at Isaac Williams' ranch in Chino.

"Who was leading the party?" Gillespie asked him.

"A man named Wilson."

Benito Wilson, Dunavant knew, was a tough fighter who had been dispatched by Commodore Stockton to the San Bernardino country, below the Cajon, to protect the frontier against Indian attacks and any hostile parties that might be sent up from Sonora.

"He wanted me to go with them," said the supercargo. "He was certain the Californians were going to attack, but I didn't like the idea of holing up in a ranch house. . . ."

The man sat down suddenly in a heap and nothing more could be drawn from him.

Gillespie stood looking down at the dark lanes of the pueblo, his back turned to all of them.

Gilson said, "The greasers have probably sent a good part of their troops to Chino. Now is the time to smash them at Paredón Blanco."

Gillespie lifted his head and looked toward the distant campfires, but said nothing in reply.

Beside the trail between San Miguel and San Luis Obispo, having ridden almost three hundred miles in two days, without sleep, lean John Brown dropped from his horse and lay down in the grass.

He had no watch but he judged from the Big Dipper that it was about eleven o'clock. Tom Lewis, lying beside him, was already asleep, snoring flat on his back. He had picked up Tom Lewis at Las Virgenes. That was two nights ago when his horse had been shot from under him and he had walked twenty-seven miles to the ranch house before he could find another one. Tom Lewis was a good companion, a good talker, but John Brown wished that he was stronger, because then they could have ridden on instead of stopping. But he was a good companion, a good talker, and that was important.

Everyone had been good, all along the way. He had given the cigarette papers to three different men—he remembered their names: Lieutenant Talbot at Santa Barbara, Thomas Robbins and Lewis Burton—and they had given him fresh horses. It was funny what a cigarette paper with some words scribbled on it would do.

He thought about Monterey, and the pines growing down to the sea, and the girls in bright-colored dresses, but it sure seemed far away, farther than ever. He thought about Captain Gillespie for a while, wondering what was going on down there with his friends and why he had said he could make the trip in four days. Then he listened to Tom Lewis snoring and wished he was stronger. He was a good talker but not very strong.

He woke up with the Dipper shifted around and the sky black. He must have been asleep for five hours at least. He gave Tom Lewis a shove with his foot and walked to his horse, but when he got in the saddle and looked down Tom Lewis was still lying there snoring. He went over and gave him another shove. Tom Lewis sat up then, half up on one elbow, and mumbled that he couldn't go on. He was plumb jiggered out.

John Brown decided he wouldn't waste any more time with Tom Lewis, although he was a good companion and a good talker. He lifted himself to the saddle, and spurred his horse to a gallop. He showed another one of his papers at dawn and got another fresh horse and galloped on. All day, every time he came across an American, he took a paper out of his hair and traded it for a horse, a good one too—it was sure funny about those papers. He hoped he would have one left over for a souvenir.

It was black night again when he rode into Monterey, with fog drifting low so he couldn't see the pines or the sea even. The streets were deserted and he didn't see one girl. He felt pretty good riding up to the Customs House, tired and hungry, but pretty good, but when he got down from the saddle his legs wouldn't work. They were bent to the shape of every horse he had ridden in the last three days, and when he walked into the room he felt foolish as all hell, with his legs stiff as pieces of oak and all bent.

He felt like lying down, but he couldn't until they had taken off his pants and sloshed cold water on his legs and rubbed them. He felt pretty bad now, but the worst was that Commodore Stockton was not in Monterey. He was at San Francisco. That was bad news, but anyway he had come through—someone said it was four hundred and sixty miles, but someone else said it was ten miles less than that. Whichever it was, it was a long way, a long way to come and not see a girl on the street.

Then he heard them making plans—the mayor, Mr. Colton, and someone else—about sending another rider on to San Francisco, but as long as he had made it this far, he wasn't going to sit still for anything like that. The mayor, Mr. Colton, promised to wake him up after three hours, and when he did a fellow by the name of Jacob Dye gave him the loan of his best race horse.

It was sure a fine horse, the best he had ever been on, and he made good time, riding through the dark and when the sun came up, clear to San Jose. He had trouble getting another horse there, so he lost four hours that he didn't want to lose, and started off again, swearing he'd go back to Monterey sometime when it wasn't fogged up.

Word of the skirmish at Chino came to the garrison on Fort Hill that afternoon; it came piecemeal, but by nightfall the story was complete. The forces under Benito Wilson had reached the ranch at Chino the evening before and barricaded themselves, only to find that the owner, Isaac Williams, despite his assurances to the contrary, was short of powder. Some of Wilson's party, smelling a ruse, wanted to leave, but Wilson's orders prevailed. The Californians attacked at dawn with random musket fire, and in the act of leaping the dry moat which surrounded the ranch, one of their men was shot.

The death of young Ballestros incensed the Californians. Immediately they sent a party to fire the roof. With the house burning over their heads the Americans surrendered; they were then rounded up and marched toward Los Angeles in charge of Diego Sepulveda. Halfway along the road Sepulveda decided to kill all the Americans in revenge for the death of Ballestros, and was restrained, only after the utmost effort, by Varela.

The one part of the story that interested Captain Gilson was the fact that fifty men under Ramón Carillo and Varela had joined in the fight. It proved, in his opinion, the point he had made the night before.

"They left Paredón about the time we were talking," Gilson said, taking no pains to conceal his bitterness. "The sortie I suggested would have been successful."

"We were still outnumbered," Gillespie answered. "And while we were there we could have been cut off from our base."

It was dark and Dunavant was holding a lantern while the two officers supervised the emplacement of an old six-pounder that the armorers had put in condition. His hands were shaking from loss of sleep—the light fell unsteadily across the emplacement, the men grunting and sweating with their labors, across the heavy, backward-bent knees of Gilson. He wondered why Captain Gillespie had ordered the cannon set up; since noon when the first word of Chino came in by one of the Americans who had escaped it was apparent that he had made up his mind to surrender.

Dunavant glanced across the deserted town at the fires of Paredón, now bright in the clear air. When the next demand came from the Californians, probably tomorrow, Gillespie would give up. The cannon was a gesture, like the sending of John Brown to Monterey and the retreat to Fort Hill.

Holding the lantern and watching the far lights of the enemy camp, Dunavant considered his own position. He had joined the garrison, like the rest of the five Americans who had arrived in the last few days, for protection, to fight if he was called on. If the garrison was surrendered, or rather when it was, as a civilian he might be thrown into jail, unless Gillespie were to give him the status of a soldier. It might be better, he thought, to strike off and hide himself in the mountains, until reinforcements came from the North.

Later that night, lying in the hole filled with leaves that he used for a bed, listening to the tread of sentries and the horses moving around in the brush corral, he made his decision. He would stay on and take what came. The idea of hiding in the mountains, living on berries and what game he could bring down with his pistol, skulking around like a hunted animal for days and maybe weeks, made his blood churn.

The surrender took place the next afternoon, though Dr. Gilchrist, an American physician, came with the first demands from General Flores in the morning, under terms that permitted Captain Gillespie to save face. The marines were to be allowed to leave under their own flag. The cannon taken from the Californians were to be left at San Pedro, and during the march there and the embarkation on the merchantman *Vandalia* they were not to be molested.

The next day dawned with whirling clouds and a threat of rain. All night the Spaniards and Mexicans had been pouring in from the countryside. They lined the plaza and the lane out of town. The Mexican flag flew above Government House, stiff and triumphant in the driving wind from the sea.

The three officers rode down the hill, followed by the handful of marines on foot. Four of the Americans taken at Chino had been traded for the five Mexicans Gillespie had captured, and these, with Grady Dunavant, brought up the rear. The flag beat in the wind, and when they reached the plaza and the jeers of the crowd rose to a tumult, the drummers swung their sticks. The rattle of the drums was thin against the uproar that swelled through the plaza, but to Dunavant it took the edge off the bitterness of defeat.

As they turned out of the plaza and into the lane, heading toward the sea, a marine in front of him shouted, "We'll come back, you bastards. It won't be long either!"

Dunavant, gazing through the dust at the jeering faces, silently echoed his words.

Six hundred and thirty miles to the north, having arrived on the Bay of San Francisco the night before, lean John Brown sat with a jug of *aguardiente* between his feet. The commodore's ship lay anchored a half mile from the beach. John Brown had waved his hat to attract someone's notice, and now that a longboat was coming ashore, he sat on the sand waiting. He lifted the jug and took a long swig, wiped his mouth on his sleeve, and took the last two cigarette papers from his matted hair. He would give one to the commodore—that would leave him one for a souvenir.

He lifted the jug and took another drink, watching the oars of the longboat sparkle in the sun. Four days from Los Angeles to San Francisco was pretty good time, he thought, and this made him feel like having another drink. It was a good ride all right, only he wished that everything hadn't been so fogged up in Monterery.

# 30

Don Saturnino looked out across the meadows and rolling hills of the Hawk. He stood on the watchtower sweating and squinting against the late sun, resting for a moment from the labor of setting up the swivel gun that he had taken away and brought back when the gringo had disappeared.

Everything pleased his eye—the ripened grass, the broad-flowing river, the corrals filled with horses, the thousands of cattle grazing wherever he looked. And among them not a cow, steer or bull that had belonged to the gringo—he had sold them all to Don Ricardo Haro, driven the last of them away to the Cajon yesterday, including ten head of horses. Every vestige of the gringo had been removed from the house and the hills. The Hawk, at last, was as it had been.

But suddenly, as he stood there squinting and sweating, his blood coursing strong, his eye fastened on a mist of green showing beyond the mesa. His brows drew down in a heavy scowl. He took a step forward and shaded his eyes. Yes, it was something growing in a flat place back from the river, a few acres of plants growing in ordered rows. His mouth tightened. He turned and let himself down the ladder, mounted his horse and rode at a gallop across the mesa.

Frijoles! That was what he had seen from the watchtower. Three acres or more of growing frijoles, ankle-high, row after row of them, as regular as a pattern on a blanket. *Mal haya!*

He set spurs to his stallion and rode down the first row, reached the end and then started up the next row. As he wheeled toward the third row, he saw his daughter riding up from the river. Grimly he spurred his horse again. The hoofs trampled and cleft the plants. She was waiting for him when he returned, square in his path. She sat sidewise in the saddle, one hand gripping the horn, her eyes blazing out at him from under the shadows of her hat.

"We lack food since the storehouse burned," said his daughter. "We are borrowing food. This is something without reason."

He pulled up his horse. "We starve rather than eat that which is planted by a gringo. The flesh will fall from our bones before that." She looked at him levelly, and he knew, reading her thoughts, that it was not food she was concerned with. Threats, the lash, had not quenched the fire in her eyes. "The gringo has gone," he said, "with the rest. Two things happen if he returns. First, you will be locked away, and then, in due time, as God is my witness, he will be run through with a lance."

She sat for a moment looking at him. Then she said slowly, "He will return, but neither of these things will happen."

"You speak in defiance?" he said, unloosening the braided whip fastened to the pommel.

"In defiance," she answered him. "Of you and the whip and the lance. Of you and everything."

She was gone while he sat fumbling with the whip. He fought down the impulse to pursue her, turned instead with a savage oath to the task he had begun. He rode at a deliberate trot, methodically, down all the rows, and at the end he wheeled his horse and rode back. The hoofs knifed deep in the soft, rich soil; the brittle stems of the frijoles snapped and were mixed with the soil, so that when he had finished, the field was the same color as the land that surrounded it.

Savoring his deed, this final act of revenge upon the gringo who had sought to despoil his possessions, he rode homeward. He put the scene with his daughter out of his mind. He smiled under his sombrero, his jaws straining against the chin strap. He thought of the Battle of Chino and the roof burning and the gringos trooping out asking for mercy. He relived the scene in the pueblo, as it had been told to him, when the enemy surrendered and tramped away amid the jeers of the populace. He recalled the victorious reports that had been coming in all week—at Santa Barbara the gringo soldiers were hiding in the mountains; at San Diego the garrison, driven from the town, had fled for their lives and had taken refuge on a whaler lying in the harbor.

He thought of all the events of the past ten days and smiled. His only regret was that he had failed in trapping the gringo the night of the dance. He had arrived with his men in time but somehow the quarry had escaped. This was a great disappointment of his life; it would haunt him forever.

And then, galled by the memory, he lightened his spirits by planning how over the months that were to follow he would systematically even the score with all those who had befriended the gringo, Don Anselmo in particular. He knew their names, every one of them, and in time, in cleverly devised ways, he would see that they paid for their treachery.

By the time he arrived home he was in high spirits again. His eyes swept the courtyard, noting the fires in the blacksmith shop, the busy looms, the ovens sending up their streamers of smoke, and fastened finally on his eagle. The bird sat, dangling its silver chain, nibbling quietly at its plumage.

"*Ayee!*" he shouted.

The eagle cocked a cold eye at him but ceased preening its feathers. From the wicker cage under the tree Saturnino took out a mouse and tossed it wriggling into the air. Quicker than the eye, the talons snatched the prey. Saturnino emptied the cage, and as he stood admiring his golden bird—no one in the length and breadth of California owned one like him—his mind turned to the Indian girl Guadalupe.

He found her grinding corn in the granary. Rosalia was there also, and with a jerk of his head, he motioned her to leave.

Guadalupe did not look up. A shaft of sun fell through the doorway on her arms that were bared to the elbows. He looked at the dark hairs glistening on her arms and the muscles rippling beneath the skin as the pestle turned in the bowl. She held the bowl between her strong outthrust knees, and as she turned the stone her breasts, though they seemed to be of the firmness of melons, rocked gently beneath her dress.

His chest was tight but he managed to say, "What passes?"

Without looking up, she replied, "Nothing passes."

The pestle went on grinding the corn. Her hands were floured with a dust, but her arms were clean, of the same smoothness as the manzanita.

"Does it please you to be home again?"

"My home is in the mountains," she said.

Saturnino scowled. He was tired of this sort of talk. He had heard much of it in the last three months and he was very tired of it. At first it had amused him, even when they had left the Hawk and gone to the ranch in the hills he had not minded it, but now they were home and it made him very tired.

"I will send you to the mountains," he said.

The girl glanced up at him. "When?" she said, her eyes searching his face.

"Soon," he said. But as he said it, he looked down into the wild hot eyes. He saw the sunlight on her bare arms, the small dark silky hairs on her upper lip. He realized that he would never permit her to leave. "Soon," he repeated, for it suited his plans to have her think so.

Outside, he walked toward the gate. He had heard hoofs on the mesa when he was talking to Guadalupe, the shrilling of metal crickets coming up from the west, and now he saw Don Melchor Manrique striding through the gate at the other end of the courtyard. When he had heard the crickets the thought flashed through his mind that they had something to do with the gringos; he was certain of it as Don Melchor strode toward him, dressed in an iron-studded jacket.

Don Melchor spoke while they were still a dozen paces apart. "They return!" he shouted.

"Who?" Saturnino said coolly. "Who returns? It must be the Devil and his minions."

"The gringos," Don Melchor said. "They are on a ship in the harbor of San Pedro."

Saturnino laughed. "They have been there for a week. What is new about this?"

"This," Don Melchor said: "there are now two ships, one with many guns that arrived last night. Many guns and many men."

Saturnino digested the news in silence. Then he said, "The more men, the more to kill. As for the guns, they are on the ship, and without horses or oxen cannot be transported." He paused and gave Don Melchor a quick glance. "All the horses were driven from the hills last week, so I have heard. Is it true?"

"The hills were scoured and within four leagues of the harbor there is nothing that travels on four legs."

"Then the gringo will move afoot, without cannon."

"It is the truth," said Don Melchor. "And we will meet them on horseback."

Saturnino grinned. "On the backs of the best horses in the world. The best riders on the best horses."

When Don Melchor had ridden off toward the Cajon to spread the alarm, Saturnino passed the word to his *vaqueros*. In his room everything was as he had left it on his return from the Battle of Chino—his jacket, his shield, his ten-foot lance, the musket, powder and ball—everything lay at hand, for General Flores had warned all warriors to keep themselves in readiness. The moment had come sooner than expected, but it had come. Now, within the short space of a week, he would have another chance to wet his lance. The last chance, at Chino, was abortive. The gringos had given up without a fight, and just as the plans had been made to kill them on the trail, the ignorant, pock-marked Varela had interceded. Nothing like that would happen again, *por Dios!* for this time General Flores and Colonel Curel were in charge.

Attired for battle, carrying his lance and musket, he made his way to the gate, taking care to avoid his mother. (Angels of Christ! how old must he be—a man of ninety with a white beard of great length—before he ceased to quaver at her serpent's tongue?) The horses were waiting, the leathern bags on the cantles stocked with yucca cakes and strips of dried beef, the *vaqueros,* eight of his best men, impatient in the saddles.

As they rode away, the sun nudged the western hills and flung long red banners across the sky. The men, sensitive to such signs, raised their eyes and one of them said, "A good omen." Another said, "There is much blood." They were answered by a third, "The blood of the gringo."

A smile formed at the corners of Saturnino's mouth. He looked at the sky and studied the information he had obtained from Don Melchor. The country had been ransacked for muskets and pistols; enough had been found to equip more than a hundred men. Another hundred would rely on the lance. An old four-pounder, which was used on festive occasions for the firing of salutes, and which was buried in the garden of Inocencia Reyes at Stockton's first approach, had been dug up, reconditioned and mounted on wagon wheels by an English carpenter. Powder for the pedrero had been procured from the mission at San Gabriel. Under José Carillo fifty men had already ridden toward the sea to reconnoiter and harass the foe. General Flores was to follow with the cannon.

In the last red surge of the sun his smile broadened.

The *Vandalia* rode at her anchors, rising and falling on the long Pacific swells that swept under the shimmering kelp fields and into the roadstead. Beside her lay the 54-gun *Savannah.* The day was clear, the sea glassy smooth, and the last of the longboats bore toward shore, loaded with seamen and marines.

For an hour from the decks of the *Vandalia* Grady Dunavant had watched the disembarking of Captain Mervine's forces, the long line of boats plying back and forth from the ship to the beach. The final boatload was ashore and the men were assembling their equipment. Gillespie's marines were also there on the sloping white beach. There was only a motley collection of men left on the *Vandalia*—fourteen mountain men, a blacksmith, the supercargo and he. The supercargo chose to remain behind, so the sixteen of them, called forward by Gillespie, lowered themselves to the boat.

On shore, Captain Mervine's troops were ready to march. Gillespie divided his force into two parties of skirmishers, deployed one group to the left, and the other, under Captain Gilson, formed on the right, flanking the seamen and marines. With flags and to the beating of drums, the three hundred and seventy-five men turned their backs on the sea and began the march on Los Angeles. They carried short rations of water, for it was presumed that the springs had been poisoned, and traveled on foot, without cannons, because the Californians had driven every horse and ox out of the area.

Grady found himself marching behind Captain Gilson. Beside him was a young trapper, short, thin-shanked and dark as an Indian, with black hair to his shoulders. His name was Jessup, and he carried a Spencer canted across his shoulder. In addition to the Colt, Dunavant carried a brassbound, smoothbore piece, a Hawkins, which he had bought from one of the mountain men. He felt like a mountain man himself, with a powder horn filled with Dupont slung around his neck, and a leather sack of galena in his pocket.

"What d'ye aim to bring down?" Jessup wanted to know, eying the obsolete rifle.

"They shoot hard and sometimes straight," Dunavant said.

"Cap and ball for this chile," Jessup said. "I got no hankerin' for ary flints."

Dunavant had no hankerin's either, but it was a rifle and he would need it. Most of the seamen and marines had been in the first march on Los Angeles; they remembered it now on this sunlit afternoon, with the sky blue and the smell of pennyroyal rising beneath their feet—how they had failed to draw a single shot from the enemy, and how they had ridden into a deserted town. But that was almost two months ago; the temper of the Spaniards, stiffened by the *Sonoreños* and the Mexicans, had undergone a change. They had driven the Americans from Los Angeles, defeated them at Chino. He had learned some things about the temperament of the enemy, and the banter of the marines worried him. They marched in a solid square to his left, shoulder to shoulder, complaining because they were afoot, but carefree as if they were on their way to a hoedown. He didn't like Captain Mervine's square nor the holiday spirit of the men. He liked the man who was leading the right flank even less—Gilson, striding ahead, stiff-legged and confident.

At the crest of the first low hill they stopped to rest. Beyond them the grass rolled and rippled, bending downward into a swale and rising again, bordered as it reached a farther crest with thickets of dry mustard stalks. There was no movement anywhere except that of the wind in the grass, not a horse or a cow, no sign of the foe.

Jessup said, "They're runnin' same as afore."

Behind them the sea lay calm, with the curving arm of the beach showing white against the tan cliffs, and the two ships riding stern-on, small and almost lost in the shimmer of the water, and the island rising up beside them more like a shadow than what it was. He would remember the island later, and himself standing there looking back at it, at the bay and the white sand of the beach, and wondering what would happen to Mervine's square against cannon fire. Later it would be called Dead Men's Island, and many of those who were laughing now among the coarse-stalked sunflowers would be buried on the island that looked like a shadow.

The first shot came whining from the right flank. It was almost an hour later, and they were within sight of a ranch house. The sun was behind Palos Verdes and the shadows sprawled far out in front of them. At the edge of the shadows, on a rise that ran parallel to him, Dunavant saw three horsemen outlined against the sky. They were in motion, but the man in the lead fired as he rode. The ball parted the air over Jessup's head.

Jessup squinched his eyes and his mouth dropped open. "Goddam!" he said, "goddam if'n I'm not a ring-tailed coon," and fired as he spoke the words. The shot kicked up dust, short, but at Gilson's command one of the six rifles that answered him winged the nearest of the three horsemen. He fell from the saddle, crawled on his knees, then got up and staggered out of sight over the rise.

Gilson looked at Jessup. "You'll fire when I give the order." And he added, glancing sidewise at Dunavant, "You'll fire, hereafter, with the others."

Grady had not used the Hawkins; the range was long and he didn't have powder to squander on a chance shot. "I'll use my judgment about shooting," he told Gilson.

Gilson's neck reddened under its coat of dust. "If you do, you'll face trouble when we reach Los Angeles."

Grady held his tongue, but he was determined to use his rifle as he saw fit. He had had a long time to think about things—the last night on Fort Hill, the week aboard the *Vandalia*—and he had come to the conclusion that he would have no part in the feud between Gillespie and Gilson, or the one reported between Stockton and Frémont. He was a part of the army and not a part of it. He was with the army, but in another day or perhaps tonight he might be on his own. If and when he was, he wanted to have a supply of powder.

That night, lying on the ground, he made his plans. They were camped at the ranch house he had seen earlier from a distance, from which everyone had fled except a blind Indian. The ranch belonged to a Spaniard named Dominguez who had left with his family the night before. The night was warm and the fires that had been built for supper had died down. The camp was silent; the men lay sprawled about in exhaustion. The only sounds, besides the snoring, were made by the sentries and the whimpering of doves in the cottonwoods. If they reached the pueblo tomorrow or the next day, or if they didn't reach it and had to retreat, he was going back to the Hawk. With or without the army, he was going back for Luz.

In the morning, after brief alerts throughout the night when stray shots thumped the adobe walls, they were away with the sun, marching as before, with the marines and webfeet in the center, and two parties of skirmishers on the flanks. The day turned off hot. By midmorning the horizon danced with skittering waves that made visibility poor, near things far and the distance blurred and retreating. They had no trouble, however, in seeing the Californians, who began to appear in increasing numbers, skirting the plain ahead, just out of range. The occasional shots they fired from their smoothbores fell short of the marching men. One spent itself at Jessup's feet.

He reached down, picked up the ball and turned it in his fingers. "I be dogged," he said. "They're afirin' goat turds."

The trapper doubled up with laughter; everyone was laughing and joking about something. It's as though they're going to a hoedown, Grady thought again, his thin face serious, as if they had a girl in one arm and a jug in the other and could hear music beckoning to them around the next bend in the road. He didn't like the laughter and joking any more than he liked Mervine's square. They taught this formation at the Academy, he knew, but it wasn't suited to this kind of fighting, or the kind it might turn into.

The pluming smoke looked like a flower, like the sunflowers they were tramping through, only much bigger. It was yellow and had a small dark core, and it hung for a moment in the windless air, directly ahead and a half mile away. Then he heard the cannon shot careening, and saw it in a humpbacked curve drop a couple of hundred yards in front of them. As the order came to charge the emplacement, two horsemen appeared out of a gully, looped *reatas* around the carriage and dragged the cannon away, out of sight beyond the next rise.

The square and the flankers tramped on as if nothing had happened, only the laughter was louder now, and the officers joined in. Another shot followed when they had gone another half mile. This one, like the one before, dropped short, and the heavy yellow smoke hung in the air.

This sent Jessup into another fit of laughter and started another ripple running through the columns. "I kin chunk a rock straighter'n that," Jessup said.

It was all pretty funny, Jessup thought, with the cannon spouting smoke like a steamboat, and the shot lobbing up in a curve you could watch, and falling kerplunk in the grass, and the greasers riding out and snatching the cannon away. He laughed and smacked his thigh and allowed again that he could chunk straighter'n they was doing.

Dunavant didn't argue, but he could see plainly enough that it wasn't the aim that was off, so much as that the Californians were using inferior powder. When another shot fell short he felt better about everything—they might make the pueblo after all, possibly after nightfall. An officer stepped up the cadence and everyone moved faster; the sunflowers and the dried stalks of mustard made a swishing sound against their legs.

A buzzard was floating overhead, and as he followed it with his eyes, he heard the thud of the cannon again. It sounded like all the rest and he didn't bother to shift his eyes from the buzzard. Then Jessup was swearing beside him and a hush had fallen over the columns, and out of the hush someone screamed. The hush ended and it seemed as though everyone was shouting at once.

Something had happened to the square. The marines and webfeet had halted, but it wasn't that. He saw that the first rank was out of alignment, caved in at the center, and that the men who had been marching here in center were now lying among the sunflowers. The next minute the square had re-formed and was moving on, around the men on the ground, toward the enemy that had vanished again.

The word came up from the left, from lip to lip, to Jessup who said, "Four kilt, by Jesus, more'n ten hurted."

There was steady rattle of rifle fire now. The troops cursed and fired and shouted for the greasers to come on and fight. Mounted on fine horses, the Californians swung backward in circling loops, about forty men on the left, ten men in the center with the cannon, and forty men or more on the right. The air was still and scented with the odor of turpentine weed and pennyroyal. The heat increased.

Grady was far out on the right flank, on ground a little higher than the others. He had taken off his Spanish jacket and wore it around his hips, the sleeves tied in front, the heavy brassbound Hawkins held in his two hands. The enemy horsemen were like phantoms in the dancing heat, appearing and disappearing, yet always out of rifle shot. He wondered if Cesaire Curel were out there on the horizon. The tactics were clever enough to be his—the cannon set up, fired when they came within range, then pulled away and the performance repeated—but Curel was likely far to the rear, in his white gloves and polished boots. There would be no chance for a shot at Curel, not today or in this battle; sometime, but not here on the long trail to Los Angeles.

As a matter of fact there would be no chance to reach any of the foe; he knew it and Captain Mervine, and Gillespie and Gilson knew it. The army had halted now and the officers were in a group forward, talking. The shot roared low over their heads; for a moment he thought that it was going to land between them and the men. Then the center of the square sagged and he saw eight marines on the ground, four of them lying awkwardly as they had fallen, and the others crawling. . . .

The bugle was a long time in sounding, yet it came, thin and heartbreaking, against the heavy air and the stillness. The retreat was orderly, with the enemy following at a distance. They reached the ranch house at dusk and went into camp. The moans of the wounded and the soft whimpering of doves lasted all night. And at dawn they marched for the sea.

Grady Dunavant had made his plans. When they came within sight of the bay and saw the ships lying there on the glass-smooth water, he said good-by to Jessup, nothing to Gilson. He hid himself in an arroyo and stayed hidden all day. A half-dozen horsemen rode past him; once he thought he recognized Curel, and once Tepeyollotl the Indian. No one saw him and at nightfall he set out across country, heading for the North Star.

He walked all night, ate some of his provisions at sunup, lay down in the willows beside a river and slept until it was dark again. The stars were out when he started north along the river bank, and a half-moon, tipped on end, which gave little light. At the end of a mile of walking, he had the feeling that he was being followed. He was certain of it and hid himself, watching the horseman ride past within a few feet of him. At dawn he hid again, ate a little of his food, and was lying down when Tepeyollotl rode up.

He might have known that it was Joe who was following him, and that Joe would be leading an extra horse, saddled and fresh, with a Spanish brand on its flank, a musket in the sheath.

"Old woman cannon say boom," Joe said.

He was proud of the cannon. Before he told Dunavant how he had seen a man hide the first morning in the arroyo, deserted the Spaniards the next day and followed the tracks which were not like those left by the soldiers, tracks with one toe turning in like the señor's, he explained how the cannon had been dug up from Mrs. Reyes's garden and, since she was an old woman, the origin of the name.

"Old woman say boom," Joe said and imitated the sound. "Boom, boom. *Jesús Cristo!*"

"Where did the señora go?" Grady Dunavant asked. "Did she go to San Diego when I left the ranch?"

"San Diego, yes. Boat. Go away."

Dunavant got into the saddle.

"Go away. Good-by," Joe said.

Yris Llorente! She was gone at last; Grady wondered to what fate. He wished her more happiness than she would ever find.

They rode that day and at night came to a small stream running down from the hills that overlooked the Hawk. The ranch lights were faint. A thin wash of moonlight lay on the mesa, but Grady couldn't see whether or not there were horses tied at the gate. Joe said that De Zubaran and his *vaqueros* were still with the army, but there was no sense to presume that Joe was right.

They had talked while they rode, and when they reached the stream, Joe left without a word.

There were no horses at the gate. Tepeyollotl had been pretty sure that Don Saturnino was still riding with the army, because when he deserted and followed the man he had seen hiding in the arroyo, Don Saturnino was with the army standing on a hill back from the shore and watching the Americans row out to their ships. They would be watching until the ships sailed off and that might not be for many days. Then it would take Don Saturnino another day to reach home.

The gate was barred and Tepeyollotl beat on it with his fist. When it opened he walked inside, saying boldly that he wanted to see Guadalupe, that he was her brother and wanted to see her. She was in the kitchen scouring out an iron pot. She looked up at him in the doorway. He didn't have to say anything. She knew that he had come for her and she dropped the pot and followed him into the darkness. Her belongings had been packed since he had left the ranch many weeks before. She was gone only a moment and then she came back with her belongings hidden under a blanket.

They went to the gate, and there he suddenly remembered that he was to talk with the señorita. He had forgotten about her in the joy of seeing Guadalupe. She was in her room, with a light showing under the crack of the door. He knocked softly and when she opened the door he gave her the message that had been given to him. Then he walked back to the gate, closed it behind him and got into the saddle. He had brought along the extra horse for Guadalupe, but the señor had it now, so he helped her up behind him and set his heel against the horse's flank.

It was a three-day journey to where he was going, and since the horse was carrying a heavy load, he crossed the mesa at a trot. There were some horses in the corral, but he didn't want to be followed for a thief. Guadalupe said nothing while they rode across the mesa; however he could feel her breath warm on his back, and the warmth of her body through the thinness of his shirt.

As Luz saddled her horse—the best she owned, the palomino—she saw the Indian and Guadalupe riding toward the east. One of the girls, suspicious at Guadalupe's actions, had raised an alarm, but she had put an end to the matter by assuring them that it was nothing.

She had not stopped to say good-by to Carlota—her grandmother would know why she had gone. She hadn't even stopped to change her clothes or to bring the things he had left behind him—the little book written in English of which she couldn't understand a single word, the gray coat and trousers—everything she had managed to hide away beneath the mattress of her bed.

She spurred away from the corral at a hand gallop, took the opposite direction from the stream, circled back along the King's Highway only when she was below the mesa.

She saw the glint of water in the light of the half-moon falling through the willows, and as she reached it she turned the horse upstream and rode to the place where the stream came out of the hills in a series of small waterfalls. There was a glade here, lush with grass that brushed her stirrups. The air was sweet with the smell of wild jasmine. She pulled up her horse and waited, listening, straining forward in the saddle. The only sounds were the heavy breathing of her horse and the thin tinkle of the falling water.

She called and listened again. A bird fluttered out of a tree beside her. Her heart beat in her throat louder than the sound of the water and the heaving of her horse. What if she had come to the wrong place? There was another stream a league west. The Indian might have made a mistake or she might not have heard him correctly. She called again.

He came from behind her, quietly, on a horse that looked dark, but was a gray since it carried the brand of Don Anselmo who owned nothing else. His face was shadowed under his hat even when he was close to her.

He spoke in English and then, realizing that she hadn't understood, laughed at himself.

"I have brought nothing," she said. Her heart was beating louder than before and she wondered if he could hear it. "*Nada,*" she said, as his arm circled her waist, lifted her to the ground. "Oh," she said against his mouth.

# 31

A STILL, rosy light lay over the peaks, but down below them in the hidden valley that was shaped like a saucer day had not yet broken. The dregs of night hung there over the grass and the stream that came down from the peaks and wound off and disappeared through a slot in the mountains. It was like looking at objects through deep water, the edge blurred and moving under the gaze, but even while he sat on his horse with his eyes straining against the darkness, the rosy light crept across the Temescals, the grass took on texture, the stream showed white where it riffled over stones, and beyond it against the hill the outlines of the house took shape.

She had said that the house was small and dilapidated, and it was both—not more than a fair-sized barn, with a gaping hole in the roof and a corral that was half fallen down. But he had never seen anything that looked so good to him, and in the instant the light struck it, he was already planning what he would do to make it livable.

"It doesn't please you," she said, taking his silence for disappointment.

"It pleases me so much I can't talk. Everything! The stream—there'll be fish—and the pines just up the slope where I can cut timber . . . "

"The house?"

"Especially the house."

"It has no oven and there's a hole in the roof."

"We'll build one," he said, "and fix the roof."

But as they rode downward through the thickets of manzanita and lilac he said nothing about the thing that pleased him the most. The valley, not more than fifty acres in extent, was hidden, and at least ten miles from the Hawk and the King's Highway, with a range of mountains and hills between them. When they had stood in the glade last night discussing where they could go, he had objected at first to her suggestion that they come here. It had seemed too close to the ranch, and in spite of the fact that the house was used only by sheepherders in the summer when the grass grew scarce in the valley, he had preferred his own plan of going south to Pala, to the home of Renaldo Chavez. He was glad she had won out, but he said nothing about it now. Wherever they were in California, they were still in danger, and it was just as well to let the matter lie, to pretend that they weren't.

There were fish in the stream, as he had thought, and farther up where it came out of the mountains he saw ladders of brush and logs—the workings of beaver. The house was made of adobe, with no windows and a narrow door, and as they walked into the one room, pack rats scurried out between their legs; the place was alive with the whine of mud daubers, bees were hiving in the roof, and the pale tendrils of a vine had fingered their way through a crack in the wall.

She was watching his face, so he said, "By nightfall I'll have everything clean as a whistle and a patch over the roof." He looked up at the rotted timbers, at the blue sky showing through the roof, and thought to himself, It'll take a week even to make a dent in things.

She wanted him to repair the corral first.

He objected to this. "If we fix things up too much, anyone who happens along on the ridge and sees everything changed down here will get suspicious. The roof is the most important."

The sky was clear and the sun hot, but it was now going on toward the middle of October, and rain could be expected at any time. He picketed her palomino well out of sight of the ridge, left the house the way it was, running over with bees and pack-rat nests, and with her *reata* looped over the saddle horn, climbed the mountainside to the first stand of timber. Using his Green River knife, he whittled and hacked down three sapling pines, tied them with the rope and dragged them down the mountain.

He made two more trips that morning for poles, stopped only a few moments to share with Luz the last of his food, and then with her holding one end, he put up the roof poles. There was nothing to tie them with, so he notched them into place. She thought he was taking too great pains, making a careful mortice in each one, but he felt different about it. They might be here only a day or a week or even less, yet it was a home, their home, and he wanted it to be right, not something that was going to fall down on their heads. He shaved the joints carefully, the resinous sap sweet in his nostrils, as if he meant them to stand for fifty years.

At the lower end of the valley the stream fanned out into a marshy sedge; here he gathered swaths of tules, bound them with strips of willow bark and set them in place on the poles. While he was on the mountain and later, down cutting tules, she had cleaned out the pack-rat nests, so the room was pretty clean. When the roof was fixed he made a fire in the middle of the room, piling up bunches of sage and sprinkling it with a little of his powder. They went outside and watched the smoke billowing out through the door. It wasn't a good idea to be burning brush in daylight in case someone chanced along the ridge, but he did it anyway.

The room smelled of sage after the smoke cleared out, different from the rat and sheepherder smell before. She was as pleased with the new smell and the roof as a child with a trinket, smiling her quick smile and sidling up to him. She put her arm around him and held her face up for a kiss, all shining and little beads of perspiration standing out on her forehead.

He pretended that his knees weren't suddenly water, and said, "I kissed you last night." He asked her what they were going to eat for supper—the last of his provisions was gone. She still stood there smiling at him, knowing as all hell. He backed out the door and said he was going for food. He could hear her laughing when he was far up the stream.

Trout with orange bellies lay in every pool; he considered using his Hawkins on them, but finally decided against it, since he couldn't spare the powder and the noise might attract notice. Instead, he took off his shoes and rolled up his pants and waded into a pool, being careful not to muddy the water. He watched where the trout went, picked the biggest one that had hidden in a crevice in the rocks, and stooped down, ran his hand in until he could feel the flutter of the side fins, squeezed slowly and evenly, and then hard. He caught four this way and quit.

Luz had gathered her shawl full of acorns while he was gone and was sitting cross-legged by the stream grinding them on a flat stone. She had been watching him coming down the stream, and she was watching him now, more interested in him than in what she was doing. There was a smile in the corners of her mouth, and a look in her eye that made him uncomfortable. He sat down and cleaned the fish, trying to avoid her eyes, but when he looked up she would be studying him, smiling to herself.

He got up and wrapped the trout in ferns and said he was going to look for wood and make a fire.

"Do we sleep on the ground?" she asked, very innocent and casual. "You're so clever with the knife, you should be able to make a bed."

But he went up the mountain again and filled his rucksack, and a sort of sack made from his jacket, with pine needles. He made two trips, heaped up the needles in one corner of the room, spreading them out and covered them with his blanket. While he was working, she came and stood in the doorway and watched him.

"The bed isn't very wide," she said.

"It doesn't need to be."

"And there is only one blanket."

"I am sleeping by the fire," he said, avoiding her gaze.

She was laughing behind her hand. "You will be cold."

"I am used to it," he said.

"That is no reason for being cold."

He said nothing and finished the bed.

Behind the house, where it would be hidden from the ridge, he built a fire, spitted the trout and slanted them over the blaze. In the meantime she had found an old iron pot, crusted with a sheepherder's summer meal. They scoured it out in the sand of the stream bed, and made up some cakes with acorn flour, which they set out in the coals.

The trout were good, a crisp, flaky brown, but the cakes were bitter; they stuck in his throat, and when he managed to get the first one down, he said, "A while back I saw a cow and a calf up the mountain. You might go up there in the morning and throw a lasso and we'll have some milk."

Luz sat across the fire from him, with the flames making shadows in her hollow cheeks. "What will we do with milk?" she asked.

"Drink it, mix it with flour." He had always wondered why it was that no Spaniard, though there were thousands of cattle running around underfoot, ever thought of using milk. "Also for butter," he said.

Her eyes sparkled. "Butter—what is that?" she asked, saying the American word gingerly.

"You put it on cakes like these and eat it."

"It tastes like what?"

"It tastes soft and makes the cakes go down easier, though with these, not much easier."

She shuddered. "It sounds very horrible. Like the word 'butter' sounds. But I will lasso the cow so you can have some butter." She savored the word for a moment. "But I still don't think we should drink the milk. It is for calves."

She went on eating, as if she enjoyed everything, the bitter acorn cakes as much as the trout, making small sounds with her mouth as she had months ago by the Santa Ana; eating and watching him with her tawny eyes, pausing to look at the mountains that held the stars like a cup, and the firelight snaking out through the grass, and the deer that came quietly down to drink, as if everything had a special meaning for her.

He looked at her and thought, It's a hell of a thing for me to bring her here, away from her whole family, with her father and all his men on the hunt for both of us. It's not what a man should do with the girl he loves. He looked at her, the fine-turned wrists golden in the flames, the hollows at her cheeks and temples. It's not good, he thought, but I'd do it again.

She got up and went down to the stream to wash her hands, striding long through the grass, like a boy. Watching her disappear in the darkness he remembered the other time by the river and how he had watched her, with his blood beating in his ears. It was beating now, but it was different now from then.

When she came back she stood by the fire and yawned, raising her arms in a matching gesture of sleepiness. She shook out her hair so that it fell on her wide shoulders, with its blackness streaked with firelight. She yawned again. Without getting to his feet he threw more wood on the fire. He sat there staring into the fire, not looking at her, even when she told him she was going to bed. He felt like a fool, but he sat listening to her steps in the grass, the opening of the door, aware that it hadn't closed. She came back to the corner of the house and asked him if he would be warm enough. She came back twice more on one pretext or another, calling to him through the dark. The last time he didn't answer her. If she came again . . .

She didn't but he could hear her scratching around in the empty room. The fire died down and the air grew chill. He threw on more wood and lay down with his back to the blaze, listening to the sounds in the house—or were they the sounds from the stream, he wondered? Wondering, he fell asleep, and woke with the fire still burning and the cry of a lion fading away up the mountain.

The cry came again from the pines above him; then he saw her coming across the small meadow, carrying the blanket. He pretended to be asleep when she knelt beside him, though he was shivering with the cold. She wanted to tell him that she was frightened, but he kept his eyes closed and lay still, breathing regularly—she was one girl that wouldn't be frightened by a lion, and he was not going to be taken in.

She spread the blanket, pulled it over him and lay down between him and the fire, curving her legs along the back of his legs, and putting one hand gently on his shoulder.

The mountain lion called again and was answered far up the mountain, but the hand on his shoulder didn't move, as he knew it wouldn't.

"You are cold," she said. "Cold and not asleep."

"I was asleep until you waked me up."

"I haven't been to sleep at all," she said.

"Then it is time."

"It is cold in there," she said, and shivered.

"In both places. Tomorrow I'll go down to Wolfe's and get blankets."

The hand on his shoulder tightened. "You'll not go from here, anywhere, for blankets or anything else, for food or powder or for any other reason."

"Then we'll starve and freeze both."

"The mountains are full of game. One deer will last for weeks."

"That takes care of everything except the blankets and the freezing."

"Tomorrow you can make the bed larger and put a board down the middle, as is done in Massachusetts."

She started to laugh, and he wondered how she knew about Massachusetts, but didn't ask her. He could feel the warmth of her body through his clothes and her breasts lying tightly against him.

"I love you," she said calmly.

He turned over on his back, away from her, and started to speak.

"I have always loved you," she said, "from the first morning on the trail, and later on the river, and every time after that, even the day when you were going to the ranch and we were leaving. Then and now, and particularly now. Very much at this moment."

"And so it is with me," he said, not as calm as she was.

"Then you will kiss me?"

He lay and said nothing, smelling the wood smoke in her hair that lay against his shoulder, and the smell of ferns as always.

"You can kiss a small kiss," she said.

"Neither a small one nor a large."

"On the cheek."

"Neither there nor anywhere else."

"One?"

"Neither one nor two."

"Then you can sleep," she said.

"That is good."

"And when you are asleep I will kiss you then."

He did not answer. He looked up at the stars streaming across the sky, feeling her eyes on him in the darkness, and said nothing. He could stand the cold and the acorn flour, but not much more of this.

The next morning he shot a buck and carted it down the mountain on his horse, skinned it and cut strips to smoke over the fire and some to dry. While he was doing this she roped the cow and brought it in with the calf trotting at its heels. They had to keep the cow roped and snubbed close to a corral post. She stood by laughing at the antics, at him and the whole performance, and when he was through, with less than a pint to show for his efforts, he understood the Spaniard's attitude toward milk. It wasn't very good milk, either.

In the afternoon he surveyed the house for a fireplace. He went about the job as if he were going to live there the rest of his life, marking the course of the mud and stone chimney on the outside of the south wall where it couldn't be seen from the ridge, and laying out the opening on the inside, high and wide enough to take a three-foot log. She came in while he was down on his knees drawing the outline of the fireplace with his knife.

She knelt beside him and looked at the marks he had made and then at him.

"It's a fireplace," he explained.

She drew in her breath. "It is bad luck to have a fireplace under a roof."

"You have one at the Hawk."

"It was built by Don Cristóbal, and as everyone knows it brought him bad luck. No other Spaniard in the valley has a fireplace inside the house."

He sat back on his heels and glanced at her; she was serious. "Where I was brought up," he said, "we had a fireplace. The only misfortune I can think of was that it was a big one and I had to cut wood for it."

"That was in America," she promptly said. "We live in California."

"One of these days," he said, "California will be a part of America."

He knew that she wouldn't like this, and he was right, she didn't. Without a word she jumped up and went striding out the door, clanking her spurs, toward the stream, where she sat herself down on a rock and tossed pebbles in the water. She was still tossing pebbles when he came back to the house with the first armful of stones for the chimney, but when he returned with the second load, she was waiting for him, smiling.

"Perhaps," she said, "it will make a difference about the fireplace if California is a part of America. If this happens, then it won't be bad luck any longer."

Her reasoning was a little difficult to follow and he didn't like the way she stressed the word "if," but he decided to let the matter drop. She had started a chain of thought, however, and during the rest of the afternoon while he gathered stones, with her helping him, he dwelt on it. After all, it might be weeks or even months before Stockton could organize his forces. This meant that they might have to live on here in a hand-to-mouth existence, without salt or corn meal or utensils, short on powder, no blankets with winter coming on. And besides these considerations, the thought persisted and grew in him that his help might be needed.

He said nothing about what he was thinking, but she knew, and when after supper he got up and went out across the meadow to where his horse was picketed, she went with him.

"You are going to Wolfe's," she said.

He threw the saddle on and cinched it, without looking at her. Then he said, "I'll be back tomorrow with everything we need."

"You are going to find out about the fighting. If there is fighting you will stay."

He kissed her for the first time in two days, but her lips were cold under his and her body was stiff. "Whatever I find," he said, "I'll come back. If there's fighting, I'll take you to Pala, to the home of Chavez, who is my friend. I'll be back tomorrow night."

She waved to him as he crossed the stream, and when he got to the top of the ridge she was still standing where he had left her, a spot in the darkening meadow, her hand raised to him. He traveled fast along the ridge, taking a sight on the hills above Jim Wolfe's before night fell, and then riding down the mountain until he came to the King's Highway. The moon was not up and he saw no one.

Wolfe's dogs picked him up a half hour before he came to the ranch, circling him and yelping until he drew up to the gate, and Wolfe called them off. Wolfe carried a rifle; he closed the gate and barred it, and as they walked toward the courtyard Grady found out everything he wanted to know about Stockton and the others. The *Savannah* was still anchored at San Pedro. The Californians were in two camps, one in the Palos Verdes overlooking the anchorage, the other at Los Cerritos, inland a short way and south of the bay. There were rumors that Stockton was in San Francisco making ready to sail in the *Congress*.

On the *portale* Wolfe paused. "There's a young priest inside—Father Cabrera—from San Gabriel Mission. He's on the way to Capistrano, spying as he goes. I don't trust him farther'n I can throw a cat, so don't talk. Just keep quiet and pretend you're one of my men."

They went on until they came to the *sala*. Here Wolfe paused again to get Dunavant's story. He shook his head when he heard it. "You're asking for a peck of trouble," he grunted. "I'm dogged glad I'm not in your boots—bad as things are here, with my wife keepin' me from gettin' hauled off every day."

The priest was holding a cup of wine. He put it down as Dunavant came in. He was young and dark, with the coloring of a *Sonoreño*. His head was round and shaved close to his skull, and he had a heavy stubble on his round chin. He was short but muscularly built, with wide feet and long yellow toenails sticking out of his sandals. His eyes were dark and red-lidded. He looked Dunavant over carefully, mumbled a greeting, and began to drink his wine, studying him with his mean eyes.

Grady drank a cup of wine, listened to the talk and said nothing. The talk concerned cattle, a deal the priest wanted to make for two hundred head later in the fall, but he could see Cabrera's thoughts moving slowly behind the red-lidded eyes, evaluating him, wondering why it was that he had never seen this gringo before, why he was here at an hour after midnight! Cabrera's mind kept working all the time he was talking about the cattle. As he got up to go to bed, he settled his robe around his thick calves, ran his fist along the stubble of his chin and said, the hard, opaque eyes narrowed on Dunavant, "How is it, señor, that we have not met until tonight? I pass this way frequently, but do not remember you."

"For the reason," Grady Dunavant said, "that I have been in Sonora, in Hermosillo, selling horses."

"Hermosillo is my home," said the young priest. "A place of great beauty." The dark eyes flicked over Dunavant's face like the tongue of a snake. "You were not introduced to me and I therefore do not know your name."

Dunavant said, "James Miller."

"A pleasant sleep, Señor Miller. In the morning we will talk about Hermosillo and what transpires there."

In the morning before dawn with the two *botas* crammed full of supplies, a quantity of powder and ball, an ax in the sheath beside his Hawkins, and Jim Wolfe's blessings, Grady rode away from the gate. He rode leisurely, avoiding the Camino Real, south for better than five miles, and there in a clump of live oaks, on a slight rise where he could observe anyone who passed on the trail below him, he pulled up and waited for Father Cabrera.

He came, after a full hour by Grady's watch, riding at a smart clip on a brown powerful horse, his robes pulled back on his knees. Grady Dunavant waited until he had passed before he started out after him. He permitted the priest to reach the stream that came out of the hills, the same stream that ran through the hidden valley, then he cut down out of the brush and overtook him.

The priest jerked around in the saddle as he heard the hoofs behind him.

Dunavant said, "We didn't have a chance to talk about Hermosillo, Father Cabrera. It is a beautiful city and there is much to say. If you will get down from your horse for a moment we will resume the journey and discuss the city of your birth at length."

The hard red-lidded eyes fastened on Grady Dunavant walking toward him, on the Colt held waist-high and cocked.

"Stand with your back to me," Dunavant said, when the priest slipped out of the saddle. "Stand still and do not move, with your hands clasped behind your head. Do not move, for if you do you will not learn the latest news of Hermosillo."

The priest's neck was sweating and sweat ran along the fingers held behind the short neck. Dunavant tied the blindfold tight and moved the young man forward with the Colt against his back. He held the stirrup, helped Father Cabrera into the saddle, headed the horse in the opposite direction and, having mounted, followed him.

After a short distance he told the priest to rein to the left. They traveled a half mile over a series of low hills, returned in a wide loop the way they had come, turned again before they reached the Camino Real, and then with the sun overhead followed the stream into the mountains.

Dunavant took the long way home. He left the stream halfway up the mountainside, made a series of switchbacks and came to the valley from the south ridge. It was night when they rode downward through the pines. He could see the fire beside the house.

"Hermosillo," he said, "is far."

The priest had not uttered a word on the journey, but he said now, "I know who you are. I have spent the last six hours thinking about your name. It is not James Miller."

"It is James Miller," Grady Dunavant said, "and we are arriving at Hermosillo."

He called to Luz. She answered him, standing up with the fire at her back, and as he rode toward her, seeing her tall there against the fire, with the light on her hair, he wanted to shout.

"We have a windfall," he said. "We have a guest." He helped Father Cabrera from the saddle. He fumbled in the rucksack, took out the priest's breviary and put it in his hand. "He is Father Cabrera and he has kindly agreed to marry us."

The fire put a nimbus around the priest's cropped head. "Without eyes," he said, "I cannot read."

He was a powerful young man and by this time sufficiently enraged to do anything, once he could see what there was to do. "You seem to remember my name," Grady said. "It is probable, therefore, that you will remember what is in your breviary. Speak as you remember it, and God will forgive the circumstances and the mistakes."

The priest had to be prompted again, this time more pointedly, but he finally began to intone the words in his sullen *Sonoreño* voice. He looked very impressive with his broad shoulders, with the halo of light around his head and the wind stirring his robes. The stars were bright, floating high above the circle of the mountains. Grady looked at the stars and the firelight flickering over the pines and Luz standing behind him and thought, No man ever had a finer wedding.

The trip up the mountain and down the other side was longer to Grady Dunavant than the trip from Santa Fe. He was tempted to release Cabrera at the stream, but he went on until they reached the hills above Jim Wolfe's, headed west and circled back into a thicket of scrub oak, below a low range that ran at right angles to the Temescals.

Here he dismounted and untied the blindfold. The sky was turning gray; in the faint light the young priest looked at him hard and long.

"I will remember you," he said. "And your name as well, which is not James Miller."

"My thanks for your services," Dunavant said. "Ride on to Jim Wolfe's and refresh yourself. When the war is finished I will see that you get a fine image for your chapel."

He waited until the priest was out of sight.

It was midmorning before he made his way into the valley. The sun was butter-yellow on the grass, and the stream chuckled over the stones. Luz was by the fire cooking breakfast. He grounded the reins beside the house and walked toward her. She did not look up; she was pretending to be busy, but her hair was carefully combed and she wore a ribbon knotted through it.

"Good morning, Mrs. Dunavant," he said. He put his hand on her arm and straightened her up. "I forgot to kiss you last night—only two times in the last three days, as a matter of fact."

"We will eat now," she said, struggling in his arms, but not with great purpose. "And anyway, Mr. Dunavant, I am not married to you. Banns must be published. . . . "

He laughed, and the sound went up the mountain and came back in a clear echo. "You are as married as you ever will be," he said, lifting her from her feet and starting through the meadow.

# 32

METAL CRICKETS shrilled in the morning stillness. Pennons that tipped the lances fluttered in the wind. Rowels and *conchas* and silver headstalls flashed in the sun. The stallions strained against the Spanish bits. The victors were coming home.

With his boots thrust deep in the hooded stirrups, enormous in his iron-studded jacket, Don Saturnino led his men into the valley. Behind him was the triumph of Dominguez. The foe had been vanquished, driven from the field, forced to flee in ignominious defeat to their ships. In the whole of the South, from the Tehachapis to San Diego, not the tread of a single gringo desecrated the soil. Mayhap the call would come again, but the measure of the enemy had been taken; if need be, it would be taken once more, another time, finally, with the gringos dead on the field. In triumph and anticipation his nostrils flared, his long bony face, rimed with the dirt and sweat of battle, shone.

"*Ayee!*" he shouted into the morning.

"*Ayee!*" shouted his men.

"*Santiago!*" he cried.

"*Santiago!*" his men cried after him.

"*Santiago* and victory!"

"*Santiago* and victory!"

He gripped the high-peaked saddle with one hand, held the reins taut upon his thigh. Afar lay the mesa; the grazing cattle already showed his brand. The King's Highway stretched away beyond the reach of the eye, to the Hawk, to the Santa Ana, untrammeled and safe. He upended the skin of wine, filled his mouth and rinsed it, spat the wine into the dust, drank deeply and passed the skin.

"*Bien haya,*" Saturnino said. "Blessed is He."

"*Bien haya,*" the men said, drinking.

The clot of dust that hung above the trees grew into a horseman, a man in robes, a priest on a brown lathered horse.

"*Hola!*" Saturnino shouted, sending his voice ahead. "How goes it, Father? Have your ears detected the news? Do you savor it in the morning air? Is it writ upon the sky? *Hola,* there, Father Cabrera, speak up."

The priest turned and rode to meet him. His robe was bedraggled, a red welt lay across his round forehead. He looked at Saturnino like a man in a stupor, deprived of speech, his eyes restless in his head.

"You have heard?" Saturnino asked him.

The priest nodded, glanced toward the mountains in the south and those in the north, as if he were trying to get his bearings, and then at Saturnino.

"Where does a stream flow out of the mountains?" the priest said in his clipped husky voice. "Where is it that there is a stream and pines growing?"

Saturnino tugged at his chin strap and laughed. "This sounds like a riddle, Father. It is early in the day for riddles."

"This is no riddle," the priest said in anger.

"If it is not, I am at a loss to answer, for there are such things in many places. In the San Bernardinos, in the San Jacintos, the Santa Rosas, the Sierra Madres."

"In the Temescals?"

"Likewise there."

Saturnino passed the skin of wine. The priest refused it and said, "I have heard the voice of your daughter many times. Therefore, hearing it again, I am not one to be fooled."

Father Cabrera was looking at the mountains again. Saturnino spun one of his rowels against the stirrup and glanced at his men. The priest was a small partaker of wine, so this would not account for his actions. Had the young man become separated from his wits?

"Ride with us to the ranch," Saturnino said. "We will pursue the subject at leisure."

"When I say what I am about to say you will not wish to ride to the ranch."

Like a bolt traveling through the sky, the thought struck Don Saturnino. It was something to do with his daughter, this that the priest was saying. She had run away, hidden in the mountains, but why should the priest be uncertain?

"Enough of these riddles, Cabrera. Take hold of your wits and speak!"

He listened to the priest's story without a change of expression. When the tale was finished he said, "We go to the ranch. We will eat and get supplies and fresh horses. Then we will ride."

Spurring his stallion he left Cabrera sitting there looking around at the mountains, and thundered along the Camino Real. Let the priest wonder, he thought; it would serve him right for not daring to withstand the gringo's threats. Pines and a stream flowing. This could be many places, and yet only one place—on the lower ranch, the sheepherder's house in the valley, the small valley of the Temescals.

At the gate he threw his reins to Tiburcio and gave instructions to saddle fresh horses. He walked into the courtyard and straight to where his eagle sat in the sunlight that sifted down through the ash tree.

"Ho, here, Águila," he said. "How goes it with thee?"

The bird slanted a wary eye at him, looked at him from one side and the other, lifted its wings—they required clipping again, Saturnino noticed, for they had grown and almost spanned the nine feet they naturally were—and made a dry sound in its throat.

"Your plumage is not of a good color," Saturnino said. "You have not been fed as I ordered, but we will attend to that, sir."

He also wanted to see Guadalupe before he went into the mountains to be gone he knew not how long, but that must wait, like the feeding of his eagle.

His mother's voice called his name, shrilly, twice repeated. Swearing, he obeyed the summons. Carlota was in her room. She was sitting at the window, munching on a cake and sipping a cup of frothy chocolate.

"From the speed of your return," she said, "the clattering across the mesa, it appears that you are being pursued by the Americans. Or is it because you are anxious to see me, as you were before you left."

"For neither reason," he said. "Your friends now hide in ships."

"The news has preceded you. But about the business of the ships—other ships will come, until there are many, and when there are many you will need to ride forth again. Someday you will ride out and not return. In the meantime the ranch lacks attention."

He measured his voice and said, "The ranch lacks more than attention."

Carlota prodded her servant with her cane. He rose from the floor and went off for another bowl of chocolate. "She left three nights ago."

"With your permission."

"It was not asked. If it had been asked, it would have been given. I have seen much of the American. He is superior to others who have come here—to Don Julio and his city ways, to one and all of those who came with guitars and squatted in the courtyard and yowled like tomcats. She is gone and she is in good hands. The manner of her going fills me with envy, that it is not me instead. There is much to occupy your attention on the Hawk. Occupy it and do not molest them."

"You can depend on it, old lady, that I would go in search if I knew where to search. For no other reason do I swallow this insult."

He backed toward the door, the sharp eyes of his mother following him. "I have need to talk with Don Ricardo," he said. "A business of horses, which may require my presence until morning."

He had reached the door when she called him back. He stood in the doorway, choking on his anger but outwardly calm, and waited for her to speak.

"Guadalupe," she said, taking the bowl of chocolate from the Indian, "also has gone. She left several days ago with her brother and has gone to the Santa Rosas."

It was a blow that rocked him to his boots. He opened his mouth to speak and found no words. The room in which his mother sat, the earth beneath his feet, the world of sky and air, disappeared as if in a fiery breath. He backed away, stumbled at the edge of the *portale*, caught himself and strode on through the courtyard, past the eagle that beat its half-raised wings, on through the gate to his horse.

The mesa, the river, the sand dunes beyond, were all behind him before he was aware that he sat astride the stallion he had ridden into battle. The Temescals rose blue and misty on his right hand, but he did not cast one glance toward them. His eyes were fixed on the east, the dim, far shape of El Toro and the Santa Rosas.

It never occurred to him that Guadalupe would go anywhere except to the Santa Rosas; even when he stopped at noon for food and was told by his friend Torreon that a girl and a one-armed man had passed the ranch two days before and had taken a side trail toward Palomar, he was disposed to doubt the information. But Torreon was positive, and finally, though with reluctance, he set out toward Palomar.

He rode hard, having borrowed a fresh horse, and in late afternoon came on a man who said he had encountered the two Indians early that morning, camped beside the lake. Saturnino passed the lake after midnight and changed horses at Pala Mission as the sun rose. The way forked here, one trail leading to the sea, the other to Palomar, and having been told by the Indian who saddled his horse that the couple had left the Mission the night before and taken the trail to the sea, he spurred in the opposite direction.

His distrust of the Indian was justified, for he picked up their trail at the first ranch house, again after three hours of fast riding, and with the sun overhead saw them jogging along through a valley a mile or so below. He slackened his pace, dropped down the rise, took a short cut through an arroyo and came out once more on the trail a short distance behind them.

They had seen him and were riding faster now, at a hand gallop, on a horse without speed. The one-armed Indian he had long since recognized, from the descriptions gained along the way, as the servant who had left with Yris Llorente the night of the dance. The girl astride behind the Indian clasped him while she looked back at Saturnino over her shoulder, in a seizure of fear.

He presumed that the Indian carried a knife, and as he set rowels to his horse, unfastened the rope from the saddle horn and shook a loop in it, he saw the man reach down and fumble at his legging. The *reata* sped out flat and true. It hung in the air, settled as the Indian straightened, twanged taut when Saturnino snubbed the rope and brought his horse to a rearing halt.

They fell backward, the knife hurtling from the Indian's grasp, and lay stunned on the grass. It was a short task to secure their arms. He cut two lengths from the end of the rope and bound their arms to their sides. He knotted the ropes carefully. The girl lay on her side, not moving, but looking at him with her teeth bared.

She had never looked more beautiful to him. "It is something that I did not choose." He smoothed the hair back from her damp forehead. "It fills me with sorrow," he said.

The journey homeward to the Hawk was slow. Three long days, with every movement of his horse an agony to a body driven beyond endurance. He had slept little during the battle, none during the pursuit; he longed to lie down and sleep for days without end, to fill his stomach and sleep. Guadalupe rode bound beside him, alert to slip her ropes. The one-armed Indian walked behind him at the end of the *reata*. There would be no sleep until they came to the ranch, and little there, for he must then gather his men and search the Temescals.

They rode through Pala at night, stopped to drink and rode on. By the lake he looked at the sullen Indian and wondered why he bothered with him, why he didn't slit his throat there in the broad sun. On to the ranch of Torreon where Don Gilberto advised him to furnish the Indian with a horse. On with the sun beating down and Guadalupe cursing and silent by turns, and the mountains swimming in his gaze, and the plodding sound of the feet behind him bleeding now in the dust. On with the moon swinging up pale and unshapen. And then the river, the mesa, the house pale in the moonlight, silent, strange to his gaze.

The gate was open. He lifted Guadalupe down, taking care to escape her teeth, and bound her to the man, looping the rope about them. He staggered forward through the gate. His feet struck something and he stopped. It was a skin of wine. There was a fire burning low in the oven, but the courtyard was deserted. He dragged the pair to the storeroom and thrust them in and fell against the door.

He stood for a long time, leaning against the door, unable to move. There was the rank bitter smell of spilled wine in the air and he realized dully that the Indians had been celebrating the victory in his absence—the Battle of Dominguez. It seemed far away in another life and not a victory.

His throat was afire and he lurched toward the well, let the leathern bucket down and managed to retrieve it. He drank great gulps of the cool water and sloshed water over his face.

The eagle stirred above him, rustling the papery leaves of the ash. He dropped the bucket and said, "I am tired, señor, very tired, but I will find food and feed you." He looked around at the silent house. The smell of wine turned his stomach. My bird, he thought in sudden pity for himself, is the only friend I have. My wife gone many years ago. Guadalupe gone. My daughter gone. A man dishonored by his mother. Only one friend, except my son Roque.

He took a step away from the well. At first he thought he had stumbled and that the tree, which moved under his eyes, had fallen on him. The rustling was the leaves of the blue ash he had planted as a child. He raised his arm instinctively, feeling what he thought were leaves. Something was gripping his shoulders with the bite of iron. Then he was aware that the leaves were not leaves and that the iron gripping his shoulders was the talons of the eagle.

The cry that rose to his throat was cut off. He lurched and fell, hearing the chain snap. He clawed at his throat and tried to release the breath that swelled his chest to bursting, rose and fell again in a gushing pool that was hot beneath his fingers.

He called the name of his son. But the cry was a whisper, softened with the welling of blood. He said the name again and remembered that Roque was not at home. He cried the name of his mother. He clawed at the curved iron at his throat. In a final desperate moment his vision cleared and he saw across the pale shine of the courtyard two figures standing in the doorway. It was the door of the storehouse and the figures stood together bound as he had bound them.

Only now did he realize that he had not barred the door. It was a great fortune, he thought, that they were there, and he called to them. The figures did not move. In the silence he heard the sound of wings and, looking up with his last strength, feeling the iron beak no longer at his throat, saw the eagle rise and soar low over the roofs, to the north. But the sound of the wings grew louder and beat through the courtyard. He was being borne away, up and away toward the mountains.

Jorge lay on a sandbank beside the river. He lay sprawled on his back with one leg drawn up and the other dangling in the water. Under his head, rolled up for a pillow, were his clothes. His sombrero was pulled down over his eyes as a shield against the glare of the sun. The water ran shallow and warm around his ankle, and sand sifted lazily between his outspread toes.

He had been asleep but now, almost awake, he was watching, through half-opened eyes, a bird scratching around in the sallows about fifty paces away. It had long legs and a long curly beak, but its body was as plump as a well-fed chicken, just the right size for eating. He looked sidewise at his musket, lying across his boots. The musket was beyond his reach; he would have to rise to get it.

Instead, he closed his eyes. Finding that he had slept enough, he opened them again, wider this time. The bird was still poking around, pausing now and again to cock its head at him. A red curlew, he decided. This meant that the month was November, for he had never seen a red curlew in any other month except November.

His eyes opened wider, blinking in the glare of the river bottom. If it was November, it meant that his brother Roque had been gone about five months. It meant also that he would be coming home from Santa Fe before long. This thought brought him to with a start.

He saw the curlew take wing, two more from cover follow. They flew together, within easy shot, over his head. He did not even glance at his musket. Months had gone by and he had not yet taken the letter to Beatriz Galindo down beyond the Temescals. Roque had written the letter to her the night before he left for Santa Fe. "She expects me for a dance next Saturday night," Roque had said, giving him the letter.

"So deliver it to her before then. And do not forget." He had hung back in hope of a bribe from Roque, saying nothing. The plan was successful. Roque had said, "I will bring you a ring from Santa Fe." The pact had been made.

Jorge sat up. It was too late now to be informing Beatriz Galindo that Roque would not be present for the dance. The dances at the Galindo ranch were always long ones, lasting many days, but to his knowledge they never lasted five months. Not delivering the letter was a very foolish thing. Now he would not receive the ring from Roque. What he would receive would be a kick in the rear end.

He rose slowly. Momentarily, as his feet touched the sand, he forgot his difficulty. The sand was blistering hot. With a howl of pain he leaped from the sandbank into the water and stood there on one foot and the other until they both had cooled off. Then the difficulty began to plague him again.

Frowning, he glanced around at the river and the trees and the sky. Soon he would have to begin thinking of an excuse to give Roque. It was true that the summer had been an eventful one, more so than usual. First, Don Cristóbal had died—but suddenly he remembered that this had happened before Roque left; then there was the excitement when the Americans captured Los Angeles, the greater excitement when Señor Dunavant had come to the ranch, and greater than that, the night the American had fled; the disappearance of his sister, and greater than all, the death of his father. . . .

Jorge wiggled his feet deeper in the cool sand. He thought about his difficulty. It was certainly possible to inform Roque about all the things that had happened during the summer, and trust to fortune. But he should have a better excuse than this, a quick one, for his brother was quick-tempered and might deliver the kick before the story was completed.

The answer came to him. It was so simple that he wondered why he had not thought of it before. He squinted from under his sombrero at the sun. Early afternoon! By riding hard he could deliver the letter to Beatriz Galindo and return a couple of hours after supper. She had a younger sister who talked too much but who was very pretty. He could tell his grandmother that he had been hunting. A pang of joy ran through him as he thought how simple things were when you put your mind to them. In this world all you needed was a brain.

His back was covered with sand where he had sweated. The sun was still hot on his shoulders. It would be hotter riding into Brea Canyon where the wind seldom blew. A few minutes' delay would not hurt his plans, now that he had taken three months to make the trip. He ran and dived parallel to the water, skittering along on his stomach and flailing his arms.

For a while he lay floating. Next summer he would raise a dam of brush and logs and in the resulting pool learn to swim. He might be able to use this knowledge when he was out fighting Indians and his horse was shot out from under him while he was fording a river. It did not matter at the moment that all the rivers were only waist-deep in winter, knee-deep in the summer, when they were not dried up. The idea of learning to swim was good. Also his plan of going to the Galindos. He felt suddenly important and grown-up. He looked down at himself. He glanced down his cheeks at the black fuzz on his upper lip. He was a man all right.

With a yell he jumped to his feet and shook himself free of water. He put on his sombrero. As he stood there enjoying the feel of the sun on his shoulders, he heard the sound of giggling. He whirled around and saw, a hundred paces or so farther along, partly masked by willows, several Indian girls standing in the river. They were from the ranch. They had seen him and their giggles were meant to call his attention to the fact. They were naked. Through the thin green foliage their wet bodies gleamed red.

Jorge did not move. The giggling continued, broken by a scream or two; the wet bodies shone through the willows. One of the girls laughed. It was low-pitched and soft, but it was a taunt, a challenge meant for him. He settled the rawhide strap under his chin. He would show this girl, all of them, that they could not taunt a De Zubaran. He would give them the scare of their lives!

In one leap he gained the bank. He sneaked along quietly until he came to the willows. Whooping, he burst through the willows and ran down the stream toward the Indians who were already screaming and floundering in every direction.

He had intended only to give them a scare, but they all had disappeared in the brush, except one girl. She was running straight up the river. Her legs were plump and she was having trouble in the loose sand. She looked back over her shoulder in mock terror. He saw that it was Isabel, the new girl who had eyes like a deer. He was gaining. He would soon overtake her; he held back just enough so that they would both be out of sight of the other girls when he caught her.

As he ran, he heard the sound of hoofs. The sound came from the trail to the northeast, which crossed the river just in front of him. He slowed down, looking for a place to hide, but the hoofs came closer. A man on horseback rode down from the bank. Jorge glanced in the direction of the fleeing girl. He stopped in his tracks. There was no use in trying to hide when the horseman had seen him, had pulled up his mount and was gazing down at him not ten steps away.

Jorge looked at his feet. Then, with all the carelessness he could muster, he looked up at the rider. With a shock he saw that it was Juan Mitla, one of the men who had gone with Roque to Santa Fe. Roque had come back; was at this moment not far away! And here he was, standing in the river, naked, with the Indian girls giggling from the brush, the letter undelivered. Thinking of Roque and his own bare behind, he sidled toward the bank, ready to spring from sight among the willows.

Juan Mitla cleared his throat and slowly looked him over. "You grow," he said.

Jorge was in no mood for compliments. *"Jesús María!* Where is Roque?"

Juan Mitla's lizard eyes regarded him. "You have learned to swear also."

"Where?" Jorge repeated in a hoarse whisper, still ready to spring.

"At Malaspina's."

The muscles in Jorge's legs relaxed. He gave his sombrero a shove and took a deep breath. He threw back his shoulders. Juan Mitla was a servant. It was none of his business that he was running around naked chasing girls. Defiance flashed in his eyes, but he felt weak inside. It was one thing to face the world in your clothes, he thought, and another to face it with only your hat on.

Slowly, deliberately, he walked away. When he was out of sight he started to run. He ran as fast as his legs would carry him. He found his clothes and dived into them, buttoned his trousers while he ran toward his horse, his jacket while he galloped across the mesa. He had forgotten his shoes, but it now was too late to go back for them. It was even too late to hunt for the letter—he could not even remember where he had left it. Anyway, there was no point, come to think of it, to deliver a five months' old letter; he would simply tell Beatriz that Roque was in Santa Fe. The important thing was to get out of sight before his brother appeared.

He swept by the lower corrals, dodging trees by a hair; rode through a flock of guinea hens that rose screeching around him in a speckled cloud of feathers and dust. But as he reached the east flanker of the house, he looked up at the parapet. On the parapet, under its poncho, was the swivel gun. He pulled up his horse and sat for an instant looking at the gun. He had never fired it, but he knew how from watching Don Saturnino. His brother was coming home. There would never be a better occasion.

He unfastened his *reata* and, edging his horse near the wall, stood up in the saddle. He swung the rope in a wide loop over his head, upward and out. In three tries he lassoed the swivel gun, pulled tight on the rope and climbed hand over hand up the wall. He opened the trap door and went down the ladder. Tinder, powder, wads, ramrod—he had better not use shot. He sped up the ladder and uncovered the swivel gun. It shone in the sun like a jewel.

The charge was ready. He poured powder in the touchhole. For a second he stood screwing up his courage. He was going to receive a kick anyway from Roque, so he might as well receive one from his grandmother as well. For another second he debated whether or not to add another charge of powder. A double charge would cause a great hullabaloo. It also might burst the barrel. Leaning forward he swung the tinder. Fire belched out from the bell-shaped mouth, followed by smoke and a jarring crash which made his teeth jump. His feet stung as if he had stepped into a patch of horse nettles.

In the courtyard below he heard voices, screams. He covered the swivel gun and arranged the rope so a single jerk would release it. He slid down to his gelding, retrieved the rope and knifed into the saddle. A horse was trotting up behind him. He glanced around. It was Juan Mitla.

"A very big noise," Mitla said.

"Do not tell Roque that you saw me." Jorge drew his finger in a fierce threatening gesture across his throat. "Say nothing."

Juan Mitla nodded.

Jorge started off at a gallop across the mesa, his sombrero bouncing on his back, his bare feet spurring the horse. It was closer to the Galindos by way of the Temescals; there was no trail from this side and it was rough going, but he had no time to waste on a leisurely trip. He plunged into the brush and zigzagged up the mountainside, unmindful of the buckthorn tearing at his face. He lost his sombrero and did not pause to find it.

On the ridge he rode at a gallop, skirting to the south through the pines. Below him was the hidden valley, the stream, the sheepherder's house. He pulled up with a yank at the reins. There by the house was a man, and beside the man, another figure that might be a woman.

Jorge rubbed his chin. He sat for a full minute gazing down into the valley. Then quietly he drew away from the ridge, into the pines, and proceeded on his way, his eyes starting out of his head.

# 33

It was late afternoon and sultry hot. Stiff with the day's heat, the brittle grass crackled underfoot. The willows that bordered the stream gave off a rank breathless smell. A sea wind was blowing in the pines, but here in the lee of the mountain, where Grady Dunavant and his wife stood admiring the mud-and-stone chimney, the air was quiet.

"The best chimney in California," Grady announced.

Luz had helped with the carrying of stones and the mixing of the mud, and she was proud of her part, the broad graceful run of the stones they had carted up from the stream bed, and the smoothed-out mortar that was already beginning to dry.

"Some chimneys do not draw well," she said.

"This one will. It's built like the one at home."

"When can we put a fire in it?"

"Not until tomorrow. It's still green."

"A little one?"

"Tomorrow," he said. "And not in the daytime." Yesterday, while they were working on the chimney, he had seen a horseman on the north ridge. Last night he had sat up with his rifle across his knees, and he had watched the ridge on and off all day. He felt pretty certain that they had not been seen, but it was sensible to presume that they had, and not to advertise their presence by smoke. "We'll light a fire tomorrow night," he said, "and cook supper over it."

"We will have a special one," Luz said. "For the fireplace."

They had been eating well out of the provisions he brought back from Jim Wolfe's—he had made three trips now—and hunting was good. Beaver could be had for the taking; there was nothing better than stewed beaver tail, no matter what Luz thought. Deer were plentiful; there were mountain pigeons that trapped easily; doves, fat quail, and the stream was full of trout.

"A banquet," he said, "to celebrate the fireplace."

She was walking upstream and he followed her. The water was lower now, barely covering the stones, and running in thin trickles from pool to pool. In the first pool, at the head of the valley where the stream came out of the live rock, he had cut trees, laced them with brush and weeds and made a dam. There the stream backed up and formed a pool waist-deep.

A trout lay on the surface, his gills moving faintly, mouthing the water. The trout veered and shot under a rock as Luz dropped her shift. She walked into the pool holding her breath, with her arms stiff at her sides, for the water was cold. In the beginning, when they had first started swimming here after the work was done for the day, she would never go near the pool until he was in it. She would undress behind a rock and stay there, and then when his back was turned, she would sneak out and submerge until only her head showed. Afterward she would wait for him to dress, and when he wasn't looking, she would reverse the process, emerging from behind the rock fully clothed. It was all very tiresome, he had thought.

"Are you my wife," he asked her after she had carried on this way for several days, "or are you someone else's wife?"

"I am Mrs. Grady Dunavant," she said, making a pretty fair try at the name.

"Then why don't you act like it. Not like Mrs. Jones."

"Mrs. Jones? *Quién es?* Who is she?"

He had a hard time explaining this jibe, so he gave up teasing her, and the strategy worked.

He sat down now and took off his clothes and waded into the pool. For the last three days, since she had become emboldened, he had tried to teach her to swim. It seemed curious to him that she didn't know how, with a river running past the ranch, but she didn't.

She was standing in the middle of the pool, and he took her by the waist and turned her over, facing the sky, and showed her how to hold her body and her legs and arms, to float. She drifted for a moment and then went down and came up, gurgling water. He held her while she caught her breath and tried it again. After a while she caught on and floated as well as he did, but by that time he was chilled through.

He lay down in the grass, watching her, and let the sun soak into him, watching her and the sky that was beginning to show a thin skim of clouds. A chipmunk, no larger than his thumb, with an orange blaze down its back and tail, came out on a ledge above his head, peered at him, flicked its tail, scurried away and came back to peer at him again. The clouds were thickening.

He got up and looked at his wife. She was golden where she lay on the water, and dancing reflections played along her skin. "Strawberries are late this season," he said, feeling his blood stronger than the sun. "And of a good size."

She didn't know what he meant.

"A good size," he said, "but perhaps they aren't sweet."

She repeated the word strawberries, making a line between her heavy eyebrows as she frowned. "Strawberries? What is it?"

He made a gesture and pointed. Then she laughed and stood up, blushing. He was pleased to see that he could get a blush out of the emboldened Mrs. Dunavant.

He waded into the pool and lifted her up and held her hard against him and carried her out and set her down lightly on her feet in the warm grass.

"Do you love me?" she said.

He kissed her on the mouth.

"Will it be always?" she asked him.

He kissed her again.

"Not with the sun shining," she said, trying to pull away from him.

"With the moon or the sun, what is the difference?" he said. Someday she would get over this, too. He kissed her again and dried her body with his hands and began to help her into her clothes.

"It is not right in the sun," she said, but with a questioning note in her voice. "Is it, do you think?"

He said nothing.

When they were both dressed the skim of clouds had overridden the sky, and by the time they reached the house there was a nip to the air and a high thin sound was passing through the pines. The leaves of sycamores were still green, but winter had come, he thought; summer had changed into winter, in an hour, without a day between that could be called autumn.

The house looked different from the way it had the first day. He had made a real bed for them, using pine saplings for the frame and strips of deer hide fastened to the frame for slats. Out of one of the blankets Jim Wolfe had given him he sewed up a mattress and filled it with pine needles. There was a curtain around the bed, made of calico that he had also borrowed from Wolfe. But most of the calico Luz used to make a dado, waist-high, around the room to keep the gypsum he had washed the walls with from coming off on their clothes. From manzanita, the curly-fibered wood that grew on the benches, he had fashioned a rack for her to keep her dishes in and hung it over the fireplace. The wood was red and looked something like mahogany.

She lighted a fat deer-tallow candle now, filling the room with a soft glow, and glanced longingly at the dark fireplace. "A small one?" she said.

Wood was already stacked in the fireplace; he sifted powder over it from his horn and struck flint. The chimney was green and would probably crack under the heat. He had taken great pains with the chimney, as he had with everything in the house, but while he had been doing it, and now as he knelt there, he knew that the house was not for a lifetime, as he pretended. They were living from day to day, from hour to hour, and there was no point in pretension or in worrying about whether the chimney would crack or not.

They did not hear the horse coming down the mountain. They were sitting on the bench in front of the fire, with their legs thrust out into the heat, watching the flames licking up the chimney, joking and laughing with each other over the tongue of smoke that licked out to the under edge of the arch, hung there and then retreated. They heard nothing until there was a knock on the door. Grady took his rifle from the corner and stood where he was while Luz opened the door.

A yellow waning light hung over the valley, and against it, in sharp outline, stood Jorge de Zubaran. As a gasp of relief came from his sister, he walked into the room, his broad hat on the back of his head, clanking his spurs and looking as important as he knew how. His gaze moved over the room, the bed, the whitewashed walls, Grady Dunavant, the fire, and finally fixed on Luz.

"I saw you yesterday from the ridge," he said. "I saw two people and no hole in the roof and I knew who it was."

Luz looked at Grady; there was mingled relief and anger on her face and, plainer than either, cunning.

"And then you went home," she said, "and told everyone what you had seen."

Jorge straightened his shoulders and, remembering his hat, took it off. "I am not one who gabbles," he said slowly and with considerable dignity. "What I know I keep to myself." His gaze drifted over the room again. "I keep it to myself, though it is not proper that you should be here with a man who is not your husband." He scowled at Grady, who to keep from laughing turned and set his rifle in the corner. "I have come, therefore, to take you home."

"We're man and wife," Grady said. "Married by Father Cabrera."

Momentarily this took the wind out of Jorge's sails, but he wasn't convinced. "I have not seen or heard of the banns."

"By a special dispensation," Luz said, "the banns were omitted."

Jorge was not to be deflated so easily. "I have never heard of banns being omitted."

"They were omitted with Carlos and Teresa. You recall that, do you not?"

Jorge didn't think that he did, though they were his own cousins. He took another tack. "There is much that has happened at the Hawk which you do not know."

"I know of Don Saturnino," Luz said, crossing herself.

"But of Roque you do not know."

"Not of Roque," Luz said, allowing her brother this one triumph. "What passes with Roque?"

Grady knelt and stirred up the fire, and while Jorge pondered an answer, he considered again the argument he had had with Luz when Wolfe brought the news of her father's death. He had wanted her to go to the funeral, but she had refused to go without him. "We can both go to the Hawk," she said, "and remain. You will not be molested by Roque when he returns or by any of the others. Wolfe is not molested, is he?" The idea of hiding behind a woman's skirts did not appeal to him, and he said so, and there the matter had ended.

He stood up, with his back to the fire, waiting for Jorge to speak.

"What passes with Roque?" Luz said.

"He is home," Jorge burst out. "It is almost two days now. And without sheep. The American soldiers came to Santa Fe when they were ready to leave with the sheep, so they left the sheep and rode fast for home."

"Did your brother bring any other news about the soldiers?" Grady asked.

"They march to California," Jorge said. "There are many of them and they have cannon. Roque and Juan Mitla hid outside the city and saw them as they rode past. Then my brother rode fast for home. And he is here and there will be a battle when they arrive, and the Americans will be beaten as they were beaten at Dominguez."

Jorge wouldn't stay for supper. Grady walked outside with him. "What has happened to Tepeyollotl?" Grady asked.

"He is married to Guadalupe. They are both at the ranch." From the saddle the boy looked down at him, setting the braided strap under his chin. "I will investigate the business of the banns," he said, "and if it is not true I will return for my sister." He picked up the reins; as he rode off through the dusk, he said over his shoulder, "And I do not believe the story of the rubies."

That night when Luz was in bed and sleeping, Dunavant took his rifle from the corner and sat down on the bench and cleaned it. Later on, lying beside his wife, he thought about the coming battle, and during the next day it was on his mind, and at the end of the week as he was making plans to go to Jim Wolfe's, Wolfe rode in. They were eating supper in front of the fire. Wolfe had little to say during the meal, and Dunavant knew that he had come with news that he didn't want to repeat in front of Luz. When they had finished eating, he made an excuse, went out of the house and took Wolfe down to the stream.

"You've heard about the troops coming from Santa Fe?" he said.

Wolfe nodded. "Genril Kearny," he said. "Heard about it this morning. Horse traders comin' from Sonora met up with the genril and a hundred men down by the Colorado. He's aimin' toward San Diego, ridin' mules and well tuckered out. Ought to get there next week."

They sat by the stream and talked and smoked their pipes out. Wolfe thought that General Kearny would end the war in California before Christmas, that by the first of the year the country would be at peace, and when he mounted his horse the last thing he said was "We'll throw a big fandango for the genril."

Dunavant listened to the hoofs climbing the mountain. He stood there listening until they were gone. Then he went back toward the light that shone through the door.

Luz was sitting on the bench in front of the fire, though he would have sworn he had seen her standing inside the door when he was walking up from the stream. She sat with her feet together and her hands in her lap, as if she had been sitting there all evening. He sat down beside her.

She didn't look at him. After a moment she said, "What did Jim Wolfe want of you?"

"Nothing," he answered.

"He came all this way to say nothing?"

"Oh, just news about what's going on."

He looked sidewise at her. She had full lips, but they were pressed together now, as thin as a Green River blade. She was looking straight ahead into the oak blaze.

"He has some more calico, if you want it," Grady said.

She didn't want any more calico and she said it by remaining silent. She sat and looked into the fire and made no comment on anything he said. Finally she got up, went to the bed and pulled the curtains closed after her.

The wind was backing smoke down the chimney, and he could hear it in the pines, a long-drawn-out sigh, oft repeated, and there was a chill in the room even with the fire going. He waited for her to get into bed and go to sleep. She was setting her boots on the floor. She was hanging up her clothes on the pegs he had fixed for her. He heard the thongs on the bed squeak as she sat down. She would be combing her hair now, sitting in her shift and holding her hair to one side and combing it, then moving her head and combing the other side.

The horses were whickering and he went outside and examined the picket pins. The sky was heavy, with no stars showing, and the wind had a bite and a feel of dampness. When he got back to the house the room was quiet except for the wind and the noise of the fire. He waited for a time, listening for her breathing, before he walked over to take his rifle from the corner.

The rifle was not in the corner. He looked around the room for it and went outside and looked, and then realized that Luz had hidden it. She was lying on her back looking up at the ceiling when he pulled the curtains.

"Where is the Hawkins?" he said.

"What do you want with it?"

"It needs cleaning."

"You've cleaned it three times the last week."

"It needs cleaning again."

"I don't know where it is," she said, and turned with her back to him.

He found the rifle finally under the bed and sat down in front of the fire. He held the rifle stock between his feet, the long barrel clamped between his knees, stretched out so that he could get a purchase on the wiping stick. The rod, wrapped in a rag that had been soaked in deer fat, came out clean. He threw the rag in the fire, placed the rifle across his knees and examined the flint. He had used the flint only once, but he replaced it with a new one.

The thongs on the bed made a faint sound. "When is it that you are leaving?" Luz said.

"Who told you that I was leaving? I haven't said so."

Finished with the flint, he fixed the set of the trigger, adjusting it to a feather touch. He pushed back the brass lid in the side of the stock. There were twenty pieces of linen in the patch box; he took out one, closed the box, picked up his powder horn from the floor and held it to the light. It was a handsome flask, made from a black buffalo horn, shaved thin as isinglass, so that every grain of powder was visible.

Luz said, "Will you leave in the night without saying good-by?"

"No," Grady said.

He put his rifle and powder horn away and undressed, snuffed out the candle and lay down beside her. The fire had died down and the wind was coming strong out of the chimney. She lay with her back turned to him, jammed up against the wall. He had decided to say nothing to her until morning. He watched the embers in the fireplace and lay quiet.

"Are you awake?" she said.

"How could I be asleep when I just came to bed?"

"Grady?"

"Yes."

"You do not have to go."

"There will be no peace for anyone until the fighting is over," he said.

She had turned, facing him. He could smell her hair and he could see out of the corner of his eye the glint of embers in it. Her body was touching his; now her face was against his shoulder and she was sobbing. He put his arm around her and held her against him, feeling his heart pound against hers.

In the morning when they rode out of the valley the ridges were covered with snow and the lower slopes held a thin sprinkling of snow that was already melting. From the ridge they saw that the far mountains were white, shadowed with blue in the canyons. The sky was clear; the sun shone like brass.

At the bottom of the slope he kissed her and watched from the brush while she rode onward toward the Hawk. Then he spurred his horse and, keeping away from the Camino Real, headed into the south.

# 34

At the end of two hours he saw a string of Spanish lancers on the trail below him, riding in the same direction. They disappeared, but a short time later he heard the clacking of metal crickets and saw six more horsemen gallop after their comrades. A few minutes passed and another band, with pennons flying, pounded north along the Camino Real. After that he holed up until dark.

Riding all night he came to Tom Risk's before dawn the next morning. The King's Highway ran through the ranch, and though the house was a mile or more off the trail, hidden behind a wooded spur, he waited for sunrise before approaching it. There were no horses at the gate. In answer to his summons a small door in the gate slid open and a pair of glittering eyes regarded him through the slit. An Indian wanted to know who he was, and after he was told said that Señor Risk had gone to San Diego, and that he had been instructed to let no one in.

The matter would have ended there except that Delfina Risk overheard the conversation. She was a sister of Jim Wolfe's wife, a few years older than Mrs. Wolfe but just as pretty, with a fine figure and big Spanish eyes, and since she was married to an American, friendly to the cause. She cuffed the Indian over the ears for his stupidity and sent him to the kitchen to fetch breakfast. She led Dunavant into the house; while he was eating she answered his question about the lancers he had seen on the trail. They were on their way to a rendezvous with the forces of Andrés Pico at San Luis Rey.

"But why?" Grady asked. "Has General Kearny entered California?"

Delfina Risk knew nothing about General Kearny. "It is Commodore Stockton," she said. "He is in San Diego. He has dispersed the garrison there and set his marines to building fortifications above the town and makes plans for a march on Los Angeles."

"Then Pico is at San Luis Rey to head him off?"

"That is what my husband thinks. That is why he started off yesterday for San Diego—to warn Commodore Stockton that the lancers are at San Luis Rey."

At this moment Dunavant changed all his plans. He had intended to go to Renaldo Chavez' and wait there for word of General Kearny and his army marching in from Santa Fe, but Chavez' ranch was near the place Pico's forces were gathering. It was a good place to stay away from. His best course was to take the back trail for San Diego.

He slept until afternoon, ate again and borrowed a fresh horse.

Delfina Risk gave him her blessing and a message for Luz. "You are fortunate," she said standing at the gate, "in your choice of wives."

He looked at her, wondering how she knew; not longer, however, than a moment or two, for he was aware, when he thought of it, that this sort of thing would travel fast from one end of the valley to the other.

"They have the ranch next to us," Delfina Risk said. "South."

"Who?"

"Señor and Señora Fraser. You are fortunate," she repeated.

Grady Dunavant, agreeing that he was, lifted himself to the saddle. He was riding away when she asked the question. She asked it again while he sat staring at her.

Cesaire Curel!

"He came to the gate last night and asked for Señor Fraser. I did not let him in. I did not like his beard or his eyes. He rode away. South, toward the Frasers. He was angry because I would not open the gate to him."

"Which way is the ranch?" Dunavant asked calmly.

"Oh, it is more than ten miles, and out of your way."

"Where is it? On the trail?"

"Not on the trail. Beyond the first stream eastward. But it is very far. *Muy lejos.*"

"It is not far," he said.

She warned him with her eyes. "It is much out of your way."

"Nor out of my way," he said, tipping his hat.

He rode fast, his shadow lengthening in front of him. The country was rough, dense with toyon, and it was night before he crossed the stream and saw the lights glimmering among the trees. The house sat on a low hill. It was small, with the walls of several rooms unfinished, and a corral below the hill. There were only a few horses in the corral, but one of them was white and it looked like the horse he had seen at Dominguez.

He slipped to the ground, tethered his gelding in the brush where it wouldn't be found, took another look at the white horse, and then let down the bars and chased all the horses out of the corral and into the brush. He put the Colt in his side pocket and climbed the hill, walking carefully, and stopped outside the square of light that fell through the window. He could see Camilla sitting against the far wall and he could hear a voice, a man talking, but not Cesaire Curel. It was possible, he thought, that Curel had already gone. But something, some strong instinct, told him that the man he was looking for was now sitting less than twenty feet away.

In the dim light he examined the Colt and put it back in his pocket and knocked on the door. He could wait outside or somewhere along the trail, waylay him as he rode past, but he preferred it this way, openly, whatever the chances, so the murderer of San Saba would know. . . .

Fraser came to the door, and Grady walked past him before the first surprise he had ever seen on that face could change to a smile of greeting. Camilla was on her feet, coming toward him. The room was smaller than it seemed from the outside, but it was well furnished; she apologized for it, as he knew she would. Curel was standing by the window, dressed in a blue, scarlet-faced jacket. The candlelight made his face look paler than it was, pale as the gloves he held in his hand.

Grady sat down in the chair Fraser pushed toward him. "I was over at Risk's," he said to Camilla, but watching Curel. "Heard you were here and came over. It's a nice place. You've done a lot in a short time."

"We've just begun," Camilla said, apologizing again for the way everything looked. "We're building three more rooms."

Camilla settled herself and began to tell him their plans for the house and ranch, but he was not listening. He was watching Curel who had seated himself on a sofa near the door. Curel was never without a weapon, the over-and-under derringer. It was small, short-barreled, and he carried it in the pocket of his waistcoat. The bulge was visible now against his tight-fitting jacket.

"What happens to the title of the ranch," Dunavant asked Fraser after Camilla had finished, "when the United States takes over California?" Fraser wanted to know what he meant. Fraser had recovered from his first surprise; he asked the question in his blandest manner, knowing perfectly well what Dunavant meant. "I mean," Dunavant said, "that Pico made a lot of grants the day before he left Los Angeles and went into hiding. They're not going to be legal when Stockton is back in Los Angeles."

"When will that be?" Fraser asked.

"Soon. In a few weeks. You know that Kearny is marching from Santa Fe."

"Not in a few weeks," Curel said. "Or in months. You seem to have forgotten Dominguez. There will be more precisely like it."

"Pomeroy," Camilla said, "can't we have a glass of wine?"

A shadow of annoyance, Dunavant noticed, passed over Pomeroy's face, but he rose obediently and left the room.

"He's very hospitable really," Camilla said. "But he has so much on his mind, with the house and everything."

Dunavant thought she sounded like her mother; he was glad for the second time that he wasn't Peter Pomeroy Fraser.

Curel said, "I didn't finish our conversation at the Hawk. Your departure . . ."

"Both are in the past."

"But the past is never finished."

"It would not interest Mrs. Fraser," Dunavant said. "We'll have an opportunity to finish the conversation another day. In the next week or two."

They looked at each other across the length of the room. Fraser passed between them, carrying a tray filled with glasses, and Curel stood up and drank leaning against the door. When Dunavant had finished his wine he rose, put his glass on the tray, picked up his hat and said that he was riding back to Risk's. Fraser and Curel had some plan on; they had been discussing it when he came in—he was certain of it. The plan wouldn't work out, and he'd meet Curel somewhere on the trail. He said good night to Camilla.

"By no means," said Fraser. "A long ride at this time of night! Wouldn't think of it. You'll not be so comfortable here, but safer, my boy, with the country full of soldiers. We'll have to put you up with Colonel Curel here, but you're old friends. . . ." He took Dunavant's hat out of his hands. "I can assure Colonel Curel that you don't snore."

Fraser laughed his quiet pleasant laugh and Camilla went bustling off, looking more like her mother every minute, to prepare the bed. Dunavant glanced at Curel. His expression had not changed. Dunavant wondered if he were thinking the same thoughts that at this moment ran like fire through his own blood. He would stay, but sometime during the night, before dawn, he would leave—either he would leave or Cesaire Curel.

The room was large, in the wing of the house that was unfinished. He presumed from the fact that there were four beds that it had been used for servants, and that the servants had been routed out to make a place for him and Curel. He had gone to bed first, snuffing out the candle, and he lay now, dressed and with his Colt lying beside him, waiting for Curel to come in.

There was no glass in the window and through it came a chill wind that smelled of rain. He could hear the sound of horses in the brush. The window though small was big enough to get through, but he had found it barred when he examined it before he got into bed. A half-moon shone through it and the bars laid shadows across the earth-and-blood floor.

He was not sure now that Curel intended to stay all night. Curel might be waiting for him to go to sleep or for the chance to slip away. There was something faintly unconvincing about Fraser's invitation. He had thought so at the time; glancing at Curel when the invitation had been made, he had seen a curious fleeting glitter in Curel's gaze. He had known then that Curel would never leave the ranch while there was a chance of being waylaid, surprised on the trail, and he would never ride out alone.

It was past midnight when Curel came to bed. He came in with a candle and undressed, laying his clothes out on one of the beds. He took a long time about it, arranging everything carefully, and fastened a silk bandage around his beard. Dunavant lay on his side and watched him. Curel never once glanced in his direction; finally he snuffed the candle and lay down.

The room was quiet and all Grady could hear was the ticking of his watch. The horses had moved farther off into the brush. The moon, setting behind the hills, still cast dim shadows. He lay and did not move, breathing slow and deep, the Colt beside him. He knew now that Curel was biding his time, waiting until he was asleep. Otherwise Curel would have made a break for it; he might have tried and found that the corral was empty. It was possible, Grady thought, that he had gone to the corral and come back only when he saw that the horses had been let loose.

He was watching the bed where Curel lay, and an hour might have passed when he heard the leather thongs creak. The moon had gone down and he could see nothing in the room, but he was certain that Curel was on his feet. There wasn't a sound but Curel was moving somewhere in the room. Dunavant got slowly out of bed. He wanted to say something, some final word to express the hatred he had borne for years, which was now a bitter dryness in his throat, but a single word would betray his position.

Curel was less than three paces away when Grady first saw the outline of his figure—his back half turned. Then Curel flung himself at Grady. The first slash of the knife caught Dunavant's sleeve. As the arm went up again Dunavant shot waist-high. The explosion beat against the walls. Then he heard the slug strike the wall and skitter back across the floor. He thought for an instant that he had missed, before he saw the man crumple to his knees.

He went to the door, expecting Fraser or Camilla, but the hall was empty. There was a light burning in the living room and he walked toward it. Fraser was standing at the door. He held a half-finished glass of wine in his hand and there was a frown on his bland forehead. In his other hand he held a pistol. It was a long-barreled Colt and he held it as if he knew what he was doing, as if he had done this before, but there was still a faint trace of apology about his manner.

Dunavant kept walking toward him. "I am going out the door," he said to Fraser, "and if you want to live you'll not use that gun. The only reason I don't shoot you is that there are worse punishments."

Fraser fired. The bullet burned across Dunavant's shoulder. The butt of the Colt caught Fraser on the temple and he went down, clutching the glass of wine. The wine spilled out on the rug. At the end of the hall Camilla was screaming; it was the same sound that Kate Howland had made the night of the brawl in the gambling room.

Dunavant let himself out and ran stumbling down the hill.

He rode out the next morning on a trail which led through the Indian village of Aguanga and through Warner's ranch, and eventually through the wild uninhabited country east of San Diego. When he rode into the Aguanga the Indians were running around in all directions. None of them spoke Spanish, and since he knew nothing of their tongue, the best he could get was a gesture indicating there were horses moving out of the village toward Warner's. After more than an hour on the trail, breathing dust, he caught the sound of hoofs and the tinkle of a bell mare.

He nudged his mount along carefully, shortening the distance, so that little by little he could hear more than the sound of hoofs and the tinkle of the bell. On the frosty air was the sound of laughter, then voices, American voices.

The tall young man in the rear was a lieutenant. His name, he said in answer to Dunavant's greeting, was Davidson, Davidson of the First Dragoons, and he wanted to know, turning sidewise in the saddle, who the hell Grady Dunavant was. He was lean as a cusk, and wore a greatcoat turned high around a thin sun-blackened face, and below the torn edges of the coat one trouser leg was chewed off at the knee. He wore a spur on a boot that showed bare toes through a broken seam. Lieutenant Davidson had a fistful of *tortillas* and a fistful of something in his mouth. His lips were sun-cracked and he spoke around whatever it was in his mouth in a slow, good-natured voice.

"Where you riding?" he asked.

"Wherever you're camped."

The lieutenant pointed with his fistful of *tortillas* in the general direction of a mountain where pines threw long morning shadows on snow, and went on eating, chewing and swallowing like a man who hadn't eaten for a week.

There were twenty or more soldiers riding on either side of the herd of Spanish horses. They were all sun-blackened like the lieutenant, in torn faded uniforms, and some of them wore spurs on bare heels. In the lead was another officer who looked familiar, with sandy hair showing under a broad turned-up campaign hat.

"Andrés Pico and his lancers are camped at San Luis Rey," Dunavant said.

The lieutenant swallowed, not interested in the information. "They're all over from here to Santa Barbara, according to Warner's major-domo, except down at San Diego. In two weeks' time we'll have them all cleaned out. In less time than that if they don't fight, and Carson says they won't."

Dunavant kept his memories to himself. He wondered if Kearny's dragoons would have to learn the same lesson that Mervine and his marines had learned at Dominguez.

"Is that Carson out front?" he said.

"Yes, and sorer than hell."

Dunavant rode forward around the thin young men in tattered uniforms on half-wild Spanish horses. All of them were eating; they looked at him out of faces that were hard and confident, fined down to bones and skin. They looked at him on his fat red gelding, at his clothes and the brassbound Hawkins, and said nothing.

Christopher Carson was riding a hammerheaded mare that rolled a saucer eye as Dunavant came up.

"Thought you were in Washington, lieutenant," Dunavant said.

Carson spat over the cocked-back ears of his mare. "Call me Bub. This damn army gives me a gripe. Wisht I'd never heerd tell."

Carson spat again in disgust and looked ahead to a valley backed by hills rolling on to the mountains where snow lay. A stream ran through the valley and among the live oaks beside the stream rose the camp smoke of the Army of the West.

He looked at the men by the fires and said, "Ridin' hell-bent-for-Betsy, with nigh to a thousand miles behind—close on sixty miles one stretch with nary water—ridin' hard and on schedule, with messages for the President."

Carson started to spit, changed his mind and went on. "Knew when I seen the dust somethin' was up. Hit war Kearny and his damn dragoons, nigh on three hundred, and going for Californy, one hundred and fifty mile out of Santa Fee."

"And here you are," Dunavant said.

Lieutenant Carson wasn't listening. "Knew when I seen the dust, for sartin when I seen Kearny. Looked at me and said, 'You're goin' back, Mr. Carson.' Tole him that I had messages for Frémont's family in Washington, not writ down but in my head. Dispatches for President Polk. Tole him that Californy was peaceful as a dead coon. Tole him that hit was nigh on a lifetime ere I seen my wife in Taos. He jes' looked at me and said, 'Fitzpatrick can take the dispatches. You're goin' back, Mr. Carson.' "

The lieutenant fell silent for a moment as they rode down toward the camp, his gaze traveling over the gaunt men, and General Kearny who stood beside the ranch house with his back turned to the wind.

At the corral Carson said, "Sent back two hundred of the men thar at Socorro, and Fitzpatrick and my dispatches."

"You got your commission from Stockton," Dunavant said, "Why didn't you tell the general that Stockton was in charge in California and under orders from the Navy?"

"Never thought," Carson said. "Wisht I had afore now. Wisht I'd said it thar. Had a good notion to desert, but didn't. Jes' came along with my tail 'tween my legs, eatin' mule meat, makin' dry marches, watchin' stock die like flies, drinkin' water fit to make a man puke."

He looked at the horses being driven into the corral. "Not much good, nohow. Took 'em at Aguanga. Wisht I'd thought to tell Kearny what you said. Mebbe it ain't too late."

"It's pretty late, lieutenant."

Carson spat in the dust. "Jes' call me Bub."

# 35

Having left Fort Leavenworth June 16, captured Santa Fe and sent back two thirds of their troops and all of their wagons at Socorro on the strength of Kit Carson's news that California was pacified, having forded the Colorado and made the crossing of the Devil's Highroad, where the spined agave tore their clothes to ribbons, where they got their first water after thirty hours, and gone on through another desert where most of their remaining stock died, and the ones that lived were urged forward by one man tugging at the halter and one pushing from behind, having rested for a day in the beautiful valley of Agua Caliente—seven men eating one sheep at one sitting and everyone bathing in the sulphur springs—the Army of the West, mounted on half-dead mules and wild horses stolen at Aguanga, under the command of Brigadier General Stephen Watts Kearny, one hundred and twenty men and five civilian volunteers, rode out of the valley on the morning of December 4.

The day had dawned murky and by the time they were on the trail to Santa Ysabel rain was falling heavily. Deep in their greatcoats, the men hunched in their saddles. The rain dripped from their hats and ran down thin dark faces. Many were close to naked and the rain, dripping down their beards, lay cold against their flesh.

They were a silent and sorry-looking outfit, Grady thought; it was only in their eyes, sunk in their heads, and on the thin faces that there was any hint that these Missouri farm boys were ready for battle.

Dunavant had given his red gelding to Captain Johnson. He was mounted on a roan mare that stepped sidewise under a hard bit and would do nothing under a soft one. His Hawkins was sheathed in a piece of sheepskin. In his pocket he carried a small leather sack of deer fat, which Luz had told him to rub on his chest if he caught a cold, and which was already beginning to spread grease on his trousers.

General Kearny, who had refused the offer of the gelding, was out in front on a gray horse that pricked its ears at every sound. There were brass rowels on his boots. He rode straight as if it weren't raining. His blue eyes, colder than the eyes of Frémont, were fixed down the valley. No one—not General Kearny or any of the officers, Carson least of all—had much faith that the Californians would stand and fight. "They're a passel of ould women," Carson had summed it up. Grady wondered again, thinking of what Carson had said, if this were to be another Dominguez.

They camped the night in the abandoned Mission of Santa Ysabel, which now belonged to a deserter from an English merchantman. Mr. Stokes had fixed himself up a comfortable house and everyone slept out of the rain in what had once been the chapel of the church. There was hot food for everyone except the officers. That night Lieutenant Emory tried to get a position on a star with his Gambey sextant but failed, and in the morning Captain Johnson sat down and made the last entry in his diary:

December 4. Marched at 9, and took route for San Diego, to communicate with naval forces and to establish our depot . . . Marched 15 miles in a rain, cold and disagreeable. . . . We heard of a party of Californians, of 80 men, encamped at a distance from this; but the informant varied 16 to 30 miles in his accounts, rendering it too uncertain to make a dash on them in the dark, stormy night; so we slept till morning.

In answer to a message General Kearny had sent to San Diego two days before, Stockton had dispatched thirty-five men under Captain Gillespie and Lieutenant Beale, and in the morning as the army was moving toward Santa María, they came on these men. Gillespie confirmed the existing information about Pico and his lancers, but late at night when they made camp in a wooded canyon Indians brought word that Pico had moved and was now nine miles away at San Pasqual.

The men crouched by the fires in the rain, waiting for the parley of officers to break up. Corporal Ramsdale allowed as they should go on since all the back trails to San Diego lay beyond them. Sergeant Moore was for pressing on too. "Maybe in the foothills we kin lick the hull mess in five minutes." It was hard to see Private Fiel across the fire, the rain and mist were so heavy, but his voice came back in agreement. Then someone, coming out of the dark, said that Captain Moore was going to take eighty men and attack. Before anyone was up that was all changed and instead Lieutenant Hammond and fifteen men were sent out to reconnoiter the enemy. "Never seen ary a general who could make up his mind," Corporal Ramsdale said and pulled his greatcoat over his head.

Grady rubbed deer fat on his chest and threw the rest away. When Lieutenant Hammond came back, having encountered some of the Californians sleeping in a hut at the foot of the canyon, and by accident alarming them and leaving an army blanket and a jacket behind him, the call "To horse!" was sounded. Grady rose in the rain and found his mount. When he was in the saddle he looked at his watch; it was two o'clock. In front of him Lieutenant Emory was worrying because two nights had passed and he hadn't been able to use his sextant. He took a reading, though, and found that the temperature was at freezing. Everyone was glad that General Kearny had decided to attack.

Emory rode forward; gradually the column lengthened out, and Grady, in the rear with the other volunteers and the baggage, could hear the vidette far below them. His horse was still stepping sidewise, and during all of the nine miles down the canyon he kept thinking of the red gelding he had lent Captain Johnson, wishing he had it back, or another one half as good.

Captain Abraham Johnson, astride the best horse he had ridden since he had left Fort Leavenworth, shook the water from his hat and remarked to General Kearney who was riding beside him that the rain seemed to be lessening.

Kearney hoped that the rain would continue, for then their movements would be concealed. It was to be a dawn surprise by Indian tactics with the objective the taking of the enemy's horses. He hoped that the rain would keep up. He looked at Lieutenant Carson.

Carson said, "You can't rightly tell about Californy weather." A man can't tell about nothing, he thought.

Captain Johnson was listening to the mutter of saddle leather, his eyes fixed beyond the twelve men riding in front of him, when he saw the shine of breakfast fires. The air was thick, though the rain had stopped, and cold. The reek of his soggy greatcoat filled his nostrils. He looked at the fires, waiting for Kearny to give the orders, and planned how he would dry his coat.

Kearny had moved beyond him to the head of the column. The command for a trot and then a charge came with the first sign of dawn; hearing it, Captain Johnson spurred forward on his red gelding, taking Carson with him. The twelve men followed, Lieutenants Warner and Emory and General Kearny fell in behind them. The spearhead of the attack galloped down the slope.

Through the gray mist Captain Johnson saw the lounging pickets rise from the campfires and, after a moment of confusion, reach for their lances. They were running for their horses. They were on their horses, fleeing in a wide circle down the valley. His hand was on the hilt of his sword, the braided rawhide that the sun had made as hard as wood. Shouting to his men he yanked on the sword; a second time and a third. The sword was rusted in its scabbard. The fleeing pickets had wheeled on rearing horses, and as he heard the cry of "*Santiago*" he drew the pistol and shouted again to the men galloping behind him. He heard the dull report of a musket and, all in one lengthened second, the ball struck.

Lieutenant Carson had slipped his rifle from its holster. As the musket ball drilled Johnson through the forehead, he pressed the trigger, pressed it again and realized that the powder was wet. Holding the rifle, he prepared to use it for a club, but the next instant his horse stumbled and he was falling. He fell on his rifle and it broke into two pieces. Scrambling for his life beneath the on-plunging hoofs of the advance guard, he crawled to one side and sat dazed in the grass.

The mist lay heavy. Through it, moving, he thought, like the legs of a girl under a thin summer dress, he saw the vague figures of the enemy riding in, lances raised. General Kearny took a lance thrust in the shoulder and fell from the saddle; took another thrust rising to his knees. Only two shots had been fired by the Californians—one had killed Captain Johnson, a soldier had been badly wounded by the other. The lancer, turning, was riding to lance Kearny for the third time. A ball from Emory's pistol knocked him to the ground.

Carson saw a rifle lying in the grass and ran for it. The powder was wet and it wouldn't fire, but he kept it for a club and looked around him, his eyes groping in the mist. The enemy had wheeled on their tough-muscled horses, away from the men who lay sprawled on the sloping ground. François Ménard dead. Captain Johnson dead. The others, all of them except two, wounded. The advance guard had been cut to pieces in three minutes of fighting.

Nary minute more than three, Carson thought, holding the rifle that wouldn't shoot. And the guard gone.

He heard the voice of Ben Moore and, whirling, saw the captain at the top of the hill looking down from his white horse, and as he looked Moore led the second wave into the valley. The Californians were racing for its lower end. Captain Moore swept past him, and Captain Gillespie, and soldiers shouting fit to split a man's ears. They strung out in a long line. The enemy was retreating. Captain Moore was a half mile past him. Carson found a horse and pounded down the trail in pursuit.

The Californians had ridden up a side trail, had disappeared, then out of the mist they came, a quarter of mile in front of him, in the rear of Ben Moore's forces, shouting "*Santiago*" again and wielding their lances. Captain Moore was down, lanced eight times, mostly through the kidneys. And Gillespie, thrashing with his sword, was down. And more soldiers than he could count were twisting in the grass. The mist was clearing a little and he couldn't see any of the foe—they had faded like Indians—but he could hear the sound of hoofs climbing the hills to his right.

Then Lieutenant Davidson came in at a gallop with his men, dragging two howitzers, but when the guns were being unlimbered, the mules that were drawing one of them bolted and headed into the enemy lines. The dawn was here and in the watery light Carson could see the driver on the lead mule sawing at the brute's mouth. The howitzer clattered up the rise and now he could discern a Californian riding to meet it. The lance caught the mule driver in the stomach and ran through him, and as he fell, he was lanced again in the kidneys, like the others.

Lieutenant Carson, hearing the last of the troops galloping down the valley, hearing the confused babble of the dying, seeing the blood in the grass around him, and the darkening blood on the shredded uniforms of the men, held his rifle that wouldn't shoot and cursed in the tongue of Owl Woman, his first wife, a daughter of White Thunder of the Cheyenne.

Coming up from the rear, with the baggage and Lieutenant Emory's barometer and Gambey sextant wrapped in sheepskin, with dry powder and a Hawkins that hadn't been fired, Grady Dunavant found him standing there in the midst of the carnage, too dazed to move.

The army camped that night, having withdrawn from the valley, on a steep hillside covered with rocks and cactus. The day had been spent in bringing in the wounded. From the first note of the bugle, which Grady had heard while he was still in the canyon, not more than ten minutes had elapsed, and in that time eighteen men had been killed and eighteen lanced. Of the lanced two were to die that night.

The rain and the heavy clouds had drawn off, but the night was heavy and bitter cold. (Lieutenant Emory's reading showed two degrees below freezing.) With the first darkness a party was sent out to bury the dead—among them Corporal Ramsdale who had said that "he never seen ary a general who could make up his mind." The camp was without provisions, cut off from water, reduced by one-third its number, the mules emaciated and the horses unmanageable, but there was a small fire, and beside it Dr. Griffin tended the wounded.

When the burial party came back Dunavant was talking to Lieutenants Beale and Carson. The men clambered up the hill silently and stood by the fire. Carson said, "I feel sad for the womenfolks back home. Sorrow's worse'n death."

The fires of the enemy showed brightly on a distant rise. The night was quiet except for the cries of the wounded and dying, and the cries of the coyotes that sat on the hills. After midnight Captain Turner, who had assumed command in place of the wounded Kearny, sent Alexis Godey and three mountain men on a detour to San Diego.

Dawn broke with an overcast sky. With General Kearny again in the saddle, they moved down from the cactus and rocks, the wounded grouped in the center on travois built by the mountain men. On the skyline the enemy rode back and forth, out of rifleshot.

But when the Army of the West had reached the lower end of the valley, had watered their stock and gathered up a herd of cattle to drive before them, a cloud of lancers beat down from their rear, swept in a circle around them and occupied a peak past which the army must go. Eight riflemen, creeping forward, dislodged them from the peak and the army moved up and camped, losing their cattle in the maneuver. General Kearny said that they would strike out in the morning and cut their way through to San Diego.

There was no water on the peak. Grady and the other civilians dug a hole and found a small seepage, which was enough for the wounded. Later in the day the enemy sent an emissary under a white flag with sugar and tea. This gesture was no surprise to Dunavant, who by now had begun to understand the workings of the Spanish mind. When the emissary had gone, the enemy horsemen circled the hill, shouting taunts. Three of the least emaciated of the mules were killed. A soldier, chewing on the stringy meat, looking around at the boulder-strewn eminence, said grimly, "Let's call it Starvation Peak." Someone else said, "Let's call it nothin' and get the hell out."

Dawn broke with frost white on the rocks and the fleshy lobes of the cactus. General Kearny made plans to move out that night, but the wounded were found to be in no condition to move. Then, nothing having been heard from Stockton, he sent Carson, Beale and his Diegueño servant off for San Diego. Carson assumed charge and after dark he took his two men and slipped down the hill. San Diego was thirty miles away over rough ground, cut by gravelly arroyos, heavy with brush and cactus.

He went quietly, Indian fashion, for at dusk he had seen enemy sentinels on the hills and knew that the whole camp was alert. What he didn't know was that Godey, who had been captured on his way back from San Diego, had told Andrés Pico that Carson was with the army, and that the Spanish captain, bent on preventing a juncture of Stockton and Kearny, had thrown a triple cordon around the peak, set a patrol riding and warned his men, *"Se escapara el lobo"*—"The wolf will escape."

Their shoes ground on the rocks and after a short way they took them off and stuffed them under their belts. Canteens clinked against the brush, so they discarded the canteens, keeping only their rifles. These required great care and they moved slowly, inching their way down the steep hill on hands and knees.

They hid behind boulders as a patrol went by, inched forward, hid again at the sound of hoofs, crawled on into a shallow ravine, where the Diegueño Indian left them to take a route of his own, and finally breasted the ravine. There Carson suddenly flattened in his tracks. A sentry had ridden up within thirty feet of them. Carson, pushing back softly with his foot, signaled Beale to hug the earth. The sentry slipped from the saddle and put his ear to the ground.

It was an Injun trick, Carson thought; he had fooled Injuns and he could fool a greaser actin' like an Injun. The sentry was in no hurry at all, crouching there on all fours with his rear stuck up in the air, like a stinkbug. There was nary sound anywhere, except that he could hear Beale's heart flapping hard against his ribs.

The sentry stood up, brushed his knees, took out flint and steel and lighted a cigarette. The light flared over the rocks and the gaunt shapes of the prickly pear. Beale thought it was a signal. He cupped his hand over Carson's ear and whispered, "We're gone. Let's jump up and fight it out." Thinking of other things, thinking slowly of Clark's Fork and the brush with the Blackfeet, of Kiowa on the Arkansas, of these and others, thinking slowly and yet while Beale was still whispering, Carson whispered back, "Not yet. I seen worse'n this afore."

When the sentry was gone the two men crawled on; finally, with the enemy patrols behind them, they began to walk. They paused only to dig cactus spines from their bleeding feet—somewhere along the way they had lost their shoes. Hell, Kit Carson thought, I'm gettin' like an old squaw—can't think of nothin'!

Back on the peak the night turned cold, with the glitter of snow on the far mountains. Emory took a reading and announced that the temperature was four degrees below freezing. To Grady Dunavant, lying wrapped in a salvaged blanket, it seemed an understatement. Beyond him lay young Streeter, with eight lance wounds in the neck, five in the chest, and a wound in each hip. Before morning Serveant Cox, who had married in June the prettiest girl at Fort Leavenworth, died though Dr. Griffin applied blisters and bled him twice.

The next day the enemy drove a band of wild horses up the hills in an effort to stampede the remaining stock. Three of the horses were shot and, being fat, were slaughtered and converted into gravy soup. During the day the Californians circled the peak, out of range as usual, waiting for thirst and hunger to force surrender. No one, least of all General Kearny, thought that the three men would get through to Stockton. At nightfall he ordered the baggage, saddles and greatcoats burned—everything that could not be carried in a haversack. When dawn came they would march.

The bonfires blazed in the night, died, and a smoky stench lay over the peak. Grady sat against a boulder with the unused Hawkins at his side. He watched the stars wheeling down a bright sky. He listened to the tick of his watch, struck flint after a time and saw that it was midnight. He dozed off and woke with the sound of shouting in his ears. The men around him were on their feet. When he stood up he heard the heavy tramp of boots on the hillside, a voice calling up in the darkness, the clink of canteens.

Someone cried, "Stockton!"

It wasn't Stockton, but it was one hundred of his sailors and eighty sweating marines.

# 36

BENT forward in the saddle against the roaring wind, Grady Dunavant rode hard through the night. It was almost a month since the Battle of San Pasqual; the Army of the West was camped on the Santa Ana. They had rested in San Diego, had trained new volunteers and had covered ninety-four miles in nine days. Now they were encamped on the Santa Ana, making ready for the final march on Los Angeles where the enemy had gathered his forces and, seven hundred strong, was waiting for battle.

The wind howled through the narrow defiles of the canyon. The air was filled with sand that stung like shot. A man in his right mind, Grady Dunavant thought, would have stayed in camp. Carson had shaken his head, watching him ride away. Grady had left his rifle with Carson and started off in the late afternoon. It was now after midnight and he was better than halfway home.

At the upper end of the cayon the wind increased; as the dawn broke with the earth and sky joined in a driving yellow wall of sand, he tethered his horse. Below him was the mesa, the dim outlines of the Camino Real. The house was obscured, but it was there below him. He lay down in a toyon thicket and slept.

Roque de Zubaran, dressed in his father's *cuera* that was too big for him, and holding his father's shield, stood in front of Doña Carlota. The call had come from General Flores. The messenger had ridden in that morning with word that six hundred gringos were marching on Los Angeles. Roque was sweating under the jacket, and the shield hung heavy on his arm. The army was waiting for him, for all true sons of California, while he squandered precious minutes listening to his grandmother.

She had not wanted him to go to San Pasqual with Andrés Pico, but he had gone. He had wet his lance many times on the hated foe. He had seen them cut to pieces and driven from hill to hill. He would have seen them starved at last if it had not been for the reinforcements that arrived in the night. Even then they would have been driven into the sea if it had not been for dissension among the Spaniards. There was still dissension—many of the warriors had already laid down their lances, feeling the cause was lost—but it wasn't lost. They would still win by their strength and the will of God.

"Birds in one flight," Doña Carlota said, speaking from the doorway, "bathe at one fountain. In this case the fountain is filled with blood."

Roque was silent.

"You have wet your lance. It is time to put it away. A day has gone. Another day comes. It is my desire that you live to see it."

"I have no desire to see the day you speak of," he said and bowed, clasping the shield in front of him.

"Then may you go with God," his grandmother said.

Luz and Jorge were waiting for him at the gate, and he bowed to them. Luz put her hand on his arm, trying to detain him. He wrenched himself free and mounted his horse. The *vaqueros* fell in behind him.

He looked down at his sister and said, "I will return with my shield or upon it."

With the wind at his back he rode fast toward the Camino Real, holding his lance upright in the stirrup.

Grady Dunavant saw the line of horsemen gallop down from the mesa, but he didn't move out from his hiding place until dark. The wind had not diminished and he was at the gate before he saw it through the driving sand.

Guadalupe opened the gate for him. Luz was in bed, asleep, with a candle burning on the table. The room was filled with smoke and drifting dust. He stood above the bed, looking down at her, her hair clouded over the pillow and her lips slightly parted. His rifle was with Carson on the Santa Ana, but for an hour he was home. He snuffed out the candle and lay down beside her. Only then did she know that he was there. He held her in his arms for a long while and neither of them spoke. The wild beating of her heart against his was louder than the crying of the wind. Her hair smelled of ferns as it always did, as it had in his thoughts during the long days he had been gone.

"The war is not over," she said, "for you."

"I'm here," he answered her, evading the question. "The soldier comes home to his bride."

She struggled out of his arms and sat upright and wanted to know about the battle, if he had been hurt and if he had used the deer fat.

"Hell," he groaned.

She wanted to know what "hell" signified. "I have heard you say it before."

His visit was turning into a talk and the talk into a language lesson. "It signifies *Jesús María, mal haya* and *caramba*—all of them and none of them and more, too."

"You are angry?"

"Mrs. Dunavant," he said, taking her in his arms again, "I didn't come home to talk."

Afterward, as she lay sleeping against his shoulder, he slipped quietly out of bed. As he opened the door she called to him. For a moment he hesitated, thinking it was better to go and pretend that he hadn't heard her. But he went back and stood by the bed.

"What is it?" he asked her, trying not to be impatient.

She stood up, held him and said in a small voice, "You can't go now." She paused, and then said in a voice that was smaller yet, "I am going to have a child."

He had to sit down on the bed, but when his knees were steady again, he got up. He stood listening to the wind. He saw the men lying in the grass at San Pasqual and heard the moans of the dying on Starvation Peak. He had a part in this thing and it had to be settled. He couldn't ask the others to do it for him, not and be very happy about it afterward.

"I'll be back in a few days," he said. "And I don't want you to go running around the country on horseback. Understand!"

She was sobbing with her face in the pillow, so he closed the door, the gate, and mounted his horse. He rode with the wind toward the west. Dawn was still an hour away.

He came upon the army the next afternoon. They were drawn up on the banks of the San Gabriel, with the 2nd Division in front, and the 1st and 3rd on the left and right flanks. The guard and a company of volunteer carbineers were in the rear, forming a Yankee Corral for the wagon train and cattle.

The enemy had already been met and driven after a few rounds of fire from a hill that barred the passage to the San Gabriel. They were now on the other side of the river on a high bank, with two nine-pounders in position.

Dunavant got his rifle from Carson and fell in with Gillespie's volunteers. Captain Gilson watched him. They had not spoken on the way up from San Diego and Gilson ignored his greeting now. The river was about a hundred yards wide at this point; the bed was streaked with quicksand. General Kearny advised against a hasty crossing but was rebuked by Commodore Stockton. "Quicksands be damned!" he shouted.

The army went forward through the knee-deep current under a hail of grape. As they gained the far bank enemy cavalry swooped down on both flanks, were turned with heavy rifle fire and retreated. When night came and the cannon were in place the marine band played "Hail Columbia." It was a different night from the first one at San Pasqual, Grady thought.

The next day was the same, with the army moving forward slowly afoot, the Californians retreating, and before noon it was apparent to everyone that victory had been won. Los Angeles was four miles away. Grady tramped along with his Hawkins over his shoulder, amused that in four battles he hadn't fired a shot. He remarked about it to Carson, and before the answer came from the slow-speaking lieutenant, who still insisted on being called "Bub," six horsemen came out of nowhere. They were riding low in the saddles and carrying lances. Carson knocked down the first one at a hundred yards or more. As Grady brought his Hawkins to bear, Gilson snatched it from his hands and fired at the second horseman. The man pitched headlong into the grass. The four remaining Californians turned and scattered in different directions.

The first man who went down was lying where he had fallen, but the other one was crawling off through the grass toward a thicket of willows. The three men started for him, Captain Gilson in the lead, with his pistol drawn, his short legs pumping through the brush. The youth turned like an animal at bay, rose to his knees, and then to his feet, the lance, broken near the head, still grasped in a bloody hand. His lips were pulled back from his teeth in a grimace of fear and hatred. He was not looking at Gilson who had stopped and was raising his pistol. The boy looked at Grady Dunavant. It was a long moment before Grady recognized him.

There was blood on his jacket and on his mouth. He raised the broken lance and took a step toward Dunavant. He began to speak but the words were unintelligible. Gilson had the pistol in front of him, his elbow slightly bent, and Grady couldn't reach it. As he struck Gilson, with the full weight of his body behind the blow, he was glad that the pistol was out of reach. His fist landed just forward of the hair that curled from under the captain's ear. Gilson sprawled on his face.

The boy had taken another step toward him, and as he spoke again, he fell forward. Grady cut the leather jacket from his body. The wound was high on the shoulder, but it was a clean hole and would heal in time. He took the pistol from Gilson's limp fingers, went back for his horse and lifted the boy across the saddle.

Carson said, "A friend of yours?"

"Someday," Grady said. The band was playing far off now toward the walls of the pueblo. Grady shook hands with Carson. "When you head east stop at the Hawk."

"I'll be goin' through sure—Kearny or no Kearny."

"Goodby, Bub."

Carson raised his rifle.

Grady Dunavant nudged the horse. He stopped at the river and bathed the boy's wound, and went on toward the Camino Real. He could no longer hear the band playing, but the walls of the town showed white in the sun. To the east and the Hawk he noticed for the first time that the wild oats were springing green on the hills.

the pistol was out of reach. His fist landed just forward of the hair that curled from under the captain's ear. Gilson sprawled on his face.

The boy had taken another step toward him, and as he spoke again, he fell forward. Grady cut the leather jacket from his body. The wound was high on the shoulder, but it was a clean hole and would heal in time. He took the pistol from Gilson's limp fingers, went back for his horse and lifted the boy across the saddle.

Carson said, "A friend of yours?"

"Someday," Grady said. The band was playing far off now toward the walls of the pueblo. Grady shook hands with Carson. "[illegible] next stop at the Hawk."

"I'll be [illegible]."

"Goodby, Baby."

Carson raised his rifle.

Grady Dunavant nudged the horse. He stopped at the river and bathed the boy's wound, and went on toward the [illegible]. He could no longer hear the band playing, but the walls of the town showed white in the sun. To the east and the Hawk he noticed for the first time that the wild oats were springing green on the hills.